Fossil Fuels in a Changing Climate

Fossil Fuels in a Changing Climate
Impacts of the Kyoto Protocol and Developing Country Participation

ULRICH BARTSCH and BENITO MÜLLER

with ASBJØRN AAHEIM

Additional Contributions

Philip Barnes
Hans Kolshus
Robert Mabro

Published by the Oxford University Press
for the Oxford Institute for Energy Studies
2000

Oxford University Press, Great Clarendon Street, Oxford OX2 6DP

Oxford University Press is a department of the University of Oxford.
It furthers the University's objective of excellence in research, scholarship
and education by publishing worldwide in

Oxford New York
Athens Auckland Bangkok Bogotá Buenos Aires Calcutta
Cape Town Chennai Dar es Salaam Delhi Florence Hong Kong
Istanbul Karachi Kuala Lumpur Madrid Melbourne
Mexico City Mumbai Nairobi Paris São Paulo
Singapore Taipei Tokyo Toronto Warsaw
with associated companies in Berlin Ibadan

Oxford is a registered trade mark of Oxford University Press
in the UK and in certain other countries

Published in the United States
by Oxford University Press Inc. New York

© Oxford Institute for Energy Studies 2000

First published 2000

British Library Cataloguing in Publication Data
Data Available

Library of Congress Cataloguing in Publication Data
Data Applied for

ISBN 0-19-730024-3

Cover designed by Oxford Designers & Illustrators from an original painting,
Abstrakte Landschaft, by Franco Müller. © 1999
Typeset by Philip Armstrong, Sheffield
Printed by Biddles, Guildford

CONTENTS

LIST OF TABLES

Appendices

LIST OF FIGURES

ACRONYMS FOR WORLD REGIONS IN THE STUDY

USA	United States of America
JPN	Japan
EUM	Member countries of the European Union
ROE	'Rest of OECD Europe' (Iceland, Norway, Switzerland)
ROO	'Rest of OECD' (Australia, Canada, New Zealand)
EIT	'Economies in Transition' (former Soviet Union and Eastern Europe)
CHN	China
IND	India
ANI	Asian Newly Industrialised region
AOE	Middle Eastern and North African oil-exporting region
LAM	Latin America
ROW	Rest of the World

The full list of countries included in these regions is in the Annex to Chapter 4

ABBREVIATIONS

$	US dollars
¢	US cents
AA	assigned amount(s)
AAU	assigned amount unit
AEEI	autonomous energy efficiency improvements
AFB	atmospheric fluidised bed unit
AFV	alternative-fuel vehicles
AGBM	Ad-Hoc Group on the Berlin Mandate
AOSIS	Alliance of Small Island States
BaU	business-as-usual
C	carbon
CCAP	Climate Change Action Plan (US)
CCGT	combined-cycle gas turbine
CCT	clean coal technology
CCTI	Climate Change Technology Initiative (US)
CDM	Clean Development Mechanism
CER	certified emission reductions (CDM)
CES	constant elasticity of substitution
CGE	computable general equilibrium (model)
CH_4	methane
CHP	combined heat and power (generation)
CICERO	Center for International Climate and Environmental Research – Oslo
CIS	Confederation of Independent States
CLIMOX	Oxford model for climate policy analysis,
CO	carbon monoxide
CO_2	carbon dioxide
CO_2e	carbon dioxide equivalent
COP	Conference of the Parties to the FCCC
COP/MOP	COP serving as Meeting of the Parties to the Kyoto Protocol
COPn	n^{th} session of COP

DC	developing country
DOE	Department of Energy (USA)
EC	European Commission
EE	energy emissions
EIA	Energy Information Agency (USA)
EPAct	Energy Policy Act (USA)
ERU	emission reduction unit (JI)
EU	European Union
FCCC	UN Framework Convention on Climate Change
FY$yyyy$	financial year $yyyy$
G77	(G77+China) Group of 77 (plus China)
GAMS	general algebraic modelling software
Gas CC	(natural) gas combined-cycle
GATT	General Agreement on Tariffs and Trade
GC	global compromise
GDG	Green Developing Group
GDP	gross domestic product
GEF	Global Environment Facility
GHG	greenhouse gas
GNP	gross national product
GTAP	Global Trade Analysis Project
GWP	global warming potential
H_2	Hydrogen
HDI	human development index
ICAO	International Civil Aviation Organization
IEA	International Energy Agency
IET	International Emission Trading
IGCC	integrated (coal) gasification combined-cycle
IMF	International Monetary Fund
IPCC	Intergovernmental Panel on Climate Change
JI	Joint Implementation
LNG	liquefied natural gas
LPG	liquefied petroleum gas (propane)
LUCF	land-use change and forestry

MITI	Ministry of Trade and Industry (Japan)
MoFA	Ministry of Foreign Affairs (Japan)
NAFTA	North American Free Trade Agreement
NGL	natural gas liquids
NO_2	nitrogen dioxide
NO_x	nitrous oxides
OECD	Organisation for Economic Co-operation and Development
OIES	Oxford Institute for Energy Studies
OPEC	Organization of Petroleum Exporting Countries
PPP	purchasing power parity
PS	preference score
PV	photovoltaic
R&D	research and development
RI	real income
RIIA	Royal Institute for International Affairs
SAR	Second Assessment Report (IPCC)
SO_2	sulphur dioxide
TFR	total fertility rate
UKCS	United Kingdom continental shelf
UN	United Nations
UNCED	UN Conference on Environment and Development (Rio 'Earth Summit')
UNDP	UN Development Programme
VAT	value added tax
VCR	Voluntary Challenge and Registry (Canada)

ORDERS OF MAGNITUDE

Units
$ = US dollar, ¢ = US cent
h = hour, d = day, yr = year
cm = cubic metre = m^3
g = gram, t = (metric) tonne = 1000kg = 10^6g
J = Joule
W = Watt
b = barrel
btu = British thermal units
oe = oil equivalent
CO_2e = carbon dioxide equivalent
ppm = parts per million

Examples
$5bn/yr = *5 billion US dollars per year*
mtoe/d = *million tonnes oil equivalent per day*
kb/d = *thousand barrels per day*
bcm = *billion cubic metres* = 10^9m^3
tcm = *trillion cubic metres* = $10^{12}m^3$
kW, MW, GW = *kilo, mega, giga Watts*
TWh = *tera Watt hours*
gC, tC = *grams, tonnes of carbon*
Gt CO_2e = *giga tonnes CO_2 equivalent*
Gg = *giga grams* = 10^9g = *thousand tonnes*

ACKNOWLEDGEMENTS

The work for this book was undertaken at the Oxford Institute for Energy Studies (OIES) in co-operation with the Center for International Climate and Environmental Research in Oslo (CICERO) over the period of one year beginning in March 1999. The research initially started as a study commissioned by the Royal Ministry of Petroleum and Energy (Norway), but authors and sponsors agreed that a wider dissemination should be sought. The Research Report completed in August 1999 was therefore edited and expanded to form this book over the following six months.

The book is the result of co-operation between different people. All the chapters in the book have benefited greatly from this co-operation, and it is therefore not possible to attribute specific chapters to contributors. However, we will give an indication of the division of labour. The main body of work was performed by Ulrich Bartsch and Benito Müller at the OIES. Ulrich Bartsch provided modelling expertise, and edited most of the chapters. Benito Müller developed the political aspects of the scenarios. He also delved deeply into the esoteric realms of greenhouse gas emitting processes to produce baseline emission data. Asbjørn Aaheim and Hans Kolshus at CICERO looked into the development of technology. Phil Barnes provided analysis of coal and gas markets. Robert Mabro has devoted much of his professional life to the functioning of the oil market. Some of his knowledge went into this book. Last but not least, he gave general guidance to a loosely knit and often stretched group of researchers. Ulrich Bartsch and Robert Mabro also wrote the conclusions. Of course, many other people deserve thanks for their help to bring this project to a presentable conclusion, and we would like to name but a few: Jürgen Blank, Joanna Depledge, Denny Ellerman, Michael Grubb, Fiona Mullins, and Kevin Rosser. We hope that the results of our labours live up to their expectations.

CHAPTER 1

INTRODUCTION

Since the 1980s, changes in the Earth's climate have attracted increasing attention both in academia and among the public at large. There remains now little doubt that the concentration of greenhouse gases in the atmosphere, and the average surface temperature of the planet are rising. Economic and social effects of rising temperatures are likely to be negative on balance, and catastrophic in some regions. A growing body of scientific evidence supports the claim that these climate changes are induced by human activity, particularly by the burning of fossil fuels.

With the Earth Summit in Rio de Janeiro in 1992, an international process was set in motion which led to the drafting of the Kyoto Protocol in 1997. In this Protocol, a number of countries commit themselves to reduce greenhouse gas emissions to an aggregate level below the baseline of 1990. Commitments apply to countries listed in an annex to the Protocol, the so-called Annex I countries. These make up the industrialised world, i.e. the members of the Organization for Economic Co-operation and Development (OECD), and countries in Eastern Europe and the Former Soviet Union. Reductions are to be achieved for the First Commitment Period covering the years 2008–12.

The purpose of this study is to assess the effects of policies to reduce greenhouse gas emissions on the markets for the fossil fuels, oil, coal, and gas. Special attention is devoted to supply, demand, and prices of oil. This book fills a major gap in the growing climate change literature. Although fossil-fuel CO_2 emissions are by far the most important contributor to global greenhouse gas emissions, the climate change literature so far has not adequately addressed the questions surrounding supply of and demand for fossil fuels. Supply and demand behaviour crucially determine the costs of policy action, and the success of the Kyoto Protocol in terms of global emission abatement. It seems therefore most timely to study the interactions between the fossil fuel markets and abatement policies.

This book also recognises the fact that the Kyoto Protocol was explicitly designed to be only a first step on the road to global emission abatement. The reduction targets in the Protocol are not sufficient to halt the increase in concentration of greenhouse gases in the atmosphere, mainly because fast-growing developing countries are not obliged to take part in the abatement efforts. So far, no official attempts have been made to design a post-Kyoto scenario in detail. If the world is serious about stabilising the concentration of greenhouse gases in the atmosphere anywhere near current levels, a wider, global agreement has to take the place of the Kyoto Protocol after the First Commitment Period in 2012. In this book we develop a scenario for such an agreement.

The crucial issue for an inclusion of developing countries into a new climate change agreement is the allocation of emission caps across the nations of the world. Because countries cannot be forced into accepting and implementing such an agreement, a compromise has to be found which is politically acceptable for a majority of the world by recognising notions of fairness and justice. We develop a plausible scenario based on a global compromise formula, which allows developing countries room to grow, and recognises the responsibilities of the industrialised world.

The methodology employed here uses policy simulations based on a model of the world economy developed at the Oxford Institute for Energy Studies (OIES). The research looks at developments over a period of two decades into the future, i.e. up to the year 2020, and at policies with implications which permeate the global economy. A consistent frame of reference was needed, capable of tracing long-term policy impacts through economic sectors, and across international boundaries, and of including relevant feedback effects. An integrated global economic model is able to perform these tasks.

The Oxford model for climate policy analysis, which we have called CLIMOX, is based on an integrated economic database developed by the Global Trade Analysis Project for the year 1995. CLIMOX is a global general equilibrium model, developed to produce projections for national and regional economies of the world, and to simulate impacts of climate policies. Projections and simulations cover the time period between the base year 1995 and the year 2020.

Based on the CLIMOX model, we describe alternative scenarios for the world. The first scenario, labelled 'Business as Usual' (BaU) relates to a world where climate change policies are not implemented; in other words, to a non-Kyoto world. It involves projections at five-year intervals up to 2020 for a set of relevant variables: population, economic growth, productivity, oil supply (both conventional and non-conventional), hydrogen supply from non-carbon sources, oil demand by region, coal and gas supply and consumption, and projections of both CO_2 and methane (CH_4) emissions. The BaU scenario is the baseline, against which outcomes of policy simulations are compared.

CLIMOX is only a model of economic relationships, and therefore gives only a partial view of the world. For example, it does not describe feedbacks between the economy and the world climate. Damage costs from climate change, or benefits from emission abatement, are thus not included in the analysis. This is an omission which we hope does not distort results too much over the time-frame of the study, which is relatively short at least in terms of global climate change.

Apart from this caveat, a disclaimer has to be issued. The present analysis uses simulation methodology, which is from the outset not designed to predict the actual state of the world twenty-five years into the future. This book is about the impact of policies on a set of economic variables, and we compare values without implementation of policies and values with implementation of policies. We are therefore mainly interested in relative changes from a baseline. We do not pretend to know the actual levels of variables, nor that CLIMOX is a crystal ball. Predictions are best left to wiser or more foolish men and women.

Structure of the Book

The book is divided into three parts. Part I sets the stage for the rest of the book, and Part III is devoted to policy scenarios. In between, Part II gives a detailed description of methodology and basic assumptions. However, for readers less interested in such detail, Part I (Chapters 2 to 4) and Part III (Chapters 10 to 17) provide all the necessary information.

The main focus of the book is on the impact of the Kyoto Protocol on oil markets, and therefore we start in Chapter 2 with a description of the Protocol, discussing its history and details of emission reduction commitments and implementation options. Chapter 3 then presents our evaluation of the functioning of oil markets, and projections of oil supply until the year 2020. All other relevant basic facts which characterise the BaU scenario are summarised in Chapter 4. Most importantly for an understanding of the rest of the book, the chapter starts with an overview of the model, and a list of the countries and regions, which are distinguished throughout the analysis.

For a more detailed understanding of methodology and assumptions, however, the reader should turn to Part II (Chapters 5 to 9). Chapter 5 describes in some detail the structure of the CLIMOX model and assumptions concerning exogenous parameters. Chapter 6 is of crucial importance for the projections of energy demand over the time horizon of the study. It is devoted to an evaluation of the development of technology. The first part looks at technology in the engineering sense, considering energy saving equipment in the two most energy intensive economic sectors – electricity generation and transport. It attempts an evaluation of the path of energy consumption in light of existing and emerging new technologies. The second part looks at technology in the macro-economic sense, i.e. the relation between the input factors labour, capital, and energy on one side, and the output of goods and services on the other. Energy intensities of production are compared and underlying causes for differences in energy efficiency are highlighted. Chapters 7 and 8 provide the background to supply of and demand for coal and gas, while Chapter 9 shows emissions of the two most important greenhouse gases, CO_2 and methane, from fossil fuels and other sectors.

The BaU scenario provides a reference for assessing the impact of climate change policies which characterise alternative states of the world. The study examines two such states in Part III. The first is labelled the Kyoto scenario and the second is the Global Compromise scenario. We trace the impact of climate change policies introduced to achieve the emission targets of the two scenarios on fossil fuel supply, demand and prices and oil revenues. These are compared with the projections of these same parameters in the reference case provided by the Business-as-Usual scenario.

The Kyoto scenario describes a situation in which the emission targets assigned to the Annex I countries in the Kyoto Protocol are attained. The Kyoto scenario is detailed in Chapter 10, and Chapter 11 shows simulation results.

The emission targets defined in the Protocol can be achieved in a variety of ways. There is a wide array of measures that countries can adopt. They can choose to use a single policy or a package of measures. They can limit their action to national policies or extend it to co-operation and trade with other countries. The Kyoto scenario identifies the different policy packages which are likely to be introduced by the various countries (or group of countries) committed to the emission targets of the Protocol. Chapter 12 in contrast looks at the impacts of an implementation of Kyoto using single policy instruments, i.e. national carbon quotas, national energy taxes, and international emission permit trading.

The second climate change scenario which we label 'Global Compromise' is explained in Chapter 13. The emission targets are more stringent than in the Kyoto case, and non-Annex I countries are now involved. The scenario is based on a compromise formula, which provides a plausible solution to the problem of allocating emission reduction targets.

The implications of the Global Compromise scenario are presented and discussed in Chapters 13 and 14.

Finally, in Chapter 15 we test the sensitivity of results to changes in crucial assumptions: the behaviour of investment in non-conventional oil, the development of oil productive capacity, the rate of economic growth, and the cartelisation of the sale of 'hot air' by countries where actual emissions are lower than targets. Chapter 16 provides a brief comparison of features of this study with those of other works on the same issues, and Chapter 17 summarises and interprets the results.

PART I

THE SETTING

CHAPTER 2

THE KYOTO PROTOCOL

2.1 Introduction

A prerequisite to modelling any impacts of the Kyoto Protocol whatsoever is to gain some understanding not only of the provisions in the Protocol itself, but also of the legal, political and institutional framework surrounding it. For this purpose, we shall now turn to a short historical excursion, detailing this framework and the process which led to the Protocol. Following that, we shall discuss in some detail the specific provisions of the Protocol itself, in particular its multifarious dimensions of 'flexibility': the multi-gas approach, the 'bubbling' provision, banking, sinks, and the mechanisms for international transfer.[1]

2.2 The Road to Kyoto

2.2.1 The Rio Earth Summit and the UN Framework Convention on Climate Change

The international climate change regime which led to the UN Framework Convention on Climate Change (UN FCCC) and the Kyoto Protocol has its origins in growing concerns in the 1980s about the potential of 'man-made changes in climate that might be adverse to the well-being of humanity', as stated in a declaration issued by the participants of the First World Climate Conference in 1979. A number of intergovernmental conferences in the late 1980s – culminating in the Noordwijk Ministerial Conference (1989), and the Second World Climate Conference (1990) – were an expression of these growing

---

1. In doing so, we are indebted to Michael Grubb's excellent and detailed exposition of the issues in his *The Kyoto Protocol: A Guide and Assessment* (London: The Royal Institute of International Affairs,1999).

concerns, as was the establishment of the Intergovernmental Panel on
Climate Change (IPCC) in 1988 by the UN Environment Programme
and the World Meteorological Organization. Following its mandate to
assess the state of existing knowledge about the climate system, the
environmental, economic, and social impacts òf climate change, and
the possible response strategies, the IPCC published its first assessment
report in 1990. It had a powerful effect on both policy-makers and the
general public and provided the basis for the negotiations on the
Climate Change Convention.

In December 1990, the UN General Assembly approved the start of
treaty negotiations for a Climate Change Framework Convention. The
fact that this decision was taken in 1990 had implications which could
not have been envisaged at the time. The reason for this is that 1990
became the 'natural' base-line year for any quantitative deliberations
in the negotiations. This was true, in particular, for emission levels.
The problem was and is that 1990 also turned out to be the starting
point of the economic collapse of the so-called economies in transition,
i.e. the former Soviet bloc countries, which means that these countries
have ever since emitted considerably less than their 1990 base line
levels, leaving them with substantial amounts of surplus ('hot air')
emission quotas.

The Intergovernmental Negotiating Committee charged with the
climate change negotiations was facing a strict deadline, namely the
UN Conference on Environment and Development to be held in Rio
de Janeiro in June 1992 (the 'Rio Earth Summit'). The fact that
negotiators from 150 countries managed to finalise this Framework
Convention in just fifteen months is quite remarkable, in particular
since many developing countries saw global warming as an issue of
little or no importance, caused by and to be dealt with by the
industrialised North. Indeed, some even saw the whole issue as a
conspiracy of the North to impede their development.

To understand why these negotiations came none the less to fruition,
and indeed to understand the content of the Framework Convention,
it is not so much the strict deadline but the context of this deadline
which is of importance: what has to be kept in mind is that the 'Earth
Summit' was much more than a conference on climate change. Indeed,
the FCCC was only one of five treaties signed at Rio, including the
'Rio Declaration on Environment and Development', a statement of
environmental and development principles, and 'Agenda 21', a
programme of action designed to give effect to those principles. The
Rio Declaration proclaims, in particular, that 'the right to development
must be fulfilled so as to equitably meet developmental and environ-

mental needs of present and future generations' (Principle 3) and that 'all States and all people shall cooperate in the essential task of eradicating poverty as an indispensable requirement for sustainable development, in order to decrease the disparities in standards of living and better meet the needs of the majority of the people of the world' (Principle 5). Against this background, it cannot be surprising to find developmental concerns enshrined in both the FCCC and the legal instruments subsequently negotiated under it. Indeed, it stands to reason that these development clauses are essential to the Convention, in the sense that without them, the Convention would not exist.

Turning to the content of the FCCC, we find that after the usual preamble and definitions (Article 1), the Parties agree in Article 2 that

> The ultimate objective of this Convention and any related legal instruments that the Conference of the Parties may adopt is to achieve ... stabilization of greenhouse gas concentrations in the atmosphere at a level that would prevent dangerous anthropogenic interference with the climate system. Such a level should be achieved within a time-frame sufficient to allow ecosystems to adapt naturally to climate change, to ensure that food production is not threatened and to enable economic development to proceed in a sustainable manner.

In order to achieve this objective, the Parties furthermore agreed in Article 3 that actions to implement the provisions of the Convention should be guided, *inter alia*, by the following considerations ('Principles'):

> 1. The Parties should protect the climate system for the benefit of present and future generations of humankind, on the basis of equity and in accordance with their common but differentiated responsibilities and respective capabilities. Accordingly, the developed country Parties should take the lead in combating climate change and the adverse effects thereof.

> 2. The specific needs and special circumstances of developing country Parties, especially those that are particularly vulnerable to the adverse effects of climate change, and of those Parties, especially developing country Parties, that would have to bear a disproportionate or abnormal burden under the Convention, should be given full consideration.

The Convention thus explicitly and unambiguously requires developed countries to take the lead in combating climate change.[2] It also requires the Parties to give full consideration to both intra- and inter-generational equity issues concerning both responsibilities and capabilities (burden sharing). The central focus of debate during the negotiations

---

2. This fact will have to be borne in mind when we turn to discuss in Chapter 10 the current hostility of the US Congress to the Kyoto Protocol.

of the Convention was on the Commitments detailed in Article 4. After an initial list of commitments concerning all Parties – such as establishing national inventories of greenhouse gas emission sources and sinks – Paragraph 4.2 turns to commitments for developed country Parties as listed in Annex I to the Convention. Each Annex I Party commits itself, in particular, to

> ... adopt national policies and take corresponding measures on the mitigation of climate change, by limiting its anthropogenic emissions of greenhouse gases and protecting and enhancing its greenhouse gas sinks and reservoirs. These policies and measures will demonstrate that developed countries are taking the lead in modifying longer-term trends in anthropogenic emissions consistent with the objective of the Convention, recognizing that the return by the end of the present decade to earlier levels of anthropogenic emissions of carbon dioxide ... would contribute to such modification ...

Having been formulated in this rather vague manner, there are different possible interpretations of what this commitment amounts to. The majority reading, however, is quite unambiguous, namely that Annex I countries are committed to return their emissions to 1990 levels by the year 2000. Amongst the other provisions of Article 4, there is at least one which has led to considerable political controversy and which deserves a special mention, namely Paragraph 4.8, stating that

> in the implementation of the commitments in this Article, the Parties shall give full consideration to what actions are necessary under the Convention, including actions related to funding, insurance and the transfer of technology, to meet the specific needs and concerns of developing country Parties arising from the adverse effects of climate change and/or the impact of the implementation of response measures, especially on:
>
> (a) Small island countries;
>
> (b) Countries with low-lying coastal areas;
>
> ...
>
> (h) Countries whose economies are highly dependent on income generated from the production, processing and export, and/or on consumption of fossil fuels and associated energy-intensive products; ...

One of the reasons for the political sensitivity of this paragraph lies in its reference to funding actions aimed at meeting the needs of developing countries arising from adverse effects of climate change and/or from adverse effects of response measures. It is clear that, in the case of small island countries and countries with low-lying coastal areas, the adverse effects in question are those of climate change and not of response measures. It would seem therefore that the funding actions in question are meant to pertain to adaptation measures. Funding pertaining to developing country needs arising from adverse effects of response measures, by contrast, clearly refers to those developing countries with economies which are likely to suffer from a downturn in production or consumption of fossil fuels. There is no agreement, however, as to what precisely is to be funded in this case. While analogy to the small island case might suggest adaptation measures – such as measures to diversify the economy – OPEC, led by Saudi Arabia, has in recent years insisted that 'funding' in this case must be interpreted as compensation of losses from projected revenues. However, the 'OPEC interpretation' has not received a particularly warm reception by the OECD countries which are essentially meant to provide the funding. None the less, the fact remains that the Convention does envisage funding for the needs of developing countries with fossil fuel economies arising from adverse effects of response measures, and the sooner a politically acceptable interpretation of this commitment is found, the better for the climate change regime.

Having been signed by 154 states (plus the EC) at Rio, the Convention entered into force on 21 March 1994, 90 days after the receipt of the 50th instrument of ratification. Remarkably, the USA was fourth in line – after Mauritius, the Seychelles and the Marshall Islands – in ratifying the FCCC. As of 6 June 1999, 178 Parties have either ratified or acceded to the Convention,[3] including all oil-producing countries with the exception of Iraq and Libya. The speed and scope of this international acceptance was truly outstanding and distinguishes the FCCC from most if not all other major international treaties.

2.2.2 The Conference of the Parties, the Berlin Mandate, and the Kyoto Protocol

Continuing its preparatory work after Rio, the Intergovernmental Negotiating Committee went on to meet and discuss matters relating to commitments, arrangements for the financial mechanism, technical and financial support to developing countries, and procedural and institutional matters. It was dissolved after its 11th session in 1995, after

---

3. 'Accession' is the act whereby a state accepts the offer or the opportunity to become a party to a treaty already negotiated and signed by other states. It has the same legal effect as ratification. Accession usually occurs after the treaty has entered into force. [Arts.2 (1) (b) and 15, Vienna Convention on the Law of Treaties 1969, as described in http://www.un.org/ Depts/ Treaty/glossary.htm]

which the Conference of the Parties (COP) became the Convention's ultimate authority at its first session (COP1) in Berlin.

This first session of the COP formally established key institutional components of the climate change regime under the Convention, namely the Subsidiary Bodies for Scientific and Technical Advice and for Implementation, and it confirmed the Global Environment Facility as financing agency. COP1 also reached an enabling compromise on the politically more controversial issue of joint implementation (see Section 2.5.2) by creating a pilot phase programme of 'activities implemented jointly'. Politically by far the most contentious decision taken at Berlin concerned the adequacy of commitments and potential next steps under the Convention. While a majority of countries accepted in preparatory discussions that commitments beyond the year 2000 were needed to address the long-term problem of climate change, it had also become clear that many OECD countries were not even on course to fulfil the year 2000 aim set out in the Convention (in Paragraph 4.2.a, see Section 2.2.1). At one end of the spectrum, oil-exporting countries represented by OPEC and some important US industry groupings were fiercely opposed to developing further reaching commitments. At the other end was the proposal tabled by the Alliance of Small Island States (AOSIS) calling for a 20 per cent cut in industrialised country CO_2 emissions by 2005. The decision finally adopted at Berlin (the 'Berlin Mandate') was that the Convention's commitments were indeed inadequate and that negotiations were to begin under what became known as the 'ad-hoc Group on the Berlin Mandate' (AGBM)[4] to enable the COP 'to take appropriate action for the period beyond 2000, including the strengthening of the commitments of Annex I Parties'. These negotiations were charged with ensuring completion 'as early as possible in 1997 with a view to adopting the results at the third session of the Parties,' which as it turned out was held in Kyoto.

The year 1995 saw another key event in the climate change story in the adoption of the Second Assessment Report (SAR) by the IPCC, written and reviewed by some 2000 experts worldwide. Published in time for COP2 held in Geneva in July 1996, it soon became widely known for its conclusion that 'the balance of evidence suggests that there is a discernible human influence on global climate'. From the moment it was published, the scientific integrity of the SAR was put into question by a small but powerful group representing predominantly

---

4. The acronym for the originally suggested 'Berlin Mandate Working Group' was felt to be slightly too German.

US industrial interests. Against this background, a speech by the head of the US delegation at COP2 proved to be decisive. Not only did he give a firm rebuttal to the SAR critics by declaring that 'we are not swayed by and strongly object to the recent allegations about the integrity of the IPCC's conclusions ... raised by naysayers and special interests bent on belittling, attacking and obfuscating climate change science', but he also made the first call by a major Annex I Party for legally binding quantified commitments by declaring that 'the US recommends that future negotiations focus on an agreement that sets a realistic, verifiable and binding medium term emissions target ... met through maximum flexibility in the selection of implementation measures, including the use of reliable activities implemented jointly, and trading mechanisms around the world'.

These sentiments were taken up in a Ministerial Declaration at COP2 which explicitly endorsed the IPCC conclusions and recognised that 'the continued rise of greenhouse gas concentrations in the atmosphere will lead to dangerous interference in the climate system'. Moreover, the declaration recognised that many Annex I Parties 'need to make additional efforts to overcome difficulties they face in achieving the aim of returning their emissions of greenhouse gases to 1990 levels by 2000' and it instructed its representatives 'to accelerate negotiations on the text of a legally-binding protocol ... for adoption at the third Conference of Parties'. Though not adopted as an official COP2 document, due to Russian, Australian and OPEC objections, this declaration became the guiding light for the negotiations leading up to COP3 at Kyoto.

On 11 December 1997, at the third session of the Conference of the Parties (COP3) in Kyoto, the text of a Protocol (the 'Kyoto Protocol') to the United Nations FCCC was adopted, and it was open for signature until 15 March 1999. By that date the Protocol had received 84 signatures. The remaining 94 Parties may accede to it at any time.

In its central provisions, the Kyoto Protocol defines certain legally binding, quantified maximum greenhouse gas emission levels. These targets, specified in Annex B of the Protocol, apply to a group of Parties to the FCCC listed in Annex I to the Convention.[5] The overall commitment by these Annex I countries is specified in Article 3 of the Protocol which stipulates that

---

5. To be more precise, the targets apply to those Annex I Parties which had ratified the FCCC by the time of Kyoto (excluding, thus Turkey and Belarus), and to those which were accepted into Annex I at Kyoto. But for the present purposes we shall use 'Annex I' throughout.

> The Parties included in Annex I shall, individually or jointly, ensure that their aggregate anthropogenic carbon dioxide equivalent emissions of the greenhouse gases listed in Annex A do not exceed their assigned amounts, calculated pursuant to their quantified emission limitation and reduction commitments inscribed in Annex B and in accordance with the provisions of this Article, with a view to reducing their overall emissions of such gases by at least 5 per cent below 1990 levels in the commitment period 2008 to 2012.[Article 3.1]

Individual targets (see Table 2.1) range from a reduction of emissions of 8 per cent below 1990 levels to an increase of 10 per cent above this base-line, adding up to a 5.2 per cent reduction below 1990 emissions. The term 'assigned amount', as used in the Protocol, refers to a Party's permitted aggregate net-emissions during the commitment period, as determined by its Annex B target. In other words, if a Party emitted 100 units in 1990, and if it is committed under Annex B to a 5 per cent reduction below this level, then it will be permitted to emit on average 95 units in each of five years in the commitment period and its assigned amount for the period will hence be 475 units.[6]

Following US insistence at COP2, the Protocol contains a number of 'flexibilities' in the manner in which Parties can implement their commitments. These will be the topic of the remaining sections of this chapter. What remains to be mentioned here is that the Protocol 'shall enter into force on the ninetieth day after the date on which not less than 55 Parties to the Convention, incorporating Parties included in Annex I which accounted in total for at least 55 per cent of the total carbon dioxide emissions for 1990 of the Parties included in Annex I, have deposited their instruments of ratification, acceptance, approval or accession' [Article 25.1]. The '55 per cent clause' was specifically adopted to ensure that the Protocol could only come into force if ratified by the majority of Annex I countries, without giving any one of them vetoing power.

2.3 Bubbles, Baskets and Banking

2.3.1 Bubbling and Basket Flexibilities

The individual targets specified in Annex B of the Kyoto Protocol are not completely rigid. Article 4 of the Protocol allows, in particular, for what has become known as 'bubbling':

---

6. Due to the nature of our model, 'assigned amount' will be used in a slightly modified manner in the modelling context (see Section 10.1).

Table 2.1: The Kyoto Protocol Commitments

Annex I Parties (with commitments)	Annex B commitments:[1] % of base year	CO_2 emissions in 1990[2] 1000-tonnes	%
USA United States	93	**4,957,022**	**36.1**
JPN Japan	94	**1,173,360**	**8.5**
EUM	92	**3,326,494**	**24.2 (100)[4]**
Germany	92 (79)[3]	1,012,443	7.4 (30.6)
UK	92 (87.5)	584,078	4.3 (17.8)
Italy	92 (93.5)	428,941	3.1 (12.8)
France	92 (100)	366,536	2.7 (11.2)
Spain	92 (115)	260,654	1.9 (7.9)
Netherlands	92 (94)	167,600	1.2 (4.9)
Belgium	92 (92.5)	113,405	0.8 (3.3)
Greece	92 (125)	82,100	0.6 (2.5)
Sweden	92 (104)	61,256	0.4 (1.7)
Austria	92 (87)	59,200	0.4 (1.7)
Finland	92 (100)	53,900	0.4 (1.7)
Denmark	92 (79)	52,100	0.4 (1.7)
Portugal	92 (127)	42,148	0.3 (1.2)
Ireland	92 (113)	30,719	0.2 (0.8)
Luxembourg	92 (72)	11,343	0.1 (0.4)
Monaco	92	71	0.0
ROO		**771,936**	**5.6**
Canada	94	457,441	3.3
Australia	108	288,965	2.1
New Zealand	100	25,530	0.2
ROE		81,513	0.6
Switzerland	92	43,600	0.3
Norway	101	35,533	0.3
Iceland	110	2,172	0.0
Liechtenstein	92	208	0.0
EIT1[5]		**3,417,981**	**24.9**
Russia*	100	2,388,720	17.4
Poland*(1988)[6]	94	414,930	3.0
Romania*(1989)[6]	92	171,103	1.2
Czech Republic*	92	169,514	1.2
Bulgaria*(1988)[6]	92	82,990	0.6
Hungary*(1985–7)[6]	94	71,673	0.5
Slovakia*	92	58,278	0.4
Estonia*	92	37,797	0.3
Latvia*	92	22,976	0.2
Croatia*[7]	95	n.a.	n.a.
Lithuania*	92	n.a.	n.a.
Slovenia*[7]	92	n.a.	n.a.
Ukraine*[7]	100	n.a.	n.a.
Total		**13,728,306**	**100**

* Economies in Transition (according to Annex I). 1 Kyoto Protocol. 2 For the purposes of Article 25 of the Kyoto Protocol FCCC/CP/1997/7/Add.1. 3 EU Bubble Targets. 4 EU percentage. 5 Annex I part of our model EIT region. 6 EIT with base year other than 1990, 7 Base year not yet agreed.

> Any Parties included in Annex I that have reached an agreement to fulfil their commitments under Article 3 jointly, shall be deemed to have met those commitments provided that their total combined aggregate anthropogenic carbon dioxide equivalent emissions of the greenhouse gases listed in Annex A do not exceed their assigned amounts.[Article 4.1]

In other words, Parties can choose to redistribute their commitments in ways which preserve their collective total. However, there are some constraints concerning this manner of redistributing targets. For one, the 'bubble targets' must be submitted with the instruments of ratification of the Parties in question, and they will remain in operation for the whole duration of the commitment period (Article 4.3). Moreover, Article 4.4 stipulates that

> if Parties acting jointly do so in the framework of, and together with, a regional economic integration organization, any alteration in the composition of the organization after adoption of this Protocol shall not affect existing commitments under this Protocol. Any alteration in the composition of the organization shall only apply for the purposes of those commitments under Article 3 that are adopted subsequent to that alteration

This means, in particular, that the EU (itself a Party to the FCCC, separate from its member states), having negotiated such a redistribution amongst its member states soon after Kyoto, 'cannot meet its commitment through expansion to include countries of central/east Europe whose emissions had declined substantially through economic transition'.[7]

A second flexibility dimension introduced into the Kyoto Protocol is given by the fact that targets are defined in terms of a basket of six greenhouse gases from identified sources, as listed in Annex A of the Protocol. Annex A is taken directly from the IPCC Guidelines on preparing national greenhouse gas inventories (see Box 2.1), with the exception that land-use change and forestry (Section 2.4) are treated separately. The six gases are compared on the basis of their 100-year global warming potential (GWP) and they are measured in 'carbon-dioxide-equivalent' (CO_2e) units.[8]

According to the second National Communications of the Annex I

---

7. Michael Grubb, *The Kyoto Protocol: A Guide and Assessment* (RIIA: London 1999), p.122.
8. The targets in Annex B refer to the total emissions of these six gases in CO_2e units. While a tonne of CO_2 will remain a ton of CO_2e (CO_2, as the reference gas, having a GWP of 1), a tonne of methane will amount to 21 tonnes of CO_2e, and a tonne of SF_6 to the staggering amount of 239 kilotons CO_2e.

Parties for 1995 (see Table 2.2), total Annex I carbon dioxide emissions accounted for 82.5 per cent, followed by methane (11.6) and nitrous oxide (3.9), with the remaining three gases totalling merely 2.1 per cent.

Table 2.2: Anthropogenic GHG Emissions of Annex I Regions in 1995

	CO_2 (Mt CO_2e)	%	CH_4 (Mt CO_2e)	%	NO_2 (Mt CO_2e)	%	Other GHGs (Mt CO_2e)	%	Total (Mt CO_2e)
USA	5,215	84.8	650	10.6	145	2.4	137	2.2	6,147
JPN	1,218	88.1	32	2.3	34	2.5	99	7.1	1,384
EUM[(a)]	3,196	79.9	456	11.4	294	7.4	52	1.3	3,998
ROE	84	76.3	15	13.6	8	7.1	3	3.0	111
ROO	824	73.0	220	19.5	74	6.6	10	0.9	1,128
OECD	10,537	82.5	1,374	10.8	555	4.3	301	2.4	12,766
EIT1[(b)]	2,969	82.3	523	14.5	78	2.2	39	1.1	3,610
Annex I	13,506	82.5	1,897	11.6	633	3.9	340	2.1	16,376

(a) Other GHG data not available from Greece, Ireland, Luxembourg, Monaco, Portugal, Spain.
(b) Other GHG data available only from Czech Republic, Russia, Slovakia.

Source: FCCC

2.3.2 'Kyoto' Banking

Under Article 3.13, Parties to the Protocol are also allowed to 'bank' unused assigned amounts in the sense that

> if the emissions of a Party included in Annex I in a commitment period are less than its assigned amount under this Article, this difference shall, on request of that Party, be added to the assigned amount for that Party for subsequent commitment periods

Banking in this manner, and even 'borrowing from the future' (a US proposal which did not make it into the Protocol), may well make economic sense. Environmentally, however, both concepts are some-what problematic. It has to be remembered that in the context of climate change, the temporal distribution of emissions (the 'emissions path') may affect the integrity of the envisaged environmental regime. It is not self-evident that emitting, say 4.5Gt CO_2e in one period and 5.5Gt CO_2e in some later period (Kyoto banking), or vice versa (US borrowing) would have the same climatic effect as emitting 5Gt in both periods. In encouraging 'early action', banking could well have a beneficial climatic effect in certain specific cases depending on the

Box 2.1: IPCC Guidelines

1 Greenhouse Gases   *(100 year) Global Warming Potentials*
- Carbon Dioxide CO_2 1
- Methane CH_4 21
- Nitrous Oxide N_2O 310
- Hydrofluorcarbons HFCs   various
- Perfluorcarbons PFCs   various
- Sulfur Hexafluoride SF_6 239000

Sectors / Source and Sink Categories
1. All Energy
    1A. Fuel Combustion Activities
        1A1. Energy Industries
        1A2. Manufacturing Industries and Construction
        1A3. Transport
        1A4. Other Sectors
        1A5. Other
    1B. Fugitive Emissions from Fuels
        1B1. Solid Fuels
        1B2. Oil and Natural Gas
2. Industrial Processes
3. Solvent and Other Product Use
4. Agriculture
    4A. Enteric Fermentation
    4B. Manure Management
    4C. Rice Cultivation
    4D. Agricultural Soils
    4E. Prescribed Burning of Savannahs
    4F. Field Burning of Agricultural Residues
    4G. Other
5. Land-Use Change & Forestry
    5A. Changes in Forest and other Woody Biomass Stocks
    5B. Forest and Grassland Conversion
    5C. Abandonment of Managed Lands
    5D. CO_2 Emissions and Removals from Soil
    5E. Other
6. Waste
    6A. Solid Waste Disposal on Land
    6B. Wastewater Handling
    6C. Waste Incineration
    6D. Other
7. Other
International Bunkers

Source: The revised 1996 IPPC Guidelines for National Greenhouse Gas
Inventories: Reporting Restrictions (as endorsed in Annex A of the Kyoto
Protocol)

amount of permits banked and the time schedule involved. In general, however, 'Kyoto' banking could equally well be harmful to the climate.[9]

It should be emphasised that the problem in question is not so much a problem of the concept of 'banking' per se, but rather one of the manner in which this procedure is envisaged to be carried out under the Kyoto Protocol. That there are environmentally less problematic alternatives will be borne out in the discussion of our Global Compromise scenario, where (Section A.13.2.2) we shall introduce a version of banking which is environmentally harmless and provides at least the same incentives for early action as the Kyoto version.

2.4 Sinks: Land-use Change and Forestry (LUCF)

The degrees of flexibility inherent in the Kyoto Protocol are by no means exhausted by the option to redistribute targets, by the possibility to focus on different gases in one's abatement efforts or by the option to bank unused parts of assigned amounts. There is, in particular, the further possibility of using 'sinks' in complying with the commitments set out in the Protocol.

Atmospheric greenhouse gas concentrations depend on very complex cycles involving not only emissions from terrestrial sources but also absorptions of the gases into what are known as terrestrial 'sinks.' In the case of CO_2, the most prominent 'carbon sinks' are organic processes in the biosphere, in particular bio-mass growth. Because atmospheric GHG concentrations depend on *net*-emissions (= actual emissions minus absorptions), and since absorptions as well as emissions can be altered through human intervention, specifically through changes in land-use and in forestry practice, it is not surprising that issues relating to such GHG sinks did enter the negotiations leading up to the Kyoto Protocol.

Given the complexities involved in estimating these sinks (Box 2.2), and the sizeable proportions of sinks claimed by the different Parties (Table 2.3), the issue of emissions/sinks from land-use change and forestry proved to be highly contentious and occupied an important part of the first week at Kyoto. Finally, it was decided to drop both land-use change and forestry from the list of GHG sectors (in Annex A)

---

9. Of course, if the periods between which these transfers of assigned amounts occur are themselves rather short and adjacent, then the problem may be marginal, given the long-run nature of the climate change problem.

Box 2.2: IPCC Land-use Change and Forestry Example

	2000	01	02	03	04	...	17	18	19	20	21	22	23	...37	38	39	40
Plot																	
1	200	-5	0	0	-10		-10	-10	-10	-10	0	0	0	0	0	0	0
2	0	200	-5	0	0		-10	-10	-10	-10	-10	0	0	0	0	0	0
3	0	0	200	-5	0		-10	-10	-10	-10	-10	-10	0	0	0	0	0
4	0	0	0	200	-5		-10	-10	-10	-10	-10	-10	-10	0	0	0	0
5	0	0	0	0	200		-10	-10	-10	-10	-10	-10	-10	0	0	0	0
⋮																	
13	0	0	0	0	0		-10	-10	-10	-10	-10	-10	-10	0	0	0	0
14	0	0	0	0	0		-10	-10	-10	-10	-10	-10	-10	0	0	0	0
15	0	0	0	0	0		0	-10	-10	-10	-10	-10	-10	0	0	0	0
16	0	0	0	0	0		0	0	-10	-10	-10	-10	-10	0	0	0	0
17	0	0	0	0	0		-5	0	0	-10	-10	-10	-10	0	0	0	0
18	0	0	0	0	0		200	-5	0	0	-10	-10	-10	-10	0	0	0
19	0	0	0	0	0		0	200	-5	0	0	-10	-10	-10	-10	0	0
20	0	0	0	0	0		0	0	200	-5	0	0	-10	-10	-10	-10	0
Total	200	195	195	195	185		55	45	35	-165	-170	-170	-170	-30	-20	-10	0

Yearly Carbon Flux by Plot in tC/ha (positive = emissions, negative = sink absorbtion)

Within a 20-year time frame, say 2000–2019, one hectare of a forest is cleared each year for agricultural purposes (all of the vegetation is completely burned at the time of clearing). The forest has a biomass of 200tC/ha. The cleared land is used as pasture, established the year after the clearing (with 5tC/ha) and abandoned after three years. After being abandoned, the land re-grows linearly at 10tC/ha per year, but only up to 75 per cent of its original biomass (reached after 15 years).

Each plot will thus exhibit the same carbon flux pattern, relative to the year in which it is cleared. Before the clearance, the carbon flow is zero. In the clearance period, 200t are emitted. In the next period, when the pasture is being established, the plot absorbs 5t. While it is used as

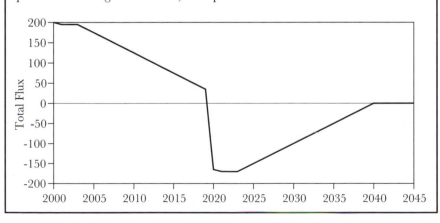

Box 2.2: *continued*

pasture, the carbon flux from the plot is again zero. After being abandoned, it again becomes a sink (10t/yr) until after 15 years, the re-growth reaches maturity. Thereafter the plot has again a zero flux.

The aggregate flux in any one period is, of course, the sum of the fluxes of the plots which have undergone a change in use. In the 20-year period in which this change is carried out, the total flux is positive, starting at 200t and steadily decreasing to 35t. In total, the practice results in 2.38 kt/C of emissions. However, in the next 20 years, the area in question is actually a carbon sink, starting with an absorption of 165t, which again steadily decreases to 10t in 2039. In 2040 and thereafter, the effects of the change in land-use more than 20 years earlier finally ceases to have an effect, i.e. the carbon flux from the area returns to nil, as it was before

---

Table 2.3: Anthropogenic CO_2 Emissions from and Removals by Land-use Change and Forestry by Region. 1995

	Total Emissions (Mt CO_2)	Sinks (Mt CO_2)	% of Total Emissions
USA[a]	5,215	-428	-8.2
JPN	1,218	-95	-7.8
EUM[c]	3,196	-186	-5.8
ROE[d]	84	-19	-22.2
ROO[e]	824	-43	-5.2
OECD Total	10,537	-770	-7.3
EIT1[b]	2,945	-720	-24.4
Annex I Total	13,482	-1,490	-11.1

Source: Second National communications. (a) US figures only. (b) EIT1 = Annex I countries of EIT. The only sink figures available for Lithuania, Slovenia, and Ukraine are for 90, which were taken over for 95. No figures available for Romania and Croatia. (c) No sink figures for Greece. (d) No sink figures for Iceland. (e) No sink figures for Canada

to be considered under the Protocol and instead address them in separate clauses. The compromise on LUCF hammered out at Kyoto states that:

The net changes in greenhouse gas emissions by sources and removals by sinks resulting from direct human-induced land-use change and forestry activities, limited to afforestation, reforestation and deforestation since 1990, measured as verifiable changes in carbon stocks in each commitment period, shall be used to meet the commitments under this Article of each Party included in Annex I.[Article 3.3]

This clause was clarified at the subsequent Subsidiary Body meeting as meaning that assigned amounts should be adjusted by verifiable changes in carbon stocks during the first commitment period resulting from direct anthropogenic activities of afforestation, reforestation and deforestation since 1 January 1990.

2.5   Mechanisms for International Transfer

2.5.1   *The Need for International Transfers*

It is widely recognised that the marginal costs of cutting greenhouse gas emissions differ considerably across countries, which is partly because countries differ with respect to endowments with natural resources, climate, structure of production, and so on (as discussed in Chapter 6). Until recently greenhouse gas emissions have essentially been a 'free good'. Because of the differences in abatement costs, reducing emissions in some countries will be much more expensive than in others.

International transfers of emission savings, or emission trading, would greatly reduce overall costs of implementation. Transfers would allow countries with high costs to pay for abatement in countries with low costs. In principle the high cost country would be willing to pay any price lower than its own marginal abatement cost to interact in this way with the low cost country. The low cost country, on the other hand, would be willing to accept the deal for any price higher than its own marginal abatement cost. In principle, both countries would therefore gain from the deal, and achieve their targets (or, rather, their joint target) at a lower total cost than if the targets were met by separate measures in each country. In an ideal world without distortions, marginal abatement costs would be equalised between countries.

Since CO_2 emissions are related to the use of fossil fuels, and countries differ strongly with regard to the mix of fossil fuels they use, restrictions on emission trading imply that too much effort is spent on reducing the demand for fossil fuels which are expensive to replace, while not enough is done to reduce the demand for those that may be replaced at a low cost.

2.5.2   The 'Flexibility' or 'Kyoto Mechanisms'

The Kyoto Protocol accepts three distinct mechanisms for international transfer of net emission savings – initially known as 'flexibility mechanisms', a term which has since been superseded by 'Kyoto mechanisms' – namely: international emission trading (IET), project joint implementation (JI), and the clean development mechanism (CDM).[10] The precise definition of these mechanisms is still under discussion and will not be finalised until the sixth session of the Conference of the Parties (COP6) to be held late in 2000 in The Hague. This and the complexity of the issues involved are the reasons why we can only give a rough outline in terms of the specifications which have actually been adopted in the Kyoto protocol.

Arguably the best known, but at the same time the least specified of these mechanisms is that of international emission trading. Historically, a number of such trading programmes have been in operation in domestic contexts, the largest being the US Acid Rain Program to reduce SO_2 emissions.[11] The lack of specificity in the Kyoto Protocol is political in origin. Due to internal dissent about early crediting, supplementarity, and competitiveness, the OECD was only able to table a reasonably detailed emission trading article at the very end of the Kyoto conference. Given adamant G77 opposition,[12] it was however omitted and replaced by what became Article 17 of the Protocol (see Box 2.3)

In contrast to IET, the other two international transfer mechanisms admitted under the Protocol (JI and CDM) are 'project level' mechanisms. They are not defined directly in terms of exchanging parts of assigned amounts (i.e. of national quotas), but rather in terms

---

10. A general account of the concepts involved in emission permit trading can be found in article 1.4.7.7 'Definition, Development, and Deployment of Tradable Permits' in the forthcoming UNESCO *Encyclopedia of Life Support Systems (EOLSS)*.

11. The results from the first years of operation since 1995 have shown compliance with relatively strict environmental goals to be much less costly than initially predicted (less than half the initial EPA estimates).

12. 'The G77 adamantly refused to accept an article on emissions trading. Chairman Estrada rejected the OECD's complex text on the grounds that it was submitted too late; in reality, he knew that every sentence would be opposed as a matter of principle ... developing-country opposition to emissions trading was rooted in principles, fed by anger that it might enable the United States to avoid significant domestic action, and magnified by resentment about the prospective Russian windfall'(Grubb, op. cit.:95).

Box 2.3: Article 17 (International Emissions Trading)

The Conference of the Parties shall define the relevant principles, modalities, rules and guidelines, in particular for verification, reporting and accountability for emissions trading. The Parties included in Annex B may participate in emissions trading for the purposes of fulfilling their commitments under Article 3. Any such trading shall be supplemental to domestic actions for the purpose of meeting quantified emission limitation and reduction commitments under that Article.

---

of carrying out projects generating emission savings (or sink enhancements) which are additional to climate change measures that would otherwise have been undertaken in the country hosting the project. Being project based, these mechanisms are often interpreted in terms of technology transfers. As such, many of the potential host countries prefer them to the pure monetary transfers involved in IET. The 'additionality' clause, however, makes these project level mechanisms rather unwieldy to handle, for in many cases it is not at all clear what this additionality actually means, let alone whether it is satisfied. These uncertainties are not only problematic from the environmental point of view, they could also deter potential investors fearing that the fruit of their project investments would ultimately not be recognised.

Both project level mechanisms suffer from these problems, but they do so in differing degrees. Since JI, as defined in Article 6 of the Protocol (Box 2.4), is restricted to transfers within Annex I, the mentioned uncertainties are mitigated by the fact that the Parties certifying the created 'emission reduction units' (ERUs) will have to debit them from their assigned amounts. In other words, a Party deciding to host a JI project and certifying this project to generate x tonnes CO_2e ERUs, will have to reduce its assigned amount by x tonnes. Accordingly it would be 'shooting itself in the foot' if it were to certify an inflated reduction figure. As in the case of IET (but unlike the CDM),[13] credits obtained by way of JI are subject to an explicit supplementarity condition (Art. 6.1.d), in that they are intended to be 'supplemental to domestic action' of the acquiring Party. Again, we are dealing with a condition which through its vagueness may have facilitated the Kyoto negotiations, but only at the price of postponing

---

13. The fact that this sort of supplementarity is referred to in the specifications of those mechanisms which are intra-Annex I, but not in the Article governing the CDM (with its potential for North-South technology and investment transfer) is indeed a noteworthy curiosity of the Kyoto Protocol.

Box 2.4: Article 6 (Joint Implementation)

1. For the purpose of meeting its commitments under Article 3, any Party included in Annex I may transfer to, or acquire from, any other such Party emission reduction units resulting from projects aimed at reducing anthropogenic emissions by sources or enhancing anthropogenic removals by sinks of greenhouse gases in any sector of the economy, provided that:

(a) Any such project has the approval of the Parties involved;
(b) Any such project provides a reduction in emissions by sources, or an enhancement of removals by sinks, that is additional to any that would otherwise occur;
(c) It does not acquire any emission reduction units if it is not in compliance with its obligations [concerning the compilation of emission inventories and reporting]; and
(d) The acquisition of emission reduction units shall be supplemental to domestic actions for the purposes of meeting commitments under Article 3.

2. The Conference of the Parties serving as the meeting of the Parties to this Protocol may, at its first session or as soon as practicable thereafter, further elaborate guidelines for the implementation of this Article, including for verification and reporting.

3. A Party included in Annex I may authorize legal entities to participate, under its responsibility, in actions leading to the generation, transfer or acquisition under this Article of emission reduction units.

4. If a question of implementation by a Party included in Annex I of the requirements referred to in this Article is identified in accordance with the relevant provisions of Article 8 [on expert review], transfers and acquisitions of emission reduction units may continue to be made after the question has been identified, provided that any such units may not be used by a Party to meet its commitments under Article 3 until any issue of compliance is resolved.

---

the real conflict between those Parties in favour of unrestricted flexibility and those flatly opposing flexibility per se. The gist of what this notion of 'supplementarity' may mean can be gauged from the above-mentioned OECD proposed Article on IET, which included the instruction that 'a Party shall not transfer or acquire more than x% of its emissions allowed in any budget period'.[14] The potential conflict

---

14. As quoted in Grubb op.cit.:130.

built into the vagueness of these supplementarity conditions did not take long to erupt, as is witnessed by the current vociferous arguments concerning the formula proposed by the EU (see Sections 10.2.3 and 11.2.3) which roughly amounts to a 50 per cent cap on the use of the transfer mechanisms (i.e. $x = 50$).

The third international transfer procedure adopted in the Kyoto Protocol, the Clean Development Mechanism, has rightly been dubbed the 'Kyoto surprise'. It originated from a proposal put forward in June 1997 by Brazil, stipulating that Annex I countries should be financially penalised for non-compliance with their commitments. The fines were meant to be levied in proportion to the degree of non-compliance with a suggested level of $10 per tonne of excess carbon-equivalent emitted. The penalties raised in this manner were to be paid into a 'Clean Development Fund', intended primarily to finance emission limitation projects in developing countries. The idea that OECD countries would agree to this sort of financial penalty was, of course, ambitious from the beginning. However, by introducing projects which would save emissions equivalent to the degree of non-compliance (instead of 'fixed-rate' penalties), and by removing the Fund's compulsory element (referring to 'contributions to compliance', rather than 'penalties for non-compliance'), the Clean Development Fund became the Clean Development Mechanism.

Given these origins, it is not surprising that the CDM 'mission statement', Article 12 of the Kyoto Protocol (Box 2.5) puts a strong emphasis on the developmental purpose of the mechanism, in that projects undertaken are meant to assist non-Annex I countries 'in achieving sustainable development'. One of the key differences between the CDM and JI (as specified in the Protocol) lies in the fact that in Article 12.10, the former explicitly allows for so-called 'early crediting' between 2000 and the beginning of the first commitment period in 2008. An example may be helpful to illustrate the working of this early crediting. Assume a Party A (the 'acquiring Party') invests in a number of projects in a country H (the 'host country') which come on-line in 2000 and have the effect of reducing H's emissions by 10 units per year. Assume, furthermore, that A's assigned amount for the first commitment period is 100 units (i.e. an average of 20 units per year), and that the life-time of the projects goes beyond the end of this period. Without 'early crediting', A could therefore still claim reduction units from H, but only the 50 units which the projects saved during the commitment period. Thus without early crediting A could add 50 units to its original assigned amount (its 'Reference Level' in Figure 2.1), leaving it with a new target of 150 units. With early crediting,

Box 2.5: Article 12 (The Clean Development Mechanism)

1. A clean development mechanism is hereby defined.
2. The purpose of the clean development mechanism shall be to assist Parties not included in Annex I in achieving sustainable development and in contributing to the ultimate objective of the Convention, and to assist Parties included in Annex I in achieving compliance with their quantified emission limitation and reduction commitments under Article 3.
3. Under the clean development mechanism:
(a) Parties not included in Annex I will benefit from project activities resulting in certified emission reductions (CERs); and
(b) Parties included in Annex I may use the CERs accruing from such project activities to contribute to compliance with part of their quantified emission limitation and reduction commitments under Article 3, as determined by the Conference of the Parties serving as the meeting of the Parties to this Protocol (COP/MOP).
4. The clean development mechanism shall be subject to the authority and guidance of the COP/MOP and be supervised by an executive board of the clean development mechanism.
5. Emission reductions resulting from each project activity shall be certified by operational entities to be designated by the COP/MOP, on the basis of:
(a) Voluntary participation approved by each Party involved;
(b) Real, measurable, and long-term benefits related to the mitigation of climate change; and
(c) Reductions in emissions that are additional to any that would occur in the absence of the certified project activity.
6. The clean development mechanism shall assist in arranging funding of certified project activities as necessary.
7. The COP/MOP shall, at its first session, elaborate modalities and procedures with the objective of ensuring transparency, efficiency and accountability through independent auditing and verification of project activities.
8. The COP/MOP shall ensure that a share of the proceeds from certified project activities is used to cover administrative expenses as well as to assist developing country Parties that are particularly vulnerable to the adverse effects of climate change to meet the costs of adaptation.
9. Participation under the clean development mechanism, including in activities mentioned in paragraph 3(a) above and in the acquisition of CERs, may involve private and/or public entities, and is to be subject to whatever guidance may be provided by the executive board of the clean development mechanism.
10. CERs obtained during the period from the year 2000 up to the beginning of the first commitment period can be used to assist in achieving compliance in the first commitment period.

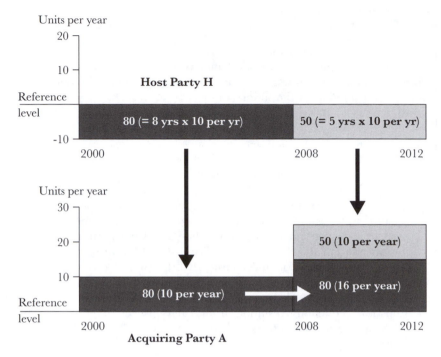

Figure 2.1:   Early Crediting and Kyoto Banking

however, A would have an additional claim to the cumulative emissions saved by the projects before 2008, namely 80 units, implying that it would now have an assigned amount of 230 units. Clearly, early crediting is in the interest of the acquiring Party. It is also in the interest of the host Party, for it begins receiving investments or technologies well before the beginning of the first 'accountancy' period. But is it in the interest of the environment?

In order to assess this question, and the environmental compatibility of the three mechanisms in general, it is useful to have them described in a unified conceptual framework. As concerns their climatic impacts, both JI and (an 'environmentally friendly' interpretation of) the CDM can actually be reduced to IET. Given the climatic benignity of emission trading,[15] this means that all three mechanisms are, in principle at least, compatible with the aims of the climate change regime. Before we turn to how matters look in practice, let us briefly explain how the said reduction is to be achieved.

---

15. IET is indeed completely harmless in this respect, provided that the geographic origin of GHG emissions can actually be ignored as far as *global* warming is concerned.

Box 2.6: Article 3 on Accounting International Transfers

3.10 Any emission reduction units, or any part of an assigned amount, which a Party acquires from another Party in accordance with the provisions of Article 6 [JI] or of Article 17 [IET] shall be added to the assigned amount for the acquiring Party.

3.11 Any emission reduction units, or any part of an assigned amount, which a Party transfers to another Party in accordance with the provisions of Article 6 [JI] or of Article 17 [IET] shall be subtracted from the assigned amount for the transferring Party.

3.12 Any certified emission reductions which a Party acquires from another Party in accordance with the provisions of Article 12 [CDM] shall be added to the assigned amount for the acquiring Party.

It is not difficult to see that concerning climatic effects – which are obviously not troubled by the source of finance for the emission savings in question, nor by the question of whether they were achieved in addition to what had otherwise been planned – ex-post trading in ERUs is essentially the same as the international trading of assigned amounts. Thus by having 50 units validated as ERUs , our host *H* will not only have to hand over 50 units to *A*, – who will be able to add them to its assigned amount (Box 2.6) – but also to subtract 50 units from its original assigned amount (its 'Reference Level' in Figure 2.1), leaving it with a new target 50 units below this level. The effect of this transaction on compliance is thus the same for either side as if the 50 units had been traded accordingly. And the same is true for the effect on the global climate.

The CDM, however, can only be reduced to IET under an 'environmentally friendly' interpretation. One way of doing so is to interpret 'having no commitments' in terms of having a 'non-abatement target'. By this we mean that Parties without actual commitments are assumed to receive (hypothetical) assigned amounts covering exactly their 'Business-as-Usual' emissions, that is to say, the emissions which would have occurred in the absence of any changes due to climate change measures or the climate change regime. Under this interpretation, the ex-post trading under the CDM can be made to work exactly like JI: if the 50 project units are verified as CERs, our host *H* (this time a non-Annex I Party with a 'non-abatement target') will have ensured that the appropriate emission savings have actually been achieved. By handing these 50 CER units over to *A*, *H* will have to reduce its original assigned amount – given by its Business-as-Usual (BaU) emissions – by 50 units, in conformity with the principle of conserving the global total of assigned amounts, followed both by JI and IET. Thus after the transaction, H is left with an assigned amount of BaU – 50 units. And if H would have been in 'compliance' in the absence of the CDM projects, then it will obviously be so after the transfer of the CERs.

The conditional form of this last statement might seem somewhat puzzling. After all, if our 'non-abatement targets' are given by what Parties actually emit, how could they possibly fail to 'comply'? Indeed they could not. However, we consciously did not define these targets as *actual*, but as BaU emissions. The reason for this was simply to ensure the environmental integrity of the system with particular regard to the problem of carbon leakage. The point is that by accepting emission intensive 'carbon fugitives', a Party's actual emissions will increase over and above its BaU level. In the absence of compensating abatement actions, such a Party will thus fail to comply even if it has one of our 'non-abatement targets'. Accordingly it would not be permitted to transfer its CERs (in full), at least not under our environmentally friendly interpretation of the CDM.[16]

In practice, however, it is very unlikely that the non-Annex I countries would accept this consequence. As a matter of fact, given the obvious problems that would be involved in establishing a Party's BaU emissions, it is highly unlikely that this version of the CDM could actually be applied at all. In short, the version of the CDM which can be interpreted as a limiting case of IET and thus shown to have the same environmentally benign character is, in practice, not workable for both political and epistemic reasons. However, it is still useful for the purpose of analysis, not only because it allows us to pinpoint certain weaknesses in the general conception of the CDM, but also because it can be used to analyse the issue of 'early crediting' in a revealing general manner.

After all, we have shown that, from an environmental point of view, both the CDM (in our interpretation) and JI are essentially the same, indeed they are both equivalent to IET in the relevant commitment period. Moreover, the method of introducing hypothetical 'non-abatement targets' used in demonstrating this equivalence for our

---

16. Had our 'non-abatement targets' been defined in terms of actual emissions, there would be no such restriction. More important, however, is the fact that in this case, it would in principle be possible for all Parties to be in compliance without any emission abatement at all.

version of the CDM lends itself very naturally to be applied to the time-span in which early crediting is meant to take place. If we do so, we will find that, from an environmental perspective, (verified) early crediting – be it under JI or the CDM – can be described as buying parts of assigned amounts in this pre-Kyoto period and banking them in the manner suggested in Figure 2.1. This immediately highlights the fact that early credits, whichever their provenance, will involve the environmental problem associated with banking discussed in Section 2.3.2. However, it also brings out another set of problems which may be less self-evident.

We have to remember that the argument we used to establish the equivalence between these (hypothetical) transfers in the pre-Kyoto period and the environmentally harmless trade in assigned amounts was crucially based on the assumption that the project based mechanisms in question are of the above-mentioned 'environmentally friendly' kind. Given the problems concerning the practical applicability of this type of mechanism, it stands to reason that early credits, in practice, will be susceptible not only to the environmental problems of banking, but also to the ones we have identified with reference to the CDM. In particular, there is the danger of host Parties intentionally inflating their emissions during the early crediting period just to have them removed through early crediting projects. Importantly, this problem is not confined to early crediting through the CDM, but applies in equal measure to early credits obtained under the otherwise environmentally harmless JI. For these reasons we believe that it would make environmental sense, on the one hand, to promote IET and JI and, on the other, to monitor closely and possibly even cap the use of banking, early crediting and the CDM.[17]

---

17. We do not wish to reject banking, early crediting and the CDM outright, for there are, of course, other reasons, mainly to do with creating incentives for abatement actions, which speak in their favour as far as the climate is concerned. All we suggest is that the environmental dangers inherent in these instruments must be recognised and that environmentally speaking IET and JI are, on the whole, preferable.

CHAPTER 3

OIL PRODUCTION CAPACITY AND SUPPLIES

3.1 Introduction

The purpose of this chapter is to identify and analyse the factors that influence the development of crude oil production capacity in the period to 2020. We are not concerned here with determining the path of actual production at every point in time during the period under consideration. Actual supplies are determined together with demand and prices by an interaction deemed to be simultaneous and punctual, although in reality it involves lags and shifts of both the demand and supply schedules. One would need therefore to establish separately the structure of these schedules (that is their shape at a given point in time and the likely changes in both shape and position over time) and then examine their interaction with the help of a model.

We are concerned here with specific aspects of the supply issue, namely the determinants of capacity and the likely evolution of capacity in the next twenty years. We begin by defining and discussing a number of propositions that are central to the understanding of the supply/capacity issue.

3.2 Capacity versus Reserves

At any given point in time crude oil supplies are subject to a constraint set by the size of the production and lifting capacity extant in the producing countries, irrespective of the size of proven reserves. Capacity provides an indication of the sustainable upper limit to production.

It is important to stress that capacity is *not* an absolutely rigid datum partly because there are many different concepts of capacity. Actual production may well exceed the upper limit that a certain capacity concept seems to involve; and there are circumstances which technically constrain production below the limit suggested by that or another concept. Capacity, therefore, should not be identified with production. Production also is not identical to supplies. Supplies defined as the volumes put on the market may be smaller or larger than output because stocks provide some flexibility. Although stock changes can have a very strong impact on price movements in the short term their quantitative importance in petroleum is rather small. In a world that currently consumes more than 70 million barrels per day (mb/d) of crude oil, stock changes rarely exceed 2 mb/d, that is less than 3 per cent of the output flow.

Let us examine here a number of capacity concepts.

(a) Appliances or plants have a *rated technical capacity* which is the rate of utilisation recommended by their manufacturers. This is supposed to ensure the good performance of the appliance or plant in question and prolong its life expectancy. One can always utilise a piece of equipment at a higher rate than that posted by the manufacturer at a possible cost, however, in terms of performance or length of life.

(b) In petroleum the optimum rate of production from an oil field crucially depends on the characteristics of the natural reservoir. This optimum rate tends to change over time. The production facilities installed on an oil field are unlikely to display at all times a rated technical capacity equal to the rate of optimum extraction. Facilities may be therefore upgraded or increased (e.g. by the drilling of wells and so on) when they fall short of the requirements of optimum field production; and, on the contrary, remain underutilised when they are in excess of requirements.

(c) Regulations regarding safety, and more significantly the flaring of associated gas, can result in wide discrepancies between the optimum rate of extraction determined by pressures within the natural reservoir, the rated technical capacity for extraction from installed facilities and actual output. In the case of a prohibition of (or limits on) gas flaring, the gas reinjection equipment would set the actual constraint on output. It is important to know, therefore, when a reference is made to optimum rates of production whether the implicit criterion is reservoir behaviour or the available capacity of gas reinjection equipment. This distinction is very important in the case of Saudi Arabia, for example, where the current capacity estimate of 10 mb/d most probably refers to the volume that can be produced without flaring more natural gas than permitted. In an emergency the flaring regulation can be relaxed and production could be increased to 11.0 if not 12.0 mb/d.

(d) A further distinction needs to be made between production and lifting capacity. Actual output volumes are constrained by the smaller of these two capacities. In general, most exporting countries will have adequate lifting capacity defined as the difference between maximum possible output and the lowest expected level of domestic utilisation. During the Iraq/Iran war, however, significant discrepancies emerged between production and lifting capacity because of bombing damages caused to export terminals in the Gulf and because of the threat to tankers due to naval warfare.

(e) The concept of 'surge capacity' is sometimes mentioned. As any engineer knows it is always possible to produce, albeit for a limited time, a higher volume than allowed for by rated or optimum capacity. It is important, however, to distinguish between genuine 'surge capacity', that is increases in output above the normal operation of the system at full capacity, and increases in output brought about by bringing on stream 'shut-in' or idle capacity. After the invasion of Kuwait by Iraq and the consequential loss of some 4.5 mb/d of oil production, almost every producing country increased its crude oil output. Some of them, particularly Saudi Arabia and Abu Dhabi, brought back on stream large volumes of capacity that were lying idle; others, such as Mexico for example, which were operating at full capacity still managed to increase output.

Having defined various capacity concepts, let us now discuss the relationship between capacity and reserves. The fundamental proposition, here, is that there is no correlation between the size of extant capacity and that of proven reserves. The very wide range of reserves to production ratios in the world proves the point. In other words, reserves are exploited very intensively in some parts of the world (UK, USA, Norway and so on), and at very low rates in other parts (e.g. Saudi Arabia, Kuwait, Iraq). If the reserve/production ratio of the USA (which is estimated at eight years) were adopted by Saudi Arabia, its oil production would be of the staggering order of 80–90 mb/d!

Capacity is the result of past investment decisions related to past discoveries and to the knowledge of field behaviour acquired during development and production but is not entirely determined by these two factors. As any other investment, creating crude oil production capacity is also determined by the familiar host of economic and political variables: expected profitability, availability of and/or access to funds, depletion policies and so on. Expected profitability depends on assessment of geological prospects, price, costs and interest rate forecasts, fiscal regime, and in the case of private investment also length of secure tenure and other contract terms. The investment behaviour of national oil companies is not identical to that of private corporations because of fundamental differences in their respective relationship with governments. And there are differences from one national company to another, and differences in the behaviour of private companies depending on size, international exposure, attitude to risk and nationality. To give just one particular example, on a specific factor, Exxon's attitude to risks is very different from Mobil's and it will be interesting to find out which of the two attitudes will prevail now that these companies have merged.

In general, national oil corporations tend to restrict investments and end up operating with much higher reserves to production ratio than private oil corporations. The exploitation is that much more intensive where property rights extend to mineral resources buried under land that is privately owned, as is the case in the USA.

Reserves are an indication of long-term, in some cases of very long-term, potential while capacity defines short-term constraints. We can thus expect oil production to be much higher in Saudi Arabia than in the North Sea in the long term, while today Saudi production is only 30 per cent larger than the North Sea despite the fact that Saudi reserves are 18 to 20 fold greater than those of the North Sea.

3.3   Time Lags and Shocks

A common characteristic of all investments is that they involve time lags between the date at which the decision to invest is made and the date at which the capacity thus installed begins to yield an output. In energy, these time lags tend to be long. Lags cause cycles of plenty and famine. When lags are long and the number of projects is not large the cycles of shortages and gluts can be very pronounced.

A stable oil world is one in which investment in productive capacity matches the growth of actual demand while still ensuring that the system holds a small surplus. Prices tend to explode when the market begins to fear that the growth in demand will rapidly eat up the idle capacity extant in the system. This phenomenon, although largely ignored by analysts, was nevertheless at the root of the price explosions of 1973 and 1979. And oil prices tend to collapse when the volume of idle capacity becomes so large as to defeat OPEC's ability to manage production.

But how to ensure that investment in capacity will match the growth in oil demand in such a perfect way? The multiplicity of investors, the time lags, the uncertain demand prospects, the dependence of investors on new field discoveries, technological developments and conditions of access to oil provinces, all conspire to make a moderately reasonable (never mind an ideal) match virtually impossible.

Add to all that the irregular but inevitable occurrence of political shocks. Recall that in the past fifty years we witnessed the Iranian nationalisations under Mossadeq, the Suez crisis, the 1967 Arab-Israeli war, the 1973 war, the Iranian Revolution of 1979, the Iraq-Iran war of the 1980s and the Iraqi invasion of Kuwait in 1990. We also had restrictions on oil production and exports resulting from either US or international sanctions on Iraq, Libya, Iran and other countries. All these events were potentially disruptive and several caused significant crises.

To expect the oil world to be free from political shocks in the next twenty years would be incredibly optimistic. Yet it is impossible to forecast the timing, location and impact of such shocks on the supply of oil.

3.4 Producers' Policies

A central feature of the oil world is that both the big natural reserves and the large export volumes are mostly in (or from) countries which depend to an extraordinarily high degree on export revenues for government expenditures and foreign-exchange earnings. This is the case of all OPEC countries with the exception of Indonesia, all the non-OPEC countries of the third world with one or two exceptions, as well as Russia and other oil countries of the former Soviet Union.

This high degree of dependence is unlikely to vanish in the foreseeable future except perhaps in one or two countries. The implication is that the major oil-exporting countries will always have a vital interest in attempting to manage prices and to exercise caution when investing in capacity. But, here again, price management will never be perfect in the sense that long response lags may follow instances of price collapses (as in 1986 and 1998–9) and that significant price rises may not elicit a swift response of investment in capacity. On the other hand, caution about investment in capacity in the interest of price management may give way to the familiar temptation of seeking greater output. However, the dependence on oil revenues tends to prevail in the end and to put the brake on ambitious output or capacity objectives if these cause a price collapse. But the whole sequence of actions and policy responses involves lags and therefore disruptions.

The critical policy issue as regards supplies in the next twenty years is that of the opening-up of the upstream sector of major oil-exporting countries to private foreign oil corporations. The countries which at present are totally closed are Saudi Arabia and Mexico. Russia is open in principle but virtually closed in practice. Iraq has been negotiating with foreign companies for investment after the lifting of sanctions, but sanctions are still in force. Iran is inviting foreign investors on terms that are so harsh as to discourage most. Those who have been willing to accept them so far have done it in the belief that once in the country their chances to obtain better terms in the future will significantly increase. Perhaps yes and perhaps no. In Venezuela, the *apertura* regime which attracted so many foreign investors may well be revised by the Chavez government and become less attractive. Kuwait, after long hesitations and debates will offer some production-sharing contracts disguised as service contracts. Foreign companies have been operating in Algeria and Qatar since the late 1980s and have scored successes in finding or developing oilfields.

Whatever the outcome of these very mixed developments, the critical issue is the reconciliation of the conflicting objectives of private investors seeking maximum profits and host governments seeking maximum fiscal revenues or rent. Private investors operate in a competitive structure and seek to optimise output given costs, taxes and prices. Governments seek to maximise the fiscal take which depends on export volume and the unit tax. Companies consider themselves to be price takers, and therefore optimise their production without regard to its possible impact on prices. Government revenues are more responsive to price than output, which makes government (even if they become temporarily misguided on occasions by a desire to defend or expand market shares) ultimately concerned about the impact of production on prices.

The question, therefore, is whether governments which invite foreign investors to the upstream, will enshrine in the relevant contracts residual statutory powers to impose production limits whenever the governments wish to implement a policy aiming at stabilising or raising oil prices.

3.5 Geological Potential

Economists treat reserves as an economic concept virtually ignoring the role of Nature. Geologists treat reserves and possible production profiles as a fact of Nature ignoring economic factors. Both groups

seem to have little understanding of the role of technology. Economists
believe that in the long run technology, or more precisely technical
progress, is the antidote of scarcity. Technical progress removes
Nature's constraints, brings about substitutes, increases productivity
and reduces costs and creates this fluid flexibility which underpins the
assumptions of neo-classical production and growth theories. This is
true to a point, particularly if time, that is the chronological path, is
of no concern. Everything is possible in the long run. The difficulty,
however, is that the long term is a bit like the horizon, always there
but never within reach. For the geologists the focus is on what Nature
has in store. Some of them will tell us that oil in various forms and at
various depths under land or seas is plentiful. This was, for example,
Peter Odell's view at least in the past.[1] The assumption is that costs do
not matter. Others, on the contrary, tell us that conventional oil exists
in finite quantities. Production will therefore peak at some point and
then sharply decline. This is Campbell's and Laherrère's message which
has been publicised recently very forcefully and very widely.[2]

These two geologists reminded us correctly that oil production in
the past twenty years has outpaced the rate of discoveries. This is an
important fact which suggests that decline will sooner or later set in.
They initially indicated that the peak might be reached as early as in
year 2000 and later modified the prediction delaying the onset of
decline to the year 2005. However, they did not seem to take two
important factors into account. The first is that the world holds huge
reserves of non-conventional oil which will be exploited when the
scarcity of conventional oil pushes prices up and keeps them for a long
while above, say, $25 per barrel. The second is that technology which
is available today enables considerable increases in recovery factors.
To raise the recovery factor of oil in the ground from 30 per cent to
50 per cent is akin to an increase in proven recoverable reserves of 66
per cent from an estimate based on old technology. These two
considerations suggest that the expected 'natural' peak may well be
delayed by at least ten or fifteen years.

3.6 Prospects of Capacity Expansion by Country

The upshot of the previous discussion is that the oil supply path is
unlikely to be smooth, largely because of the uncertainties and time

1. P. R. Odell and K. E. Rosing, *The Future of Oil* (London: Kegan Paul, 1983).
2. *The World Oil Supply 1930–2050*, 3 vols. (Geneva: Petro-consultants, 1995)

lags that affect investment, and partly because of the likely occurrence of political shocks. The system has however some inherent flexibility because capacity, however defined, is never absolutely rigid in the short term. Production always tends to increase by more than expected in an emergency.

The supply system is continually under strains. It is constantly subject to the conflicting forces of (a) competition in areas involving small producing countries and/or private oil companies and (b) output management where core OPEC members and a few key non-OPEC countries have a vital interest in reducing production whenever excess supplies put downward pressure on prices. Significant oil price movements (distinguished here from the normal volatility of futures markets) tend to be related to the volume and changes in the volume of surplus capacity. As mentioned earlier, the stability of the oil supply system requires it to keep a certain amount of idle capacity, say 2 mb/d or thereabouts. This 'buffer' is usually held by the Gulf countries. Prices will inevitably rise whenever the market perceives a reduction in the size of this buffer or anticipates that it will be gradually reduced by demand growing at a faster rate than investments in capacity expansion.

A significant rise in the volume of idle capacity may not cause the market to bid prices down if that rise is due to a deliberate exporters' policy of output restrictions. On the other hand, the existence of a large volume of surplus capacity makes it difficult for OPEC members to resist 'cheating' temptations and, more importantly, to reach agreement on quota allocation in response to a price crisis.

There is no mechanism, specifically a co-operative scheme for co-ordinating decisions on capacity investments, which would ensure that the volume of idle capacity is precisely that required to keep the system stable.

When looking at the long run we may be able to ignore both short- and medium-term supply (and accordingly price) fluctuations, and treat the long-term path for oil output and/or production capacity as a smooth trend line. This is acceptable so long as the analyst does not lose sight of the assumption that the focus is exclusively on the end-point of the path and not on the path itself. But the analyst who wishes to form a view on the whole development will want both (a) to treat the path as a smooth one for modelling purposes and (b) to gain insights (which are per force of a qualitative nature) on the vagaries of the path. This is where the difficulty lies. We shall now try to marry the two approaches here.

For a long-run forecast of capacity or production, the size of reserves and the possible onset of oilfield decline do matter. In the medium term the ability to take advantage of the reserve potential is strongly influenced by the initial conditions (if a country has, say, a 2 mb/d capacity today while its reserves could easily carry 10 mb/d of capacity, the speed at which this potential can be realised critically depends on the initial capacity), the institutional structure (national oil corporations or private oil companies), access to capital and so on. There are also political constraints (e.g. international sanctions) which may block decision making for a fairly long time (the sanctions on Iraq were imposed in 1991 and those in Cuba, not an oil country, however, some forty years ago!).

Our view is that natural decline will adversely affect production in the USA and the North Sea some time during the beginning of the long period ending in 2020. The decline has characterised oil production in the US lower 48 states for many years, and the whole of US liquid production, despite the addition of Alaska, since 1986. Deepwater developments offshore in the gulf of Texas may reverse for a while the decline but the long-term trend involves significant reductions in the US output of conventional oil.

In the North Sea the decline is expected to hit the UK before it begins to affect Norway. UKCS oil production has already displayed the classical two-peak saddle pattern, and it will be very surprising if a third peak emerges at some point. The area has been exploited very intensively and advantage has been taken of advances in exploration and production technologies, much more than in most other parts of the world. Only major discoveries west of the Shetlands would reverse for a while the impending decline.

Official estimates expect production in Norway to peak in 2001. Even if they reflect caution, the fact remains that the peak, however delayed, is still in sight.

In the Middle East, Dubai's production has already declined significantly. Egypt's seems to have peaked in 1993 at 0.945 mb/d. A gentle decline, now 20,000 b/d per annum, has set in after that year. Syria's production is already beginning to lose steam. It is expected that Oman's will peak soon.

Among OPEC member countries the troubled producer is Indonesia but this may well be due to institutional and managerial problems rather than to a paucity of reserves.

The areas outside OPEC and the countries mentioned above, which are the current focus of attention of the industry are the countries of the Caspian region, the west coast of Africa, and Latin American countries such as Brazil, Colombia and Argentina.

A significant production increase cannot be expected from the Caspian before 2005. There will be production growth in Angola, which may add 1 mb/d to the current output level by 2005. Growth of production in Brazil, Colombia and Argentina is likely to occur between now and 2010 after which date decline may set in. The additional volumes in these three countries by 2010 (taking 1997 as a base) may be of the order of 0.7 mb/d. A more optimistic view might put the increase at 1.0 mb/d.

Any long-run perspective on supplies must take Russia into account. Performance in this country has been disappointing so far. Russian companies have not yet managed to invest and re-organise the industry in a way that reverses the decline trend started after 1987 (Russia was then producing 11.48 mb/d while production in 1997 was only 6.93 mb/d). Foreign companies, despite the great hopes when the Berlin wall was demolished, have not yet succeeded in gaining significant access to the upstream sector in Russia. The situation will probably change in the years ahead when Russia will finally manage to put its house in order. One could assume that a significant revival of Russian production will not manifest itself before 2007 or 2008, after which Russia could become a very significant supplier.

In North America, other than the USA, one can expect increases of about 1 mb/d in Canada and 1.3 or 1.4 mb/d in Mexico by 2020. Canada is, with Venezuela, a prime candidate for supplying non-conventional oil should conventional oil fall short of demand in the longer period. If oil prices rise to levels that make investments in non-conventional oil profitable and demand expectations turn out to be strong, we would see a very significant supply response from non-conventional oil.

As is well known, the big reserve potential outside the former Soviet Union is in the Gulf and Arabian Peninsula region and in Venezuela. The key countries will always remain Saudi Arabia, Kuwait, Abu Dhabi, Iran and Iraq.

At present development in Iraq is constrained by sanctions. These could be lifted any time or continue to be imposed for many more years indeed. Once lifted, and provided the Iraqi political situation turns out to be stable, significant new production capacity will appear in Iraq after a lag of two to four years. It is thus impossible to predict the date of this resumption. All that can be said is that it could not possibly happen before 2002–2003. A more likely guess is 2005–2006.

In Iran the external political constraint has been effectively lifted. The more serious obstacle to the involvement of foreign investors relates to domestic politics. To placate the opposition of the fundamentalist parties, the government has introduced very harsh terms in the contracts proposed to the foreign oil companies. Although French companies such as Total and Elf, and more recently Shell, have signed agreements in the hope of obtaining better terms in the future, it is not obvious that the Iranian prospects will seem attractive to a number of major oil companies. If investors are forthcoming, Iran's production may well rise to a peak of 5.0 or 5.3 mb/d by 2010 or soon after.

Kuwait has the potential to go up to about 3.0 mb/d and Venezuela to 6 mb/d of conventional oil. Abu Dhabi may add to its current output up to 0.8 mb/d. The Saudi potential is huge. Capacity could be built to 20.0 mb/d or beyond. But will Saudi Arabia go that far? The critical issue does not relate to the reserves potential but to the nature and characteristics of the investment path.

A picture emerges when taking all these points together. Expansion of oil supplies in the period to 2005 depends largely on the main OPEC countries and some of the 'old' non-OPEC countries such as Mexico and Norway. Whether gluts or shortages will characterise the period to 2005 depends on the timing of two independent sets of events: economic recovery in Asia and the lifting of sanctions on Iraq. An early economic recovery associated with delays in developments in Iraq and Iran would tighten the oil market. A delayed recovery associated with an early lifting of sanctions would result in a slack oil market. In either case OPEC will have an important role to play rushing the development of capacity in one instance, and controlling tightly production in the other.

The period after 2005 may see the emergence of substantial additional supplies in the Caspian and Russia depending on the success of developments in deep offshore technology in various oil provinces. But these capacity increases may not be sufficient by themselves to meet requirements if oil demand growth returns to an annual rate of 2 to 3 per cent. OPEC countries and one or two 'old' non-OPEC would easily fill the gap however.

Natural decline may well begin to be felt in the aggregate around 2015. Campbell and Laherrère expect it to happen much earlier, perhaps in 2005. The optimists (and there are more than a few) believe on the contrary that the reserve potential is sufficiently large and technical progress sufficiently dynamic to postpone for a long time the onset of a decline.

Two important factors must be taken into consideration in this context, however. The favourable one is that a decline in the production profile of conventional oil (unless extremely steep which is unlikely in the period to 2020) can be easily compensated for by developments in the non-conventional oil sector. The unfavourable factor is that the giant oilfields in the old provinces, such as the Middle East or Venezuela, are showing signs of fatigue. To realise their production potential may prove to be increasingly costly and quite demanding in management skills and the application of new technology. For these reasons the expansion of effective capacity may not end up by being as large as thought by those who focus exclusively on the enormous size of natural reserves available in the Middle East and the former Soviet Union.

3.7 A Base-Case Projection of Oil Production Capacity

Table 3.1 presents estimates of oil production capacity in 2010, 2015 and 2020. It also shows data of actual oil production in 1995. Oil here means hydrocarbon liquids, that is crude oil and NGLs. The estimates for capacity in 2010, 2015 and 2020 refer exclusively to conventional oil. Oil that will be obtained from shale, tar sand and other such sources, that is non-conventional oil, and which may become (depending on prices and demand expectations) a non-negligible source of supplies in the future, is not included. By definition, processing gains, not being part of capacity at the field, are not included in these data.

There are several sources for oil production data but the numbers they report are rarely identical. Readers familiar with one particular source sometimes feel uncomfortable when they are presented with data from another origin. There is not much we can do about this problem since we have to use a single source. We have selected for this study the 1995 data provided by the Energy Information Administration which is part of the US Department of Energy. The differences between this source and BP Amoco *Statistical Review of World Energy* (1999) which is also authoritative are not very large except for the USA. The EIA puts USA oil production in 1995 at 8.626 mb/d while BP Amoco has 8.320 mb/d. There is a difference in the total production number with BP Amoco recording almost 68 mb/d and the EIA 68.65 mb/d in 1995.

The base case projections for 2010, 2015 and 2020 reflect a judgement on the development of production capacity that is likely to occur given the following assumptions. First, as argued in this chapter the investment path will not be smooth partly because of myopia about future demand and price movements, partly because of political

Table 3.1: Oil Supplies 1995 and Capacity Projections 2010–2020, Thousand Barrels per Day

	1995	*2010*	*2015*	*2020*
USA	8,626	7,700	6,500	5,700
Canada	2,386	3,000	3,300	3,500
Mexico	3,064	4,000	4,800	4,800
Total North America	**14,076**	**14,700**	**14,600**	**14,000**
Argentina	757	1,000	1,100	900
Brazil	890	1,200	1,350	1,250
Colombia	593	850	850	700
Ecuador	401	300	250	200
Peru	131	90	70	60
Trinidad & Tobago	131	90	70	60
Venezuela	2,899	5,600	6,200	6,000
Other S. & Cent. America	102	50	40	30
Total S. & Cent. America	**5,904**	**9,180**	**9,930**	**9,200**
Denmark	186	100	70	50
Italy	97	90	70	50
Norway	2,905	3,000	2,400	1,700
Romania	141	90	60	50
United Kingdom	2,756	1,500	1,000	700
Other Europe	565	300	250	200
Total Europe	**6,650**	**5,080**	**3,850**	**2,750**
Caspian	760	2,000	3,300	3,200
Russian Federation	6,175	8,000	9,000	8,500
Other Former Soviet Union	205	100	100	100
Total Former Soviet Union	**7,140**	**10,100**	**12,400**	**11,800**
Iran	3,703	4,800	5,000	4,500
Iraq	585	5,000	5,500	6,000
Kuwait	2,152	2,800	2,800	2,800
Oman	861	600	500	400
Qatar	497	700	650	600
Saudi Arabia	8,933	13,000	16,000	17,000
Syria	584	300	150	100
United Arab Emirates	2,393	3,500	3,500	3,500
Yemen	345	200	150	100
Other Middle East	50	50	50	50
Total Middle East	**20,103**	**30,950**	**34,300**	**35,050**
Algeria	1,347	1,800	2,100	1,800
Egypt	980	500	400	300
Libya	1,430	1,800	2,100	1,800
Nigeria	1,993	2,800	3,000	2,700
Other West Africa	1,333	1,700	1,900	1,800
Other Africa	282	160	120	100
Total Africa	**7,365**	**8,760**	**9,620**	**8,500**

Table 3.1: *Continued*

	1995	2010	2015	2020
Australia	614	600	600	570
Brunei	176	100	80	60
China	2,990	4,000	3,600	3,300
India	750	600	600	550
Indonesia	1,579	900	700	600
Malaysia	702	600	450	400
Papua New Guinea	100	50	50	50
Vietnam	173	150	150	100
Other Asia Pacific	241	300	250	200
Total Asia Pacific	**7,325**	**7,300**	**6,480**	**5830**
Total OPEC	**26,379**	**40,500**	**45,050**	**45,000**
Total NOPEC (excl. FSU)	**35,044**	**35,470**	**33,730**	**30,330**
Total World	**68,563**	**86,070**	**91,180**	**87,130**

Note: Supplies for the base year 1995 obtained from the base solution to the CLIMOX model as shown in the chapters reporting simulation results differ slightly from actual supplies shown here. This is due to the fact that the solution for the base year for a large general equilibrium model like CLIMOX does not exactly reproduce the base data put into it. The discrepancies in this case are very small, showing a good calibration of the model.

Source: USDOE, Energy Information Administration for 1995, estimates for projections by Robert Mabro.

factors and partly because of a reluctance by the large OPEC producers to invest too early lest they end up holding surplus capacity.

Secondly, capacity does not represent maximum possible production. Actual output may turn out to be higher. In other words, our model allows for some price elasticity of supplies. This means that given our base case capacity data the production results are determined endogenously together with demand and prices. In practice, the supply elasticity is the result of additional investments not taken into account in the base case projections and of an increase in the rate of operations of extant capacity.

Thirdly, we assume that a natural decline in conventional oil production will begin to set in after 2015. This is a more optimistic assumption than Campbell's and Laherrère's. Whenever this decline sets in, non-conventional oil will increasingly be brought in to fill the gap (but there will be some unavoidable time lags initially). Because of this assumption our estimate of base case capacity in 2020 is lower than in 2015. It is possible, however, that producers will respond to this decline by attempting to reverse it for a while with more investments in advanced technologies. A second peak may thus emerge, but allowing for time lags we assume that this will occur just after 2020, that is outside our period, and probably for a short time.

The projections in Table 3.1 may appear to some to be rather pessimistic. Our judgement is that they are consistent with past trends at least in so far as the period 1995–2015 is concerned. The average annual increase is projected to be of the order of 1.1 mb/d. in this period. In carrying out some sensitivity analyses in Chapter 15, we have simulated a higher 'base case' capacity for 2015, which implies an average annual increase of slightly less than 1.5 mb/d. It is difficult to imagine a situation in which the average annual increase will be well outside the 1.1–1.5 mb/d bracket; and our preference still remains for the lower end of this range.

Judgement may differ more significantly however on the timing of the decline postulated here to occur after 2015 and on the likely response to this inevitable phenomenon. In the sensitivity analysis we assume that the decline is postponed and that capacity continues to increase until 2020, reaching a little more than 103 mb/d.

3.8 Conclusions

The oil supply problem is not fundamentally a 'physical' issue for the period considered, except towards the end of our 2020 horizon. But non-conventional oil will then come to the rescue. Nature is generous and the human mind is inventive. Scarcity is not an attribute of things but arises from the limitation of time. Technology develops in the long run; substitutes are found in the long run; episodic shifts that take the world from one technological state to another occur in the long run. If we set our sights on some distant horizon we can assume that we shall end up safely there. The problem is not that we shall not have enough oil to take us to 2020 but that the road is likely to be bumpy and subject to a number of economic and political shocks.

The serious worry is about investment in capacity. Expectations, lack of funds, myopia about future developments, political factors and crises all conspire to restrain to some extent the build-up of capacity. On the other hand, variations in the demand for oil due to economic booms and recessions and to policy factors create, given the available capacity at the relevant periods of time, successive episodes of tightness and slack in the supply/demand balance. The paradox is that excess supplies may frequently emerge in the short run while investments may not meet fully long-term requirements. This is the familiar problem of an apparent contradiction between phases of the cycle and the trend.

It is important to remember in any interpretation of results that a twenty-year period is *not* a very long time relative to the development horizon of the oil-exporting countries of the third world; and not a very long time for the clumsy adjustment process that characterises the world of oil.

CHAPTER 4

METHODOLOGY AND 'BUSINESS-AS-USUAL' PROJECTIONS

4.1 Introduction

The research for this book uses a large simulation model, the CLIMOX model, to compare values for economic parameters without implementation of climate change policies, with values for alternative states of the world in which climate change is addressed. This chapter introduces CLIMOX, and presents projections for economies, fossil fuels, and emissions in a Business-as-Usual (BaU) scenario. The scenario is intended to portray a world in which the greenhouse gas problem is not addressed. Under this scenario, local pollution remains an important incentive for public policies and technological development, but policies directed specifically against greenhouse gas emissions are not implemented. We will here summarise basic assumptions about economic growth, technological progress, fossil fuel supplies and demand, and emissions. In Part III of the book, simulation outcomes are compared against the baseline parameters shown here.

4.2 The Oxford Model for Climate Policy Analysis (CLIMOX)

The projections and simulations in this book are produced from the Oxford model for climate policy analysis (CLIMOX) developed at the Oxford Institute for Energy Studies. It is a global computable general equilibrium (CGE) model which is based on an integrated database, GTAP V.4, of regional factor supply data, input-output tables, and an international trade matrix.[1] The database distinguishes 45 countries and 50 commodities and the CLIMOX model can be adapted to different aggregations of these countries and sectors. This section gives

---

1. The database has been developed by the Global Trade Analysis Project (GTAP) for the year 1995.

an overview of the model, and more details can be found in Chapter 5.

The model was developed at OIES on the basis of two earlier models, the GREEN model developed at the OECD, and the GTAP model, which comes with the database. GTAP is a very simple, one-period CGE model. It was translated into a format suitable for the software used for CLIMOX by Thomas Rutherford.[2] The earlier version of the GREEN model available to us was developed in the early 1990s for environmental policy analysis and was based on 1985 data. The OECD has subsequently updated the model, also based on the GTAP database. Both versions are programmed in C, and we were able to use a translation of GREEN into GAMS format from the Massachusetts Institute of Technology (MIT).[3] Although we took the MIT translation as a blueprint for some of the refinements of the simple GTAP model during the development of CLIMOX, our model is significantly different in structure from the OECD model.

The CLIMOX model consists of a system of non-linear equations, producing equilibrium levels of quantities and prices for factors and goods endogenously. Goods supplies are determined by production functions, relating inputs of labour, capital, a fixed factor, and intermediate goods to single outputs. Production factors are owned by a household sector for each region. Labour and fixed factor supplies are given exogenously, whereas capital is produced through savings. The household sector demands final consumption goods as determined by a linear expenditure system.

The model solves for single periods, which are taken to represent five-year averages. After each solve, stock variables, in particular labour and capital supply, are updated to give the basis for the next five-year point. The basis for the model is neo-classical economic theory, which means the economies in the model maintain full employment, through costless re-allocation of labour between sectors, and competitive adjustment of wage rates. This picture of a smoothly functioning economy can only be justified in terms of medium-term averages, which is why each model solution is interpreted as an average point for a five-year period.

---

2. CLIMOX is programmed in the General Algebraic Modelling System, Mathematical Programming System for General Equilibrium (GAMS/MPSGE). See T. Rutherford (Oct. 1998), GTAPinGAMS: The Data Set and Static Model, University of Colorado, http://robles.colorado.edu/~tomruth/gtapingams/gtapgams.psz.
3. The translation was the first version of the Emission Prediction and Policy Analysis (EPPA) model; the latest version of EPPA is also based on GTAP.

Like all CGE models, CLIMOX is a simulation model, and not a forecasting model. It is therefore calibrated, not estimated. Forecasting models are based on equations which usually have been estimated from a large data set, and attempt to project actual events into the future. They are usually short-term in nature, i.e. for periods below five years, and they are usually limited in the number of regions and sectors, to allow estimation. Their focus is on the absolute values of variables.

Simulation models in contrast place great emphasis on depicting economic behaviour, and are more long-term in nature. CGE models depict the 'centre of gravity' of economies, not the ups and downs of the real world. Model solutions therefore should be interpreted as average points for a period. The focus is more on the functional relationships between economic agents, and on directions of change, than on actual levels of variables. The models are used to indicate the relative changes from a baseline for variables, which are the result of changes in policy instruments.

4.3 Regions and Economic Sectors

In order to limit the complexity of the analysis and reporting the results, CLIMOX uses aggregations of the GTAP database. For the present analysis, the world is aggregated into twelve regions, following relevant economic, energy-related and political lines. Four countries are represented individually, which are the USA, Japan (*JPN*), China (*CHN*), and India (*IND*). In addition, we distinguish the European Union (*EUM*), the Rest of OECD Europe (*ROE*: Norway, Switzerland, Iceland), the Rest of the OECD (*ROO*: Australia, Canada, New Zealand), the Economies in Transition (*EIT*: including the Former Soviet Union, Eastern and Central Europe), Asian Newly Industrialised countries (*ANI*: Indonesia, Korea, Malaysia, Philippines, Singapore, Thailand, Taiwan), the Middle East and North African Oil Exporting Region (*AOE*), Latin America (*LAM*), and the Rest of the World (*ROW*). A full list of countries is attached in Annex 4.1.

The countries and regions USA, the EU, Japan, ROE, ROO, and EIT, correspond roughly to the Annex I countries.[1] Middle East and North Africa (AOE), and the Latin American countries (LAM) contain the major oil-exporting developing countries, whereas the ROE region

---

1. EIT contains some non-Annex I Parties due to limitations of the GTAP database.

contains Norway as the most important OECD oil-exporting country. China and India are modelled individually because of their large population sizes and importance for the world economy and emissions profiles in the twenty-first century. The Rest of the World region in the model represents most poor developing countries in Sub-Saharan Africa and Asia.

The OIES simulation model further distinguishes twelve commodity sectors in each region or country. The non-energy sectors are agriculture, livestock, paddy rice, energy intensive manufactures, other goods (including non-transport services), and transport. The energy sectors are oil, refined oil, gas, coal, electricity, and a utility sector for the distribution of gas. Industrial sectors and private households do not consume crude oil, which is only used in the refinery sector.

This sectoral aggregation distinguishes the three fossil fuels as sources of CO_2 and fugitive fuel methane, and the livestock and paddy rice sectors as sources of agricultural methane. Industries are distinguished into primary energy (oil, coal, gas) secondary energy producing (refining, electricity generation), distribution in the case of gas, and three types of energy using (energy intensive, other industries and services, and transport).

4.4 Economic Growth

Economic growth is determined by growth in the supply of labour and capital, technological progress, and increases in the availability of resources. Population growth assumptions which determine the growth of regional labour supplies are based on UN population projections. Technical progress is both of the general, Hicks-neutral variety which increases factor productivity, and progress in energy efficiency which reduces the amount of energy needed to produce a given unit of output. Growth in the capital stock is determined by national savings, and CLIMOX is investment driven, i.e. household savings adjust to exogenous assumptions of investment demand for funds. Also, we have assumed rates of growth in government demand for goods and services.

Capital stock growth, technological progress, and government demand growth have been calibrated to produce certain economic growth rates in the base run of the model. We assume economic growth in the world to average 2.5 per cent of GDP over the 25-year horizon of this analysis as shown in Table 5.7 in Chapter 5. The continuing slump in the Economies in Transition is assumed to cost them 1.4 per cent of GDP per year between 1995 and 2000. From then on, we assume robust growth of 4–5 per cent. Indian economic growth is also high, although it falls behind growth in the Asian Newly Industrialised, and the Middle East/North Africa regions. The optimistic growth projections for the latter region rest on the strong population growth, and the strong increase in oil production in the region which will, at least in part, necessitate the inflow of foreign capital. We do not see a major change in the sluggish performance of the small developing countries in Sub-Saharan Africa which dominates the ROW region.

4.5 Fossil Fuel Production and Demand

Of paramount importance for the analysis of climate change policies is the level of fossil fuel supply and demand expected over the analysis horizon, as this is the single most important factor determining the extent of man-made greenhouse gas emissions. We will therefore summarise here the projections of fossil fuel supplies over the next 25 years, developed with the simulation model against the background of the discussions in Chapters 3, 7, and 8.

4.5.1 Oil

Production. The growth of fossil fuel production capacities in the model is largely determined exogenously. Production of fossil fuels uses intermediate inputs, labour, capital, and a fixed factor, representing resources and collecting any resource rent contained in the producer prices. Fixed factor supplies increase at an exogenous rate, representing a given reserve depletion profile. Some price elasticity of supply exists, and therefore the model determines both quantities and prices endogenously.

The production of conventional oil is fairly inelastic, with a very limited price response due to substitution of capital for resources. In the simulations this flexibility amounts to some 8 mb/d (million barrels per day) of conventional oil production at most, out of a total production of more than 90 mb/d towards the end of the period.

From the year 2010 onwards, conventional oil production is supplemented by the production of non-conventional oil, and oil products are supplemented by hydrogen for fuel cell applications. There are therefore two alternative sources of liquid fuels in the model; non-conventional oil and hydrogen (H_2). Non-conventional oil is oil produced from tar sands, heavy oil, shale oil, and so on, but also oil produced using new technology such as gas-to-liquids. Non-conventional oil is not produced in the base year, because it is more expensive than conventional oil. It is drawn into the global oil market once the price of conventional oil rises. The rate of production then reacts much more flexibly to demand than the production of conventional oil.

The hydrogen in the model and in the rest of this book is used as a generic term for very low-carbon alternatives to liquid hydrocarbon fuels, such as hydrogen produced with wind, hydro, or photovoltaic electricity – as opposed to hydrogen produced from fossil fuels directly or using fossil fuel generated electricity, ethanol, bio-mass diesel, and so on. Hydrogen in the model is therefore a real 'backstop' technology, which gains competitiveness with emission policies. In the base year 1995, hydrogen production is inefficient because costs are assumed to be 15 per cent above costs of refined oil.

The reasoning behind this specification of oil supply is a lack of price responsiveness over the medium term in the production of conventional crude. Investment and later production decisions are in the majority long-term in nature and not strongly influenced by price movements. Investment decisions for non-conventional crude and hydrogen are dependent on demand expectations over the long term because of the high costs involved. The model actually produces a strong supply response of non-conventional oil supply. This is to be

Table 4.1: Production of Conventional and Non-conventional Oil by Region, BaU, 1995–2020. Thousand Barrels per Day

	1995	2000	2005	2010	2015	2020
USA	8,626	8,327	8,193	7,982	6,867	6,240
EUM	3,316	2,781	2,258	1,702	1,174	852
ROE	2,905	3,219	3,112	3,027	2,492	1,847
ROO	3,071	3,244	3,459	3,737	4,070	4,318
ROO NON-CONV	0	0	0	0	490	1,659
EIT	7,339	7,990	9,224	10,567	12,901	12,574
EIT NON-CONV	0	0	0	982	2,737	3,727
CHN	2,990	3,329	3,696	3,927	3,773	3,536
IND	750	701	650	580	584	548
ANI	2,375	2,204	1,966	1,672	1,307	1,168
AOE	23,951	27,692	31,083	35,594	39,493	39,812
LAM	8,799	11,712	14,924	17,585	19,740	19,015
LAM NON-CONV.	0	0	0	0	426	1,544
ROW	4,364	4,193	4,050	3,844	4,030	3,598
ROW NON-CONV.	0	0	0	0	88	1,543
TOTAL CONV	68,486	75,392	82,616	90,216	96,431	93,508
TOTAL NON-CONV	0	0	0	982	3,741	8,473
TOTAL	68,486	75,392	82,616	91,198	100,172	101,981

Table 4.2: Production of Hydrogen by Region, BaU, 1995–2020. Thousand Barrels per Day Oil Equivalent

	2005	2010	2015	2020
USA	0	0	0	1,314
JPN	0	0	164	630
EUM	0	120	447	1,160
ROO	0	0	53	164
EIT	0	0	0	0
ANI	51	324	735	1,512
TOTAL	51	444	1,399	4,781

interpreted as the response of decision makers to the expectations of oil demand over the model horizons. If Kyoto policies are implemented and consequently oil demand drops below the BaU projections, non-conventional oil capacity is not built, and hydrogen becomes attractive. Tables 4.1 and 4.2 show oil supply profiles for the BaU scenario as derived in Chapter 3.

Total conventional oil supply increases from 68.5 mb/d in 1995 to 90.2 mb/d in 2010, and 93.5 mb/d in 2020. In 2010, 1 mb/d of non-conventional oil are produced, whereas hydrogen production is 0.4 mb/d. By the end of the model horizon, 8.5 mb/d of non-conventional oil are produced, alongside 4.8 mb/d oil-equivalent of hydrogen. The hydrogen in the model therefore captures about 5 per cent of the market for liquid fuels by the end of the projections horizon. This projection is lower than our assessment of the potential market share of hydrogen in general, because it applies only to hydrogen produced using non-carbon energy, as mentioned above. The total potential for hydrogen, in fuel cell vehicles or stationary applications, might well be more than double that amount.

Demand. Projections for the demand for oil are shown in Table 4.3. The table shows regional demand projections as obtained from the simulation model. It should be remembered that the model produces quantities and prices endogenously, given certain exogenous parameters. The supply flexibility for oil (discussed above), and the demand elasticities (given by the household demand system and production technology) produce the demand profiles shown in Table 4.3.

Crude oil demand increases in the USA from 15.1 mb/d in 1995 to 19.5 mb/d in 2020, an average annual growth of 1 per cent. The European Union will increase its demand for oil from 12.6 to 13.9 mb/d between 1995 and 2020, a growth of 0.4 per cent per year on average. Consumption in Japan and the Rest of OECD Europe region

Table 4.3: Oil Demand, BaU, 1995–2020. Thousand Barrels per Day

	1995	*2000*	*2005*	*2010*	*2015*	*2020*
USA	15,106	16,386	17,484	18,794	20,166	19,467
JPN	4,555	4,773	4,979	5,197	5,241	4,765
EUM	12,574	13,210	13,690	14,207	14,567	13,910
ROE	552	596	633	659	679	652
ROO	2,453	2,601	2,737	2,904	3,047	3,027
EIT	4,558	3,864	4,241	4,998	5,975	6,582
CHN	3,106	3,629	4,162	4,788	5,451	5,873
IND	1,224	1,422	1,625	1,860	2,115	2,272
ANI	5,007	5,827	6,689	7,560	8,460	8,679
AOE	8,853	11,070	12,878	15,129	17,607	19,156
LAM	6,335	7,438	8,531	9,684	10,898	11,433
ROW	4,164	4,577	4,968	5,419	5,966	6,166
TOTAL	68,486	75,392	82,616	91,198	100,172	101,981

will increase very slowly, at rates around 0.2 per cent per year. The developing countries, with the exception of the Rest of the World region (dominated by Sub-Saharan Africa), will demand around 2.4 per cent more per year, increasing their share in world oil demand from 42 to 48 per cent until 2020. Oil demand in the Economies in Transition declines between 1995 and 2005, increases only 0.5 mb/d over the 1995 level in 2010, and reaches 6.6 mb/d in 2020. Average

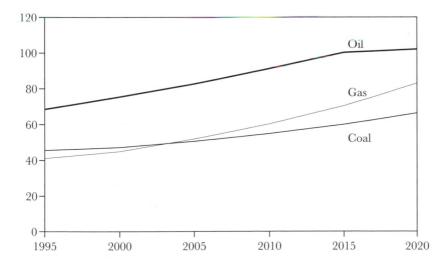

Figure 4.1: Fossil Fuel Production, BaU, 1995–2020. Million Barrels per Day Oil Equivalent

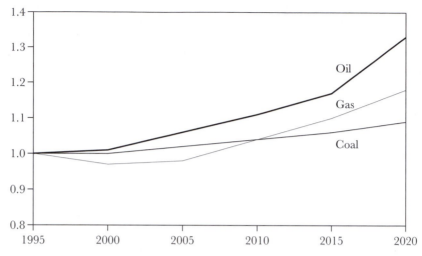

Figure 4.2: Fossil Fuel Price Indices, BaU, 1995 = 1

growth over the period is 1.5 per cent per year, starting with a negative rate of –3.1 per cent in the first ten years. World oil demand and supply grow at 1.6 per cent per year on average. Figure 4.1 summarises production of fossil fuels for the Business-as-Usual scenario.

Figure 4.2 shows price projections for the three fossil fuels resulting from the interplay of supply and demand in CLIMOX. For the Business-as-Usual scenario, our assumptions of the development of production capacity of conventional and non-conventional oil, and of hydrogen, together with the economic growth produced in the model, result in the prices shown in the figure. CLIMOX therefore projects an increase in the price of oil from the base year 1995 by 11 per cent in 2010, and 33 per cent in 2020 in real terms. This means, taking an average price of oil in 1995 of $18 per barrel, that the oil price reaches $20 per barrel in 2010, and $24 per barrel in 2020, in constant 1995 Dollars.

4.5.2   Coal

In contrast to oil, coal supplies are more flexible. Reserves are abundant, and production is less strongly limited by resources, which is reflected in the model by a higher elasticity (0.5) of substitution between capital and the reserve factor in the production function. With increasing demand resulting from economic growth, coal supplies increase over the model horizon. Tables 4.4 and 4.5 show production and consumption levels for coal.

Table 4.4: Production of Coal, BaU, 1995–2020. Million Tonnes Oil Equivalent per Year

	1995	2000	2005	2010	2015	2020
USA	554	566	586	611	640	679
JPN	4	3	3	3	3	4
EUM	127	104	84	68	54	43
ROE	0	0	0	0	0	0
ROO	174	182	194	208	224	244
EIT	340	305	323	350	380	409
CHN	662	744	846	965	1,104	1,272
IND	152	160	169	180	193	209
ANI	41	48	56	65	76	89
AOE	1	1	1	1	1	1
LAM	25	31	38	47	58	72
ROW	192	205	220	237	256	277
TOTAL	2,272	2,350	2,521	2,736	2,990	3,300

Table 4.5: Demand for Coal, BaU, 1995–2020. Million Tonnes Oil Equivalent per Year

	1995	2000	2005	2010	2015	2020
USA	509	526	544	563	584	617
JPN	75	75	75	75	75	75
EUM	227	214	205	200	198	198
ROE	1	1	1	1	1	1
ROO	74	75	77	79	81	83
EIT	325	278	287	314	352	388
CHN	647	732	840	965	1,110	1,283
IND	159	173	191	209	229	254
ANI	68	76	87	100	115	134
AOE	8	9	11	12	14	16
LAM	20	21	22	24	26	29
ROW	161	169	180	192	205	220
TOTAL	2,272	2,350	2,521	2,736	2,990	3,300

There seems little disagreement in the literature about the reserve availability of coal. A different issue is the location of reserves and the availability of a transport infrastructure needed to bring these to markets. We assume a near doubling of coal production in China, which will use almost all of this production domestically. China thus becomes by far the biggest coal producer, delivering about one-third of the world total. North American coal production increases only slowly, whereas Australia increases the share of exports in total production for the ROO region. Coal is declining strongly in the European Union, as Britain and Germany end coal support and reserves dwindle. European coal production declines to one-third of its 1995 level, from 127 million toe (tonnes oil equivalent) to 43m toe by 2020. The average price of coal increases slowly, as input and transport costs increase. The price of coal increases from the 1995 level by 4 per cent until 2010 and 8 per cent until 2020.

4.5.3 Gas

As for coal, reserves of gas are in principle abundant, but distance to demand centres poses the question of transport capacity and transport costs. This seems a stronger constraint on gas use than on coal use, and therefore the model assumes a lower supply elasticity for gas than for coal. Also, in some regional markets, reserves might be limited, for example in the USA. Tables 4.6 and 4.7 show BaU production and consumption levels for natural gas over the model horizon. Gas prices shown in Figure 4.2 fall between 1995 and 2000, a result of new capacity additions and liberalisation in major gas-consuming regions. In 2010, as the supply situation tightens, gas prices are on average 4 per cent above the 1995 levels, and increase by 18 per cent until 2020.

Table 4.6: Production of Gas, BaU, 1995–2020. Billion Cubic Metres per Year

	1995	2000	2005	2010	2015	2020
USA	541	561	585	614	644	678
JPN	2	2	2	3	3	3
EUM	207	212	219	234	250	267
ROE	34	51	76	81	85	89
ROO	199	220	245	276	309	347
EIT	744	761	913	1,091	1,290	1,513
CHN	20	25	35	50	70	103
IND	20	24	27	31	36	43
ANI	111	138	170	211	261	324
AOE	237	280	317	364	426	503
LAM	102	137	184	253	350	487
ROW	56	73	95	127	170	228
TOTAL	2,273	2,482	2,870	3,335	3,894	4,585

Table 4.7: Demand for Gas, BaU, 1995–2020. Billion Cubic Metres per Year

	1995	2000	2005	2010	2015	2020
USA	628	686	749	822	905	1,014
JPN	69	83	96	109	123	141
EUM	341	378	417	449	483	531
ROE	6	7	7	8	8	8
ROO	109	121	134	147	162	180
EIT	661	641	767	933	1,128	1,318
CHN	20	27	38	55	80	121
IND	21	25	30	36	44	55
ANI	74	91	113	142	179	235
AOE	186	229	276	334	402	491
LAM	104	129	162	205	263	347
ROW	55	66	80	96	116	145
TOTAL	2,273	2,482	2,870	3,335	3,894	4,585

4.6 Emission Projections

In Chapter 9 we discuss emissions of greenhouse gases incorporated into the analysis. The data calculated by CLIMOX are denominated in international Dollars, and some auxiliary coefficients are needed to turn values into physical quantities of fossil fuels and greenhouse gas emissions. The model then accounts for CO_2 emissions from the burning of oil, coal, and gas at the point of consumption. In addition, we have included methane emissions. In the energy sectors these result from incomplete combustion, and from fuel leaks during mining and transportation. Coal bed methane and leaks from gas distribution systems are the main sources of energy methane.

Non-energy sectors are also major sources for greenhouse gas emissions. The agricultural sector produces large amounts of green-house gases, in particular methane from livestock husbandry and rice cultivation, but also CO_2 released from the soil under certain practices. Cement production is another major non-energy source of CO_2. CLIMOX recognises CO_2 and methane emissions from the energy sectors in the simulations, whereas non-energy greenhouse gases are ignored. We have used the model to produce projections for these non-energy gases. Global energy emissions are projected to increase from 23.6Gt in 1995 to 36.8Gt in 2020 (see Table 9.1 in Chapter 9). This means an average growth of 1.8 per cent per year.

Annex 4.1: List of Countries Included in the Regions of the Model

USA

United States of America	American Samoa
Guam	Northern Mariana Islands
Puerto Rico	United States Virgin Islands

JPN
Japan

EUM 'EU Members'

United Kingdom	Germany
Denmark	Sweden
Finland	Austria
Belgium	France
Greece	Ireland
Italy	Luxembourg
Netherlands	Portugal
Spain	Monaco
Channel Islands	Isle of Man
French Guiana	Gibraltar
Guadeloupe	Holy See
Martinique	Reunion
Saint Pierre and Miquelon	San Marino

ROE 'Rest of OECD Europe'*

Iceland	Liechtenstein
Norway	Switzerland
Svalbard and Jan Mayen Is	

ROO 'Rest of OECD'*

Australia	New Zealand
Canada	Heard & McDonald Islands
Norfolk Island	

EIT 'Economies in Transition'

Croatia	Bulgaria
Czech Republic	Hungary
Poland	Romania
Slovakia	Slovenia
Estonia	Latvia

---

* ROE and ROO represent 1990 OECD Countries with Annex B Commitments

Lithuania	Russian Federation
Ukraine	Armenia
Azerbaijan	Belarus
Georgia	Kazakhstan
Kyrgyzstan	Moldova
Tajikistan	Turkmenistan
Uzbekistan	

CHN

China	Hong Kong

IND

India

ANI 'Asian newly industrialised'

East Timor	Indonesia
Korea (Rep. of)	Malaysia
Philippines	Singapore
Thailand	Taiwan

AOE 'The Middle East and North African Oil Exporting Region'

Iran	Iraq
Kuwait	Oman
Qatar	Saudi Arabia
United Arab Emirates	Syria
Yemen	Algeria
Egypt	Libyan Arab Jamahiriya
Bahrain	Gaza Strip
Israel	Jordan
Lebanon	Tunisia

LAM 'Latin American'

Mexico	Venezuela
Colombia	Bolivia
Ecuador	Peru
Argentina	Brazil
Chile	Uruguay
Guyana	Paraguay
Surinam	

ROW 'Rest of world'

Viet Nam	Sri Lanka
Bangladesh	Bhutan
Maldives	Nepal
Pakistan	Anguila
Antigua & Barbuda	Aruba
Bahamas	Barbados

Belize	British Virgin Islands
Cayman Islands	Costa Rica
Cuba	Dominica
Dominican Republic	El Salvador
Grenada	Guatemala
Haiti	Honduras
Jamaica	Montserrat
Netherlands Antilles	Nicaragua
Panama	Saint Christopher and Nevis
Saint Lucia	Saint Vincent and the Grenadines
Trinidad and Tobago	Turks and Caicos Isl.
Turkey	Morocco
Western Sahara	Botswana
Lesotho	Namibia
South Africa	Swaziland
Angola	Malawi
Mauritius	Mozambique
Tanzania (United Rep. of)	Zambia
Zimbabwe	Benin
Burkina Faso	Burundi
Cameroon	Cape Verde
Central African Republic	Chad
Comoros	Congo
Congo, Dem. Rep. of the	Côte d'Ivoire
Djibouti	Equatorial Guinea
Eritrea	Ethiopia
Gabon	Gambia
Ghana	Guinea
Guinea-Bissau	Kenya
Liberia	Madagascar
Mali	Mauritania
Mayotte	Niger
Nigeria	Rwanda
Sao Tome and Principe	Senegal
Seychelles	Sierra Leone
Somalia	Sudan
Togo	Uganda
Afghanistan	Albania
Andorra	Bermuda
Bosnia and Herzegovina	British Indian Ocean Territories
Brunei	Cambodia
Christmas Island	Cocos (Keeling) Islands
Cook Islands	Cyprus
Falkland Islands	Faroe Islands
Fiji	French Polynesia
Greenland	Johnston Island
Kiribati	Korea (Dem. People's Rep. of Korea)

Lao People's Dem. Rep

Macedonia, former Yugoslav Republic of

Marshall Islands

Mongolia

Nauru

Niue

Palau

Pitcairn Islands

Solomon Islands

Tonga

Vanuatu

Wallis and Futuna Isl.

Yugoslavia

Macao

Malta

Micronesia, Federated States of

Myanmar

New Caledonia

Pacific Islands

Papua New Guinea

Saint Helena

Tokelau

Tuvalu

Wake Island

Western Samoa

PART II

METHODOLOGY AND ASSUMPTIONS

CHAPTER 5

THE OXFORD MODEL FOR CLIMATE POLICY ANALYSIS (CLIMOX)

5.1 Introduction

In the previous chapter we have given a short overview of the simulation model developed for this book. We will give a more detailed description in this chapter. Section 5.2 starts with an overview of the equations of the very basic GTAP model, which was the starting point in the development of CLIMOX. The next section summarises some adjustments of the GTAP database, which were deemed necessary in order to achieve a realistic representation of fossil fuel production. Refinements of production and demand equations in CLIMOX are shown in Section 5.4. Section 5.5 explains the dynamic structure of the CLIMOX, and documents assumptions about population, techno-logical progress, energy efficiency improvements, economic growth, and increases in fossil fuel production capacity. The model includes non-conventional oil and hydrogen as alternatives to conventional fuels, as described in Section 5.6. The last section discusses how emissions and emission reduction policies are treated in the model.

5.2 The GTAP Equilibrium Model

Computable General Equilibrium (CGE) models are based on the Arrow-Debreu interpretation of Walras's laws of general equilibrium. The CLIMOX is programmed using the Mathematical Programming System for General Equilibrium (MPSGE) modelling tool for the GAMS software developed by Thomas Rutherford. CGE models are represented as a sequence of explicit demand and supply functions for factors and goods, and an equilibrium is defined by market clearance, and zero-profit functions, which are solved as mixed complementarity problems. CLIMOX is a refinement of Rutherford's version of the GTAP model, programmed in MPSGE and GAMS. We present here basic features of Rutherford's GTAP model.[1] These are, first, the demand functions for intermediate goods and production factors, then private and government consumption demand, and third, international trade in goods. The household budget equilibrium, market clearance conditions, and zero profit conditions close the model.

5.2.1 Intermediate and Factor Demands

Producers have the choice between supplying domestic or foreign markets. In the GTAP model, domestic and export goods are joint products with a constant elasticity of transformation. The transformation function is

$$Y_{ir} = \left[\alpha_{ir}^{Y} D_{ir}^{1+1/\eta} + \beta_{ir}^{Y} X_{ir}^{1+1/\eta} \right]^{1/(1+1/\eta)}$$

where Y is total output of good i in region r, D is domestic, and X export supply, η is the elasticity of transformation. With competitive producers, supplies for a given total output are dependent on domestic and export prices:

$$D_{ir} = Y_{ir} a_{ir}^{D} (p_{ir}^{D}, p_{ir}^{X})$$

$$X_{ir} = Y_{ir} a_{ir}^{X} (p_{ir}^{D}, p_{ir}^{X})$$

This gives us supplies of goods. Note that for CLIMOX, the elasticity of transformation η is infinite, i.e. domestic and export goods are perfect substitutes.

Intermediate inputs to production are determined by input-output coefficients a_{ijr}, implying a Leontief technology in physical inputs. Intermediate demand is

$$ID_{ir} = \sum_{j} Y_{jr} a_{ijr}$$

Goods sold in the domestic market, including intermediate goods, are composites of goods produced domestically and imports. Following Armington,[2] domestic users have a choice between the two types of

---

1. This section is a summary of his description of the model; see T. Rutherford (October1998), GTAPinGAMS: The Data Set and Static Model, University of Colorado, http://robles.colorado.edu/~tomruth/gtapingams/gtapgams. psz. p. 3 ff.
2. P. Armington, 'A Theory of Demand for Products Distinguished by Place of Production,' *IMF Staff Papers*, 16, 1969, 159–78.

goods, which is represented by a constant-elasticity-of-substitution choice function:

$$ID_{ir} = \left[a_{ir}^I DI_{ir}^\rho + \beta_{ir}^I MI_{ir}^\rho \right]^{1/\rho}$$

where DI is domestic and MI is imported intermediate goods.

In the basic model version, producers minimise unit cost given factor prices and applicable taxes. Factor demands are obtained from the following optimisation:

$$\min_f \sum p_{fr}^F (1 + t_{fir}^F) FD_{fir} \quad s.t. \quad \psi_{ir} \prod_f FD_{fir}^{\theta_{fir}} = Y_{ir}$$

where Y is given exogenously. Under the assumption of linear homogeneity of the production function, factor demands are the product of activity level and compensated factor demand functions depending on factor prices and taxes:

$$FD_{fir} = Y_{ir} a_{fir}^F (p_r^F, t_{ir}^F)$$

5.2.2 Public and Private Demand

Aggregate public sector output is exogenous, but the composition of the aggregate is price-responsive. Public sector demand for goods is derived from a Cobb-Douglas aggregation function:

$$G_r = \Gamma_r \prod_i GD_{ir}^{\theta_{ir}^G}$$

As mentioned above, all goods sold domestically are Armington aggregates of domestically produced goods and imports, therefore public sector demand is given by exogenous aggregate demand, and domestic and import prices, and taxes.

$$GD_{ir} = \overline{G}_r a_{ir}^G (p_{ir}^D, p_{ir}^M, t_{ir}^G)$$

Private households maximise a Cobb-Douglas utility function:

$$U_r = \sum_i \theta_{ir}^C \log(CD_{ir})$$

Again, households demand Armington aggregates of domestic and imported goods. Demand functions depend on aggregate expenditure, and the price of the aggregate goods gross of taxes.

$$CD_{ir} = \frac{\theta_{ir}^C M_r}{p_{ir}^C (1 + t_{ir}^C)}$$

5.2.3 International Trade

Imported goods are composites of imports from the different regions of the model. For the three types of commodities, intermediate goods, public and private consumption goods, the percentage of composition of domestic and imported goods may differ, but the regional origin of the imported goods is the same within the import aggregate. The total import composite is therefore determined by a constant elasticity of substitution (CES) aggregation across imports from different regions. Taxes and a transportation margin apply on bilateral trade in the model, where transportation inputs are Cobb-Douglas aggregates of international inputs supplied by different countries. Bilateral trade flows then result from cost-minimising choice given f.o.b. export prices, export tax rates, and import tariffs. Demand for bilateral imports is given as

$$M_{irs} = M_{is} a_{irs}^M (p_{ir}^X, t_{irs}^X, p^T, t_{irs}^M)$$

5.2.4 Household Budget Equilibrium

The model has one aggregate consumer in each region, who earns payments to factors, and tax revenues, and pays investments, public sector demand, and net capital outflows. The balance is aggregate consumption expenditure:

$$M_r = \sum_f p_{fr}^F F_{fr} \qquad\qquad \text{factor income}$$

$$+ \sum_i t_{ir}^Y (p_{ir}^D D_{ir} + p_{ir}^X X_{ir}) \qquad \text{indirect taxes}$$

$$+ \sum_{ij} t_{ijr}^{ID} p_{ir}^{ID} Y_{jr} a_{ijr} \qquad\qquad \text{taxes on intermediate goods}$$

$$+ \sum_{fi} t_{fir}^F p_{fr}^F FD_{fir} \qquad\qquad \text{factor tax income}$$

$$+ \sum_i t_{ir}^G p_{ir}^{GD} GD_{ir} \qquad\qquad \text{public tax income}$$

$$+ \sum_i t_{ir}^C p_{ir}^{CD} CD_{ir} \qquad\qquad \text{consumption tax income}$$

$$+\sum_{is} t_{irs}^{X} p_{irs}^{X} M_{irs} \qquad \text{export tax income}$$

$$+\sum_{is} t_{isr}^{M} (p_{is}^{X} M_{isr}(1+t_{isr}^{X}) + p^{T} T_{isr}) \quad \text{tariff revenue}$$

$$-\sum_{i} p_{ir}^{D} I_{ir} \qquad \text{investment demand}$$

$$-\sum_{i} p_{ir}^{G}(1+t_{ir}^{G})GD_{ir} \qquad \text{public sector demand}$$

$$- p_{n}^{C} B_{r} \qquad \text{current account balance}$$

Capital flows (or the current account balance) are exogenous, denominated in the numeraire price index and held fixed in the simulations.

5.2.5 Market Clearance

Having defined demands for goods and factors, we can now define conditions for market clearance: for each type of commodity and factor, supply has to equal demand in the equilibrium solution. For example, domestic supply equals demand for intermediate inputs to production, public and private demand, and domestic investment.

$$D_{ir} = DI_{ir} + DG_{ir} + DC_{ir} + I_{ir}$$

$$= ID_{ir} a_{ir}^{D,I} + GD_{ir} a_{ir}^{D,G} + CD_{ir} a_{ir}^{D,C} + I_{ir}$$

where the different factors represent compensated demand functions for domestic inputs by sub-markets, each of which are functions of domestic and import prices.

Other market clearance equations are included for import commodities (Armington aggregate of regional imports must equal demand for intermediate, public and private consumption), exports (export supply equals import demand across trading partners plus demand for transport services), primary factors (exogenous endowments equal primary factor demand in production), and supply of the Armington aggregation of domestic and imported goods has to equal demand for intermediate goods, public and private consumption.

5.2.6 Zero Profit Conditions

Producers behave competitively under constant returns to scale. Profits therefore have to be zero in equilibrium. This means that the value of output has to be equal to the value of domestic and foreign sales, net of taxes:

$$(p_{ir}^D a_{ir}^D + p_{ir}^X a_{ir}^X)(1 - t_{ir}^Y) = \sum_f a_{fir}^F p_{fr}^F (1 + t_{fir}^F) + \sum_j a_{jir} p_{jr}^{ID}(1 + t_{jir}^{ID})$$

Likewise, zero profits are earned in international trade, where Armington functions transform domestic and imported goods into aggregates for intermediate, public, and private demand. Equilibrium identities can be written in reduced form:

$$p_{ir}^I = c(p_{ir}^D, p_{ir}^M, \alpha_{ir}^I, \beta_{ir}^I)$$

$$p_{ir}^G = c(p_{ir}^D, p_{ir}^M, \alpha_{ir}^G, \beta_{ir}^G)$$

$$p_{ir}^C = c(p_{ir}^D, p_{ir}^M, \alpha_{ir}^C, \beta_{ir}^C)$$

in which

$$c(p^D, p^M, \alpha, \beta) \equiv \min_{D,M} p^D D + p^M M \quad s.t. \quad (\alpha D^\rho + \beta M^\rho)^{1/\rho} = 1$$

is the unit cost function defined by the CES aggregate of domestic and imported inputs.

With this the description of the basic GTAP model is complete. We now have production and consumption of goods, based on endowments of production factors, and have stated the conditions under which equilibrium prevails in all markets. The coefficients of the functions are either estimated on the basis of the original data set, or given exogenously.

The beauty of using CES functions for all major relationships is that we only need a set of elasticity values for the different functions, while the rest of the coefficients can directly be taken from the data set. This consists of regional social accounting matrices, and an international trade matrix. The data set is balanced from the outset, and is taken to represent a general equilibrium of the world economy. Calibration of the model means that the function parameters are determined to reproduce the data set.

5.3 Adjusting GTAP

Version 4 of the GTAP database represents the world economy for the year 1995 in 45 countries and 50 commodities. The database was originally developed for the Uruguay Round of negotiations under the GATT system, and therefore has a very detailed treatment of the agricultural sector. A few difficulties became apparent in GTAP in the energy sectors. A new version of GTAP is under preparation where special care has been taken to arrive at an accurate representation of production and use of fossil fuels, given that GTAP is becoming something of a standard for energy-environmental modelling. However, the new version is to be released in the first half of the year 2000, and therefore this research had to use version 4.

Some ad hoc adjustments were made to take care of three of the more obvious difficulties with the database. Firstly, we adjusted factor payments to capital and resources to reflect different production costs and resource rents in the different regions. Secondly, we adjusted the input-output flow of natural gas to distinguish clearly between the different fuels, and thirdly, Japanese oil production was set zero.

5.3.1 Adjustment of Factor Payments

The production costs of oil consisting of costs of physical inputs, labour and capital, are far below its price in most regions, especially in the Middle East. The price of oil therefore contains some element of rent, which can be interpreted as payment for reserve depletion.[3] Oil production in GTAP contains payments to a third production factor, the resource itself. Given the significant differences in production costs of oil, the shares of the resource factor in total factor payments should differ strongly between regions. This is not the case in GTAP version 4, where the capital share in the Middle East is far too high, and the rent is far too low. We therefore made some adjustments, reallocating factor payments away from capital and into rents. Table 5.1 shows the percentage of capital payments reallocated to rent payments for each region. This adjustment does not alter total production costs, and the database remains balanced.

5.3.2 Adjustment of Gas Inputs

In the input-output matrix of the database, a large portion of natural gas is an input in the oil refining sector, and then moves from oil refining into gas distribution. In fact, in some regions the value of

---

3. There is a large body of literature devoted to the calculation of a depletion premium and comparisons with the actual price of oil, and we do not wish to add to this literature. Readers are referred to M.A. Adelman, *The Genie out of the Bottle: World Oil since 1970* (Massachusetts Institute of Technology, MIT Press, Cambridge Mass., 1995) as a starting point.

Table 5.1: Percentage of Capital Payments Reallocated to Rent

USA	0
EUM	0
ROE	0
ROO	20
EIT	20
CHN	20
IND	20
ANI	0
AOE	70
LAM	50
ROW	20

refining output which is used in the gas distribution sector is greater than the value of natural gas used in distribution. This distorts simulation results, because the model cannot distinguish between refined oil produced in refining and natural gas moving through refining. We therefore adjusted the input-output matrix by channelling natural gas directly into the gas distribution sector and reducing refining inputs accordingly.

5.3.3 Japanese Oil Production

Japan produced 18 thousand barrels per day of oil in 1995. In GTAP, the country produces oil but factor payments to the fixed factor are zero. We therefore cannot control the development of production capacity over time, which requires a time profile for the fixed factor (see Section 5.5.5). Japanese oil production was therefore set zero.

5.4 The CLIMOX Equations

Section 5.2 described the basic model structure on which CLIMOX is built. In this section we present some additional detail. We start with the production function nesting, and continue with the derivation of household demands. Section 5.5 then describes the dynamic structure of the model.

5.4.1 Production

Goods are supplied through multi-level nested production functions of the constant elasticity of substitution (CES) type. This structure allows for distinct elasticities of substitution between different inputs at each level. Figure 5.1 shows the nesting structure and the elasticity flags used at the different levels. At the top of the production nesting, X^d (price is P^d) is produced using a Leontief technology (substitution elasticity equal to 0) combining non-energy intermediate inputs and an aggregate bundle of capital, labour, energy, and a fixed factor designated as *KLEF*. At the next level in the nesting structure, *KLEF* is produced using a CES production function combining labour and a capital, energy, and fixed factor bundle (*L:KEF*), the next level combines an energy bundle and a bundle of capital and the fixed factor (*E:KF*), and this bundle finally is determined as an aggregate of capital and the fixed factor (*K:F*).

The energy bundle *E* is a multi-level aggregation of coal, oil, refined oil, gas, and electricity. At the top level, a non-electric bundle is combined with the electric composite fuel. This is an Armington aggregation of domestic and imported electricity. At the next level, the non-electric bundle is produced from an Armington aggregate of domestic and imported coal, refined oil and gas.

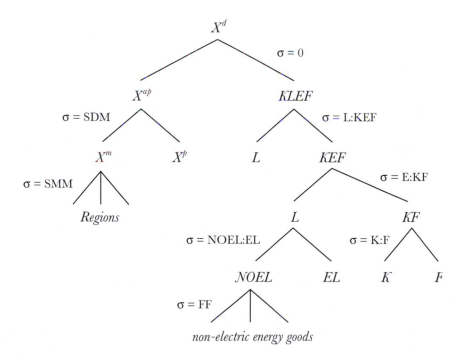

Figure 5.1: Nested CES Structure of Production in CLIMOX

The capital stock in the model economies is distinguished by vintages. Each production sector is modelled as comprising two distinct technologies, producing an homogenous good, but with different production parameters. For old capital, material inputs including the energy commodities are demanded in fixed proportions, and the substitution elasticities between labour, capital, and fixed factor are very low (0.1). Basically, substitution between the different inputs is impossible once capital has become old. The percentages of old and new capital stock are determined by the rates of saving and depreciation. Table 5.2 shows elasticities of substitution in the different sectors, and layers of the nesting structure.

Table 5.2: Substitution Elasticities in Production

	SDM	SMM	L:KEF	E:KF	K:F	NOEL:EL	FF
Agriculture	4	8	0.5	0.5	0.2	0.5	1
Rice	4	8	0.5	0.5	0.2	0.5	1
Livestock	4	8	0.5	0.5	0.8	0.5	1
Coal	4	8	0.5	0.5	0.5	0.5	0.2
Oil	20	20	0.2	0.2	0.2	0.2	0.2
Gas	20	20	0.2	0.2	0.2	0.2	0.2
Gas Distribution	4	8	0.5	0.5	0.2	0.5	2
Oil Refining	4	8	0.5	0.5	n.a.	0.5	0.2
Electricity	4	8	0.1	0.1	5	0.5	5
Energy Intensive	4	8	0.5	0.5	n.a.	0.5	5
Other Industries	4	8	0.5	0.5	n.a.	0.5	5
Transport	4	8	0.1	0.1	n.a.	0.1	0.2

Notes: See Figure 5.1 and text below for explanation of acronyms. K:F for Oil Refining, Energy Intensive, Other Industries, and Transport is not applicable, because these sectors do not employ a fixed factor.

Goods used domestically are aggregates of imported and domestic commodities (with substitution elasticity SDM in Figure 5.1), and imported commodities in their turn are composites from different regions (with elasticities SMM in Figure 5.1).

Given the import demand specification, each country or region in the model faces downward sloping demand curves for its exports, which means export demand is less than perfectly elastic with respect to price. However, substitution elasticities are fairly high, both between domestic goods and imports (SDM), and between imports from different countries (SMM). As shown in Table 5.2, SDM elasticities are 4 and SMM elasticities are 8 for most commodities, except for oil and gas where we assume almost perfect substitutability.

5.4.2 Demand

Household demand is determined through a nested demand system for one aggregate household for each region. At the top level, households decide over the split of income between savings and consumption, where initial household savings are given in GTAP, and savings growth is determined exogenously (see Section 5.5). Disposable incomes minus savings are spent on consumption. Again, total consumption expenditures are split between subsistence and non-subsistence consumption. Subsistence consumption S_i is fixed and increases with population. Aggregate non-subsistence consumption is made up of non-energy goods and an energy bundle, which is an aggregate of electricity and non-electricity energy commodities similar to the energy bundle in production.

Subsistence consumption is determined from total consumption and exogenous income elasticities by solving the equation

$$\varepsilon_{R,I}\left(M_R^0 - \sum_I S_{R,I}^0\right) = M_R^0\left(\frac{C_{R,I}^0 - S_{R,I}^0}{C_{R,I}^0}\right)$$

for S_p where
ε_I = income elasticity of demand,
M = aggregate consumption,
C_I = total consumption of good I, and
S_I = subsistence consumption of good I.

The index R stands for region. Income elasticities of demand are region and commodity specific, and vary between 0.8 and 1.2, as shown in Table 5.3.

5.5 Dynamic Macro-Economic Structure

The CLIMOX is a recursive computable general equilibrium model. This means the core static CGE is solved recursively for the different periods, with updating of stock variables between each model solution. Each equilibrium solution is assumed to represent an average for a five-year period. This time-frame is appropriate for this type of model. CGEs assume costless reallocation of capital and labour with economy-wide wage and rental rates while other structural parameters are static. This specification is realistic only over the medium term.

Table 5.3: Income Elasticities of Demand

	USA	JPN	EUM	ROE	ROO	EIT	CHN	IND	ANI	AOE	LAM	ROW
Agriculture	0.80	0.80	0.80	0.80	0.80	0.85	0.95	0.90	0.80	0.85	0.90	0.90
Rice	0.80	0.80	0.80	0.80	0.80	0.85	0.95	0.90	0.80	0.85	0.90	0.90
Livestock	0.80	0.80	0.80	0.80	0.80	0.85	0.95	0.90	0.80	0.85	0.90	0.90
Coal	0.80	0.80	0.80	0.80	0.80	0.85	0.95	0.90	0.80	0.85	0.90	0.90
Oil	0.90	0.90	0.90	0.90	0.90	0.95	0.95	0.95	0.95	0.90	0.95	0.95
Gas	1.05	1.05	1.05	1.05	1.05	1.10	1.10	1.10	1.10	1.10	1.10	1.10
Gas Distribution	1.05	1.05	1.05	1.05	1.05	1.10	1.10	1.10	1.10	1.10	1.10	1.10
Oil Refining	0.90	0.90	0.90	0.90	0.90	0.95	0.95	0.95	0.95	0.90	0.95	0.95
Electricity	0.90	0.90	0.90	0.90	0.90	0.95	0.95	0.95	0.95	0.90	0.95	0.95
Energy Intensive	1.05	1.05	1.05	1.05	1.05	1.10	1.10	1.10	1.10	1.10	1.10	1.10
Other Industries	0.93	0.94	0.95	0.95	0.91	0.96	0.89	1.02	1.02	0.99	0.90	0.91
Transport	1.20	1.20	1.20	1.20	1.20	1.20	1.20	1.20	1.20	1.20	1.20	1.20

Important exogenous trend parameters determining growth rates of stock variables and therefore also growth of economies and emissions are population and labour supply growth, energy efficiency improvements, productivity improvements, capital accumulation, and growth in fossil fuel supply potential. This section describes the derivation of the trend parameters.

5.5.1 Population Growth

The demographic assumptions for the scenarios of this study are based on the *World Population Prospects*: *The 1996 Revision*, published by the Population Division of the Department of Economic and Social Affairs of the United Nations (New York, 1998). The *1996 Revision* contains the results of the fifteenth round of UN population estimates, incorporating detailed data for 228 countries or areas. In 1995, 81 million people were added to the world population, 95 per cent of which are in developing countries. The world's population was growing at 1.48 per cent between 1990 and 1995, significantly lower than at any time since 1950.

The demographic projections incorporated in the *1996 Revision* are carried out at five-year intervals from 1995 to 2050 according to three scenarios, based on the same assumptions about mortality and international migration for each country. The difference between the scenarios lies in their assumptions concerning fertility rates.

> The three fertility variants that are prepared are referred to as high, medium and low, depending upon the assumed levels of future fertility. The high-, medium- and low-fertility variants for each country are all thought to provide reasonable and plausible future trends in fertility [...] the medium-variant projection has well described future world population growth, at least for year horizons of 20–25 years. In that sense, the medium variant projection can be thought of as 'most likely'.[4]

According to these projections – summarised in Table 5.4 – world population will increase from 5.7 billion in 1995 to 7.7 billion in 2020. Japan and the countries in the European Union have negative or very low population growth, whereas the developing countries grow considerably. The Chinese population is projected to grow from 1.2 bn to 1.4 bn, an increase of 19 per cent, the lowest growth for the developing country regions. The highest population growth will occur in the countries of Middle East and Northern Africa (AOE region),

---

4. *1996 Revision*:89

Table 5.4: Total Fertility Rates (TFR) and Population.

	TFR Births/Woman					Population million				
	1985	1995	% change since 85	2020	% change since 95	1985	1995	% change Since 85	2020	% change since 95
USA	1.8	2.1	12.6	2.1	2.4	245.5	271.2	10.5	327.3	20.7
JPN	1.8	1.5	-15.9	1.7	14.2	120.8	125.1	3.5	123.8	-1.0
EUM	1.7	1.6	-7.8	1.8	11.4	360.1	373.5	3.7	374.1	0.1
ROE	1.7	1.6	-3.6	1.8	11.4	11.0	11.8	7.7	12.6	6.9
ROO	1.8	1.8	1.4	2.0	9.8	44.8	50.8	13.4	62.9	23.8
EIT	2.4	1.8	-23.6	1.7	-6.1	374.1	390.7	4.5	392.2	0.4
CHN	2.5	1.9	-22.0	2.0	4.7	1057.6	1205.0	13.9	1429.5	18.6
IND	4.7	3.4	-28.5	2.1	-38.1	767.9	929.0	21.0	1271.6	36.9
ANI	4.2	3.2	-23.8	2.1	-33.8	353.2	414.1	17.2	544.3	31.5
AOE	5.5	4.1	-25.7	2.4	-40.5	196.5	262.5	33.6	452.0	72.2
LAM	4.0	3.1	-22.6	2.2	-30.0	122.0	148.8	22.0	208.1	39.9
ROW	6.4	5.5	-14.0	3.7	-33.6	1195.9	1504.6	25.8	2473.5	64.4
World	3.6	3.0	-17.3	2.4	-18.9	4849.5	5687.1	17.3	7671.9	34.9

where population increases from 262 to 452 million over the 25-year horizon, an increase of 72 per cent. For the model simulations, we assume labour force growth in line with population growth.

5.5.2 Energy Efficiency Improvements

The model contains autonomous energy efficiency improvements (AEEI), that is technical progress in energy use. Improvement rates are determined using progress rates to calculate efficiency indices for each year. The exogenous progress rates defined in per cent per year which are based on the background discussions of Chapter 6 are shown in Table 5.5. These are used to produce efficiency improvement indices, which are applied to commodity sectors (for energy used in production) and demand sectors (for energy used in private, government, and investment demand) and reduce the amount of energy needed to produce commodities, or aggregate commodities into final demand. Improvement indices therefore reduce the level of energy use in the CES nesting structure for production and demand. In production, improvements apply at the aggregation of the energy bundle and the bundle of capital and the fixed factor ($E{:}KF$). In demand, they apply at the aggregation of goods in the linear expenditure system for households, the government, and investment. These productivity improvements should be interpreted as disembodied technological progress, and therefore also apply to old capital.

Energy efficiency improvements are calculated as:

$$\lambda_T^E = e^{5\rho\chi^e(T-1)(1-(T-1)/100)}$$

where $\chi^e = 0.01$, to convert from improvement rate in per cent into coefficient of improvement. The factor 5 in the formula accounts for the years between period solves. From this, the efficiency indices are derived as $1/\lambda_T^E$. The formula means that AEEI decreases over time, and economies reach steady state energy demand in the long run.

5.5.3 Productivity Improvements

Labour supply in the model grows with population, and the capital stock increases with investment. Both are improved by autonomous technical progress. Similar to the derivation of energy efficiency improvements shown above, several auxiliary parameters are used here to determine the technical progress rate. The specification means that the rate of progress decreases over time to ensure that the economies reach steady state growth in the long run (100 years). First, initial and end-of-period progress rates π are given as inputs. From this, growth rates g^{lr} are determined:

$$g_T^{lr} = (1+\alpha)\frac{(\pi_0 - \pi_{T=End})}{(1+\alpha \cdot e^{5\beta(T-1)})} + \pi_{T=End}$$

where $\alpha = 0.07$, and $\beta = 0.06$.

Starting with an initial level of 1, the productivity index g^{prod} is then calculated:

$$g_{T+1}^{prod} = g_T^{prod}(1+g_T^{lr})^5$$

Labour and capital supply is updated between period model solutions by multiplication with g^{prod}. Table 5.5 shows initial productivity increases in per cent per year π_0. Table 5.6 shows productivity indices g^{prod}.

5.5.4 Economic Growth, National Savings and Capital Stock Growth

We assume economic growth in the world to average 2.5 per cent of GDP over the 25-year horizon of this analysis as shown in Table 5.7. The continuing slump in the Economies in Transition is assumed to cost them 1.4 per cent of GDP per year between 1995 and 2000. From then on, we assume robust growth of 4–5 per cent. Chinese GDP growth continues on the very strong trend shown in the years before our base year 1995, starting at 5.1 per cent per year and declining to 4.6 in 2020, with an average of 4.7 per cent. Indian

Table 5.5: Productivity Increase in Per Cent per Year

Region	Productivity Growth Rate
USA	1.6
JPN	1.8
EUM	2.0
ROE	1.7
ROO	1.2
EIT	3.9
CHN	4.9
IND	3.4
ANI	3.6
AOE	2.0
LAM	2.6
ROW	1.2

Table 5.6: Productivity Index g^{prod}. 1995=1

	2000	2005	2010	2015	2020
USA	1.08	1.17	1.27	1.37	1.47
JPN	1.09	1.19	1.30	1.42	1.54
EUM	1.10	1.22	1.34	1.47	1.62
ROE	1.09	1.18	1.28	1.39	1.51
ROO	1.06	1.13	1.20	1.27	1.34
EIT	0.90	1.10	1.40	1.79	2.18
CHN	1.27	1.61	2.03	2.55	3.18
IND	1.18	1.40	1.64	1.93	2.26
ANI	1.19	1.42	1.69	2.00	2.37
AOE	1.10	1.34	1.66	2.07	2.58
LAM	1.14	1.29	1.47	1.66	1.88
ROW	1.06	1.13	1.20	1.28	1.36

Note: The reduction in productivity for the EIT region between 1995 and the year 2000, which represents the continuing economic downturn in the area.

Table 5.7: Real GDP. Average Annual Economic Growth Rates. Billion 1995$. Per Cent

		Real GDP		Growth, Per Cent per Year
	1995	2010	2020	1995-2020
USA	7,120	9,770	11,970	2.1
JPN	5,270	6,990	8,190	1.8
EUM	8,300	11,280	13,560	2.0
ROE	450	610	720	1.9
ROO	990	1,340	1,620	2.0
EIT	790	1,170	1,850	3.4
CHN	870	1,790	2,840	4.7
IND	320	600	890	4.1
ANI	1,290	2,590	4,000	4.5
AOE	630	1,270	1,890	4.4
LAM	1,630	2,770	3,840	3.4
ROW	1,010	1,560	2,050	2.8
WORLD	28,670	41,740	53,420	2.5

economic growth is also high, although it falls behind growth in the Asian Newly Industrialised, and the Middle East/North Africa regions. The optimistic growth projections for the latter region rest on the strong population growth, and the strong increase in oil production in the region which will, at least in part, necessitate the inflow of foreign capital. We do not see a major change in the sluggish performance of

the small developing countries in Sub-Saharan Africa which dominates
the ROW region.

These economic growth assumptions had to be translated into the
macro-economic parameters which determine growth in the simulation
model. CLIMOX is investment driven, where initial investment equals
household savings given in the underlying database. Investment
demand for funds is assumed to increase over time at a fixed, exogenous
rate, shown in Table 5.8. Foreign savings are constant, and the
government budget deficit or surplus is the result of tax revenues and
exogenous expenditure growth. Household savings adjust to investment
demand for funds. Investment demand for goods (i.e. the demand for
inputs needed to produce new capital equipment) is determined by a
linear expenditure system. Capital accumulation is derived from net
savings. Government demand for goods and services is growing at
exogenous rates below the savings rate, which over time implies
decreasing government shares in the economies.

Table 5.8: Annual Growth Rates of Investment and Government Expenditure.
Per Cent

	Investment	*Government*
USA	1.8	1.3
JPN	1.8	1.6
EUM	2.0	1.8
ROE	1.8	0.5
ROO	1.8	1.4
EIT	3.8	3.8
CHN	4.6	4.4
IND	3.8	3.6
ANI	4.5	4.2
AOE	3.5	2.4
LAM	3.3	3.1
ROW	1.8	1.2

Productivity improvements, investment and government growth rates
are calibrated exogenously. Using iterative modelling, they have been
fitted so as to produce economic growth for the regions in accordance
with the assumptions in Table 5.7. The interplay between effective
labour supply growth and capital accumulation has been given some
attention in order to produce balanced growth, where wages and
capital rentals remain roughly at the same level. The model
specification means that world GDP growth is more or less exogenous.

This simple macro-economic structure has been chosen for several reasons. It might have been feasible to implement a more elaborate structure with endogenously determined growth rates. Yet these growth rates would none the less depend entirely on initial assumptions about parameters. The type of model used here does not lend itself to an adequate endogenous representation of economic growth, which would require a dynamic growth model. The most important determining factor of economic growth in the real world is decisions about capital accumulation, both on the side of firms deciding on investment demand for funds, and on the side of investors deciding on savings. Economic theories regarding determination of investment and savings abound, and there seems to be a chicken-and-egg problem. In the end, interest rates adjust to equate savings and investment. A model capable of producing economic growth endogenously has to include a fairly elaborate specification of the international capital markets, money, nominal exchange rates, and forward looking expectations. This lies far beyond the scope of this book.

5.5.5 Growth in Fossil Fuel Supply Potential

The GTAP database contains payments to labour, capital and a third factor from production of goods. In the case of fossil fuels, this third factor is interpreted as the resource, and supply is fixed for each period. Between periods, supply is updated using fossil fuel supply projections produced for this book. Details are shown in Chapters 3, 7 and 8.

5.6 Alternative Energy

There are two alternative sources of energy in the model, non-conventional oil, and hydrogen. These are perfect substitutes for oil, and refined oil, respectively. Only non-conventional oil produces CO_2, hydrogen is a carbon-free backstop. The alternative energy commodities are produced in simple two level CES production structures. A fixed factor is introduced to represent infrastructure constraints. The production functions then combine the fixed factor with capital on the first level, and combine the aggregate with an intermediate good and labour on the second level. Substitution elasticities between fixed factor and capital are 0.2, whereas the fixed-factor-capital aggregate, labour, and intermediate input are used in fixed proportions.

The factor shares for labour and capital for each of the alternative energy goods are the same as the shares in the goods they are replacing, e.g. the capital share in hydrogen is the same as in refined oil, and so on. The fixed factor is initially assigned a value of 1 per cent of the capital share. The intermediate input for non-conventional oil is the 'Other Industries' commodity, and hydrogen is produced using electricity. The intermediate input level is one minus the sum of factor payments. The resulting initial value-added is unity for each of the alternative fuels.

The alternative energy sources are calibrated to be inefficient in the base solution. The degree of competitiveness is controlled by mark-ups on input factors. Labour and capital requirements are multiplied with the mark-ups thereby increasing the initial price, for example to 1.15 in the case of hydrogen. The refined oil competitor therefore is not produced until the price of refined oil increases above 1.15.

Market penetration is controlled by the availability of the fixed factor, both in terms of initial level and supply elasticity. These have been calibrated in order to produce a realistic market penetration for the alternative fuels over time. The alternative technologies are not available before the year 2000. Production profiles for non-conventional oil are shown in Chapter 3; projections for hydrogen in the Business-as-Usual scenario are repeated in Table 5.9.

Table 5.9: Production of Hydrogen by Region, BaU. 1995–2020. Thousand Barrels per Day Oil Equivalent

	2005	2010	2015	2020
USA	0	0	0	1,314
JPN	0	0	164	630
EUM	0	120	447	1,160
ROO	0	0	53	164
EIT	0	0	0	0
ANI	51	324	735	1,512
TOTAL	51	444	1,399	4,781

Hydrogen production is inefficient in the base year, and becomes competitive only in 2005 when oil prices rise. Market entry for 2005 with 50 thousand barrels oil equivalent is at a very low level, the experimental stage of the new technology. Production rises to more than 400 thousand barrels in 2010, and reaches 4.8 million barrels oil equivalent per day in 2020.

It should be remembered that the hydrogen modelled in CLIMOX is produced without CO_2 emissions, i.e. using renewable energy sources. This is currently very expensive. The late market entry and slow build-up of production reflects the fact that the technology is currently only in a laboratory stage, and substantial innovations are necessary to make it commercial. Hydrogen produced with conventional electricity could enter the market earlier, but would not be a backstop technology in the sense required here. We expect the total market share of fuel cell applications therefore to be much higher than what is implied by the hydrogen production profile shown in Table 5.9 and in later chapters.

5.7   Policy Simulations: Taxes and Flexibility Mechanisms in the CLIMOX Model

CLIMOX is used for policy simulations. It contains indirect and direct tax parameters. For the present analysis, climate change measures are represented in the model by national CO_2 emission quotas, CO_2 taxes, energy taxes, and international CO_2 quotas. National and international emissions permit trading can be simulated.

For policy simulations, a policy instrument, e.g. a tax rate, is changed and model solutions are obtained. The resulting data are compared with model solutions without the change in the tax instrument. In order to conduct policy simulations for the present project, a baseline had to be developed for the time-frame of the study, with which simulation outcomes can be compared. This is the BaU scenario, described in Chapter 4 and Part II of this book. In this section, we describe how climate policies are represented in the model.

The model takes into account the emissions from fossil fuel use. The greenhouse gases in the model are CO_2 and methane (CH_4) and the sources are the burning of fossil fuels for CO_2 and fugitive fuels for methane (in CO_2 equivalent units). In order to determine emissions in CLIMOX, several conversions are necessary. The model contains only values of inputs and goods in 1995 US Dollars, which have to be converted into physical units. Fossil fuel production and both intermediate and final consumption are converted into barrels, tons, and cubic metres, using region-specific fuel prices. For combustion emissions, quantities of fossil fuels consumed are converted into emissions using region-specific coefficients of CO_2 content. Fugitive fuel emissions are determined from fossil fuel production by converting quantities into emissions of CO_2 equivalent units of methane, using region-specific leakage rates.[5] Putting a price on CO_2 equivalents later

---

5. Fugitive fuel methane emissions from natural gas transport, in particular, are driven by the 'production' of the gas distribution sector.

on in the policy simulations therefore increases the production costs because of fugitive-fuel CH_4, and the consumer prices of fossil fuels because of CO_2 emissions from fuel burning.

The model also can be used to give projections for methane emissions from rice cultivation, the livestock sector, and waste management. However, because of the diverse nature of emission sources and abatement possibilities, these emissions are not considered in emission policies in the simulations. Emission policies in the model are exclusively directed against emissions from the energy sectors.

The model allows for the simulation of carbon taxes (or 'carbon-equivalent' taxes[6]), energy taxes, and carbon permits, both internationally tradable or non-tradable. Energy taxes are levied per unit of energy at the point of final use. They do not distinguish between the sources of the energy units, i.e. whether produced from fossil fuels, and from which fossil fuels. They therefore do not take account of the different carbon contents of the different fossil fuels. The carbon content of coal is 30 to 40 per cent higher than that of oil or gas, and in addition the energy conversion efficiency of coal using equipment is usually somewhat lower than that of oil or gas using equipment. The CO_2 emissions resulting from the production of a unit of energy from coal are therefore much larger than emissions from energy produced from the other fuels.

Carbon taxes or tradable permits are based on units of CO_2e, and therefore take adequate account of the relevant differences between fuels. Domestically tradable CO_2e emission permits and carbon taxes are equivalent at least for modelling purposes. We assume that under a trading system, all energy users are allowed and able to trade emission permits, including individual households, and trading is implemented efficiently and with very low transaction costs. In this domestic context, the government is taken to auction initially an amount of emission permits (in suitable denominations, e.g. tons of CO_2e) which is equal to the national quota or assigned amount specified in the relevant international agreement (e.g. the Kyoto Protocol). The auctioning system leads to an efficient determination of permit prices, which are equal to the marginal costs of abatement of a unit of CO_2e. An adequate institutional and administrative setting ensures that the

---

6. The term 'carbon tax', in its narrow sense, refers to a tax levied on the carbon content of emissions. However, in this narrow sense it is typically only used in the context of CO_2 emissions. If such a tax is also applied to different greenhouse gases, as in the case of our model, then the relevant unit is that of CO_2e. See Section 2.3.1.

emission target is reached (for example, sellers of fossil fuels have to show emission permits they received from buyers by the end of the year, so fossil fuels cannot be available without permits).

Carbon taxes are excise duties levied per ton of CO_2e at the point of sale. Reaching the emission targets with levies is much more difficult to implement efficiently than permit trading, because it requires knowledge of the exact demand response to the levies. The government would have to set levies to an amount which induces users of fossil fuels to reduce demand by the amount required to reach the (Kyoto) targets.

In a simulation model, carbon taxes or levies can be determined iteratively, until the tax levels are found under which emission targets are reached. To simulate a system of domestically traded emission permits on the other hand, the modeller places a constraint on the amount of emissions allowed. The model contains equations for emission permits. Permit supply is given exogenously and permits are owned by the household sector (which is equivalent to a revenue-neutral government auction of permits). Permit demand is calculated from fossil fuel demand (CO_2 emissions) and fossil fuel production/distribution (CH_4 emissions). The model then solves for the price of the emission permits which equilibrates permit supply and demand. The permit price increases the user cost of fossil fuels by exactly the same amount as the carbon levy determined iteratively. The permit price is the dual of the carbon tax.

The CLIMOX model can also be used to simulate international trading of emission permits. Instead of national emission constraints, the modeller places a cap on the sum of emissions of a region of countries, e.g. the Annex I countries for the Kyoto scenario. The model solves for the international permit price, which will be equal to the marginal abatement cost in each country. This necessarily assumes a permit trading scheme on the domestic level, or carbon taxes determined at exactly the right level, in order to equalise abatement costs across countries. The household sector in each country still owns the nationally allocated quotas or assigned amounts in emission permits specified in the Kyoto Protocol. This ensures that costs of internationally bought permits are paid by the buying countries and reduce their national incomes, and proceeds from sales go to the selling countries and increase their national incomes.

The Kyoto Protocol allows for international flexibility to reach the set targets. This includes international trading of emission permits, joint implementation of emission reduction projects between Annex I countries, and the Clean Development Mechanism (CDM), whereby

Annex I countries undertake emission reduction measures in non-Annex I countries. For modelling purposes, the first two mechanisms are equivalent, under one condition: that international emission trading does not involve 'hot air'; in other words that traded permits represent actual emission reductions from Business-as-Usual. International permit trading involves monetary transfers from the buying country to the selling country, and the selling country reduces emissions. This is in effect the same as Joint Implementation, where the buying country invests money in the selling country to reduce emissions in that country.

The 'hot air' issue is of some importance both for the Kyoto Protocol implementation and the Global Compromise scenario developed in Chapter 13. In the Kyoto Protocol, assigned emission amounts for the first commitment period for some countries in the EIT region in the model are well below emissions as projected in the Business-as-Usual case. This means the region can sell international emission permits without actual emission reductions from BaU. These permit sales are obviously different from Joint Implementation. Because of the additional benefits expected from Joint Implementation, and because of increasing monetary transfers associated with monopolistic behaviour, it has to be assumed that countries with 'hot air' would attempt to limit the supply of this 'hot air' to the international trading system.

The Clean Development Mechanism is much more difficult to incorporate into the model than international permit trading. Under trading, the countries involved have individual assigned amounts of emission permits, which constitute the supply of permits in the model. Demand is derived, and the model solves for an equilibrium price. For CDM, the permit suppliers have no assigned emission amounts. The model therefore cannot calculate an equilibrium price endogenously. Instead, the modeller has to make an assumption about the possible emission reductions achievable through CDM in a given country, for example 5 per cent of the projected Business-as-Usual emissions. The modeller then enters 95 per cent of BaU emissions as assigned amount of permits for the country, and the country takes part in the international trading. CDM in this setting becomes the same as Joint Implementation, and is again equivalent to international permit trading as far as the macro model is concerned.

For this study however, we have decided against this rather arbitrary addition of CDM into the analysis. The CDM will involve distinct projects in developing countries. The engineering costs of these projects, which would probably involve some amount of new infrastructure in addition to, for example, power generation plants, are difficult to assess.

In addition, the institutional and administrative difficulties involved are bound to be large, which increases costs and delays projects. These factors are difficult to take into consideration appropriately in a macro model, and arbitrary assumptions would have to be used. Instead, we have developed the Global Compromise scenario, where developing countries fully join the international emission reduction efforts.

CHAPTER 6

TECHNOLOGICAL CHANGE AND ENERGY INTENSITY

6.1 Introduction

Reductions in greenhouse gas emissions will have to be achieved either through a reduction in the activities causing the emissions, which involves high costs, or the introduction of new technologies to reduce emission intensities, by allowing the production of goods and services with less polluting processes. There is generally a widespread optimism among analysts that substantial reductions can be achieved with new technologies; yet the uncertainty about this potential is substantial.

Technological standards vary widely in different countries and regions of the world. It is clear that some regions are technologically less advanced and can reduce emissions by catching up with best-practice technologies used in more advanced regions. Some technological change is therefore possible without the development of new technologies, but rather with the adaptation of existing knowledge. More advanced regions, however, will have to rely mostly on the development and introduction of new technologies.

Technological change that affects the use of fossil fuels will emerge regardless of the Kyoto Protocol, but may also be introduced as a part of, or a response to, climate policies. To which extent technologies affect fuel use depends on the uses to which different specific technologies will be put; on whether a given country or region is able to make use of new technology; and on how quickly the different technologies can penetrate the markets. We will here attempt an assessment of the future impact of technological change, using first, an inventory of the new technologies likely to emerge in the future. Secondly, the extent of technological progress possible in the different regions is evaluated against the background of the technological status quo.

In the macro-economic modelling framework used in this study, technologies are implicit in parameters chosen for production and demand functions. Technological change and reductions in polluting activities depend most strongly on the assumed elasticity parameters shown in Chapter 5. In addition, some new and currently unavailable technologies are included in the model. These refer to alternative sources of energy which are also discussed in Chapter 5. The challenge for the modeller is that this study concerns developments twenty years into the future, under new policy regimes, and with technological options which are not clear at present. The modelling choices and assumptions described earlier are based on our evaluation of what the future will look like and this chapter gives the background to this evaluation.

In Section 6.2 we discuss technologies which are currently at the forefront of development, and might become important within the time horizon of the model. We then turn to a discussion of techno-logical change at the macro level of the CLIMOX model in Section 6.3. By comparing the technological standards across the regions in the model in terms of the efficiency of energy use, we try to evaluate which countries or regions can reduce greenhouse gas emissions through the adoption of best-practice technologies – i.e. without reduction in the level of general economic activities, and without major efforts in the development of genuinely new technologies – and which countries will have to rely on the new technologies described in Section 6.2.

6.2 Technological Progress[1]

Technological progress is a potent force that can change both the rate and the pattern of energy use in the world. New and improved energy technologies are expected to play a key role in reducing future

---

1. Main sources for this section are:
    ABB, ABB Renewable Energy Status and Prospects, 1998. http://www. abb.no/
    IEA, 'Electric Technologies. Bridge to the 21st Century and a Sustainable Future', Report of an IEA workshop, 1997.
    IEA, *World Energy Outlook*, 1998.
    IEA, Heat Pump Centre, 1998 (http://heatpumpcentre.org/).
    IEA, Key World Energy Statistics, 1998 (http://www.iea.org/stats/files/ keystats/stats_98.htm)
    IPCC, *Impacts, Adaptations and Mitigation of Climate Change: Scientific-Technical Analyses*. Contribution of Working Group II to the Second Assessment Report of the Intergovernmental Panel on Climate Change, 1996.
    IPCC, 'Technologies, Policies and Measures for Mitigating Climate Change', IPCC Technical Paper I, 1996.

greenhouse gas emissions, especially CO_2 emissions. The term potential
is frequently used when discussing technologies. The IPCC distinguishes
between the technical potential (the result of application of best
available technology), the economic potential (the result that can be
achieved cost-effectively), and the policy potential (the result that can
reasonably be achieved as a result of policies and measures). This
section describes technologies that are likely to be available (in both a
technical and an economic sense) within the time-frame of this study.
We concentrate on stationary energy supply and transport, the two
most energy intensive economic sectors. Determining which technologies are likely to mature is no easy task, as the time lags between
invention and innovation, and between innovation and adoption, in
many instances are very long.

6.2.1 Stationary Energy Supply

Because of its energy intensity and size, power generation represents
a major contributor to GHG emissions. Important issues in this sector
are the possibilities for substitution from high-carbon to low-carbon
generation, the potential for enhanced energy efficiency and the
development of alternative energy sources.

The theoretical potential for energy efficiency improvements is very
large. The global average efficiency of fossil-fuelled power generation
is about 30 per cent, and the average efficiency in the OECD countries
is about 35 per cent.

Combined-cycle gas turbines (CCGT) have high efficiency and low emissions.
They also have low construction costs, are available in a range of
small to medium sizes, have short construction times (two to three
years), and are straightforward to build and operate. CCGTs could
account for a significant share in the production of electricity in the
near future. Fast market penetration is likely in countries and regions
where gas is available and/or cheap, such as Europe, North America
and the Economies in Transition.

Integrated gasification combined cycles (IGCC) are the major innovation for
coal, residual oil, and biomass power generation. Coal is likely to
retain a strong position in power generation where gas is unavailable
or expensive. Coal is favoured in those developing countries where it
is abundant, such as China and India, and in locations close to low-
cost coal production, such as Australia, South Africa and parts of
North America. There is a large potential in developing countries to

use clean coal technologies and there are already signs of deployment of such technologies. Table 6.1 compares coal and gas technologies in terms of energy efficiency, investment and generating costs, and CO_2 emissions. It shows that natural gas turbines use 10 per cent more of the energy contained in the fuel, and cost less than half the latest IGCC coal technology.

Fuel Cells. Fuel cells convert chemical energy into electricity without first burning the fuel to produce heat using hydrogen as fuel. They are highly efficient with demonstration units showing conversion efficiencies of 40–70 per cent and more than 80 per cent in cogeneration. But the level of greenhouse gas emissions depends on how the hydrogen is produced.

Substantial resources have recently been channelled into fuel cell research and the results are promising. Installation cost estimates for fuel cells vary considerably; for example a 450 kW prototype has costs as low as 1400 \$/kW while cells in the range required for the transport sector (30–40 MW) still remain costly.[2] One estimate expects fuel cells to account for as much as a tenth of the global market for power generation equipment, worth about \$50 bn a year within a decade.[3] So far, it seems unlikely that large-scale requirements for hydrogen could be produced without using fossil fuels. The environmental performance of a fuel cell system is then probably not much better than conventional power generation with additional cleaning technologies.

Combined Heat and Power (CHP). Replacing separate heat and power generation with CHP offers significant improvements in fuel efficiencies and mitigation of GHG emissions. Producing a kWh (and some given amount of heat) from hard coal in a CHP system can reduce emissions by almost 30 per cent compared with producing both separately. Emissions can be reduced by almost two-thirds if the CHP system utilises natural gas. CHP has applications in the industrial, residential, and commercial sectors, and heat-plus-power efficiencies are typically 80–90 per cent.

Heat pumps use a relatively small amount of high quality drive energy to transfer heat from natural surroundings to a building or an industrial

2. Ø. Dahle (ed.), Energy Future Forum. A CICERO report on the conference held in Oslo (Oslo, CICERO, May 1998).
3. *The Economist*, 'Fuel Cells Meet Big Business', 24 July 1999, 64–70.

Table 6.1: Comparison of Coal and Gas Power Generation Systems under European Conditions

Plant type	*Coal* Typical with de-SOx and de-NOx	*Coal* IGCC	*Coal* IGCC with CO$_2$ capture	*Natural gas* Combined cycle	*Natural gas* Combined cycle with CO$_2$ capture
Status	Conventional	Demonstration	Available technology	Established technology	Available technology
Efficiency (%)	38–40	44–46	34–36	50–55	44–45
Investment Cost ($/kW)	1,300	1,800	2,995	750	1,420
Electricity cost (¢/kWh)	4.6	4.8	5.6	3.8	5.8
CO^2 emission (g C/kWh)	230	220	20	110	20

Sources: various

application, but can also be used for cooling. Heat pumps driven by electricity for heating buildings typically supply 100 kWh of heat with just 20–40 kWh of electricity. But many industrial heat pumps can achieve higher performance by supplying the same amount of heat with only 3–10 kWh of electricity. The IEA estimates that about 35–50 per cent fuel could be saved using heat pumps.

Nuclear Power. There are currently 430 reactors operating in the world, with an installed generating capacity of 345 GW. Nuclear electricity accounted for 2416 TWh in 1996. The investment costs for construction of nuclear units are the main component of the total cost of nuclear-generated electricity. They are sensitive to technical parameters, regulation aspects, and the cost of capital. The direct nuclear electricity generation costs vary across a number of countries from 2.5 to 6¢/kWh. There has been progress in modernising existing nuclear plants, in addressing safety and efficiency issues, and in extending plant lifetime. Progress in increasing the power of existing plants by 15 per cent and extending their life to sixty years will reduce the costs of nuclear energy.[4]

To satisfy increasingly demanding safety and waste-management requirements, more advanced reactors are being designed and developed. Life-cycle analysis shows that CO_2 emissions from nuclear power generation are 35 times lower than oil-fired power generation, and six times lower than some wind and solar technologies. Nuclear power's acceptability has decreased in the last few decades, and the general public has been reluctant to see the building of new nuclear power plants. The main concerns are fear of large-scale catastrophes, storage of nuclear waste, and the misuse of fissile material. Continuing popular concerns are likely to be a severe constraint on nuclear power generation in many countries, and nuclear is therefore not seen as providing a way to reduce greenhouse gas emissions.

Renewables. Impressive technical gains in renewable energy utilisation have been made during the past decade. Renewable sources of energy used sustainably have no or only small emissions of GHGs, and increased use of renewable sources of energy could therefore offer substantial reductions of GHG emissions.

---

4. G. Doucet, 'The Energy Industry-Embracing the 21st Century. Notes on Emerging Issues', World Energy Council. Speech given at the 6th Annual Handelsblatt Conference, Berlin, 19 January 1995.

(a) Hydro Energy. Hydroelectricity is the only renewable resource used on a large scale for electricity. The efficiency of hydro power plants is very high, from 70 to 90 per cent. The production of hydroelectricity was 2,622 TWh in 1995, and Table 6.2 shows the regional distribution in 1996.

The largest producers are Canada, the United States, Brazil and China. Worldwide there are about 700 GW of installed hydropower in large plants (>10 MW), and 20 GW installed in small plants. The technically feasible potential of the world's available hydro resources ranges from about 12,000 to 14,000 TWh per year. Approximately 50 per cent of the world's remaining large-scale hydro potential could be economic after considering social, environmental, geological and cost factors.

Based on investment costs for hydro projects in 70 developing countries for the 1990s, the cost of new hydroelectricity delivered to final use is, on average, 7.8¢/kWh. According to ABB, the installation costs for hydroelectricity range from $600/kW to about $2000/kW.

Table 6. 2: Regional Shares of Hydroelectric Production in 1996. Per Cent

Region	Share of World Production
OECD	53.0
Latin America	19.4
Former Soviet Union	8.6
China	7.5
Asia	6.5
Africa	2.4
Non OECD Europe	2.0
Middle East	0.6

Source: IEA

(b) Wind Energy. This is the world's fastest growing energy source, but still has only a small share of the 3,000 GW of worldwide installed generation capacity. There were 5 GW of installed wind power worldwide at the beginning of 1996, and capacity growth is concentrated in Europe and Asia. The cost of energy from wind power has a wide range, from 4.3 to 10¢/kWh, but future costs as low as 3.2¢/kWh have been calculated by the IPCC. The mitigation costs of wind power would be $93/t C.[5] Wind energy

5. Assuming conventional coal electricity costs of 5¢/kWh, wind power costs of 7.15¢/kWh, and emissions avoided of 230 g C/kWh.

costs vary with location and wind conditions. With wind velocity of 5.8 m/sec and a discount rate of 6 per cent, the price of wind-generated electricity is on average about 5 ¢/kWh. Increasing the velocity to 8.5 m/sec would drop this price to 3.3 ¢/kWh. The future prospects for wind power are very good, and it has been estimated that 10 GW in additional capacity will be installed during the period 1996–2000.

(c) Solar Energy. Solar power plants generally use two technologies, photovoltaic (PV) panels, and solar-thermal systems. Electricity generation from solar energy amounts to less than 0.02 per cent of total global production. The general rule is that an insolation of at least 1700 kWh/m^2 per year is necessary to reach acceptable production cost levels with large solar-thermal installations. Areas fulfilling this condition are the North African deserts, the Arabian Peninsula, major parts of India, Central and Western Australia, the high plateaux of the Andes, northern Brazil, and south-western USA. Only southern Spain and some Mediterranean islands meet the criterion in Europe.

The generation of electricity with PV cells is an elegant, noiseless and non-emitting, but expensive process for generating electricity directly. PV is already competitive as a stand-alone power source remote from electric utility grids, but has not been competitive in bulk electric grid-connected applications. The system capital costs are $7,000–10,000/kW and the electricity cost is ¢23–33/kWh, even in areas of high insolation. However, it is expected that the cost of PV systems will improve significantly through R&D, as well as with economies of scale.

The annual potential of solar energy in well-defined niche markets is estimated to be 16–22 EJ by 2020 to 2025. Whether this potential will be realised will depend on the cost and performance improvements of solar electric technologies. A 50 MW power plant based on 1995 technology with installed costs of $2,300/kW would have generating costs of about ¢8–9/kWh in areas of good insolation. The corresponding mitigation costs, when compared with coal-fired electricity, would range from $130 to $170/t C avoided.

(d) Biomass Energy. Electricity generation from biomass can take place in units from a few kilowatts for rural village or agricultural applications, to tens of megawatts for present industrial applications, to hundreds of megawatts for advanced industrial applications. Future biomass inputs for electricity generation in the Annex I countries are expected to cost around \$2/GJ. With this cost and small-scale production, electricity can be generated for ¢10–15/kWh. The mitigation costs, on the basis of replacing coal with biomass, would range between \$200 and \$400/tC avoided. Research on advanced biomass conversion technologies as well as biomass plantations is conducted, but further R&D is necessary for these to become technically mature and economically viable. Table 6.3 summarises cost estimates for mitigation of GHGs with the alternative technologies discussed here based on own calculations and the IPCC.[6]

Table 6.3: Mitigation Costs of Stationary Energy Sources. \$ per Tonne of Carbon

Energy Source	Mitigation Costs
IGCC	200
IGCC with CO_2 capture	48
CCGT	-67
CCGT with CO_2 capture	57
Nuclear	< 120
Hydro	120
Wind	93
Solar	130–170
Biomass	200–400

Sources: Calculations based on Table 6.1 and IPCC

6.2.2 Transport

The transport sector is growing rapidly and changes in vehicle energy intensity or energy source could contribute strongly to a reduction in GHG emissions. There are many options to reduce or limit the growth of emissions from transport.

Several proven and emerging fuel saving technologies exist for passenger cars. Conventional four-stroke gasoline engines have potential energy savings of 15 to 30 per cent with current commercial technology. Options include wider adoption of multivalve engine

---

6. The IPCC costs are often used as a reference, but there are studies (e.g. E. Mills et al, 'Getting Started – No-Regrets Strategies for Reducing Greenhouse Gas Emissions', *Energy Policy*, 1991, 19(6), 527–42) which conclude that many technologies represent no-regret options (negative costs).

technology, which is nearly universal in Japan, widespread in Europe, but still relatively uncommon in North America.

A 15 to 25 per cent fuel consumption saving is possible using diesel engines instead of similar-displacement spark-ignition engines. But resistance to diesel passenger cars remains strong in North America. Regular checks on tyre pressure, engine oil, and tuning can save energy, and studies have shown a fuel saving between 2 and 10 per cent immediately after engine tuning.

Alternative fuels represent an important option in the transport sector. In the past, alternative-fuel vehicles (AFVs) have been developed as a means of reducing oil consumption. They are currently being promoted as a means of reducing urban air pollution, but some types of AFVs can contribute to meeting both these goals. Estimated life-cycle GHG emission ranges for several fuels, and cost estimates for using some of the alternative-fuel vehicles are shown in Table 6.4.

Table 6.4: Life-cycle GHG Emissions and Costs for Alternative Fuel Cars

Fuel	Emission (gCO_2e/km)	Vehicle cost ($)	Fuel cost ($/l gasoline equivalent)	Cost in excess of gasoline vehicle (¢29/km)
Gasoline	222–282	15,168	0.26	0
Diesel	173–266	15,168–17,443	0.26	-3.99
Liquified petroleum gases	180–203	15,384–16,083	0.19–0.26	-1.57
Compressed natural gas	164–253	15,600–16,083	0.18–0.24	-1.18
Methanol from natural gas	250–252	15,168–16,128	0.25–0.35	-2.17
Ethanol from sugar cane	70–123	15,168–16,128	0.35–0.38	-2.06
Liquid hydrogen	29–88	18,048–19,968	0.38–1.44	4.10–13.97
Electric vehicle	151–208	20,928–24,768	0.48–0.96	6.81–14.74

Source: various

Some of the fuels listed are already cost-competitive with gasoline. Liquefied petroleum gases (also referred to as propane) was the first alternative fuel to be widely accepted as a gasoline or diesel substitute. It has achieved the largest market share of any alternative transport fuel, and on a life-cycle basis, vehicles using LPG produce less CO_2 emissions than comparable gasoline vehicles. Natural gas vehicles offer potential environmental, energy security and economic benefits, but are characterised by some drawbacks. Compared to conventional fuel vehicles, the acquisition costs are higher, the travel range is only about half, and the refuelling infrastructure is limited.

Methanol can be produced from natural gas, coal, wood or biomass, but natural gas is the least expensive of the feedstocks. The most commonly used methanol motor fuel is M85, a blend of 85 per cent methanol and 15 per cent unleaded gasoline. Combustion of M85 generally results in lower CO_2, and NO_x emissions, but CO_2 emissions from production and distribution of methanol are higher than for gasoline. M85 has therefore little, if any, role to play in reducing GHG emissions.

Ethanol can be produced from several biomass feedstock containing simple sugars, starch or cellulose. Vehicle emission test results generally show significant reductions in CO, modest reductions in VOC and little or no reduction in NO_x emissions compared to gasoline. The data on CO_2 emissions are not conclusive, but the potential for reduction seems small.

Hydrogen could be important as a motor fuel. A hydrogen fuel cell vehicle emits virtually no GHGs, particulates, or CO, but life-cycle emissions depend strongly on the production technology for hydrogen. There are several factors (technological, political and environmental) that may determine hydrogen's future, but it is difficult to predict their role over the next twenty years. Since the technology and infrastructure are still lacking, it is uncertain when hydrogen will become widely commercial. We do not expect this to happen before 2010, with a significant market share developing somewhere around 2020.

Electric vehicles are more efficient, and thus generally less polluting than internal-combustion vehicles. The electric motor is directly connected to the wheels, so it consumes no energy while the car is at rest, increasing the effective efficiency by roughly one-fifth. Regenerative braking schemes can return as much as half an electric vehicle's kinetic energy to the storage cells. This gives it a major advantage in urban traffic. Furthermore, more than 90 per cent of the energy in its storage cells is converted to motive force, whereas less than 25 per cent of the energy in a litre of gasoline is utilised by internal-combustion drives.

Electric vehicles have a large potential to reduce urban air pollution, but the life-cycle emissions of such vehicles depend on the energy sources used for electricity generation. Table 6.4 shows that electric vehicles emit less CO_2 equivalents, but have significant excess costs when compared with ordinary gasoline vehicles. Hybrid vehicles, combining small internal-combustion engines with electric motors and electricity storage devices, will also reduce emissions.[7]

The electric vehicles on the market in the United States in the late 1990s are expected to cost two to three times as much as comparable gasoline-powered vehicles.[8] The future evolution of this technology and of the market for electric vehicles is uncertain. Important factors are the extent of cost reductions that can be achieved in batteries and electric motors, and the extent to which battery-recharging rates, energy densities, and power densities can be improved.

Summarising the above discussion, it becomes clear that the technological options for the transport sector are numerous, and there is no doubt that reducing both fuel use and GHG emissions from this sector is possible. The fuel-saving technologies could mature autonomously as they save money for the consumers, whereas other technologies might depend on environmental policies for major breakthroughs. Some alternative fuels are already competitive with gasoline in terms of costs, while electric vehicles and hydrogen fuel cells remain too costly to be competitive. Table 6.5 shows the mitigation costs for the alternative fuels introduced earlier.

Table 6.5: Mitigation Costs for Alternative Fuel Vehicles. $ per Tonne of Carbon

Fuel	Cost of Mitigation
Diesel	1,858
Liquified petroleum gases	143
Compressed natural gas	262
Methanol from natural gas	13,396
Ethanol from sugarcane	203
Liquid hydrogen	1,714
Electric vehicle	5,454

Source: Calculated from Table 6.4.

It is clear that LPG, ethanol and natural gas are the cheapest alternatives for mitigating GHG, while the other options stand out as extremely costly. But even the cheapest alternatives in the transport sector are more costly than the most expensive options in the stationary energy supply sector. Alternative fuels are therefore not considered to be likely options for mitigating GHG, at least until costs are significantly

7. D. Sperling, 'The Case for Electric Vehicles', *Scientific American*, November 1996. (http://www.sciam.com/1196issue/1196sperling.html)

8. M. Helfinger, et al., 'The Role of Transportation Technologies in Reducing Greenhouse Gas Emissions', prepared by Pilorusso Research & Consulting Inc., 1995.

reduced. Fuel cells are an alternative, but still need time to become commercial.

6.2.3 Conclusions

The possibilities for reducing emissions by introducing new technologies are many, but very difficult to assess. They depend not only on how successful engineers will be in making less emission-intensive technologies commercial. Also the demand for new technologies is likely to be important. There is great uncertainty over the extent to which implementation of the Kyoto Protocol will spur research and development to find new and less emission-intensive technologies.

Another uncertain factor is that some new technologies will be introduced regardless of the implementation of climate policies, while some will be introduced as a response to it. Since we do not know which will be introduced in which case, it is hard to say what the impact of climate policy will be on technological progress. Most of the technologies discussed in the previous sections not only reduce emissions of CO_2, but yield additional advantages, such as reducing local pollutants or energy use. Hence, there are incentives for further research and development even if the Kyoto Protocol is not implemented, but the incentives will be enhanced by climate policies.

Yet another uncertainty relates to the fact that many technologies potentially in the pipeline require that several problems be solved. The impact of the technology will be highly dependent on which, and how many, of these problems are solved within the time-frame studied. A good example is provided by the potential for fuel cells in transport. Fuel cell technology is in rapid change, and may totally revolutionise the transport sector by changing the energy source in cars from gasoline to hydrogen. To make the technology commercial, the costs have to be brought down to approximately one-tenth of today's levels.[9] A big share of this reduction may, however, be obtained by the economies of large-scale production.

Fuel cells will reduce substantially the energy use in cars by increasing the effectiveness of energy use, thereby reducing emissions. However, the amount of emissions will also depend critically on how hydrogen is produced. The easiest, or cheapest, way is gasoline, but most experts predict the use of methanol, which is somewhat more expensive but leads to lower emissions. The ideal from an

---

9. R.F. Service, 'Bringing Fuel Cells down to Earth', *Science* 285, 30 July 1999, 682–5.

environmental point of view is, however, to produce hydrogen from water. This requires a quite different technological breakthrough, but could, if successful, remove most of the pollution from transport.

Although the uncertainties related to fuel cell technology are particularly large, they are also substantial with regard to implementing the other technologies considered in the last two sections. In order to highlight just how large the uncertainties are, Figure 6.1 shows estimated 90 per cent confidence intervals for the unit costs of CO_2 emission reductions for each of the transport technologies. The estimates are based on Monte Carlo simulations of the reported 'low' and 'high' estimates for costs and energy savings for each of the technologies.

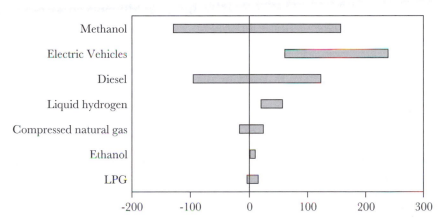

Figure 6.1: Estimated Confidence Intervals for the Unit Costs of Emission Cuts by Transport Technology. $/t CO_2

As we can see from Figure 6.1, the cost ranges due to uncertainties are very large. In general, most of the interval for each of the technologies shows positive costs. It might be economically beneficial to increase the use of diesel cars or use methanol, but it might also be very expensive. The large uncertainty associated with these technologies is explained by uncertainty about the potential for emission reductions: if they are only small, the cost per ton of CO_2 reduced may become very large. For ethanol and LPG the unit costs range from zero to $100 per ton of carbon. The cost of compressed natural gas may be negative, but may also turn out to be more than $100 per ton of carbon. Regarded as a climate measure, electric vehicles seem unattractive, with costs ranging from more than $250 to approximately $900 per ton of carbon. Note, however, that the main environmental benefits from electric vehicles are most likely to be a reduction in local pollutants.

We do not have data for the electricity sector to calculate the uncertainties. According to Table 6.3, the costs of reducing CO_2 emissions from fossil fuel power stations range from –\$67 to \$200 per ton of carbon dependent on technology. The potential is, however, limited, and depends on the technology in existing plants. The same applies to hydropower in the Annex I regions, while solar and wind power will cost above \$100 per ton of carbon. In general, it seems much cheaper to reduce emissions from stationary power production, than from the transport sector.

6.3   Energy Efficiency Across Regions in a Macro-economic Framework

6.3.1 Introduction

At the macro-economic level, technology is the relation between inputs of goods and factors and outputs of goods and services. Macro-economic models usually distinguish several production factors, in particular labour and capital, but not technologies as an engineer would describe them, i.e. particular machines and processes. Using the macro-economic approach, this section compares technological standards across the countries and regions in CLIMOX, based on the GTAP database and additional data. The aim is to identify countries or regions that can reduce greenhouse gas emissions relatively easily by adopting best-practice technologies, and countries or regions that are at the forefront of technological development and where emission reductions will have to be achieved through substitution of production inputs, shifts in economic activities, and introduction of the new technologies shown in the last section.

The point of departure is the description of production technology in the sense it is represented in CLIMOX, which allows a standard of technology to be defined and compared on a country or a regional level. A textbook discussion of how technology is represented in macro-economic models is given in Box 1. We then compare energy and emission efficiency across countries and regions.

We could assess technological standards across regions by comparing the share of energy or emissions as production factors in a unit of GDP. Clearly, there are a lot of problems with such an assessment, and we will at least have to adjust for the following factors.

(a) Countries and regions use different sources of energy. This may explain why the emissions per unit of energy use differ. Some regions for example possess large hydropower resources, which may be the reason why emissions in these regions are low in international comparison, although energy use is not.

(b) The composition of GDP differs because of the division of labour among regions. For example, some regions have a comparative advantage in producing energy intensive products, which are being exported. This may explain a higher use of energy per unit of GDP. To evaluate the importance of this effect, we compare the composition of GDP by main sectors in the countries and regions in the model.

(c) Energy prices differ between regions, due to differences in endowments of natural resources, and in domestic taxation. In countries with low energy prices energy use is expected to be higher than in countries with high energy prices, without implying differences in efficiency of energy use.

(d) Technologies differ with the level of development of countries and regions, which can to some extent be measured through the capital stock. At each level of development, there is some level of energy use and emissions that can be regarded as efficient. We therefore adjust inputs of energy and labour per unit of GDP by an indicator for economic development using the capital stock as proxy.

These adjustments should allow us to make a more appropriate evaluation of (1) those countries or regions that are inefficient in their uses of energy, and could improve through adopting best practices; (2)

Box 6.1: Technology and Cost Minimisation
in Macroeconomic Models

The production technology in macro-economic models is represented by a production function $x = f(v_1, v_2)$, where x is output, and v_1 and v_2 are input factors. The technology can be characterised by the rate at which one input factor can substitute another, without affecting the output. Let x_0 be a fixed level of production. Then, the function $v_1 = f^{-1}(v_2; x_0)$ is the production isoquant, and two examples are shown in the figure below as curved lines. Isoquants are a characterisation of the technology: a sharply curved function implies that a certain level of production can be sustained only with a relatively fixed proportion of the two input factors, while a less curved function represents a technology with high flexibility.

Box 6.1: *continued*

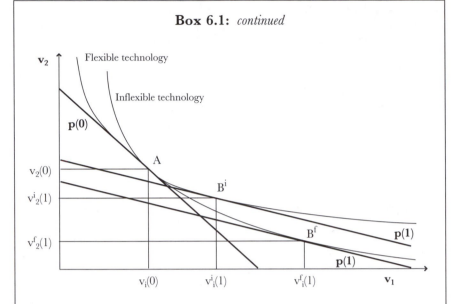

The demand for the two inputs, v_1 and v_2, is found by minimising the cost of production. With fixed cost, the input of v_2 can be drawn as a declining linear relationship, $p(.)$, to v_1. We can call this line the cost curve. Its slope depends on the prices of v_1 and v_2, and the total cost is equal to the area below the cost curve. The maximum level of output for a given cost is found at the point where the cost curve is tangent to the iso production curve which represents the technology. Hence if total costs are $p(0)$, maximum production is A.

In point A, the same output is produced with both the flexible and the inflexible technology at the same total cost $p(0)$. Any other combination of v_1 and v_2 to produce the same quantity (stay on the same production curves) would lead to higher costs (a larger area under the cost curve) for both technologies if the prices remained the same. Assume, however, that prices change such that the slope of the cost curve shifts to $p(1)$. For the inflexible technology, this leads to a new combination of the input factors to B^i, thereby reducing input of v_2 and increasing the input of v_1. The same applies in the flexible technology, however with a much more vigorous change. Thus, reduction in the use of v_2 (e.g. energy) is much more significant. In addition, while the two technologies produce the given output with the same cost under $p(0)$, the flexible technology produces at lower cost than the inflexible technology under $p(1)$.Elasticities of substitution of different inputs in production are therefore important determinants of the extent of adjustment to climate policies, and the costs of these policies.

those regions that can be considered efficient but technologically backwards, and could improve by investing in new capital but embodying existing technologies; and (3) those regions that are technologically advanced and could improve mainly by introducing new technologies.

This section continues as follows. We start in Section 6.3.2 with a presentation of the use of different sources of energy and emissions across regions. Section 6.3.3 brings in the aspect of sectoral composition of GDP, and energy prices are discussed in Section 6.3.4. Section 6.3.5 illuminates the relation between energy intensity and technology. In Section 6.3.6, we finally adjust energy intensities for the level of development by looking at variations in the capital stock. The conclusions are given in Section 6.4. The main focus is on the Annex I countries.

It should be kept in mind that this book looks at impacts of emission reductions on the fossil fuel market, and measures to reduce emissions from energy use are therefore of greatest interest. Other options to reduce greenhouse gas emissions are available to a different degree in the regions, but little is known about abatement options and costs. Emissions from non-energy sources, both for CO_2 and other gases, have hardly ever been subject to constraints in the past, and emission reductions were not profitable. In contrast, fossil fuels have always been costly, and great efforts have been undertaken to increase energy efficiency, with emission reductions as side effect. Therefore, in contrast to energy-related emissions, there may be abatement options available at very low costs for non-energy emissions.

In addition to a reduction in the emissions of greenhouse gases, the Kyoto Protocol allows for measures to enhance absorption of these gases in the seas, the soil, or biomass, so-called sinks, to be used as measures to meet the targets. It is far from clear at the moment how sinks will be calculated, but policies to enhance them may turn out to be a major option in some regions. Neither non-energy nor sink options can be evaluated properly in the macro-economic analysis used in this book. If they indeed turn out to be competitive, their adoption would substantially change the impacts on fossil fuel markets shown here.

6.3.2 Energy Use and Carbon Emissions per Capita

Energy use per capita differs strongly across regions, mainly because of differences in the standard of living, but also in the mix of energy sources used. Figure 6.2 shows the use of fossil fuel per capita across regions. There is a clear dichotomy in the level of energy use between Annex I, and non-Annex I regions, or between developed and developing countries. In the USA and the ROO region, consumption of fossil fuels per capita is four to five times the world average. The per capita consumption of fossil fuel in developed regions ranges from 230 kg oil equivalent (kg oe) to 640 kg oe per year. In the less developed regions the consumption of fossil fuel per capita is less than 100 kg oe per year, with the exception of the Middle East oil exporters, where the consumption reaches nearly 150 kg oe per capita per year.

As shown in Figure 6.3, emissions per unit of energy used vary from less than 2.4 tonnes CO_2 per tonne oil equivalent (tCO_2/toe) in

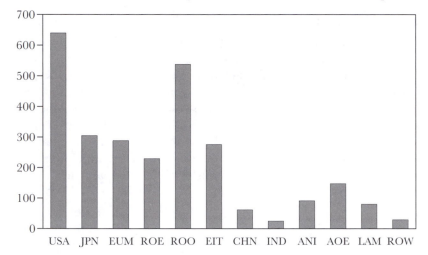

Figure 6. 2: Total Use of Fossil Fuel per Capita by Region. Kg Oil Equivalent.

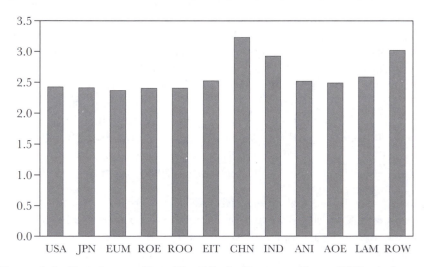

Figure 6. 3: Emissions per Use of Fossil Fuels. Tonne per Tonne Oil Equivalent CO_2

the EU countries to more than 3.2 tCO_2/toe in China. Across the Annex I countries, emissions per unit of energy are relatively constant, approximately 2.4 tCO_2/toe.

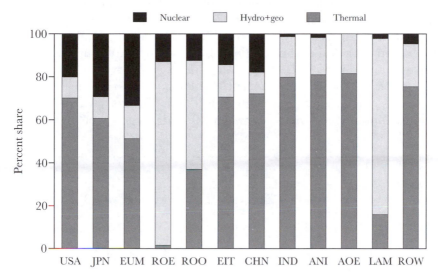

Figure 6.4: Energy Sources in Production of Electricity by Region

Sources: various

These differences are due to the high level of coal use in developing countries, and to the use of large amounts of non-fossil energy in some regions. As shown in Figure 6.4, ROE and Latin America base their electricity production on 'clean' sources, such as hydropower and geothermal heat. Nuclear power contributes a large share of the electricity supply mainly in developed regions. Finally, biomass contributes substantially to energy supply outside the electricity sector in developing countries, particularly in private households.

The figures shown here indicate that per capita emissions of CO_2 depend strongly on affluence. However, some country-specific factors, such as carbon content of the fossil fuel mix and the use of non-fossil energy resources, influence emissions.

6.3.3 Sectoral Distribution of Energy Use Across Regions

Differences in energy intensity of GDP can partly be due to the global division of labour. That is, a region may have a high intensity of fossil fuel use per unit of GDP because the countries produce products with a high energy content for the world market. These sectors are likely to be on the technology frontier, because they are exposed to international competition.

In Figure 6.5 the demand for fossil fuels in the Annex I regions is shown for eight sectors. With the exception of Japan and the Economies in Transition, households and the governmental sector are the main users of fossil fuels in all regions. The share in the ROE region is lower than in the other three regions, because households use electricity instead of primary fuels. In Japan, energy intensive industries are responsible for nearly 50 per cent of total use of fossil fuels. This is extremely high compared with the other regions, where energy intensive industries demand between 10 and 25 per cent.

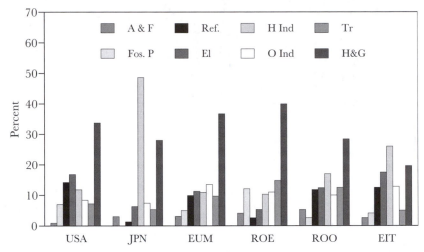

Figure 6.5: Distribution of Energy Demand by Sector in Annex I Countries

The aggregated sectors are: A&F: Agriculture, livestock and forestry, Fos P: Production of coal, oil and gas, Ref: Oil refineries, El: Production of electricity, H Ind: Heavy intensive industries, O Ind: Other industries, Tr: transport, H&G: Households and governmental sector

The large share of heavy industry in Japan explains why the use of fossil fuels per unit of GDP is higher than one would expect given energy prices and technological development. It should also be noted that the electricity sector in the USA uses a significantly higher share of total fossil use than in other regions, because it produces a larger share of its electricity from thermal power plants than the other regions.

In general, the decomposition of energy use by sector does not add much to the explanation of the variations of energy intensities across regions, except in the case of Japan. A further decomposition of sectors might have given different results, but is beyond the scope of this study.

6.3.4 Energy Prices and Energy Demand

Although the markets for fossil fuels are to a large extent world markets, domestic prices differ substantially across countries and regions. This is partly due to variations in transport costs, which are particularly relevant for gas and electricity. Another reason is variations in energy subsidies and taxes. Hence, a different intensity of energy use across regions may reflect different relative prices, such that a low price indicates high intensity and vice versa.

Figure 6.6 shows average prices of fossil fuels by region. Although energy prices vary considerably, there is no evident correspondence between energy prices and level of development. Low prices are found in the USA, the big Asian countries with the exception of Japan, the ROE region and to some extent Latin America. The price of coal in most regions is lower than the price of other fossil fuels. However, in the EU, the Middle East and North Africa, and Latin America gas is the cheapest fuel. Refined petroleum products are the most expensive in all regions. The differences between the prices of coal, oil and gas are largest in the Economies in Transition, in India and in the Rest of the World. It should therefore be expected that coal would contribute a relatively large share of fossil fuel consumption in these

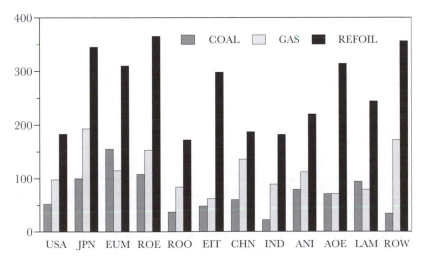

Figure 6.6:   Average Prices of Fossil Fuels by Energy Carrier and Region. $/TJ

regions. Figure 6.6 partly confirms this, as both the Rest of the World and India have high emissions per unit of fossil fuel use.

6.3.5 Energy Intensity and Technology

Figure 6.7 plots energy inputs against inputs of labour per unit of GDP (measured in international currency based on purchasing power parities) across regions. Each observation can be interpreted as a point on the iso-production curve of the production function for each region. A movement towards the origin therefore indicates an improvement of the technology applied to produce the national product. Following the discussion in Box 6.1, a movement along a convex, downward sloping line in the diagram should be due to variations in relative prices.

According to Figure 6.7, the developed countries use their resources of labour and energy much more efficiently than less developed countries. Technology in this context is considered to be a 'mirror' of the capital stock. In other words, large capital stocks in rich countries enable an efficient use of energy and labour. Thus, the standard of technology is apparently related to the level of economic development of the region or country.

Figure 6.7 shows that the USA and the ROE region represent the technology frontier among all regions. A major reason for the low

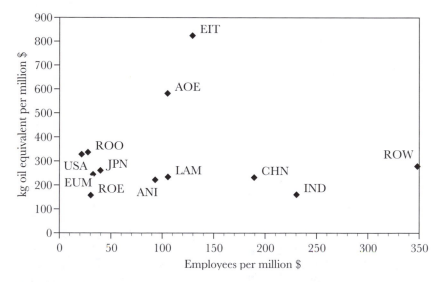

Figure 6.7: Input of Fossil Energy and Labour per Unit of PPP-based GDP by Region

Sources: various

intensity of fossil fuels in ROE is, however, the reserves of alternative energy sources for the production of electricity, shown in Figure 6.4.

The highest energy intensities are found in the Economies in Transition, the USA, and the ROO region. For the USA, the high energy intensity may be due to low energy prices, while the country produces close to the technology frontier. This also applies to the EU member states, which have lower intensity of energy, but use more labour than the USA to produce their GDP.

Figure 6.7 also indicates that Japan and the ROO region are less energy efficient than the rest. In particular in the ROO region, labour use is similar, but energy use is more intensive than in the other regions. For Japan, a high labour intensity may be due to low labour costs, which, in principle, may put them on the same level of technology as the USA. Nevertheless, the seemingly low energy efficiency in Japan is surprising, considering the high price and restricted availability of energy. As we have seen in Figure 6.5, this is at least partly due to a high share of energy intensive industries in the GDP.

China and India may be on the same level of technology, but China uses less labour and more energy because energy is less expensive relative to labour than in India. However, the Rest of the World region uses less efficient technology, since they use more labour and energy to produce a unit of their GDP. Note that labour productivity varies much more than energy intensity across regions; labour productivity varies by a factor of more than 1:10, as compared with energy efficiency, which varies by a factor of 1:5, and less than 1:3 if we disregard outliers AOE and EIT.

This observation supports the assumption that the intensity of the use of input factors depends on relative prices, since there are reasons to believe that the prices of labour vary much more than the prices of fossil fuels because fossil fuels are more mobile than labour.

Looking back to the discussion of substitution of inputs in Box 6.1, we can say that observations in Figure 6.7 which lie closer to the origin indicate higher efficiency in the use of labour and energy. However, some points lie close together, and the interpretation is more difficult. We can see that the USA may be on the technology frontier and yet less advanced than Japan, depending on the relative prices of labour and energy. Japan, on the other hand, may be less advanced than all other Annex I regions, except for the Economies in Transition. For the other regions, the largest potential for enhancing the efficiency of energy use is found in the Economies in Transition and the Middle East.

In order to say more about differences in technologies and efficiency of energy use, we have already looked at different sources of energy, variations in energy prices, and variations in composition of GDP. The next section completes the picture by looking at differences in energy use due to variations in the level of development.

6.3.6 Energy Intensity and Economic Development

At each stage of development, different capital equipment and thereby technology is used. The search for patterns in the use of resources and the level of development goes back to studies of macroeconomic growth pioneered by Simon Kuznets in 1955.[10] His hypothesis was that the distribution of income at first becomes less equitable as development proceeds, and does not improve until industry accounts for a rather large share of national income. Consequently, the income elasticity of capital use should decline with the level of national income, from above 1 to less than one. The relation between capital and output per capita can therefore be described by an inverse U-curve.

In recent years, Kuznets' hypothesis has been the subject of renewed interest within environmental economics. If energy and capital are complementary, the energy intensity for per capita GDP is also inversely U-shaped, and therefore also the level of emissions. Figure 6.8 plots the relationship between energy use per capita and GDP per capita for the twelve regions defined in this study. While the observations for the Annex I regions are spread out over a relatively large area, non-Annex I regions exhibit a strong positive relationship between GDP and energy use per capita.

A regression line for energy use per capita versus GDP per capita based on the 45 regions in the GTAP database is also shown in Figure 6.8. The regression confirms the U-shape of this relationship.[11] In countries with low income per capita, the use of fossil fuels increases by approximately 35 kg oil equivalent per $1000 increase in per capita income. At an income level of $10,000, per capita energy consumption begins to level out, and reaches a maximum at an income level of approximately $22,500. Energy use per capita is then nearly 425 kg oil equivalent. With further increases in income, per capita energy use falls.

We can now compare energy use in the different regions relative to

10. S. Kuznets, 'Economic Growth and Income Inequality', *American Economic Review*, 45, March 1955, 1–28.
11. A quadratic relationship, $y=x(a+bx)$, between MJ energy/capita (y) and GDP/capita (x) is assumed. R^2 is 0.66, the estimates were $a = 1.61$ (0.16) and $b = -0.036$ (0.0058) (standard errors in paranthesis).

averages for their level of income as defined by the regression curve. The EIT and ROO regions, and the USA have much higher energy intensities than the other regions, given their levels of per capita GDP. Also in Japan, the energy consumption is higher than the average, while the EU and the ROW region lie below average.

If we compare the prices in Figure 6.6 with the energy use in Figure 6.2, we can see that regions with low energy prices tend to have above average energy use per capita, whereas regions with high prices use less energy. One might therefore ask whether differences in input intensities are the result of different relative prices of energy.

To approach an answer to this, we therefore adjust the input intensities for labour and energy shown in Figure 6.7 by variations in the level of development according to the estimated Kuznets curve in Figure 6.8. This provides an approximation of the intensities that would have applied if all regions were at the same level of development. The resulting intensities for the Annex I regions are shown in Figure 6.9. The intensities are calculated as if per capita GDP in all regions was $15,000.

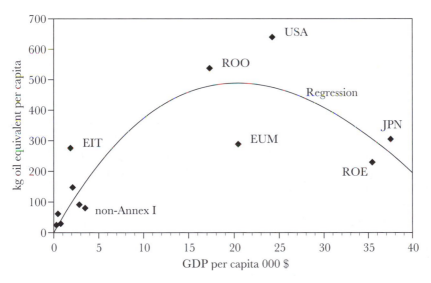

Figure 6.8: Relationship between the Use of Fossil Energy per Capita and National Level of Income by Region – Regression of a Kuznets Curve.

To evaluate the importance of energy prices we estimate the price of energy relative to the price of labour, and draw the curves representing the relative prices of energy and labour in each region.

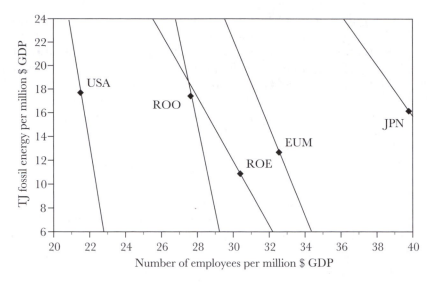

Figure 6.9:   Input of Energy and Labour Required to Produce 1 million $ GDP
and Relative Prices of Labour and Energy by Region.

Figure 6.9 thus comes as close as we can to the textbook version of
substitution possibilities for production technologies. The price lines
represent the tangents to the production possibility frontiers as shown
in Box 6.1. Hence, the technology in region A is more efficient than
in region B if the production locus for B is both above and to the right
of the observation for A. In other cases, differences may be due to
variations in prices.

The comparisons in Figure 6.9 lead to surprising results. Japan
seems relatively inefficient with a large potential for improving technology, whereas the USA is the country with the highest efficiency in
energy use, given energy prices and level of per capita income. The
ROO and ROE regions are roughly at an equal technological level,
although energy use is much higher in the former region than in the
European countries. This can be explained to a large extent by the
fact that the figure includes fossil energy only, while the ROE region
uses a great amount of alternative energy for their electricity sector,
hydro power in particular. Hence, the fossil energy consumption is
low. This makes it difficult to evaluate the technology in these regions.
However, the potential for further development of 'clean' electricity is
small.

The high level of energy consumption in the USA and ROO to a
large extent may be explained by their low energy prices. In particular,
we can conclude that ROO with its high level of energy consumption

seems to be closer to the technology frontier than ROE, which has the lowest intensity for the use of fossil fuels, provided that the regions are able to produce their GDP with the same technology. This conclusion is strengthened if we take into account the sectoral composition of the ROO region, where energy intensive activities use a large share of fossil fuels. A large part of the difference can therefore be explained by different prices.

The European Union according to Figure 6.9 is less efficient in the use of resources than other industrialised countries, and both the EU and Japan probably could reduce energy use and emissions by adopting best-practice technologies from other countries. However, in Japan, the potential for improving efficiency is most significant for labour. It is not likely that Japan would be able to reduce its energy consumption without a substantial reduction in the energy intensive industries.

From these results it seems that the EU is the only region which can gain from taking well-known existing technology into use in order to increase the effectiveness of energy. Other studies show that such opportunities are available in the electricity sector and by modernisation of industries in the eastern part of Germany.[12] For the other regions, the picture is less clear-cut. We should add that the EIT region and the non-Annex I regions turn out to be much less efficient than the Annex I regions. There is clearly a large potential for applying existing technologies in these regions in order to reduce CO_2 emissions, for instance by the use of the Clean Development Mechanism.

6.4   Conclusions

There are substantial variations in technological standards across regions, which can be explained mainly by differences in the levels of development. To increase the efficiency of energy use, measured as the amount of fossil energy necessary to produce a unit of GDP, some advantages can be obtained by introducing best-practice technologies in use elsewhere. This reduces substantially any uncertainty about the choice of technology parameters, and implies that a parameterisation of the technology based on historical data, such as we have done in the macroeconomic model, may be acceptable.

But developing regions inevitably will have to make large investments to achieve major advances. These investments also involve energy use,

---

12. H.A. Aaheim and C. Bretteville, 'Sources of Conflicts in Climate Policy within the EU. An Economic Analysis,' CICERO Working Paper, 3, 1999.

and it is hard to say how 'costly' an increase in GDP eventually turns out to be in terms of energy use. For the Annex I regions, further improvements will partly have to rely on new investments, although some differences between regions can be observed. The most evident is of course that the Economies in Transition may improve the performance of their economy by shifting to known technologies, and by undergoing structural changes. It seems, also, that the EU members may gain from substituting parts of their technologies by more modern equipment. The variations in energy intensity between the other Annex I regions can be explained either by prices, the share of energy intensive activities in the economy and the availability of 'clean' sources of electricity, such as hydropower. Low energy prices increase energy intensity in the USA and ROO region. A high demand from heavy industry increases energy use in Japan and the ROO region, and 'clean' electricity lowers energy intensity in the ROE region.

Future development depends largely on innovation in these regions. A broad range of new technologies with a large number of different applications is likely to emerge in the future, as discussed in Section 6.2. For example, different inventions in various manufacturing industries may contribute substantially to a reduction in energy use and emissions of greenhouse gases, even on a regional scale. The potential is probably largest for those regions with a high level of energy consumption in the industry sectors, such as Japan and the ROO region. However, in some cases the break-through of a certain technology may have a significant impact throughout the world. This will be particularly relevant in transport and generation of electricity.

CHAPTER 7

COAL AND ITS FUTURE

7.1 Introduction

During the 1990s, in terms of actual heat value supplied, total production of coal has remained fairly stable at around 2.2 to 2.3 billion tonnes oil equivalent per annum. Coal's overall share of world primary energy consumption has shrunk only slightly over these years and is currently 26 per cent compared with 28 per cent ten years ago.

The most important market for coal is in the generation of electricity. Nearly 40 per cent of the OECD's electricity is generated in coal-fired power stations. Power stations usually represent the largest and often the fastest growing demand for energy. Coal is also a major input to the steel industry, and still competes with other fuels in a number of countries for home heating and industrial purposes.

The continuing use of coal in all its markets is threatened by environmental concerns reflected in tightening regulations and international agreements. Coal is particularly vulnerable, because it contributes 38 per cent of the world's total carbon emissions from commercial fuels, and is also a major source of sulphur dioxide and nitrous oxides emissions as well as particulates and other environmental hazards.

This chapter looks at the key elements of coal supply, including the resource base, the supply situation, cost and quality in relation to competing fuels, the international trade in coal and the future production outlook. The second section looks at the demand for coal, including the regional pattern of consumption, coal's use in its main markets and environmental issues. This is followed by some brief conclusions.

7.2 Coal Availability and Supply

7.2.1 The Resource Base

Coal resources, as reported, are often inconsistent, incomplete and may be decidedly ancient in origin. But it is clear that the resource base is very substantial. Table 7.1 summarises the latest 'proven reserves of coal' from the BP Amoco *Statistical Review of World Energy*. These reserves alone, if used at current rates of consumption, would last well over 200 years. Naturally these estimates hide an enormous variation in mineability, quality and cost.

Table 7.1: Proven Reserves of Coal at end 1998. Billion Tonnes Oil Equivalent

	Hard Coal	*Lignite*	*Total*	*Share (%)*
USA	111.3	135.3	246.6	25.1
JPN	0.8	-	0.8	0.1
EUM	25.3	46.9	72.2	7.3
ROE	-	-	-	0.0
ROO	51.8	47.8	99.6	10.1
EIT	112.8	148.6	261.4	26.5
ANI	1.1	6.7	7.8	0.8
CHN	62.2	52.3	114.5	11.6
IND	72.7	2.0	74.7	7.6
AOE	0.5	-	0.5	0.1
LAM	8.7	14.1	22.8	2.3
ROW	62.3	21.0	83.3	8.5
OECD	206.5	240.6	447.1	45.4
Total World	509.5	474.7	984.2	100.0

Source: BP Amoco *Statistical Review of World Energy* (1999)

Over 50 per cent of coal reserves are in just three countries, USA, Russia and China, but reserves are spread more evenly and in a different pattern throughout the regions and countries than oil or gas. This has, in the past at least, given coal an advantage over imported alternatives such as oil or gas.

Coal is undoubtedly in great physical abundance and current production facilities using the transportation infrastructure already in place, seem likely to satisfy future demand under most reasonable scenarios. The price signals in recent years of falling prices in real terms and the apparently easy availability of low cost resources away from the traditional mining areas, make economic scarcity highly unlikely in future.

7.2.2 Regional Supply Situation

Through the 1990s, world production has continued to increase although in terms of total heat supplied it has remained fairly stable. As a result, coal's share of global energy supplies is now around 26 per cent compared with 59 per cent in 1950.

The range of potential coal availability over the long term is enormous, greater than any other conventional energy source. Environmental conditions, perceptions of national energy security and the cost of other preferred fuels will be significant determinants of the level of future production. A key factor will be the overall rate of growth in electricity demand.

Table 7.2 shows projections of coal production from the CLIMOX model for the Business-as-Usual scenario. The projections result from the interplay of supply and demand in the model. On the supply side, coal is produced using intermediate inputs, i.e. labour, capital, and a fixed factor. Exogenous capacity growth factors are assumed in the model, which increase the availability of the fixed factor in the production function for each country or region. Substitutability between fixed factor and capital is 0.5, to reflect the fact that coal production technology is more flexible than oil technology. Demand consists of input demand in production and household demand and is determined by economic growth and technological advances. International trade in coal is limited, and hampered by high transport costs and finite elasticities of substitution between imports from different countries and between imports and domestic supplies. In contrast, international substitution is much easier in the oil and gas markets.

Table 7.2: World Coal Production. Million Tonnes Oil Equivalent

| | Production, million tons oil equivalent | | | | | | Growth, % per year |
	1995	2000	2005	2010	2015	2020	1995–2020
USA	554	566	586	611	640	679	0.8
JPN	4	3	3	3	3	4	0.1
EUM	127	104	84	68	54	43	-4.2
ROE	0	0	0	0	0	0	0.3
ROO	174	182	194	208	224	244	1.4
EIT	340	305	323	350	380	409	0.7
CHN	662	744	846	965	1,104	1,272	2.6
IND	152	160	169	180	193	209	1.3
ANI	41	48	56	65	76	89	3.2
AOE	1	1	1	1	1	1	1.7
LAM	25	31	38	47	58	72	4.4
ROW	192	205	220	237	256	277	1.5
TOTAL	2,272	2,350	2,521	2,736	2,990	3,300	1.5

For many years, well over 70 per cent of the world's coal supply has come from just six countries. But of these, China, where it is still the basic energy source, and the USA are dominant in terms of production. These two countries alone currently produce 55 per cent of the world's hard coal and lignite expressed in common heat units. Outside of China and the USA, only India, Australia, South Africa and Russia produce more than 100 million toe per annum. As shown in Table 7.2, world coal production is projected to increase from the current 2.3 bn tonnes oil equivalent to 2.7 and 3.3 bn tonnes in 2010 and 2020 respectively.

Production of coal in the old established and traditional high cost European countries of Germany, UK, Poland, France and Spain has fallen by some 200 million toe over the last ten years. Plans in Germany suggest that coal production will be halved over the next five years, although UK production, which is no longer directly subsidised, may possibly manage to maintain production fairly close to current levels. In France it is expected that all mines will be closed by 2005 and in Spain, the only other major hard coal producer in western Europe, production of their mainly high sulphur coal is set to continue to fall drastically. Overall, coal production in the EUM region falls from 130 mtoe in 1995 to 70 and 40 mtoe in 2010 and 2020.

Coal demand in China is expected to grow rapidly, but environmental concerns, together with the country's political and economic uncertainty, make the future development of the Chinese coal industry very uncertain. Two-thirds of coal reserves are found in the three northern provinces. The concentration of China's coal mines far from consumers in the more economically advanced and rapidly growing southern and eastern coastal provinces gives rise to considerable transport problems. These remain a significant impediment to the development and utilisation of Chinese coal. Nevertheless, coal still has to supply a major part of Chinese energy requirements, and production over the modelling horizon is set to double, from 660 mtoe in 1995, to 970 and 1270 mtoe in 2010 and 2020.

The USA is the world's second largest coal producer with a well developed modern infrastructure, strong domestic demand and excess export capacity available. Coal quality varies, from high quality anthracite and other hard coals in the Appalachians on the eastern seaboard to low calorific value, high and low sulphur coal in the mid-West.

In recent years, there has been substantial cost cutting through productivity gains and industry concentration. However, the industry remains disadvantaged in many regions by the long distances and high overall costs of inland transport. There is also a growing burden on costs represented by taxes, royalties and regulatory compliance costs. However, the role of the USA in the world market as a short-run swing producer is likely to continue for many years. Although exports represent only 10 per cent of the country's total production, mines can be quickly brought back into operation and production increased when exports seem likely to earn more than the local market, and vice versa. We project USA production to increase slowly, from 550 mtoe in 1995 to 610 and 680 mtoe in 2010 and 2020 respectively, a growth of 0.8 per cent per year on average over the 25-year period.

Coal production in Russia has been declining since the collapse of the Soviet Union. Gas has also been steadily eroding much of the domestic market. Most of the mines have been transformed into joint stock companies or associations and there is now some foreign participation. Uncertainty about political stability, inadequate legislation, continuing labour problems and substantial economic difficulties are all delaying investment. Any increase in Russian seaborne export tonnages is severely limited without new investment in port capacity. The projections in Table 7.2 show EIT production in 1995 of 340 mtoe, declining to 300 mtoe in 2000, and then slowly rising to 410 mtoe in 2020.

In India, coal production has increased by over 7 per cent per annum since 1980 and by nearly 160 million toe over the last ten years. Most of this growth has come from surface mining, which accounts for over 70 per cent of production. The most significant deposits are in the north east of India but quality is variable. Overall, there is very little good quality coal and the bulk of reserves has a very high ash content. As in China, scarcely any steam coal is washed and screened for upgrading. Shortages have arisen due to the inability of the transport structure to keep pace with demand and imports have become necessary despite available production capacity. Production is projected to rise from 150 mtoe in 1995 to 180 and 210 in 2010 and 2020, which means import demand increases to 50 mtoe by the end of the modelling horizon.

In the past, South Africa was generally believed to have the lowest production costs of any major coal exporter. As an exporter, it also benefits from its geographical location equidistant from both European and Asian markets. Production is expected to increase substantially over the next few years and expansion is continuing at existing mines.

Australia contains vast low cost and high quality coal resources and the country is well placed to substantially increase exports. There is also a thriving domestic demand for coal. Production, which is largely under private ownership, has risen by some 60 million toe over the last ten years and is continuing to grow rapidly. Australia exports three-quarters of its production and is the world's leading coal exporter although most growth is currently coming from metallurgical coal. The overwhelming bulk of Australian hard coal is produced in the eastern states of Queensland and New South Wales, which are located close to the main and fast expanding coal-importing countries of Asia.

The newer, largely exporting, producing countries such as Colombia, Indonesia and Venezuela have increased their production substantially in recent years, although from very low or non-existent bases. In global terms they are still relatively insignificant.

We assume a near doubling of coal production in China, which will use almost all of this production domestically. China thus becomes by far the biggest coal producer, delivering about one-third of the world total. North American coal production increases only slowly, whereas Australia increases the share of exports in total production for the ROO region. Coal is declining strongly in the European Union. The Asian Newly Industrialised countries double, and Latin America nearly triples coal production, but both remain small producers on the world scale.

7.2.3 The Cost of Coal

The cost of producing coal and supplying it to markets varies greatly, as one might expect from an energy source which is far from homogenous and has a very substantial and widespread resource base. Table 7.3 gives an indication of the costs of steam coal, the main competitor with oil and gas, moving into international trade from leading exporting countries.

The costs of internationally traded coal appear very competitive when compared with ex mine costs in most of the old European coal mining and consuming areas. The cost of mining coal from the handful of remaining coal-producing countries in Europe and Japan is, on average, considerably higher and they are generally unable to compete with imported coal.

Operating and maintenance costs involved in coal production, particularly for labour intensive underground mining, are a much greater proportion of unit costs than with most other forms of fossil fuel. However, in the main coal-exporting countries, producers have apparently been able to achieve very substantial productivity increases in recent years primarily through technological innovation, changes in industrial and labour practices and closing low productivity mines. Further significant technological advances in coal extraction and

Table 7.3: Indicative Export Costs for Steam Coal. 1997 $ per Tonne of Coal

	Mine Operating Cost	FOB Total Cost	Ocean Freight to Japan	Cif Total Cost Japan	Ocean Freight NW Europe	CIF Total Cost NW Europe
Australia						
Queensland (S)	10.5 – 25.5	27.2 – 38.9	5.2 – 6.7	33.5 – 45.0	8.3 – 11.3	36.8 – 48.5
NSW (U)	15.0 – 27.5	24.3 – 38.9	5.95 – 7.5	31.2 – 45.8	9.0 – 12.5	34.7 – 49.3
USA	18.0 – 28.5	32.3 – 40.9	11.7 – 15.0	45.6 – 54.2	5.2 – 6.5	38.1 – 46.7
Appalachia (U)						
Appalachia (S)	22.5 – 30.5	29.0 – 38.5	12.9 – 16.0	39.0 – 53.0	6.3 – 8.9	31.9 – 45.9
Colombia (S)	22.5 – 33.0	27.0 – 37.8			5.4 – 6.5	33.4 – 43.7
Indonesia (S)	13.5 – 26.5	24.8 – 41.0	3.5 – 8.0	29.0 – 45.2	7.3 – 8.8	32.8 – 49.0
South Africa (S)	14.5 – 21.5	22.9 – 35.9	6.9 – 8.4	30.7 – 43.7	6.0 – 7.9	29.8 – 42.8
Venezuela (S)	22.0 – 27.5	29.4 – 40.0			7.0 – 9.5	37.7 – 38.3
W Canada (S)	18.5 – 22.5	33.0 – 44.5	6.4 – 7.3	39.4 – 50.8	8.5 – 10.3	42.6 – 54.1

(S) Surface mines   (U) Underground mines

Notes: Mine operating costs include all operating costs for saleable coal, taxes and royalties, but exclude return on investment. The internationally traded coal shown, represents a range of delivered costs to NW Europe of around $30 to $55 per tonne which in terms of fuel oil is roughly equivalent to around $45 to $75 per tonne. This compares with an average spot price of fuel oil (3.5 per cent sulphur) delivered in NW Europe during 1997 of $90 to $95 per tonne and between $65 and $70 per tonne in the first half of 1998.

Source: OECD/IEA Coal Information (1998)

upgrading processes seem unlikely, over the next few years at least, although the trend to larger mines using the latest techniques will continue to keep costs down. Mining costs for the major exporters to Asian markets such as Australia are expected to continue to fall in real terms.[1]

Prices for steam coal are generally related to those of its main competitor, fuel oil, but because of surplus capacity they have often tended in practice to be determined largely by coal to coal competition. There has been a general move by steam coal buyers away from term contracts to spot purchases and tenders. Spot pricing for steam coal, related mainly to trade in individual cargoes and other small tonnages, has increased over the last few years, especially in the Far East. In Europe this has been largely brought about by the general over-supply position and the widening choice of production sources as well as the increasing range of coals that generators are now able and willing to burn.

7.3   The Demand for Coal

The impression is sometimes given that coal use is rapidly fading into history. The reality, in recent years, is that its overall consumption has remained remarkably robust although the geographical pattern of consumption and the pattern of end use have changed considerably. Table 7.4 shows coal consumption for 1995 and projections from the CLIMOX model. In the model, coal demand depends on economic growth, technological and energy efficiency advances, and the price of coal and its competitors.

The fast growing Asian developing countries such as India, China, Taiwan and South Korea are relatively intensive coal users and their demand for it has grown rapidly with their economies. In those four countries alone, coal consumption has increased by over 200 million toe over the last ten years. This was slightly more than the increase in oil consumption of 185 million toe and considerably more than the natural gas increase of 35 million toe. Nearly two-thirds of the world's coal consumption is accounted for by just four countries – China, USA, India and Russia.

Coal demand grows fast in China, where consumption doubles over the modelling horizon, a growth rate of 2.8 per cent per year on average. Demand in the Asian Newly Industrialised countries also

---

1. Coal Industry Advisory Board, *The Future Role of Coal* (1999).

Table 7.4: World Coal Consumption, 1995–2000. Million Tonnes Oil Equivalent

	1995	2000	Consumption, million tonnes oil equivalent 2005	2010	2015	2020	Growth, % per year 1995–2020
USA	509	526	544	563	584	617	0.8
JPN	75	75	75	75	75	75	0.0
EUM	227	214	205	200	198	198	-0.5
ROE	1	1	1	1	1	1	0.0
ROO	74	75	77	79	81	83	0.5
EIT	325	278	287	314	352	388	0.7
CHN	647	732	840	965	1,110	1,283	2.8
IND	159	173	191	209	229	254	1.9
ANI	68	76	87	100	115	134	2.7
AOE	8	9	11	12	14	16	3.0
LAM	20	21	22	24	26	29	1.6
ROW	161	169	180	192	205	220	1.3
TOTAL	2,272	2,350	2,521	2,736	2,990	3,300	1.5

grows by 2.7 per cent per year, whereas Indian demand grows at nearly 2 per cent. China will remain the biggest user of coal in the world, increasing its share from 28 to 39 per cent of global coal use.

The overwhelming bulk of the world's coal demand is for steam coal for burning under boilers to produce electricity or heat for public distribution or by industries for their own use. Specialised metallurgical coal used in the iron and steel industry represents only some 15 per cent of hard coal demand in the OECD and in the world as a whole. This proportion is steadily falling as new processes for producing steel or using non-metallurgical coal are introduced and as other materials are substituted for steel. In recent years, increasing amounts of steam coal have been used as a substitute for coke in blast furnaces through pulverised coal injection.

The transformation in the pattern of coal use in the OECD over a thirteen-year period is shown in Table 7.5. Direct use of coal in end-use markets is now down to 14 per cent from 34 per cent in 1973. The change from the 1950s when coal was used across the range of small and large industries, for home heating and even for transport, has, of course, been even more dramatic. Energy use in the fast growing new economies has leapfrogged this historic route and steam coal, without innovative new technologies, can only look to electricity generation for any kind of future growth.

Electricity generation is the largest single area of demand for primary energy, where all energy sources can be used to provide the same

Table 7.5: Coal Consumption in the OECD by Main Markets. Percentage Shares

	1973	1996
Iron and steel	10.8	5.1
Chemicals	2.2	1.1
Cement etc.	1.6	2.6
Paper, pulp etc.	1.0	0.5
Other industries	5.2	2.2
Total industry	20.8	11.5
Residential	8.5	2.1
Others	4.5	0.7
Total end use markets	33.8	14.3
Electricity Generation etc,	53.5	77.5
Gas works	0.9	0.1
Transformation losses etc.	11.8	8.1
Total	100.0	100.0

Source: OECD/IEA Coal Information (1998)

product, electricity. As a result it is also where inter-fuel competition is often at its most fierce. Although additional coal-fired power stations came on line last year in both developed and developing countries, the future construction of new capacity, in OECD countries at least, is expected to remain low. The increasing availability of relatively low cost natural gas presents an enormous challenge to the future of the coal industry in its main market. However, the type of fuel used for power generation is still in many countries, both industrialised and developing, the result of political decisions based on other than strictly economic grounds. Overall in the OECD, coal's share of electricity generated has remained remarkably stable; it was 39 per cent in 1997 compared with 40 per cent in 1980 and 38 per cent in 1973.

The cost of environmental protection for new supply projects or retrofitting existing plant is a growing area of uncertainty. Significant gains in efficiency and emission levels can be achieved by a range of clean coal technologies (CCTs) that are in various stages of commercialisation. Atmospheric fluidised bed units (AFBs) are commercially proven but give very little efficiency improvement over sub-critical pulverised coal units. They do, however, produce less emissions, are capable of handling a wide range of coals and are suitable for retrofitting in to existing power plants.

Comparisons of electricity generating costs are always very uncertain and easily manipulated to give the desired result. However, coal can be competitive for base load power generation even at present oil and gas prices but the source and quality of the coal is paramount. The relatively high capital cost of plant and certain technical characteristics make coal generally suitable only for base or intermediate load generation. Table 7.6 compares costs for electricity generation for different technologies.

Table 7.6: Cost and Climate Impact of Coal for Electricity Generation Compared with Other Sources

	Capital Cost ¢/kwh	Total Cost ¢/kwh	Construction Time in Years	Climate Impact
Coal	2.0 – 4.3	3.8 – 6.9	3 – 5	High
IGCC	3.3 – 4.5	7.5 – 8.9	5 – 7	Medium
Fuel Oil	2.0 – 2.5	4.8 – 5.7	3 – 5	Medium
Gas Turbine	0.8 – 1.1	3.4 – 3.9	1.1 – 2.0	Low
Gas CC	1.4 – 1.9	3.1	3.1 – 3.8	Low
Nuclear	3.8 – 10.0	5.3 – 11.8	3 – 5	Low

Notes:

Cost computed on the basis of an 8 per cent after tax earning power. Plant operating at base load.
IGCC = Integrated coal gasification combined cycle
Gas CC = Natural gas combined cycle

Source: OIES Review of Energy Costs (1991)

The use of coal almost everywhere will continue to concentrate on those few applications and in those countries where it has a competitive edge or cannot easily be replaced due to the applied technological application. Its use outside of power plants and highly energy intensive industries such as steel and cement is likely to diminish even more in future.

7.4 Conclusions

On a global scale, coal is still significant with a contribution to primary energy demand that is at present only exceeded by oil. But, although coal resources are spread widely, consumption is increasingly concentrating in a handful of countries and in a few main uses. The bulk of growth in demand in recent years has come from countries within the Asia-Pacific region, largely China and India, and from the USA. These three countries consumed 59 per cent of the world's coal in 1998, measured in common heat units.

Demand for coal in all but a few countries has also become concentrated within a fairly narrow range of market outlets. These are largely those applications where a basic low cost source of heat is required on a large scale. The demand for specialised coking coal for the steel industry continues to increase slowly but is under long-term threat. Growth is becoming increasingly focused on one market, power generation, where coal at present generates over a third of the world's electricity. Over 75 per cent of coal consumed in the OECD is for power generation and this proportion seems set to continue to increase.

In a few countries, such as China and India, mainly indigenous coal is still used widely across the market spectrum. Inevitably, with modernisation, increased prosperity and industry restructuring, they would seem to be destined to move along the same route followed by the OECD countries.

It seems likely that coal, outside the fading traditional high cost producing areas, will remain a very competitive fuel for large-scale under-boiler use in solely economic terms. But, without innovative technological advances, coal will continue to be at a disadvantage technically as well as on environmental grounds against its main competitors.

CHAPTER 8

NATURAL GAS

8.1 Introduction

Reserves of natural gas are abundant and, overall, may well represent a larger potential source of energy than oil. Development in many areas has been constrained by the high capital cost of most supply projects and the infrastructure needed for distribution, their relative inflexibility and the lengthy process of development usually involved. Where projects involve international movement and linkage of supply in one country to markets in another, then these problems are exacerbated.

Despite the constraints, natural gas consumption has grown in recent years rather faster than either oil or coal and this is set to continue. It now supplies almost a quarter of the world's commercial energy needs. A number of countries rely on gas for over 40 or 50 per cent of their primary energy needs and it competes commercially with other fuels in almost all markets, except transport. Electricity generation has represented the fastest growing source of demand for gas in recent years.

In Section 8.2 we look at the key elements of gas supply, including the resource base, the supply situation, cost and price structure and the future outlook. A section on the demand for natural gas considers the regional and market pattern of gas use and the future development of demand and is followed by some brief conclusions.

8.2 Natural Gas Availability and Supply

8.2.1 The Resource Base

Gas reserves were of the order of 146 trillion cubic metres (tcm) or 130 billion toe at the end of 1998.[1] At present rates of consumption,

---

1. *Oil and Gas Journal*, 1 January 1999.

global gas supplies could be expected to last for nearly 65 years compared with oil for just over 40 years. Over the last ten years proven reserves of natural gas have been increasing at an average 2.7 per cent per annum, with new reserves being added at an annual rate in excess of production.

Most of the net increase in reserves in recent years is attributed to developing countries (see Table 8.1). Reserves of the industrialised countries of the OECD have actually declined. There has been virtually no change in the estimated size of reserves in the economies in transition of the former Soviet Union over the last five years.

Table 8.1:   Proven Reserves of Natural Gas. 1979–1999. Trillion Cubic Metres

	at 1.1.79	at 1.1.89	at 1.1.99	% at 1.1.99
USA	5.8	5.3	4.7	3.2
JPN	n.a.	n.a.	n.a.	n.a.
EUM	4.4	6.5	4.8	3.2
ROE	0.7	2.4	1.2	0.8
ROO	2.6	3.2	3.2	2.2
EIT	25.8	42.5	57.3	39.1
ANI	1.6	4.1	5.0	3.4
CHN	0.7	0.9	1.4	1.0
IND	0.1	0.7	0.5	0.3
AOE	24.5	37.5	55.4	37.9
LAM	3.2	6.7	8.0	5.5
ROW	1.5	2.2	4.9	3.4
Total World	70.9	112.0	146.4	100.0
(OECD)	13.5	16.4	14.4	9.8

Source: *Oil and Gas Journal* 28 December 1998; BP Amoco *Statistical Review of World Energy* (1999)

There is a wider geographical distribution of natural gas reserves (which are currently registered in over 80 countries) than for oil. But, almost 40 per cent of total reserves is in the countries of the former Soviet Union and half of this is contained in three super giant fields. Nearly another 40 per cent of currently proven reserves are in the Middle East and North Africa. On present estimates, Russia and Iran alone account for almost half of the world's proven gas reserves.

In many sedimentary basins, oil and gas accumulations are closely associated and related to the same geological conditions. Thus major gas formations are generally known in basins which have been intensively explored for oil, although there may be deeper formations that have not been sufficiently penetrated. Over the coming years, gas reserves will certainly be augmented by deep exploration in existing fields. Furthermore, in many parts of the world where gas resources are known to exist a lack of infrastructure to move the gas to consumers means that they are not currently considered to be economic. It seems likely that this gas will be increasingly exploited as markets develop nearer to it or if the various liquids from gas technologies become commercially viable.

8.2.2 Regional Supply Situation

In the early 1970s, the USA was the single largest producer of gas, producing and consuming over half the world's natural gas. This proportion has fallen steadily over the years to around a quarter, in the face of substantial production growth in western Europe, the former Soviet Union and a range of other countries. Russia is currently the largest single producing country despite falling production in recent years, with the USA now running a close second. Between them they still account for almost half of the world's production but their share is falling in the face of rapidly increasing production from other regional sources. Fourteen major gas-producing countries, Canada, UK, Algeria, Indonesia, the Netherlands, Uzbekistan, Iran, Norway, Saudi Arabia, Malaysia, UAE, Australia, Argentina and Venezuela, currently account for an additional 35 per cent of world production. Growth in gas production has been particularly rapid in a handful of the newly industrialised Asian economies and in Latin America in recent years.

Table 8.2 shows projections for gas production from the CLIMOX Business-as-Usual scenario. Similar to the market for coal described in the last chapter, production projections are the result of the interplay of supply and demand in the model. The supply side is driven by exogenous growth of a fixed factor for the production of gas in each of the countries and regions in the model, and an elasticity of substitution between the fixed factor and capital of 0.5. The demand for gas consists of input demand from industries and household demand, and the most important factors for the level of demand are economic growth and technological change.

World gas production according to the EIA was 2270 bcm in 1995. The model projections show this to increase to 3330 bcm in 2010 and 4590 in 2020. The USA is a mature producer of natural gas and its future gas supply potential one of the most contentious of any country. Contrary to many past expectations, production has continued to increase in recent years and is now above the levels of the early 1980s. Domestic production is expected to increase from 540 bcm to more

Table 8.2:   Natural Gas Production. 1995–2020. Billion Cubic Metres

	1995	*2000*	*2005*	*2010*	*2015*	*2020*	*Growth, % per year 1995–2020*
			Gas Production in bcm				
USA	541	561	585	614	644	678	0.9
JPN	2	2	2	3	3	3	0.4
EUM	207	212	219	234	250	267	1.0
ROE	34	51	76	81	85	89	3.9
ROO	199	220	245	276	309	347	2.2
EIT	744	761	913	1,091	1,290	1,513	2.9
CHN	20	25	35	50	70	103	6.9
IND	20	24	27	31	36	43	3.0
ANI	111	138	170	211	261	324	4.4
AOE	237	280	317	364	426	503	3.1
LAM	102	137	184	253	350	487	6.5
ROW	56	73	95	127	170	228	5.8
TOTAL	2,273	2,482	2,870	3,335	3,894	4,585	2.8

than 600 and 680 bcm in 2010 and 2020 respectively, an average growth rate of just under 1 per cent per year.

Production in the EU member countries (EUM region) is dominated by the UK and the Netherlands although Denmark is self-sufficient and exports modest amounts of gas. There is also some production in Germany and Italy, although both are far from self-sufficient, and in a handful of other countries such as Spain and Ireland. Relatively little new productive capacity is available within continental Europe and onshore production is in decline, but abundant reserves are available from the North Sea with the possibility of some major new areas in the future. We estimate gas production to grow from 210 bcm in 1995 to 230 and 270 in 2010 and 2020 respectively, an annual growth of 1 per cent.

Gas production in the rest of Europe (ROE region) is all from Norway, which contains the largest offshore field in Europe (Troll). Total Norwegian production has increased rapidly since this field started production in 1996. There are a large number of other major fields under development or for which development plans have been approved. Current development plans foresee a production plateau of 75 bcm, but this is likely to increase in the near future. We project production to increase to close to 90 bcm by 2020.

The ROO region consists overwhelmingly of two major gas-producing countries that are widely separated by geography and background. Canadian gas reserves are spread widely but are generally in fairly small pools. Australia contains large volumes of natural gas reserves and is strategically placed to supply key Asian markets. The potential to meet both domestic and export demand is substantial, from reserves in the Carnarvon, Bonaparte and several other basins. Australia has plans to expand its LNG production – including proposals to develop the Gorgon fields on the North West Shelf for export to China's Guangdong province as well as building a plant to supply gas to remote areas in the West Kimberley region of Australia itself. The region produced 200 bcm of gas in 1995, and this is projected to increase to 280 and 350 bcm in 2010 and 2020.

Natural gas production in the Economies in Transition (EIT region) is dominated by the countries of the former Soviet Union. Almost 40 per cent of the world's gas reserves are in Russia, Ukraine, Kazakhstan and Turkmenistan. Reserves in Russia have been upgraded in recent years due to significant new discoveries. Many areas remain under-explored and it seems certain that Russia's resource base could allow it to continue to play a major role in the international market as well as meet the eventual upturn in domestic demand. Political stability and financial and legal factors, more than any others, will determine whether Russia and the other producers of the old Soviet Union can capitalise on their strengths. Turkmenistan was once the second largest gas producer in the EIT and the only other country exporting gas. It depends however on a transit route through Russia and has had to curtail exports due to non-payment by the importing countries. Eventually it could become an important supplier to Europe and possibly also to the Asian market, including China. We therefore project gas production in the region to more than double over the model horizon, from 740 bcm in 1995 to 1500 bcm in 2020, with exports increasing from 80 to 200 bcm.

The newly industrialised nations of Asia (ANI region) include the gas-producing and consuming countries of Indonesia and Malaysia and the rapidly growing, gas-importing economies of the Philippines, South Korea, Singapore, Thailand and Taiwan. The latter two countries also have some production of their own. The region exported some 40 bcm of gas in 1995 and production is likely to be more than adequate for expected domestic needs as well as meeting demand from importers elsewhere. Gas is currently exported from the region, largely by Indonesia to Japan, and is also imported from Australia and to a lesser extent from the Middle East. Production is projected to increase from 110 bcm to 210 and 320 bcm in 2010 and 2020.

Until recently gas development in China has been ignored in favour of oil. However, China is becoming increasingly interested in pursuing the development of its natural gas infrastructure. Although growth over the next few years seems likely to be slow, China appears to have substantial potential for expanding gas production and, according to official forecasts, it could treble by 2010 and reach 100 bcm in 2020. The growth rate reaches an average of 7 per cent per year, but this level of expansion of indigenous production would not be sufficient to meet demand. However, it is likely that the country will both import and export, as gas fields will be remote from domestic areas of demand.

Although the AOE region, consisting of the Middle East and North African oil-exporting countries, is second only to the countries of the former USSR in the size of its reserve base, it accounts for only 12 per cent of world production. Production actually consumed commercially in the Middle East, as opposed to the large volumes flared or reinjected, has increased substantially in recent years despite cuts in associated crude production. The Gulf states in particular make gas their main source of domestic energy. Gas production is projected to increase from 240 bcm in 1995 to 360 and 500 bcm in 2010 and 2020 respectively.

Most Latin American countries (LAM region) have some gas production. By far the biggest producers are Mexico, Venezuela and Argentina; in 1998 they accounted for just over 75 per cent of total gas production in the region. Production in both Venezuela and Argentina has been increasing rapidly in recent years and in both countries natural gas makes a major contribution to meeting primary energy demand. Gas production is 100 bcm in 1995, and should increase to 250 and 490 bcm in 2010 and 2020, an average annual growth of 6.5 per cent.

The Rest of the World region (ROW), as defined for the model, is in the context of natural gas a rather eclectic group of countries. It includes some with no foreseeable potential for gas production; a current major LNG exporter, Brunei; and producers such as Pakistan and Bangladesh where all production goes for domestic consumption and future potential is modest. It also includes Nigeria, with over a third of Africa's total reserves and more gas than Indonesia or Iraq. Nigerian gas production has risen significantly in recent years although only around 15 per cent of production is actually used by local industry and the oil companies; the rest is flared or reinjected. We project regional production to increase from 56 bcm to 130 and 230 bcm in 2010 and 2020.

8.2.2 The Cost of Gas

Many, if not all, of the readily available estimates of the cost of natural gas production and transportation, as with oil, are uncertain in their reliability. Where gas is produced with oil, the cost of production has to be allocated over the joint products. If the associated gas is perceived as a by-product of oil production, costs tend to be understated. The costs of non-associated gas, which is increasing in importance in future gas supplies, usually reflect the full costs of exploring and developing a gas field and bringing gas to the wellhead and the market.

Estimates of the unit cost of producing gas differ considerably both within producing countries and across regions. In the USA and Canada, production costs would appear to range from $0.20 per Mbtu to $2 per Mbtu for some offshore Gulf production, although the potential supply still available within this cost range is open to debate. In contrast, estimates of the production cost of indigenous European gas (regions EUM and ROE) vary between $0.10 and $2.20 per Mbtu with Dutch gas being at the low end of the scale, gas from the UK in the middle and Norwegian gas at the high end. Table 8.3, derived largely from estimates published by the IEA, gives an indication of the cost of European gas compared with the cost of gas imported into continental western Europe from an indicative range of existing and possible sources.

Table 8.3:   Comparative Unit Costs of Natural Gas delivered to Western Europe. 1993$ per Mbtu

	Production costs	*Transport costs**	*Border costs*
Netherlands. Groningen	0.10	0.15	0.25
UK via Interconnector	1.20	0.60	1.80
Netherlands. North Sea	1.00	0.60	1.60
Norway. Troll-Emden	1.20	0.76	1.96
Algeria. LNG	0.50	1.49	1.99
Algeria. Transmed	0.50	0.89	1.39
Russia. W. Siberia	0.50	2.72	3.22
Russia. Yamal	0.75	2.62	3.37
Nigeria. LNG	0.70	2.70	3.40
Middle East. LNG	0.50	3.05	3.55
Turkmenistan	0.50	3.90	4.40

* includes transit costs where applicable

Source: Adapted from J.P. Pauwels in IEA *Oil, Gas and Coal Outlook* (1995)

This rough comparison confirms, as might be expected, that the least costly gas is that piped to Europe from the North Sea Basin, followed by Algerian gas, and then Russian. The problem with gas supplies to Europe is not resource limitations amongst potential suppliers, but the need to transport the gas over long distances by LNG tanker or pipeline.

In the case of Japan, imports are, at present, entirely by LNG tanker. For LNG projects generally to expand significantly in future, their costs would need to continue dropping through technical, financial or strategic measures. The gain derived from economies of scale from liquefaction and shipping has been considerable. The scope for savings on pipeline costs, which depend very heavily on high load factors, does not appear to be so great as for LNG, except perhaps through the acceptance of lower rates of return than is customary.

In contrast to oil, there is at present no 'world price' for gas. Gas markets are regionalised largely into three major international trading zones, mainly because gas is so expensive to transport. There are significant differences between import price levels in the three main regional gas-consuming areas. North America is virtually self-sufficient; Asia/Oceania depends largely on internal trade and some Middle East imports; whilst western Europe is supplied by internal trade together with imports largely from Russia and North Africa. This has led to different levels of import prices between the regions. Table 8.4 gives an indication of the spread and historical movement of some average gas prices in key regions, compared with the price for crude oil. This fragmentation of the world into three gas-consuming areas is likely to diminish in importance, as the market for LNG grows. Excess capacity in production and shipping is likely to develop, which will allow arbitrage between the different markets. The CLIMOX model does not distinguish between regional gas markets. However, transport costs and finite substitution elasticities pose barriers to global trade.

Table 8.4: Average Gas and Crude Oil Prices. 1990–1998. $ per Mbtu

| | LNG | | Natural Gas | | Crude Oil |
	Japan cif	EU cif	UK*	USA **	OECD cif
1990	3.64	2.82		1.64	3.82
1991	3.99	3.18		1.47	3.33
1992	3.62	2.76		1.77	3.19
1993	3.52	2.53		2.10	2.82
1994	3.18	2.24		1.92	2.70
1995	3.46	2.37		1.69	2.96
1996	3.66	2.43	1.84	2.76	3.54
1997	3.91	2.65	2.03	2.53	3.29
1998	3.06	2.27	1.92	2.08	2.18

* Heren index   ** Henry Hub
Source: BP Amoco *Statistical Review of World Energy* (1999)

8.3 The Demand for Gas

8.3.1 The Pattern of Gas Use

Through the 1990s, gas use has grown at around 2.0 per cent only. None the less, growth has been faster than for oil or coal. As a result, the share of natural gas in the world's consumption of primary energy is now almost 24 per cent and has risen in all major regions. Demand is continuing to grow rapidly worldwide and gas seems set to displace coal as the second largest source of the world's energy within a few years. Table 8.5 shows projections for natural gas production to 2020 and Table 8.6 shows 1996 gas consumption by end-use in key regions of the world.

The USA now consumes some 27 per cent of the world's gas. In the 1990s there has been an absolute reduction in consumption in Russia and above average gas penetration in the Asian newly industrialised countries (ANI region) and in the oil-exporting countries of the Middle East and North Africa (AOE region). Despite this, the USA together with the countries of the former Soviet Union and Eastern Europe, still account for over 50 per cent of world gas consumption between them. Gas use in China and India has scarcely grown in relative terms and is, as yet, of little significance in global terms.

In the OECD countries the residential and commercial market, largely space heating, represents the single major use of gas, followed

Table 8.5: World Natural Gas Consumption, 1995–2020. Billion Cubic Metres

	1995	2000	Gas Consumption in bcm 2005	2010	2015	2020	Growth, % per year 1995–2020
USA	628	686	749	822	905	1,014	1.9
JPN	69	83	96	109	123	141	2.9
EUM	341	378	417	449	483	531	1.8
ROE	6	7	7	8	8	8	1.2
ROO	109	121	134	147	162	180	2.0
EIT	661	641	767	933	1,128	1,318	2.8
CHN	20	27	38	55	80	121	7.5
IND	21	25	30	36	44	55	4.0
ANI	74	91	113	142	179	235	4.7
AOE	186	229	276	334	402	491	4.0
LAM	104	129	162	205	263	347	4.9
ROW	55	66	80	96	116	145	3.9
TOTAL	2,273	2,482	2,870	3,335	3,894	4,585	2.8

Table 8.6: Natural Gas Consumption by main End-use Markets in 1996. Per Cent

	OECD	USA	Russia	UK	Germany	Japan
Industry	27.3	25.9	31.2	19.8	30.7	2.1
Residential/Commercial	35.0	38.2	16.3	45.6	43.2	n.a.
Others	4.1	3.3	n.a.	7.2	3.7	0.1
Total end use	66.4	67.4	47.5	72.6	77.6	2.2
Elec. Gen	23.0	23.3	35.8	20.4	18.4	67.4
Energy sector	7.4	9.3	15.6	7.0	2.4	0.6
Losses etc	3.2	n.a.	1.1	n.a.	1.6	29.8
Total	100.0	100.0	100.0	100.0	100.0	100.0

Source: Cedigaz *Natural Gas in the World* (1998) and OECD *Energy Balances*

by gas used in industry and for electricity generation. Natural gas is not used directly in the residential sector in Japan for various structural and organisational reasons, despite the heavy home heating load. Gas is used indirectly to a limited extent through being moved into the manufactured gas systems which supply much of the residential and commercial space heating.

8.3.2 The Future of Gas Use

It is in power generation that much of the future growth potential for natural gas in the industrialised countries, especially in Europe, would seem to lie. The high efficiency, particularly of combined-cycle gas turbines and their low emissions of CO_2 and SO_2 make them particularly attractive for generating electricity in environmentally committed countries. Much of the future of natural gas consumption therefore rests on the pace of overall electricity demand and the age and pattern of present generating capacity.

In the USA, the expected retirement of aged nuclear plants is likely to add to the basic benefits of natural gas use and encourage increased growth in the power sector. The gas market is highly integrated across North America and is becoming increasingly so with the advent of NAFTA. There is a high degree of fairly transparent competition and switching by gas, with competitive fuel price changes, from industrial use to electricity generation and vice versa. If gas prices can remain competitive, considerable scope remains for gas penetration in many industrial applications. Gas consumption in the USA is projected to increase to 820 and 1000 bcm in 2010 and 2020.

The European gas market is becoming more integrated and this will inevitably act as an encouragement for greater gas penetration where markets are not saturated. There are a number of countries in western Europe, such as Greece, Spain, Portugal, where gas use is still relatively new but the infrastructure and supply arrangements are expanding rapidly. For example, gas supplies less than 1 per cent of industrial energy needs in Greece at present. The scope for substitution is considerable and should help to counteract any saturation in some of the markets of the older gas-using countries. The shift towards the Mediterranean countries within the European gas market seems set to continue. Overall gas consumption in the EUM region is projected to reach 450 and 530 bcm in 2010 and 2020.

Gas consumption has been falling in recent years in most east European countries, except Poland and Slovenia, due to the state of their economies. But many east European countries are gaining access to larger and more diversified sources of gas. Their growing integration into the European network with the inevitable upturn in their economic fortunes can eventually only contribute to greater gas use.

Gas's share of total primary energy consumption in Russia has been increasing in recent years and now stands at 55 per cent, although actual consumption volumes have been falling steadily since the collapse of the Soviet Union. It seems unlikely, however, that such a huge economy as Russia's, with its wealth of resources, will not eventually need to increase its gas use substantially to support economic growth as well as substituting for coal with all its labour and transport problems. Reflecting the strong growth after 2005 that we assume in the EIT region, gas use increases by an average of 2.8 per cent per year over the 25-year model horizon, to reach more than double the 1995 figure in 2020.

Gas demand growth is projected to be fastest in China, with an average annual growth of 7.5 per cent. Still, the Chinese market will remain very small, less than half of current European consumption. The Middle East (AOE) and Latin America will become major gas-consuming areas, with 490 and 350 bcm respectively in 2020.

Liberalisation of the gas market in many countries of Latin America is already boosting demand in a region where gas use overall is still very low. Demand is being driven largely by the industrial and power generation sectors. Current plans to expand gas-fired capacity are, in part, being driven by a need to diversify power sources.

Overall demand for gas in Japan and the newly industrialised Asian economies has been affected by the downturn in Asian economies. However, although this has meant delaying and cancelling projects, there are signs of a recovery in growth, both of the economies and of gas demand. In Japan, there is also considerable potential in the residential market if the present monopolistic, rigid and inefficient towns' gas systems are finally replaced.

One of the more obvious solutions to meeting China's surging economic development, whilst alleviating the pollution caused by its massive use of coal and reducing the need to import oil, is to increase the use of natural gas. This will involve a mixture of strategies such as increasing indigenous production and importing gas from abroad by pipeline or LNG tanker. The practical problems of moving from the present tiny 2 per cent share of gas in primary energy consumption are, of course, enormous.

Many local authorities within China are apparently pushing for the greater use of gas, especially in semi-independent power stations in the booming south east. But there is at present very little domestic pipeline infrastructure and gas is largely piped to areas adjacent to the fields. Most households even in Beijing use largely coal or gas manufactured from coal as a cooking and heating fuel, if they can afford it. Plans to expand the gas infrastructure are ambitious and include a transmission and distribution network for Beijing to convert large numbers of households to natural gas. There are also moves to cut the subsidy on coal production and put limits on its use in order to clean up the environment. However, without real and substantial price increases, any gas expansion plans will face serious difficulty in attracting foreign finance and producers will have little incentive, especially in the face of rising costs. Unfortunately, fiscal incentives and a gas regulatory law to oversee pricing and sales agreements have yet to appear. The Chinese determination to succeed in diversifying its energy base should not be underestimated but it seems likely to be some time before gas use, even in the new economic areas, will be really significant. We therefore expect gas use to reach 60 bcm and 120 bcm in 2010 and 2020 respectively.

In India, gas consumption is also relatively small and coal dominates many of the main end-use sectors. There are some firm projects for expanding gas imports largely to feed power plants. India's growing economic and political strength and stability should see a substantial above average increase in gas use over the next decade or so.

In the rest of the world, Turkey is one of the fastest developing gas markets. Natural gas use has more than doubled over the past six years and there is a growing and diversified array of suppliers. Natural gas is now used widely in industry, the residential sector and in the power sector; whereas in the early 1980s it was not used at all in either the power sector or in industry and only in insignificant volumes in the residential market. There is still considerable scope for increased gas penetration and displacement of coal; above average growth for gas in this dynamic country seems likely.

8.4 Conclusions

As with any other energy source, there are many uncertainties about the future development of natural gas and speculation as to its future can be misleading. However, some important elements point to the future direction of natural gas development and the extent of its long-term contribution to the energy economies of the world.

Natural gas has already become a source of energy for almost all major market applications, except transport. Electricity generation, the market in which gas has significant advantages and where its penetration is rapid, is the largest and fastest growing energy market in almost every country. The industrial and residential markets also offer considerable scope for growth and substitution, especially outside the older gas-using countries of the OECD.

CHAPTER 9

ANTHROPOGENIC GREENHOUSE GAS EMISSIONS

9.1 Introduction

Humankind has always generated gases that contribute to the terrestrial greenhouse effect; and for a very long time, these man-made or 'anthropogenic' emissions remained quite marginal and could not possibly have had an effect on the global climate. In the present century, however, the size of these emissions has changed dramatically. To see this, one only needs to look at the evolution of the most important anthropogenic GHG source: carbon dioxide (CO_2) from fossil fuel combustion (Figure 9.1). More than 95 per cent of these emissions since 1750 have been emitted in the present century. In 1900, global CO_2 fossil fuel combustion emissions amounted to about

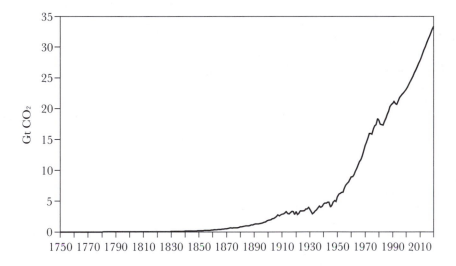

Figure 9.1:   Yearly Carbon Dioxide Emissions from Fossil Fuel Combustion

Sources: 1750–1994: Carbon Dioxide Information Analysis Center (CDIAC), 1995: FCCC, 1996–2020: OIES Projections.

2Gt, rising steadily – with the exception of major economic crises such as the two World Wars, the 1930s depression, the oil crises, and the collapse of the Soviet Union – to 22Gt in 1995, and are projected to rise under BaU conditions to 33Gt by 2020. While the definitive verdict on whether these emissions do or do not have an adverse effect on the terrestrial climate system is still unknown, the figures clearly need to be taken seriously.

As concerns potential global warming effects, CO_2 and methane (CH_4) are by far the most important of the six GHGs currently under consideration in climate change negotiations. When measured in global warming equivalence terms,[1] the combined global emissions of CO_2 and CH_4 amount to approximately 98 per cent of total GHG emissions, with CO_2 accounting for a lion's share of 74 per cent. In OECD countries – having above average CO_2 emissions of 83 per cent and below average CH_4 emissions of 11 per cent (Table A1.1) – this total is 94 per cent and thus slightly below the global figure.

9.2 Carbon Dioxide Emissions

Over 95 per cent of 1995 global CO_2 emissions[2] of 22.9Gt were energy emissions, overwhelmingly generated by fossil fuel combustion (Table A1.2). According to FCCC figures (Table A1.3), the sectoral distribution of these combustion emissions in OECD countries in descending order of magnitude was as follows: Energy Industries (Power Generation) 35.4 per cent; Transport 28.0 per cent; Industry 20.9 per cent; Small Combustion (Household and Commerce) 15.0 per cent.

In 1995, global CO_2 *energy* emissions were 21.8Gt, 47 per cent of which originated in OECD countries. Under BaU assumptions, these emisssions are projected to reach a level of 33Gt in 2020, 38 per cent of which is from the OECD region. The combustion of crude oil and petroleum products generates the largest share of these emissions, both

---

1. In order to aggregate different GHGs into single emission parameters, the amounts have to be weighted in accordance with the 'virulence' of their global warming effects. This is generally achieved by using the so-called '(100 year) global warming potentials' (GWP), measured relative to the effect of CO_2. Being the standard, CO_2 has a GWP of 1, while the GWP of CH_4, in accordance with the IPCC, is taken to be 21. In other words, 1 mass unit of CH_4 is assumed to have the same effect as 21 units of CO_2, which is why it will be added to CO_2 amounts as 21 units CO_2e ('CO_2-equivalent').
2. For stylistic reasons, we shall generally omit the qualifier 'anthropogenic' if it is self-evident from the context.

in 1995 and 2020, namely 42.1 and 40.5 per cent, respectively. Emissions from coal combustion decrease in relative size from 37.9 to 33.4 per cent, while emissions from combustion and flaring of gases increase their share from 20 to 26.1 per cent.

9.3   Methane Emissions

The global level of methane emissions in 1995 was estimated to be around 7Gt CO_2e, i.e about a quarter of all GHG emissions, and is projected to rise under BaU conditions to more than double (15.5 Gt) in 2020.[3] Methane emissions can broadly be divided into three main source categories as shown in Figure 9.2. The largest is Agriculture which represented 48 per cent of emissions in 1995, subdivided into Livestock (28), Rice Cultivation (14), and Waste Burning (6 per cent). Waste represented 20 per cent, of which Solid Waste Disposal and Wastewater 10 per cent each. Energy produced 27 per cent of emissions, from Fugitive Fuel (26 per cent) and Fuel Combustion (1 per cent).

Although our scenarios will focus on methane emissions from energy sources, it is important to keep in mind non-energy emissions as potential abatement alternatives to options involving fossil fuels.

9.3.1   The Agricultural Sector

The agricultural sector, responsible for 48 per cent of all 1995 methane emissions, is projected to increase its share to 56 per cent in 2020.[4] Most of this increase is due to a projected tripling of rice cultivation emissions from 1Gt CO_2e in 1995 to 3Gt in 2020. Under continually or intermittently flooded conditions, rice production generates methane emissions due to anaerobic decomposition of organic matter. The IPCC has identified at least three abatement options concerning rice cultivation practices. These are irrigation management, with 10 per cent reduction potential; nutrient management, 20 per cent, and new cultivars 10 per cent.

---

3. All our methane figures are inhouse estimates, based on the IPCC *Revised 1996 Guidelines for National Greenhouse Gas Inventories*. For a more detailed account see Benito Müller and Ulrich Bartsch, *The Modelling of Anthropogenic Methane Emissions: Methodology and Estimates*, EV29 (Oxford: OIES (1999)).
4. This 2020 figure is based on quite conservative assumptions about biomass burning and could thus easily be higher.

1995

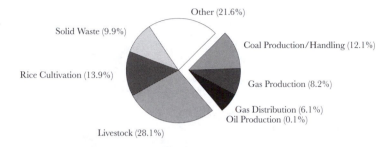

2020

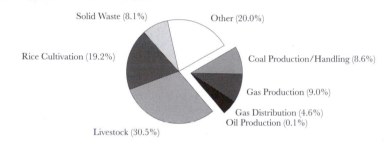

Figure 9.2:   Methane Emissions by Sector and Source. 1995 and 2020.

The category 'Other' contains all those sectors and sources for which we did not carry out regional projections: (1) fuel combustion [Energy], (2) biomass burning (= sum of deforestation and savannah burning) and agricultural waste burning [Agriculture], (3) waste water management [Waste], and (4) IPCC 'Other' category.

Given our relatively conservative estimates[5] and projections (Figure 9.3), the 40 per cent total abatement potential identified by the IPCC amounts to 0.8Gt in 2010, our model period for the Kyoto commitments. However, over 95 per cent of these emissions originate in non-Annex I countries (i.e. countries without Kyoto targets). Indeed, by 2020 China together with India are by themselves projected to emit half of them. This means that under the Kyoto Protocol, these abatement potentials could only be realised through the Clean Development Mechanism. (See Section 2.5.2)

---

5. See Müller and Bartsch (1999):19ff.

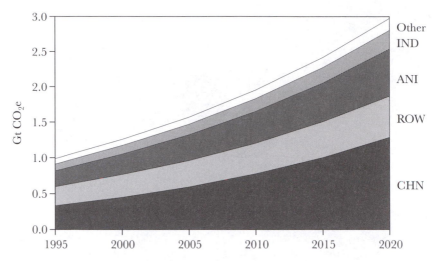

Figure 9.3: Regional Projections for Methane Rice Cultivation Emissions

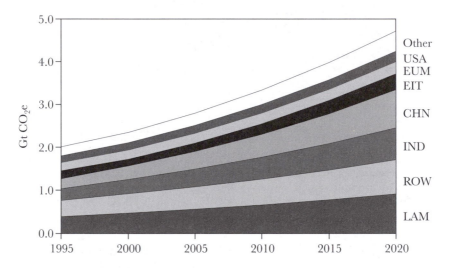

Figure 9.4: Regional Projections for Methane Livestock Emissions

The agricultural emissions from the livestock sector (shown in Figure 9.4) originate from two sources: enteric fermentation of ruminant livestock[6] and livestock manure. According to the IPCC,[7] emissions from enteric fermentation (totalling 1.7Gt CO_2e in 1995), for example,

---

6. Cattle, buffalo, sheep, goats, camels, horses, mules, asses and swine.
7. IPCC (1996), ibid.

could be reduced by means of improving diet quality and nutrient balance (30 per cent), increasing feed digestibility (3 per cent) and production-enhancing agents (3 per cent).

The IPCC also estimates a reduction potential of 21 per cent for emissions relating to manure management. The total potential for livestock emission abatement in 2010 could therefore reach 1.1Gt CO_2e. Although the regional distribution of these emissions is much less concentrated than in the case of rice, some 70 per cent still originate in non-Annex I countries.

9.3.2 The Waste Sector

By contrast waste emissions, arising principally through anaerobic conditions in solid waste disposal ('landfill') sites (Figure 9.5) and in waste water treatment,[8] originate predominantly in Annex I countries. They accounted for 63 per cent of the total 0.7Gt CO_2e landfill emissions in 1995, and the OECD countries among them for 49 per cent. The IPCC estimates a reduction potential of around 40 per cent for these landfill emissions, which, in absolute terms, means 0.3Gt in 2010.

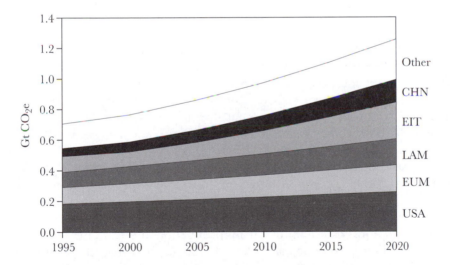

Figure 9.5:   Regional Projections for Methane. Solid Waste Disposal (Landfills)

---

8. The IPCC methodology for estimating wastewater emissions was not suitable for modelling, which is why we are unable to provide regional projections for them.

9.3.3 The Energy Sector

Methane energy emissions originate in the production, handling and combustion of fossil fuels. In contrast to CO_2 energy emissions, which are 99 per cent due to combustion, methane energy emissions are almost exclusively (99 per cent) due to fugitive fuel. The share of fugitive fuel emissions in the methane total will decrease from 26.5 per cent (1.9Gt CO_2e) in 1995 to 22.2 per cent (3.4Gt) in 2020. Throughout the time horizon of this study, gas production and distribution, followed by the emissions from coal production and handling, account for the largest shares in fugitive methane emissions. Emissions from oil production remain completely negligible throughout (see Figure 9.2).

Fugitive methane emissions from coal (0.9Gt CO_2e in 1995, 1.3Gt in 2020) are generated in the proportions of 89 per cent emissions in mining and 11 per cent in the handling of coal. The volume of fugitive methane in mining depends on the pressure on the coal mined and hence the depth of the coal seams. Underground mining releases ten times or more methane per tonne mined than surface mining. At the same time, underground mining is particularly suited for capturing these emissions. Indeed, they already have to be removed for safety reasons. At present, most of the ventilation systems simply release the fugitive methane into the atmosphere, sometimes after flaring. Instead, most of the installations could be adapted to recover and enrich the methane in order to use it as fuel. It is estimated that this could reduce emissions by 50 to 70 per cent, which, at the conservative end, would mean a reduction potential of 0.5Gt CO_2e in 2010. Figure 9.6 shows that regionally, fugitive coal emissions are again dominated by non-Annex I countries (over 65 per cent), principally China (50 per cent), although the second largest source – EIT (17 per cent) – is part of Annex I.

Fugitive methane emissions from natural gas (1.0Gt CO_2e in 1995, 2,1Gt in 2020) are concentrated in four major production regions (Figure 9.7), namely EIT (45 per cent), AOE (20 per cent), LAM (15 per cent), and USA (8 per cent). Globally these emissions divide roughly 60–40 into emissions stemming from production and from distribution, although there are considerable differences between these major contributing regions: in the non-Annex I regions (AOE and LAM), gas production is actually responsible for 80 to 90 per cent of emissions, while in the Annex I regions (USA, EIT) production and distribution contribute about equal shares.

During normal operations, fugitive methane is emitted through the practices of venting and deliberate releases from pneumatic devices

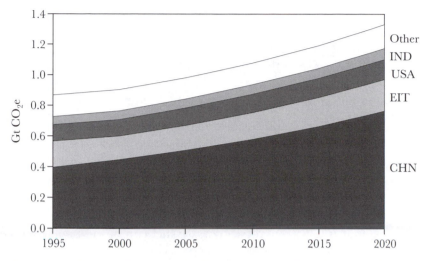

Figure 9.6: Regional Projections for Fugitive Methane Emissions from Coal
Mining and Handling

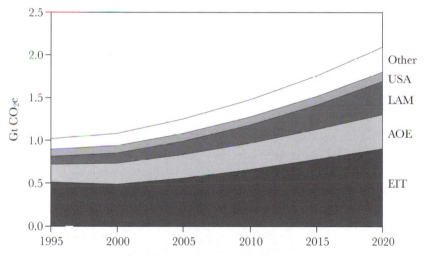

Figure 9.7: Regional Projections for Fugitive Methane Emissions from Gas
Production and Distribution

and process vents. Other emissions may arise from flaring, maintenance, system upsets and accidents. Enhanced inspection, preventative
maintenance, new design solutions, repairs and changes in routines
can greatly reduce emissions. Estimates for the reduction potential
range from 10 to 80 per cent depending on sites. Profitable reductions
are possible where small incremental investments can modify current

operations and practices and/or old or stressed systems handling large quantities of gas. Recent analyses in the United States show that emissions can be profitably reduced over the next decade by about 30 per cent. Given this and the state of production and the transportation system in the main source region (EIT), it seems reasonable to consider the midpoint (45 per cent) of the above-mentioned reduction potential range as benchmark, thus leaving us with a 2010 reduction potential of 0.7Gt CO_2e.[9]

9.4 Energy Emission Projections

The greenhouse gases modelled in our policy analyses are energy emissions, that is CO_2 generated by fossil fuel combustion and fugitive fuels methane (CH_4). The production and consumption levels of fossil fuels described in Chapters 3, 7 and 8 produce the CO_2 and methane emissions shown in this section. Global energy emissions are projected to increase from 23.6Gt in 1995 to 36.8Gt in 2020 (Table 9.1). This means an average growth of 1.8 per cent per year. As previously discussed, energy consumption in the non-Annex I countries grows faster than in the OECD countries, and therefore also emissions. In the OECD countries, emissions grow between 0.3 and 1.1 per cent per

Table 9.1: BaU Energy Emissions (Combustion CO_2 + Fugitive Fuel CH_4). Million Tonnes CO_2e

	1995	2000	2005	2010	2015	2020
USA	5,307	5,613	5,921	6,257	6,617	6,859
JPN	1,149	1,209	1,256	1,297	1,314	1,279
EUM	3,146	3,219	3,301	3,368	3,420	3,429
ROE	74	80	86	90	93	95
ROO	830	874	920	968	1,012	1,050
EIT	3,994	3,579	3,993	4,632	5,412	6,135
CHN	3,322	3,741	4,266	4,882	5,599	6,447
IND	891	980	1,083	1,197	1,324	1,473
ANI	1,181	1,365	1,580	1,809	2,065	2,323
AOE	1,353	1,651	1,958	2,311	2,703	3,123
LAM	1,088	1,280	1,500	1,762	2,077	2,443
ROW	1,343	1,454	1,586	1,731	1,905	2,092
TOTAL	23,679	25,044	27,450	30,305	33,541	36,750

9. A summary of methane reduction potentials of all sources and sectors is given in Table A1.8.

year, 1.7 per cent in the EIT region, and between 2 and 3 per cent in the non-Annex I countries. Emissions in the USA will reach 7.1Gt in 2020, followed closely by China and the Economies in Transition. This shows clearly the inefficiency of energy use in China and the EIT region, which will still have much lower GDP than the USA, yet generate almost as much energy emissions. This remains the case even though they are assumed to have high energy efficiency improvement rates. For China, this is partly due to the very high share of coal in their energy mix, whereas in the EIT region, high leakage of methane from natural gas production and transportation is a major factor.

Of the regions in the projections, the Middle East and North Africa (AOE) has the highest average growth in emissions, due to relatively high economic growth rates and low energy efficiency improvement. Another striking detail in Table 9.1 is the very low contribution of the Rest of OECD Europe region (Norway, Switzerland, Iceland) to the global greenhouse gas emissions. Apart from being small in terms of economies, the region consists of countries with unusually low energy emissions per capita and per unit of GDP relative to Annex I. In all three countries, electricity generation makes wide use of renewable, non-carbon energy sources, in particular hydropower in Norway and Switzerland, and geothermal energy in Iceland.

Figure 9.8 shows emission profiles for the USA, the European Union, and the Economies in Transition region, showing the historical record from 1980 to 1995, and our projections for the Business-as-Usual case

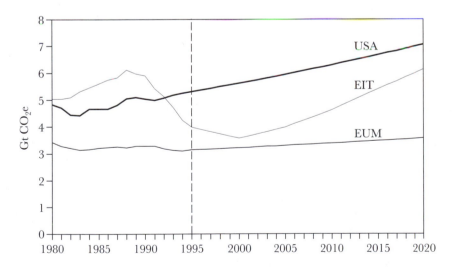

Figure 9.8: BaU Energy Emission Projections

until 2020. EIT emissions reached a peak in 1988, rising above 6Gt CO_2e. The economic turmoil which followed the collapse of the Soviet Union decreased emissions to about 4Gt CO_2e in 1995, the base year for the projections. According to the projections, emissions will only surpass 1988 levels towards the end of the projections horizon.

PART III

POLICY SCENARIOS AND SIMULATION RESULTS

CHAPTER 10

THE KYOTO SCENARIO: DESCRIPTION

10.1 Introduction

Our Kyoto scenario is aimed at evaluating the effects on fossil fuel markets of what – in the light of present knowledge – we judge to be the 'most likely' Kyoto Protocol implementation. Given the flexibility inherent in this Protocol, its targets can be met in a large variety of ways, some obviously more efficient than others. In Chapter 12, we will be looking at the effects of different implementation instruments. At present our interest is to look at the impacts of those sets of policies which have been proposed or adopted by the governments concerned. To this end we outline the policy declarations of the Annex I governments in Section 10.2, concluding with a summary of the way in which these policies are to be represented in our model (Section 10.3). Whether or not governments will actually implement these proposed policies is, of course, a different matter. Our Kyoto scenario is 'most likely' only insofar as the implementation of a declared policy should be at least as likely as that of any other policy.

The emission targets (assigned amounts) of our model regions for the Kyoto period 2010 are, of course, given by the sum total of the energy emissions (EE) assigned to the relevant countries under the percentages specified in Annex B of the Kyoto Protocol. Under this aggregation, our regions are assigned targets ranging from 8 per cent (EUM) to 0.1 per cent (ROO) below 1990 levels. In keeping with the nature of our five-year model intervals, the assigned amounts listed in Table 10.1 are to be read as yearly averages for the first commitment period, i.e. the five-year period centred around 2010. In other words, the Parties/regions would actually be assigned five times this amount, to be counted against the sum total of emissions during this five-year period.

The participation of non-Annex I Parties in abatement efforts will be discussed in our third ('Global Compromise') scenario, which is

Table 10.1: The Kyoto Scenario Energy Emissions Targets (Assigned Amounts). Million Tonnes and Per Cent

	Energy Emissions 1990		Target	Target
	CO_2 (Mt)	CH_4 (Mt CO_2e)	% of 1990	(Mt CO_2e)
USA	4,906	179	93.0	4,729
JPN	1,053	7	94.0	996
EUM	3,160	82	92.0	2,983
ROE	71	1	96.6	70
ROO	723	43	99.9	765
EIT	4,827	1,187	98.1	5,900

Sources: The CO_2 estimates are taken from the FCCC summary of the national communications (except for the EIT figure, which was based on the same sources as the 1995 EIT estimate). The CH_4 figures, in turn, are OIES estimates.

why we propose to retain the Business-as-Usual assumptions concerning the non-Annex I regions for the present purposes. The only question left open concerning this Kyoto scenario is therefore the behaviour of Annex I Parties after the Kyoto commitment period, i.e. between 2012 and the time horizon of our model in 2020. The problem here is that, even though the Protocol acknowledges that there will be other commitment periods, it says nothing at all about the timing of these periods, let alone about the relevant abatement targets. Given our two assumptions – i.e. the implementation of the Protocol and the non-participation of non-Annex I Parties – it would not seem unreasonable to assume that Annex I countries might be willing to continue in their efforts, in order to avoid a complete breakdown of the FCCC process and, ultimately, to persuade non-Annex I Parties to join an abatement regime.

If only because of the minimal transaction costs involved, a plausible way for such a continuation seems to us a 'roll-over' scenario, where Annex I Parties simply extend the provisions of the Kyoto Protocol for some time after the first commitment period. In other words, all the provisions of the Protocol, including the individual assigned amounts, as well as the 'most likely' policies, are retained for a post-Kyoto commitment. Given the 'roll-over' nature of these assumptions it is also reasonable that, for the purpose of making the most of the flexibility mechanisms, the whole of the period up to 2020 is committed. In deference to the precedent established at Kyoto, we thus assume two further commitment periods for Annex I Parties, namely from 2013 to 2017 (centred around 2015) and from 2018 to 2022 (with a mid-point at our final model period in 2020).

Finally, due to a restrictive 'sales policy' – which, according to our 'roll-over' assumptions, is to be retained for all three commitment periods – the EIT region will have considerable amounts of surplus ('hot air') permits which, under the banking provision of the Kyoto Protocol (Article 3.13), can be carried over into the second and the third commitment period, respectively. According to the provisions specified in the relevant article of the Protocol,[1] the banking procedure we propose for the present scenario is simply to add any unused assigned amounts to the Kyoto 'roll-over' targets (as specified in Table 10.1) of the region in question.

The Kyoto Protocol specifies for the Annex I countries excluding EIT an emissions level of 9,540Mt CO_2e in 2010. This requires a reduction from BaU emissions for that year of 2,440 Mt CO_2e (see Table 10.2). EIT will supply emission permits from its 'hot air' up to 2 per cent of this total, i.e. 49 Mt CO_2e, which means the region takes

Table 10.2: Emissions Permit Cartel and Banking, 2010–2020. EIT Region. Million Tonnes CO_2e

	2010	2015	2020
With International Transfers			
OECD (= Annex I excl. EIT)			
Energy Emissions in BaU	11,981	12,456	12,712
Required OECD Reductions	2,438	2,913	3,169
2 % of OECD Reductions	49	58	63
EIT Assigned Amount	5,900	5,900	5,900
EIT BaU Emissions	4,632	5,412	6,135
EIT Restricted Quota[a]	4,680	5,470	6,198
EIT Target[b]	5,900	7,120	7,550
EIT Bankable Credit[c]	1,220	1,650	1,352
Without International Transfers			
Target[b]	5,900	7,169	7,657
Bankable Credits[d]	1,269	1,757	1,523

(a) Restricted quota = BaU + 2% of OECD reductions
(b) Target = assigned amount + banked credits
(c) Bankable Credit = Target – restricted quota
(d) Bankable Credit = Target – BaU

1. 'If the emissions of a Party included in Annex I in a commitment period are less than its assigned amount under this Article, this difference shall, on request of that Party, be added to the assigned amount for that Party for subsequent commitment periods.'[Article 3.13, Kyoto Protocol]

part in international trading with a restricted quota of 4,680 Mt, instead of 5,900Mt assigned in the Kyoto Protocol. This restricted quota means the region will have 1,220Mt CO_2e unused emissions permits, which are bankable for the next commitment period.

In 2015, EIT therefore has a target of 7,120Mt CO_2e. Again, 'hot air' is limited to 2 per cent of global permit demand. The reduction requirement for the Annex I region excluding EIT in 2015 is 2,913Mt CO_2e. Adding 2 per cent of this world demand to EIT BaU emissions for 2015 produces the new restricted quota for the region of 5,569Mt. This leaves the region with a higher bankable amount than in 2010, namely 1,650Mt. The target for 2020 thus increases from its assigned amount of 5,000Mt to 7,550Mt, which means that the region in 2020 is still left with a sizeable amount of 'hot air', even though its BaU emissions have surpassed the assigned amounts. Indeed, the 2 per cent limit itself still imposes a genuine supply restriction, reducing the 'hot air' supply to 63 Mt CO_2e, with a new restricted quota of 6,198Mt CO_2e. EIT is hence not forced to undertake any actual abatement for the whole of our time horizon, although it will none the less do so for trading reasons which will be discussed in Chapter 11.

If, by contrast, international flexibility is *not* allowed in the implementation of the Kyoto Protocol, the possibility of banking means EIT will not undertake any abatement effort.[2] This is shown in the last rows of Table 10.2: EIT 2010 emissions in the BaU case are 1,268Mt below target, which is the bankable amount carried over. In 2015, banking increases to 1,757Mt, and in 2020 there are still 1,522Mt of 'hot air'.

10.2 Greenhouse Gas Policies of the Annex I Regions

10.2.1 United States[3]

The USA was amongst the first countries to take a serious interest in global warming issues. Indeed, the Senate held hearings on climate change as early as 1986. The change of reputation from leader to lingerer took place in 1990 when the USA joined a majority of

2. In reality, EIT could, of course, choose to carry out abatement measures even in the presence of its 'hot air', say if it deemed it desirable to bank more than it already can. In our model, however, abatement below assigned amounts only occurs in the context of international transfers in the period in question.

countries unwilling to accept binding targets and timetables for carbon dioxide reduction: the 'ready to take action' policy was abandoned for a 'wait on grounds of scientific uncertainty' one.

In 1993, the administration announced the Climate Change Action Plan (CCAP). Building on several pre-existing pieces of legislation – most prominently the Clean Air Act Amendments of 1990, limiting emissions from power plants, vehicles and industry, and the Energy Policy Act (EPAct) of 1992 containing, for example, energy efficiency standards and measures to promote R&D of energy efficient and renewable technologies – the CCAP combines market incentives, voluntary initiatives, and R&D programmes. It includes 47 mostly voluntary measures with specific targets pertaining to energy efficiency in the commercial, residential, industrial and transport sectors [Box 10.1]. However, the effectiveness of this plan was severely curtailed by the fact that the Senate approved less than 50 per cent of the programme funding requested by the administration. Moreover, severe cutbacks in funding were also applied to antecedent and related legislation.

In July 1997, five months before the Kyoto conference, the US Senate passed a resolution (S. Res. 98) that the USA should not be a signatory to any protocol to the UN FCCC which would 'mandate new commitments to limit or reduce greenhouse gas emissions for the Annex I Parties, unless the protocol ... also mandates new specific scheduled commitments to limit or reduce greenhouse gas emissions for Developing Country Parties within the same compliance period.' The rift between Congress and the administration was thus bound to escalate when on 12 November 1998 the USA signed up to the Protocol negotiated at Kyoto a year earlier. The opposition in Congress to this protocol led to the 'Knollenberg Amendment' in a FY1999 Appropriations Bill, stipulating that no funds may be used 'for the purpose of implementation, or in preparation for implementation, of

---

3. Main Sources:

   National Communications, http://www.unfccc.de

   D. Anderson, M. Grubb and J. Depledge, *Climate Change and the Energy Sector*, vol. 2 *The non-EU OECD Countries* (London: FT Publishing 1997).

   US Senate, *S.547 Credit For Voluntary Reductions Act*, http://www.senate.gov/~epw/

   US House of Representatives, http://www.house.gov/reform/neg/hearings/

   Resources for the Future, *Weathervane*, http://weathervane.rff.org

   IEA, *Energy Efficiency Policies 1999*, May 1999, http://www.iea.org/pubs/newslett/eneeff/table.htm

the Kyoto Protocol'. Naturally, this imposes considerable limitations on the GHG policy options left open to the administration, as witnessed by a May 1999 joint hearing of Senate and House committees[4] on the compliance of the key climate change measure in the FY2000 Budget, the Climate Change Technology Initiative (CCTI), with Knollenberg's amendment.[5]

In its FY2000 Budget Proposal, the administration earmarked $4.1 billion for climate change related measures (up 34 per cent from FY99) including, apart from the CCTI, Fuel Efficiency Tax Incentives, Partnerships for Advancing Technology in Housing and for a New Generation of Vehicles. The CCTI uses tax incentives to increase product efficiency and stimulate adoption of greener products. Owners of energy-efficient new homes would, for example, be eligible to receive tax credits between $1000 and $2000; residential and commercial users of energy-efficient equipment such as electric and natural gas heat pumps, natural gas water heaters, advanced central air conditioners, and fuel cells would be eligible to receive a 10–20 per cent credit of the cost of the investment; and consumers and businesses would be encouraged to purchase rooftop solar systems with a 15 per cent ($1000–2000) tax credit (for a sectorial analysis of these and other

---

4. The House Subcommittee on National Economic Growth, Natural Resources and Regulatory Affairs with the Senate Subcommittee on Energy Research, Development, Production and Regulation.

5. The reasons for the Congressional opposition are tellingly summarised in Knollenberg's testimony to this joint hearing: 'This fatally-flawed agreement [the Kyoto Protocol] is blatantly unfair because it exempts developing nations from making any commitment to reduce their emissions of greenhouse gases. As a result, nations like China, India, Mexico, and Brazil, … will be given a free pass while the United States is forced to struggle with the Kyoto treaty's stringent mandates.

Make no mistake: If implemented, the Kyoto treaty will result in American jobs flowing overseas. Every credible economic study on this treaty paints a dark picture for the American people. According to the Wharton Econometric Forecasting Associates (WEFA), the Kyoto treaty would cause energy prices to soar and the standard of living in our country to plummet. In a well-respected study, WEFA found that the Kyoto treaty would result in the elimination of over 2.4 million American jobs by the year 2010 and cost the average American family over $2,700 a year.

Given the lack of sound science on global climate change, there is absolutely no justification for the United States to move forward with an agreement that would place our economy at a competitive disadvantage with our foreign competitors and erode the standard of living currently enjoyed by the American people.'

Box 10.1: The US Climate Change Action Plan (CCAP) of 1993

- *Energy Supply Sector* The key energy supply objectives are: (1) To increase the use of natural gas by promoting the summer use of gas in existing coal- and oil-fired power plants, by accelerating the commercialisation of gas fuel cell technologies, and by continuing regulatory reforms of gas markets. (2) To encourage the commercial application of renewables. (3) To improve efficiency of transmission and distribution equipment. (4) To enter voluntary 'participation agreements' with utilities under which they agree to reduce emissions by a specific amount or undertake specific abatement options.
- *Residential and Commercial Sector* Under 'voluntary partnerships' the DOE is to promote building renovations and retrofits increasing energy efficiency (*Energy Star Buildings* and *Rebuild America* programmes). Financial incentives are to promote the development of more efficient consumer appliances and industrial equipment (*Golden Carrot* partnerships such as the *Super Efficient Refrigerator Program*)
- *Industry* Key voluntary partnerships programmes in the industrial sector are (1) *Climate Wise*, designed to encourage companies in developing cost-effective ways of reducing GHGs in areas such as industrial heat processes, boiler efficiency, waste heat, CHP systems and fuel switching. (2) *Motor Challenge*, a programme promoting the use of energy efficient electric motors (currently consuming more than 20 per cent of US power). (3) *Golden Carrots* for industrial equipment such as air compressors, fans and pumps.
- *Transport Sector* The CCAP is at its weakest in transport measures. In particular, it failed to contain specific measures for increasing personal vehicle fuel economy – the average fuel economy of new cars and light trucks has not improved significantly since the mid-80s, in spite of the corporate average fuel economy (*CAFE*) standards. The only substantive measures included are a reform of the federal tax subsidy for workplace parking and an efficiency labelling for tyres.
- *Forestry* The CCAP contains several programmes promoting carbon sequestration in the forestry sector, with the aim of reducing depletion and accelerating tree planting in non-industrial private forests.

GHG related policies and measures, see IEA 1999, ibid).

In view of the voluntary character of the large majority of US climate change measures, one recent development in the Congress may prove to be a turning point in US greenhouse gas policy. On Thursday 4 March 1999, Senators John Chafee (Rep. RI), Joseph Lieberman (Dem. CT), and Connie Mack (Rep. FL) introduced the Credit for Voluntary Reductions Act (see Box 10.2), aimed at enabling the administration to provide US firms with 'legal certainty that their

Box 10.2: The US Credit for Voluntary Reductions Act S.547
(Text Excerpts)

- The purpose of this Act is to encourage voluntary actions to mitigate potential environmental impacts of greenhouse gas emissions by authorizing the President to enter into binding agreements under which entities operating in the United States will receive credit, usable in any future domestic program that requires mitigation of greenhouse gas emissions, for voluntary mitigation actions taken before the end of the credit period.
- The President may enter into a legally binding early action agreement with any person under which the United States agrees to provide greenhouse gas reduction credit usable beginning in the compliance period, if the person takes an action ... that reduces greenhouse gas emissions or sequesters carbon before the end of the credit period.
- *Internationally Creditable Actions.* A participant shall receive greenhouse gas reduction credit under an early action agreement if the participant takes an action that
  (1) reduces greenhouse gas emissions or sequesters carbon before the end of the credit period; and
  (2) under any applicable international agreement, will result in an addition to the United States quantified emission limitation for the compliance period.
- *United States Initiative For Joint Implementation.* ... an early action agreement may provide that a participant shall be entitled to receive greenhouse gas reduction credit for a greenhouse gas emission reduction or carbon sequestration that ... is for a project ... accepted before December 31, 2000, under the United States Initiative for Joint Implementation; and financing for which was provided or construction of which was commenced before that date.
- *Prospective Domestic Actions.*
  Emission Reductions. A participant shall receive greenhouse gas reduction credit under an early action agreement if, during the credit period the participant's aggregate greenhouse gas emissions from domestic sources that are covered by the early action agreement; are less than the sum of the participant's annual source baselines during that period.
  Sequestration. For the purpose of receiving greenhouse gas reduction credit ... the amount by which aggregate net carbon sequestration for the credit period in a participant's domestic carbon reservoirs covered by an early action agreement exceeds the sum of the participant's annual reservoir baselines for the credit period ... shall be treated as a greenhouse gas emission reduction.
- *Domestic Section 1605 Actions.* An early action agreement may provide that a participant shall be entitled to receive 1 ton of greenhouse gas

> **Box 10.2:** *Continued*
>
> reduction credit for each ton of greenhouse gas emission reductions or carbon sequestration *for the 1991 through 1998 period* from domestic actions that are reported before January 1, 1999, under section 1605 of the Energy Policy Act of 1992; or carried out and reported before January 1, 1999, under a Federal agency program to implement the Climate Change Action Plan.
> - *Trading And Pooling.*
>   *Trading.* A participant may purchase earned greenhouse gas reduction credit from and sell the credit to any other participant; and sell the credit to any person that is not a participant.
>   *Pooling.* The regulations … may permit pooling arrangements under which a group of participants agrees to act as a single participant for the purpose of entering into an early action agreement.

self-determined course to lower greenhouse gas outputs will not put their organization at a disadvantage relative to competitors who have done nothing'.[6] While not specifically intended to bring about a ratification of the Kyoto Protocol, it stands to reason that if this act were to encourage a sizeable proportion of the private sector to acquire such early action credits, then Congress would be facing a serious lobby for the implementation of a domestic greenhouse gas programme or indeed of an international treaty with quantified emissions limitations (like the Kyoto Protocol). After all, the early action credits only become assets once such emission limitations have been introduced.

10.2.2 Japan[7]

To understand Japanese GHG policy, it is important to keep in mind that it is fundamentally seen as a part of Japan's energy policy, the overall objective of which is to achieve 'the three Es': economic growth,

---

6. Chafee in an opening statement at a hearing on the CVRA of the Senate's Committee on Environment and Public Works (29 March 1999).
7. Main sources:
   National Communications, http://www.unfccc.de
   D. Anderson, M. Grubb and J. Depledge, *Climate Change and the Energy Sector*, vol. 2 *The non-EU OECD countries* (London: FT Publishing 1997).
   Ministry of Foreign Affairs of Japan (MoFA), *Japanese Approaches to the Suppression of Greenhouse Gas Generation*, http://www.mofa.go.jp/policy/global/environment/warm/japan

energy security and environmental protection. Most countries would presumably follow Japan in putting economic growth at the head of such a list. Japan's fixation on energy security, by contrast, seems to be more idiosyncratic. The fact that energy security worries are still at the very heart of Japanese energy policy thinking can be gauged from a 1998 statement on the world energy outlook by the Ministry of Foreign Affairs:

> Developing countries' demand for energy, particularly in Asia, is expected to increase sharply in the long and medium term. On the other hand, the confirmed number of years for which energy sources can be exploited is limited, and with the development and introduction of oil-alternative energy becoming increasingly difficult, the share of OPEC countries in the supply of oil available in the world is expected to rise. Given such prospects, it would be extremely difficult to maintain an efficient supply of energy at fair prices in the long and medium term.[8]

Following the 1973 oil price shock, Japan's overriding energy policy aim was to curb its oil dependence, and the current primary energy supply projections by the Japanese government – according to which the share of coal is to be left essentially untouched – leave no doubt that this policy has not given way in any substantive manner to carbon driven policies (see Table 10.3).

Nevertheless, the Japanese government has introduced several measures under the heading of 'climate change'. First, the Action Program to Arrest Global Warming (1990), aimed 'to stabilize total

Table 10.3: Japan's Primary Energy Supply. 1973–2010. Per Cent

	1973	1986	1992	2000	2010
Coal	17.4	18.4	16.1	16.4	15.4
Oil	78.0	55.0	58.2	52.9	47.7
Gas	1.6	9.6	10.6	12.9	12.8
Nuclear	0.7	11.0	10.0	12.3	16.9
Renewables	n.a.	n.a.	1.2	2.0	3.0

Source: MoFA, Anderson *et al.*

K. Akasaka, 'Implementation Initiatives in Japan', Presentation given at the Conference on *Implementing the Kyoto Protocol* at the Royal Institute for International Affairs, London June 1999.
IEA, *Energy Efficiency Policies 1999*, May 1999, http://www.iea.org/pubs/newslett/eneeff/table.htm
8. MoFA, Ch.1, F. Energy Policy, a. Estimated Demand.

emissions of carbon dioxide in the year 2000 and beyond at about the same as in 1990'. The Basic Environment Law (1993) was intended to provide basic principles for new environmental policies concerning global issues. The 1994 Basic Environment Plan of Japan aimed at achieving the FCCC objective of stabilising greenhouse gas concentration in the atmosphere to a level not threatening the climate system. The Lead Action Program (1995), set targets for government agencies, such as a cut in waste of 25 per cent by 2000. Finally, the New Earth 21 Program proposed a reduction of emissions from current sources by 60 per cent by 2100 as an alternative to IPCC targets which were considered to be too stringent.

Apart from the occasional reference to carbon sinks and the endorsement of the Kyoto 'flexibility' mechanisms, the overwhelming majority of measures envisaged to achieve these targets are concerned with demand-side management driven by (voluntary) energy efficiency improvements. The main legislative instrument for such improvements, the Energy Conservation Law, was introduced in 1979 and has since undergone two revisions. Its 1993 revision saw, in particular, the introduction of the Sunshine and Moonlight Projects sponsoring R&D into new energy sources such as solar power generation, solar heat utilisation systems, waste heat utilisation technology, cogeneration, fuel cell batteries. The Energy Conservation Assistance Law, adopted in the same year, had the complementary aim of assisting businesses which adopted voluntary measures in pursuit of rationalising energy use and utilising recycled resources. The most recent and important development in energy efficiency, however, is the second (1998) revision of the Energy Conservation Law [Box 10.3], which means that more appliances, factories and automobiles have to comply with stricter energy efficiency standards.

Fiscal Measures. While a carbon tax proposal was put forward in 1991 by the Environment Agency and Ministry of Finance (and abandoned due to objections of industry groups and MITI), Japan's fiscal policy has been focused on measures to promote R&D and voluntary actions concerning energy efficiency improvements. As concerns the former, funding for coal and nuclear R&D far outweighs funding for renewables (shares in FY1994: 74.7 per cent nuclear, 10.5 per cent fossil fuels, and 3 per cent renewables).

Voluntary actions, unfortunately, have so far failed in achieving the intended emission reductions. One of the main reasons why they have been singled out in government policy is undoubtedly that they have been industry's favoured GHG abatement instrument. There are,

---

Box 10.3: The Japanese Energy Conservation Law

- *Residential and Commercial* The Energy Conservation Law established standards for improved energy efficiency designated 'specified equipment' (air conditioners, fluorescent lamps, televisions, copiers et cetera) and made energy efficiency labelling mandatory. Stricter standards for housing insulation will be set by the end of this fiscal year. They could save 20 per cent of energy use for air-conditioning. In 1993, offices, shops, hotels, hospitals or clinics, and schools have all been subjected to energy efficiency standards (prevention of heat loss, efficient utilisation of energy in air conditioners, mechanical ventilators, lighting systems, hot tap water equipment and elevators). A system of subsidies was introduced in 1993 to promote commercialisation of energy-saving technology such as district heating and cooling, and utilising heat from waste incineration.
- *Industry* The category of 'designated energy-management factories' is extended to those business sites with an annual fuel consumption equivalent to over 1500 kilolitres of oil or an annual electricity consumption of more than 6 GWh. The 9000 factories falling into this category are obliged to meet energy rationalisation standards set by MITI. Two alternative fiscal measures are offered to promote investment in the installation of energy-efficient equipment: (1) A tax deduction amounting to 7 per cent of the equipment acquisition cost. (2) Companies are allowed to depreciate a maximum of 30 per cent of the acquired value, in addition to the normal depreciation in the year of acquisition. Low interest loans have been instituted by institutions such as the Japan Development Bank for the installation of energy efficiency equipment. A special taxation and financial support system is to stimulate the introduction of cogeneration.
- *Transport* The second revision in 1993 saw the introduction of weight-relative automotive fuel consumption targets for FY 2000 ranging from 9 km/l to 19 km/l. On average, the fuel efficiency improvement rate of passenger cars in FY 2000 will be enhanced by 8.5 per cent compared to that in FY 1990. The second (1998) requires the Government to adopt further standards equal to more than the best performance in each size category and to include diesel vehicles. The new standards may be 25 per cent efficiency improvement (from 1995 to 2010) for gasoline cars and 15 per cent for diesel cars.

---

however, signs that this attitude may be changing. The Environment Agency, in the latest (May 1999) of a series of surveys of more than 6000 medium to large firms found that firms, for the first time, favour a tax on fossil fuels as an instrument for CO_2 emissions control.

10.2.3. European Union[9]

(a) *EU Policies*. Internationally, the EU has been one of the most pro-active Annex I players; domestically, however, it has had a distinct policy handicap. The one policy area crucial to the climate change debate, energy policy, is generally regarded as subject to the subsidiarity principle. The Union, in particular, does not have a clear legal basis for enacting EU-wide fiscal energy policy measures such as carbon or energy taxes. The application of these key GHG policy instruments has so far been the prerogative of member states. However, some important EU-wide policies have either been adopted or are currently under consideration. Chief amongst the objectives pursued is an increased energy efficiency in power generation, transport, and the domestic and commercial sectors.

In the context of the liberalisation promoted in the power generation sector, utilities are to be encouraged to adopt greater energy efficiency measures by a directive on integrated resource planning. Special emphasis is also given to the promotion of combined heat and power generation. Secondly, in 1998, the European Car Manufacturers' Association entered an agreement with the EU to cut average fuel consumption (per km) by 2008 by about 25 per cent, which the Commission estimates will provide one-sixth of the EU target reduction. A similar agreement was struck with the Japanese Automobile Manufacturers' Association in May 1999. Thirdly, under a framework directive on energy efficiency within the SAVE programme, the EU requires member states to implement policies such as minimum insulation standards for new buildings, energy certification of buildings and billing of heating costs based on actual consumption. In a recent communication, the Commission announced new legislation aimed at getting public bodies to opt for more energy efficient buildings, equipment and vehicles, with the aim of an 18 per cent cut in 1995's energy intensity by 2010.

In addition to these energy efficiency initiatives, the EU has been active in at least three other policy areas. The first of these is renewable

---

9. Main sources:

    National Communications, http://www.unfccc.de

    D. Anderson, M. Grubb and J. Depledge, *Climate Change and the Energy Sector*, vol. 1 *The European Union* (London: FT Publishing 1997).

    ENDS Environment Daily, http://www.ends.co.uk

    Climate News, http://iisd.ca

    IEA, *Energy Efficiency Policies 1999*, May 1999, http://www.iea.org/pubs/newslett/eneeff/table.htm

energy. According to a report approved by the Committee on External Economic Relations of the EU Parliament (November 1998), the global growth rate of solar power is currently at 15 per cent per annum, while wind power is projected to grow 26 per cent annually in the period 1998–2002. In a 1997 white paper, the EU set itself the aim of increasing the share of renewable energy in total power consumption from 6 per cent to 12 per cent by 2010.

The second area is civil aviation. There has been an EU proposal to 'introduce economic measures' (such as ending the global ban on aircraft fuel taxes) for lowering GHG emissions in this sector globally. This was put to the International Civil Aviation Organization (ICAO) assembly in 1998. ICAO subsequently adopted 'the possible use of economic measures such as charges and/or taxes and other market-based options' as one of the key policy areas to be investigated.

Finally, in May 1999, EU environment ministers agreed a formula regulating the use of Kyoto mechanisms which, in essence, imposes a 50 per cent cap on them, i.e. member states will not be allowed to meet more than 50 per cent of their GHG obligations by way of these mechanisms. Given Russia's apparent aim of restricting the supply of hot air permits to 2 per cent of global demand, this capping may well be achieved by the supply side alone. The Commission's environment directorate (DGXI) furthermore proposes the introduction of an EU-wide emissions trading system by 2005 – to get ready for an international system that should be running from 2008. Initially, this pilot scheme is meant to be restricted to the largest CO_2 emitters, possibly in just one sector, who would have to be subject to an emissions ceiling set out in an environmental agreement. For this purpose, interested industry associations have been invited to put forward proposals for voluntary agreements before the end of 1999.

From the point of view of the FCCC regime, one recent development is of major significance: at the fifth session of the Conference of the Parties (COP5) to the Framework convention in Bonn (November 1999), the EU and Japan officially expressed their wish for 'early ratification' of the Kyoto Protocol, in order for it to be in force by 2002. It should be noted that this could happen even if the USA fail to ratify. Indeed, at COP5, the German environment minister openly contemplated this possibility.[10]

10. In assessing the scenario of the Kyoto Protocol coming into force without US participation, it has to be kept in mind that this Protocol is primarily of political significance: the targets prescribed in Annex B, even if achieved, will not solve the climate change problem. As far as the environmental aim of the FCCC is concerned, it is really of no great importance whether the

(b) *The Member States*. The climate change programmes outlined in the National Communications by the member states all include policy objectives mirroring the EU policies on energy efficiency and renewables, although emphasis varies between the members. As almost three-quarters of the UK commitment is intended to be achieved through the power sector (62 per cent by fuel switching, 12 per cent by CHP generation and renewables), energy efficiency programmes have so far played a limited role. In Germany, by contrast, the Federal Government alone has already introduced more than 130 efficiency improvement measures in all sectors of the economy. Having only just established its National Climate Council (1998), Spain is still in the process of drawing up a strategy against climate change. The main difference between the EU and the member states is to be found in the application of fiscal instruments.

Early proposals for an EU-wide CO_2/energy tax were abandoned in 1994, partly because it was realised that the condition they were premised on, namely an analogous OECD-wide tax, was unlikely to be met, and in part because of internal insistence on the subsidiarity principle, particularly by the UK. Somewhat ironically, such tax schemes have none the less emerged as the most popular instruments to date for implementing climate change policies amongst the EU member states. The lack of co-ordination implicit in these subsidiarity fiscal reforms, however, has resulted in a plethora of different fiscal schemes across the Union, ranging from carbon (Sweden 1991) to energy schemes (UK 2001), with a variety of intermediate 'mixed' schemes (Finland 1990, Denmark 1991/96, Netherlands 1992).

Amongst the four largest emitters in the Union – jointly responsible for more than 70 per cent of CO_2 emissions in the region – two (Germany and the UK) have already adopted a carbon tax scheme and one (Italy) has announced its intention to do so. Together with the fact that of the most vociferous erstwhile key opponents (France, Spain, and the UK), all but Spain have to date been won over in support of a 1999 German presidency compromise proposal of an EU-wide energy tax (Box 10.4), this justifies the modelling assumption of energy taxation as the dominant fiscal instrument for the EUM region.

USA participates or not. The true significance of the Kyoto Protocol is in being a first step towards a regime which would achieve this aim. As such a regime will have to be global, it is important for developing country participation that industrialised countries show 'leadership' in taking the first step. The crucial question is hence whether sufficient leadership by industrialised countries would be demonstrated if the Kyoto Protocol comes into force in the absence of the USA.

Box 10.4: EU Member States Fiscal Policies

- *Germany* Having passed its final hurdle in the Bundesrat on 19 March 99, the German energy consumption tax came into effect on 1 April. It is levied on petrol, heating oil, electricity and gas. All industry sectors are liable to the same tax rate, equivalent to 20 per cent of the domestic rate. Provisions are made for subsidising renewables and under the 'coal compromise' with the EU of 97, coal subsidies are returned by 2002.
- *Italy* Excise duties on petrol, diesel, coal and mineral oils are to be increased in yearly increments over the next five years. A carbon tax on large combustion plants is introduced at an initial rate of 1000 LIT [$0.5] per tC.
- *UK* Excise duties on road fuels are to increase in real terms by yearly increments of around 5 per cent ('road fuel price escalator') and a CO_2 based duty on new cars is to be introduced in 2000. The *Climate Change Levy*, projected to save 1.5 MtC by 2010,will come into force in April 2001. It is to be levied on electricity, gas and other energy supply. Mineral oils and domestic supply are exempt, while energy intensive industries which adopt Government criteria for energy efficiency improvements will be given significant reductions.
- *1999 EU Proposal* A compromise version of the EU-energy tax proposals first put forward in 1997 ('Monti' package) under which EU-wide tax minima would be introduced on most forms of energy, with an increase of existing minimum rates for mineral oils. In order to placate objections by Spain and the UK, coal and lignite are to be zero rated, and domestic consumption would be exempt.

10.2.4 Iceland, Norway and Switzerland (The ROE Region)[11]

Iceland, Norway and Switzerland epitomise the dilemmas faced by countries with already low levels of GHG emissions for whom further reductions are either costly or require undesirable economic and environmental trade-offs. All three countries were involved in the FCCC process from an early stage, assuming the formal obligation to

---

11. Main Sources:
   National Communications, http://www.unfccc.de
   D. Anderson, M. Grubb and J. Depledge. *Climate Change and the Energy Sector*, vol II: *The Non-EU OECD Countries* (London: FT Publishing 1997).
   ENDS Environment Daily, http://www.ends.co.uk

stabilise CO_2 emissions at 1990 levels by the year 2000 and to reduce them gradually thereafter. In general, the proportion of primary energy needs in each country met by clean and renewable sources such as hydropower, geothermal or nuclear power is already very high, and as a consequence their CO_2 emissions per capita fall well below the OECD average.

Clean sources of energy provide approximately 65 per cent of total energy consumption in Iceland, 50 per cent in Norway and 37 per cent in Switzerland. Although there is limited scope for enhancing the development of clean energy resources, such projects frequently spark off local environmental controversies of their own. Substituting electricity or renewables for fossil fuel combustion, notably in the industrial sector, could potentially shave off a large percentage of national GHG emissions. In addition each country has adopted voluntary programmes to improve energy efficiency and conservation in the industrial, commercial and residential sectors. Governments are also pursuing afforestation schemes in an effort to increase carbon sequestration in sinks.

One of the most difficult challenges facing all three countries is that of reducing CO_2 emissions in the transport sector, which accounts for roughly one-third of total emissions – a significantly higher share than the OECD average of 22 per cent. Carbon taxes and vehicle levies have been implemented in Norway and Switzerland and are under serious consideration in Iceland. The problem has been that, for various reasons, demand for ground transportation has proved relatively in-sensitive to price increases. Additional large tax increases are regarded as politically unpopular and, considering low demand elasticities, of questionable effectiveness.

Attitudes to climate change policy are conditioned by the small size of these countries' economies and the prominent role of internationally competitive activities such as fishing (Iceland and Norway), tourism (Switzerland) or petroleum (Norway), all of which could be adversely affected by the strict application of GHG reduction policies. Also, the high ratio of renewables to non-renewables in the energy mix means that a relatively small number of sectors and enterprises would have to carry a disproportionate share of the burden for implementing national GHG reduction targets. Despite a strong commitment in principle to addressing the issue of climate change, given the lack of viable options for significantly reducing GHG emissions, it is unlikely that Iceland and Norway will meet their FCCC stabilisation targets in 2000, although Switzerland may come close to doing so.

10.2.5 Australia, Canada and New Zealand (The ROO Region)[12]

Despite the disparity in the scale of their economies, territories and populations, Canada, Australia and New Zealand share a number of similarities with regard to climate change policy (see Table 10.4). In terms of economic structure, all three countries are open, relatively energy intensive, and strongly orientated to natural resource exports and primary processing. As a result, per capita GHG emissions for all three rank among the highest of the Annex I countries (New Zealand is exceptional in that the main GHG is methane from the agricultural sector rather than CO_2). Demographically, in comparison to the rest of the OECD they combine higher than average rates of population growth with lower than average population density, implying rapidly rising primary energy demand and resilient demand for private transport. Prices for electricity and petrol are relatively low, encouraging increased consumption and inefficient usage. The climate change policies of all three rely to varying degrees on their potentially large sink capacity in forests and other vegetation, although for Canada and Australia land use change, forestry and fires presently constitute a net source of CO_2 emissions.

Canada, Australia and New Zealand stand to be seriously affected by climate change, and it was partly this concern that motivated them to join the first wave of countries in adopting ambitious stabilisation and reduction targets for GHG emissions. In retrospect the three governments appear to have been too sanguine about their ability to deliver major reductions in the absence of correspondingly high levels of economic and political investment. As these costs became more apparent and powerful domestic interest groups mobilised to oppose fiscal or regulatory measures, their initial enthusiasm yielded to a more cautious appraisal of national GHG objectives. According to current estimates, Canada's GHG emissions will exceed 1990 levels by 8 per cent in 2000 and 19 per cent in 2010; Australia's by 7 per cent in 2000 and 28 per cent in 2010; and New Zealand's by 22–25 per cent in 2000. Not surprisingly, although each country has reiterated its commitment to stabilise and ultimately reduce its emissions of greenhouse gas, all three are opposed to legally binding reduction

---

12. Main Sources:

National Communications, http://www.unfccc.de

D. Anderson, M. Grubb and J. Depledge. *Climate Change and the Energy Sector*, vol II: *The Non-EU OECD Countries* (London: FT Publishing 1997).

ENDS Environment Daily, http://www.ends.co.uk

CIA World Factbook 1998, http://www.cia.gov

Table 10.4: Climate Change Indicators. The ROO Region

	1997 Population (millions)	Area (000 sq. kilometres)	1997 GDP (billion $ PPP)	Annex I ranking 1996 per capita emissions
Canada	30.6	9,976	698	6
Australia	18.5	7,686	394	3
New Zealand	3.6	268	63	4

Source: *CIA World Factbook* 1998; FCCC

commitments. Australia and New Zealand have been particularly strong supporters of emissions trading schemes.

The ramifications of this in terms of policy have been an emphasis on voluntary programmes, market mechanisms and 'no regrets' measures in preference to taxation or regulation. The latter are not necessarily to be ruled out should the current approach prove insufficient, but this will depend both on the domestic political environment and whether movement in the multilateral negotiations prompts governments to take more robust action.

The climate change policies adopted to date by Canada, Australia and New Zealand have several features in common. First is their reliance on voluntary, non-binding, cross-sectoral agreements with industry aimed at enhancing energy efficiency and curbing emissions. Partners in the Canadian programme, Voluntary Challenge and Registry (VCR), represent 50 per cent of national GHG emissions; those in Australia's Greenhouse Challenge 45 per cent; while participants in the New Zealand programme represent 45 per cent of CO_2 emissions. These initiatives are accompanied by a 'government leadership' component intended to set an example for the private sector by improving energy efficiency in public sector operations. Second, is the drive to improve energy efficiency in the residential and commercial sector through amendments to the building code, the adoption of minimum efficiency standards, and appliance labelling. Third, is the penetration of gas and renewables in electricity supply, in most cases an indirect by-product of power sector liberalisation rather than the deliberate result of GHG-related policies. Fourth, is the encouragement of sustainable land management practices in agriculture and forestry. This has led, in some cases, to an over-reliance on sinks in CO_2 abatement strategies: for example, sinks account for 80 per cent of CO_2 reductions in New Zealand's plan and 45 per cent in Australia's. Lastly, in the transport sector, the fastest-growing source of CO_2 emissions in all three countries, government policies have focused on setting voluntary fuel efficiency standards and programmes to promote fuel efficiency and alternatives. Carbon taxes or new public transport initiatives have not been forthcoming.

Two political factors are likely to be of continuing influence as these countries elaborate more comprehensive climate change policies. The first is the relationship between the national government, provincial and local authorities. In the case of Canada and Australia, national and provincial governments share joint responsibility in many areas related to climate change policy, and part of the incoherence of current GHG policies can be traced to a lack of close co-ordination between them. In Canada the government has had difficulty agreeing on a common approach to climate change with the provinces, while in Australia the Commonwealth has tried to set broad policy lines – for example, in encouraging substitution of coal for gas in power generation – only to find state governments unresponsive. In both cases more needs to be done by national governments to foster consensus at the provincial and local level where many climate change measures will be implemented. (In New Zealand the government view that climate change policy is its exclusive domain so far has not been seriously challenged.)

The second political factor likely to figure into the GHG policies of Canada and Australia in particular is that of how the FCCC process will affect domestic hydrocarbon industries. In 1997 Canadian oil production averaged 2.6 million b/d, while Australia is the world's largest net exporter of coal. Their approach to climate change policy, domestically and in the multilateral negotiations, is likely to reflect some of the ambiguity of their own situation as countries especially vulnerable to climate change which are also important producers of hydrocarbons in their own right.

10.2.6 Economies in Transition (The EIT Region)[13]

(a) *Russia and Ukraine*. The Russian Federation and the Ukraine, together producing just over 70 per cent of CO_2 combustion emissions, have to be regarded as the key to GHG policy in the EIT region.

---

13. Main Sources:

National Communications, http://www.unfccc.de

I. Househam, J. Hauff, F. Missfeldt and M. Grubb, *Climate Change and the Energy Sector*, vol. 3 *The Economies in Transition* (London: FT Publishing 1998).

Box 10.5: Russian Power Generation

Total current electric generation capacity in the Russian Federation is 205 gigawatts, down from 213 gigawatts in 1990. Without significant investments and equipment upgrades, as well as rationalization of inefficient and obsolete capacity, regional power shortages will become more widespread. While 6 gigawatts of new plant capacity were being built annually from 1981–1985, only 1 gigawatt per year was built during the past 5 years. Within 5 years, half of the non-nuclear power stations will have exceeded their rated service lives. Installation of new power lines also has dropped markedly. Russian officials estimate that the country will need $3 billion to $5 billion in new capital annually from 1998 to 2000, and $6 billion to $11 billion annually from 2001 to 2005 to carry out its capacity expansion plans. Financing of this investment will be difficult to secure internally, especially in light of continuing payments collection problem by the power companies.

Source: EIA, http://www.eia.doe.gov/emeu/cabs/russia.html

Unfortunately, the common theme between the two seems to be a conspicuous lack of such policies, with the one notable exception of Ukraine's introduction of an energy audit, mandating the 'rational' use of energy. And yet, there is a tremendous potential for relatively low-cost emission reductions, in particular in the energy sector. For example, in 1995 fugitive fuel emissions of the Russian Federation alone amounted to 297 Mt CO_2e (CO_2: 17.9 Mt, CH_4: 279.3 Mt CO_2e) or 8 per cent of the Annex I EIT emissions. The scope for emission reductions by way of efficiency improvements in the power generation sector is also enormous.

As can be seen in Box 10.5, the problem is that the domestic economic situation prevents the implementation of these measures without foreign investment. Ordinarily, such investment would be unlikely in the absence of further moves towards market oriented structures, in particular in the field occupied by the giant Russian energy monopolies. At present this would be difficult to achieve given

---

ENDS Environment Daily, http://www.ends.co.uk

Climate News, http://iisd.ca

IEA, *Energy Efficiency Policies 1999*, May 1999, http://www.iea.org/pubs/newslett/eneeff/table.htm

Kyoto Protocol and Russian Energy (*Second Issue*) (Moscow: Institute of Energy Strategy, Ministry of Fuel and Energy of the Russian Federation, March 1999).

the prevailing political structures. However, in the context of the Kyoto Protocol with its 'flexibility mechanisms', such investments become a much more realistic prospect, if one keeps in mind that, for example, the above-mentioned Russian fugitive fuel emissions are equivalent to 40 per cent of what the USA would have had to reduce in 1995 in order to return their emissions to the Kyoto level.

With regard to the international trading scheme envisaged under the Kyoto Protocol, arguably the most important policy proposal is contained in a study (*Kyoto Protocol and Russian Energy*, March 1999) by the Institute of Energy Strategy of the Ministry of Fuel and Energy of the Russian Federation. In this study, Russia – which together with the Ukraine is projected to possess the lion's share of the hot air potentially available for trading under the Kyoto regime – states that it intends to restrict its sale of hot air permits to a maximum volume of 2 to 4 per cent of OECD demand in the first commitment period. The rationale for this restriction is at least threefold. In the first instance it is meant to minimise the risk of not being able to deliver the goods under a forward trading scheme supported by the Russian government.[14] Secondly, it is explicit that the quota of hot air put on the market 'should be *significantly smaller than the potential demand* in developed countries [in order] to support the market price'. This is not merely to maximise income, but, as the third motivation, to keep alive the potential for joint implementation projects.[15] The fear is, of course, that if the market were swamped with hot air permits, their price might plummet below levels at which JI would still be an attractive option.

(*b*) *Central and Eastern Europe.* The countries of Central and Eastern Europe generally have as their policy goals the transition to a market economy, to join the EU, to reduce local pollution levels, to improve

---

14. The 'forward sales' envisaged by Russia 'mean that a buyer pays now, but gets the commodity (AAU) only within the first budget period (i.e. in 2008 or the subsequent 4 years.) The seller has to guarantee delivery in time. The price and the amount of the commodity for delivery are fixed.'[*Kyoto Protocol and Russian Energy*] The envisaged hot air supply restriction, in this context, is meant to ensure delivery in time. The supply restrictions in question were indeed stated in the context of such a forward sales proposal, but it would clearly make no sense if they were not kept for the 'spot sales' during the commitment period itself.

15. Russia realises that 'in a stable and well developed financial, legal and taxation system, JI agreements are probably not useful, but in a transition economy situation, they are key instruments of cooperation' which is why it currently sees JI as 'absolutely necessary' (ibid.)

energy efficiency and to reduce the extent of their dependency on energy imports, particularly those from Russia. Most of the measures undertaken to achieve these goals will have the side effect of reducing CO_2 emissions.

State ownership of energy companies is still typical, although those companies are increasingly being disaggregated. Some countries, for instance Romania and the Baltic states, explicitly include Integrated Resource Planning and demand-side management in their national energy strategies. Larger CO_2 emitters in the region, namely Poland, the Czech Republic and Hungary, have proceeded along the path of liberalisation in order to attract investment rapidly. The expansion of gas supply and consumption, particularly for domestic use and district heating, is a priority, and should be facilitated by Gazprom's goal of increasing gas exports which must transit Central and Eastern Europe. The gradual introduction of metering for heat and electricity consumption and rapid progress towards cost recovery will also be of importance.

In the case of power generation, most states in Central and Eastern Europe have introduced emission limits for acid gases and particulates, initially often for new plant, but envisaged to be progressively applied to existing installations. Many plants have been expensively retrofitted with equipment such as fluidised bed combustion, electrostatic precipitators, making their closure less likely despite their low efficiency and use of carbon-intensive fuel. Unless a significant number of plants is eventually closed, or switched to gas firing, otherwise beneficial anti-pollution measures are likely to have an adverse effect on the CO_2 emissions of power generation in particular.

In the domestic and commercial sector, energy efficiency standards for equipment and for buildings are becoming increasingly common, although they are unlikely to have a rapid effect due to their dependence on the turnover rate for capital stock. In the case of buildings, where the largest savings of up to 50 per cent could be made, the turnover rate is unlikely to be high and most buildings could not be reconstructed economically. Similarly, appliance labelling for energy efficiency, to be introduced in accordance with EU requirements, will take some time to have an appreciable effect.

Central and Eastern European countries have generally recognised the adverse pollution impact of the transport sector, particularly associated with the use of older vehicles. Most have therefore banned the import of cars with two-stroke engines and all other cars older than approximately three years. If unofficial imports can be controlled, such a measure should dampen the extent of emission increases as a result of the private transport explosion. Russia and the Ukraine have not taken measures in this area.

In most Central and Eastern European countries a wide range of fiscal measures have been introduced, with the aim of achieving their energy goals. VAT reductions and reduced import duty for goods and equipment necessary for efficiency or for the development of renewable energy are very common. VAT rates also vary by fuel in some states. Symbolic carbon taxes are in place in Poland and Slovenia, but have no political support in most states in the region.

Soft financing is often available for energy efficiency improvements or renewable developments, both from domestic sources and via international lending institutions. This is particularly important in relation to small-scale investments for which the cost of capital would normally be prohibitively high. Price reform, with prices still typically set by governments, has progressed to the point where prices generally approach the immediate cost of supply (short-run marginal cost), although they do not yet provide for future investment and profit (long-run marginal cost).

10.3 Summary of the Model Assumptions

In order to implement the relevant policies in our model, we shall make the following assumptions:

In the United States (USA), the policy is based on voluntary agreements to increase energy efficiency and, above all, on the use of the flexibility mechanisms, in particular emissions trading. Energy efficiency improvements ('no regrets') options, will decrease energy use by 10 per cent until 2010.

In the Kyoto scenario, Japan (JPN) is to attain its target emissions by energy efficiency improvements, emissions trading and fuel switching. Should this not be sufficient, then a carbon tax should be applied. According to the Ministry of Foreign Affairs, Japan's BaU emissions projection for the Kyoto commitment period is approximately 26 per cent above its 1990 level. To achieve its target of 6 per cent below this level, Japan intends to make a reduction of 28.5 per cent (of 1990) by domestic abatement measures, and to achieve the remaining 5.5 per cent by creating sinks (3.7 per cent) and trading (1.8 per cent). In the simulations, Japan reduces energy demand by 5 per cent until 2010 through 'no regrets' efficiency improvements. The domestic abatement target places a cap on trading

The greenhouse gas policies of the European Union (EUM) are a combination of energy taxation, doubling of renewables and energy efficiency improvements (particularly in the transport sector), and using flexibility mechanisms (with 50 per cent cap). Energy taxes start as a 5 per cent levy on the average unit of energy in 2000, increase to 10 per cent in 2005, and remain at that level until 2020. Energy taxes apply to industry as well as private households, but are not paid for energy inputs into the refining industry, gas distribution, and electricity generation. 'No regrets' efficiency improvements decrease energy use by 6 per cent until 2010.

In the Rest of OECD Europe region (ROE), the countries recognise that they can gain most by international flexibility mechanisms. International trading is therefore used to the fullest extent. In addition, energy efficiency measures at home decrease energy use by 2 per cent until 2010, a relatively low 'no regrets' potential, reflecting the already high energy efficiency in the region.

As in the ROE region, the countries in the Rest of OECD region (ROO) make full use of international flexibility through traded carbon permits. Energy efficiency improvements are assumed to reduce energy demand by 7 per cent until 2010.

The role of the Economies in Transition (EIT) is to supply emission credits through (1) selling of 'hot air' credits but not more than 2 per cent of global demand, and (2) providing opportunities to obtain joint-implementation credits, first of all for projects reducing fugitive fuel emissions. The cap on 'hot air' trading means a reduction of the Kyoto target of 1.47 to 1.2 times the 1995 level of emissions. The 'no regrets' potential for the region is assumed to be quite large, with efficiency improvements reducing energy demand by 12 per cent by 2010.

CHAPTER 11

THE 'MOST LIKELY' KYOTO SCENARIO: IMPLICATIONS

11.1 Introduction

The 'most likely' implementation of the Kyoto Protocol, as described in Chapter 10, will reduce global emissions by only about 8 per cent from the Business-as-Usual levels projected for 2010 and 2020. Annex I countries reduce emissions, while non-Annex I countries, in particular fast-growing China and India, increase emissions to more or less the same extent as in the BaU scenario.

The implementation of the Kyoto Protocol is therefore not sufficient to halt the increase in global greenhouse gas emissions. World emissions continue to rise. Emissions in the Annex I region fall by 14 and 16 per cent from the projected BaU levels in 2010 and 2020 respectively, but even in this region emissions increase above the 1995 base year level by more than 8 per cent until 2020, despite a decline between 1995 and 2010 of 300 Million tonnes CO_2 equivalent (Mt CO_2e).

Thus, the very region committed to reduce emissions under the Kyoto Protocol reaches the end of the projections horizon with higher emissions than in 1995. This is because the 'hot air' problem discussed in Chapter 10 allows the EIT region, which is part of Annex I, to emit substantially more in 2010 than in 1995. Because of international emission permit trading, limits on the supply of 'hot air', and 'banking' of unused permits,the Annex I region as a whole will reduce emissions in 2010, but not in 2020 as compared with the base year 1995.

This chapter presents, first, the emission reductions for the main countries and regions in the Kyoto scenario; secondly, the implications of emission reductions for the fossil fuel markets; and thirdly the implications for oil revenues by region.

11.2 Emission Reductions

11.2.1 Emissions by Region

Emissions trading between regions means that emissions will remain above their assigned amounts in the Kyoto Protocol in some regions, which will be buyers of emission permits, and in some regions emissions will be below the targets, making them sellers. Figures 11.1 and 11.2

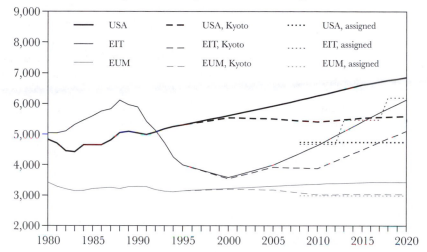

Figure 11.1: Energy CO_2 and Fugitive-Fuel CH_4 Emissions, BaU and Kyoto. Million Tonnes CO_2e

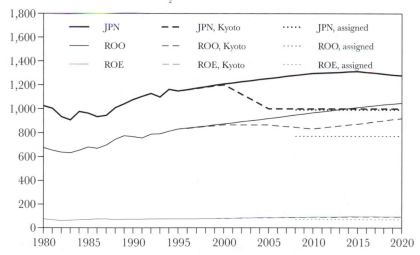

Figure 11.2: Energy CO_2 and Fugitive-Fuel CH_4 Emissions, BaU and Kyoto. Million Tonnes CO_2e

show emission trajectories for the Annex I countries. The graphs show the historical record from 1980 to 1995, and projections up to the year 2020. They show Business-as-Usual emissions, 'most likely' emissions following the implementation of the Kyoto Protocol, and dotted lines for the assigned amounts in the Kyoto Protocol.

The Economies in Transition (EIT) is the only region selling emission permits in 2010 and the following periods. Business-as-Usual emissions for EIT are below the assigned amounts in 2010, which means the region can sell emission permits without any abatement effort (the 'hot air' problem). As described in Chapter 10, we assume that the region limits the amount of 'hot air' emission permits it sells internationally. The retained permits from 2010 can be banked, and the region therefore has more room for growth in emissions in the subsequent years.

BaU emissions reach the original Kyoto target in about 2015, but banking of unused emission permits from 2010 means the region still has 'hot air' in 2015 and 2020. Figure 11.1 shows clearly the increasing amounts of emission permits assigned to the EIT region, increasing from 4700 Mt to 6200 Mt CO_2e between 2010 and 2020. These assigned amounts are 49–63 Mt above the region's BaU emissions, as specified in the 'hot air' cartel assumption.

When emission permit trading becomes an option, CO_2e becomes a valuable commodity in the region. Emission abatement at home means that more permits can be sold internationally. Emissions in the region therefore fall below the BaU line, as it becomes profitable to reduce them and sell additional permits, up to the point where marginal abatement costs are equal to the permit price. The Economies in Transition therefore reduce emissions substantially below the BaU line, by 750 Mt or 17 per cent of BaU emissions already in 2010. The permit cartel means that the region has 49 Mt of 'hot air' to sell, so in total it sells about 800 Mt of CO_2e in emission permits. In 2020, this is increased to about 1110 Mt.

The main buyers of emission permits are the big OECD countries, whereas the Rest of OECD Europe (ROE) region plays only a minor role. In absolute terms, the USA buys most of the permits, about three-quarters of the total. The EU reduces emissions substantially, albeit less than the other Annex I countries in percentage terms.

The Kyoto Protocol defines emission targets for the Annex I countries only, with non-Annex I countries free to increase emissions. Reductions in international energy prices and changes in international trade flows due to relocation of industries mean that non-Annex I countries increase emissions from the BaU projections. This leakage is found to be small: total Annex I emission reductions from BaU levels are 2400 Mt and 3100 Mt CO_2e in 2010 and 2020. Non-Annex I countries increase emissions by 30 Mt and 110 Mt in the two periods, i.e. 'leakages' are 2 and 4 per cent of total emission reductions.

11.2.2 Emissions Trading and Abatement Costs

Permit trading in theory allows the equalisation of marginal emission abatement costs across regions. Regions with high abatement costs buy more permits relative to their required emission reductions, i.e. they abate less at home, than regions with low abatement costs. By looking at abatement cost curves in this section, we can predict the pattern of trade in permits, and the relative benefits from trading for the different regions.

Figure 11.3 shows abatement cost curves for the USA, Japan, the EU, the Rest of the OECD (ROO), and the Economies in Transition (EIT). The curves are obtained by simulating hypothetical domestic emission constraints reducing BaU emissions by 10, 20, and 30 per cent in a given year, here 2010. The figure shows shadow prices for the emission constraints in 1995 Dollars per ton of CO_2 equivalent. It becomes apparent that the USA and EIT have relatively low emission abatement costs, starting at $5 and increasing to about $25 per ton of CO_2 equivalent for emission reductions between 10 and 30 per cent.

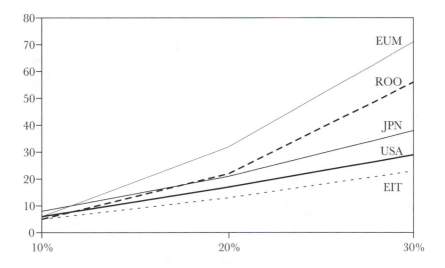

Figure 11.3:   Cost Curves for Emission Reductions, 10–30 Per Cent below BaU. 2010. $ per Tonne CO_2e

Abatement costs in the EU start at $6 and increase to $70 per ton, whereas in the Rest of OECD region they range between $5 and $56 per tonne, due to the low share of coal and already high energy efficiency in this region. Abatement costs in the ROE region are very much higher than for the regions in Figure 11.3.

The differences in abatement costs shown in Figure 11.3 explain the benefits from international trade in emission permits: regions with relatively high domestic abatement costs can pay regions with relatively low costs to reduce their emissions. Regions with high costs buy a high amount of permits and therefore reduce domestic emissions relatively little, whereas regions with low abatement costs reduce domestic emissions substantially, and either buy very few or even sell emission permits. This leads in principle to an efficient implementation of emission reductions, because reductions are undertaken where it is least costly. Figure 11.4 shows the emission reductions expected from the Kyoto Protocol in per cent of BaU emissions in 2010.

The permit trading expected under the 'most likely' implementation of the Kyoto Protocol does not lead to a complete equalisation of marginal abatement costs because of trading restrictions and additional domestic measures (energy efficiency improvements, energy taxes, investment in nuclear; see Chapter 10). Nevertheless, this trading leads to significant benefits in particular for the ROE region. As shown in Figure 11.4, the Rest of Europe region benefits most from trading as it will need to reduce its own emissions by less than 3 per cent, as

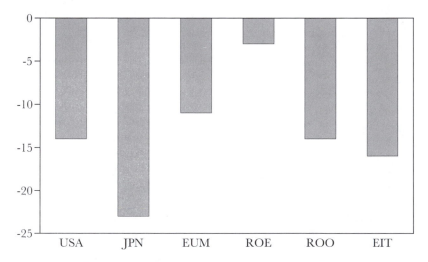

Figure 11.4:   Energy CO_2 and Fugitive-fuel CH_4 Emissions, Reductions in 2010. Per Cent below BaU

compared with around 14 per cent for the USA and 23 per cent for Japan. Reductions in the USA are relatively cheap given low energy costs in the base case. Reductions in Japan are large because of additional domestic measures and restrictions on trading. The additional domestic measures which some regions implement in the Kyoto scenario increase the costs incurred by them by restricting trading. On the other hand, the lower level of demand for emission permits resulting from these measures keeps emission permit prices relatively low, and therefore benefits regions such as the USA and the Rest of OECD Europe which do not restrict trading.

The restricted permit trading allowed under the 'most likely' implementation scenario leads to permit prices of $10 in 2010, and $11 in 2020 per ton of CO_2 equivalent (or between $37 and $41 per ton of carbon). Restrictions on trading keep the domestic price above the international price in Japan until 2020, whereas in the EU additional domestic measures, e.g. energy taxes and energy efficiency improvements, are sufficient to reduce emissions below the domestic target. The proposed cap on trading between the EU and other regions – 50 per cent of the required emission reductions – is therefore not binding in the simulations. Even with a fairly high amount of international permit trading, all the regions undertake considerable abatement efforts at home. More discussions on the EU proposal for restrictions on international emissions trading will follow in the next subsection.

11.2.3 The EU Proposal for Restrictions on Permit Trading

In our Kyoto scenario, the EU limits trading to 50 per cent of required reductions, which means domestic abatement has to cover at least half the difference between the region's BaU emissions and the Kyoto assigned amount. This is an interpretation of the EU 'recommendations on supplementarity in the use of the Kyoto Mechanisms': On 17 May 1999, the EU Council of Ministers agreed on a Community strategy concerning climate change. This includes proposals to limit both permit buying or joint implementation, and the share of assigned amounts a country may sell. The limit for permit acquisition is defined in relation to assigned amounts and baseline emissions. Assigned amounts in the Kyoto Protocol are defined cumulatively over a period of five years. The EU proposal limits permit buying to 5 per cent of the arithmetic middle between 1990 emissions and the assigned amounts, or half of the difference between the actual annual emissions of any year between 1994 and 2002 (multiplied by 5), and a country's assigned amount, whichever is higher. For our purposes, we have translated the EU formulae in order to fit the model specifications as

(1)   2.5 per cent of the sum of assigned amount and 1990 emissions, or
(2)   0.5 times the difference between emissions in 2000 and the assigned amount.

According to the EU proposal, permit selling would be restricted as in (1). Table 11.1 shows the resulting caps on acquisition or sales of permits or limits on the extent of joint implementation resulting from the formulae (figures obtained by the IEA are shown in comparison[1]). For the Kyoto scenario, we have interpreted the EU cap proposal loosely: the EU restricts own permit buying to 50 per cent of required abatement, but other countries do not agree to the EU proposal, and the region remains the only Party to the Kyoto Protocol with trading restrictions, except for Japan, where trading is restricted even more severely.

Table 11.1: The EU Cap on the Use of Flexibility in 2010

	EU Cap on Acquisition (OIES) Mt CO_2e	Required Domestic Action (% of abatement effort) OIES	IEA	EU Cap on Sales Mt CO_2e	% of Hot Air
USA	405,686	73	67		
JPN	103,179	66	36		
EUM	155,627	60	58		
ROE	4,812	76	0		
ROO	50,362	75	69		
EIT				297,855	23.5

Source for IEA: Richard Baron et al., 'A Preliminary Analysis of the EU Proposals on the Kyoto Mechanisms' IEA 28 May 99

In the Kyoto scenario, the EU cap on trading is not binding, i.e. domestic emissions abatement fulfils more than half of the EU's required reduction. In fact, required reduction (the difference between

1. Richard Baron et al.(1999), 'A Preliminary Analysis of the EU Proposals on the Kyoto Mechanisms' IEA 28 May 99. IEA figures are based on energy CO_2 alone. The differences for JPN and ROE are mainly due to differences in 2010 BaU emissions.For example, the IEA envisages that Switzerland (the only ROE country with listed IEA BaU emissions) would reach its Kyoto level under BaU conditions, thus leading to an IEA EU cap on acquisition of 721 per cent of the reduction requirements of this country.

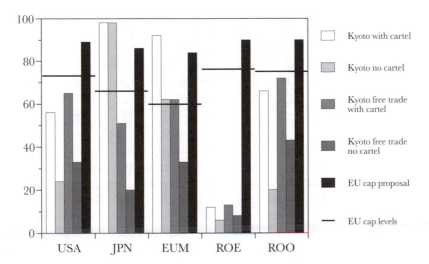

Figure 11.5:   Domestic Abatement in Per Cent of Total Required Reductions

BaU emissions and the Kyoto target for the EU) is 385 Mt of CO_2e, whereas domestic emission abatement is 354 Mt in 2010. This means domestic action fulfils 92 per cent of the requirements.

We have performed some additional simulations to assess the EU proposal, shown by five bars for each region in Figure 11.5. The bars show domestic abatement as percentages of total required amounts for the OECD countries for different assumptions concerning trade restrictions and 'hot air'. In the first simulation, the Kyoto scenario, the EIT region limits the supply of permits. The second simulation is a Kyoto scenario without 'hot air' cartel; the third, a Kyoto scenario without any other restrictions, but with 'hot air' cartel; the fourth, a Kyoto scenario without any restrictions on trading; the fifth simulation is a Kyoto scenario with caps on trading as shown in Table 11.1.

(1) *The basic Kyoto scenario.* The USA fulfils 56 per cent of its requirements through domestic abatement, while Japan fulfils 98 per cent (the country limits trading to 2 per cent), the ROE region achieves 12 per cent at home and buys 88 per cent of their requirements abroad, the ROO region reaches 66 per cent of the target through domestic action. All the regions except ROE therefore reach targets mainly through domestic action.

(2) *Kyoto without 'hot air' cartel.* Without the 'hot air' cartel, the EIT region sells all available emission permits internationally. This reduces the international permit price considerably, and therefore also the incentive to abate domestically. Nevertheless, domestic

action still fulfils 62 per cent of EU requirements, 24 per cent of the USA requirements, 20 per cent of ROO's.

The next two simulations shown in Figure 11.5 depict a 'free trade' world: in the Kyoto scenario, Japan limits trading to 2 per cent of required amounts, and the EU imposes energy taxes on domestic users. We show the results of two simulations without these additional measures, keeping the EIT 'hot air' cartel in simulation 3.

(3) *Kyoto with cartel, no additional restrictions.* Japanese domestic action achieves 51 per cent of the required amount, whereas in the USA and the EU, 65 and 62 per cent respectively of required reductions are achieved through domestic measures.

(4   *Kyoto without any trade restrictions.* We have dropped the 'hot air' cartel assumption and simulated truly free trading. This is a case where EU domestic action accounts for only 33 per cent of the required amount, far below the proposed trading limit.

(5) *Kyoto with the EU trading cap proposal.* In the final simulation, trading is far more limited because of restrictions on permit selling by EIT. This restriction is so severe, that domestic action in the EU is again above the minimum amount permitted, i.e. the cap is not binding in the EU, and the EU benefits from very low permit prices, while the USA, ROO, and in particular the ROE region suffer from very high domestic abatement costs.

Concluding from these simulations, it is clear that EU energy taxes in the Kyoto scenario increase domestic abatement, while an EIT 'hot air' cartel increases the international permit price, again supporting domestic action. Domestic abatement in the EU is thus always well above 50 per cent of requirements. Our Kyoto scenario cap on trading is therefore not binding except for a world without any additional restrictions on trading. If trading restrictions are applied throughout the Annex I region shown in the last paragraph, the EU cap is again non-binding.

11.3 Impacts on the Fossil Fuel Markets

11.3.1 Comparison Between the Three Fossil Fuels

Comparing the impacts on the three fossil fuels as summarised in Table 11.2, and discussed in the remainder of this chapter, produces surprising results: the quantitative impact on gas is about as large as

Table 11.2: Impact of Kyoto on Fossil Fuels, Reductions from BaU. Million Barrels per Day Oil Equivalent

	2010	2020
Oil	-3.0	-5.3
Coal	-4.4	-4.4
Gas	-4.0	-4.8

that on coal, and the impact on oil is smaller in 2010, but larger in 2020 than the impacts on coal or gas. Some discussions of the factors responsible for these results might be helpful from the outset.

The implementation of the Kyoto policies increases domestic prices of fossil fuels through carbon and energy levies, which depend on the carbon and energy contents of the fuels. It is assumed that the main instrument of implementation of the Kyoto Protocol is tradable carbon permits, which are sold at a uniform price per unit of carbon (or CO_2e) throughout the Annex I region (with the exception of Japan, which restricts trading and increases the domestic price of permits in 2010). Economic agents base their decisions on final prices of energy, which are determined by producer prices, transport costs, taxation (consumption taxes and input taxes), and carbon permits. Uniform prices of carbon permits affect the three fuels differently, because (a) initial domestic prices differ strongly whether we look at prices per unit of energy or prices per unit of carbon; and (b) because of different elasticities of substitution between different fuels in production, and between goods in consumption, and because of different elasticities of demand with respect to consumer incomes.

Figure 11.6 shows the differences between prices for coal and gas, and refined oil and gas, in per cent of the gas prices. Price differences are shown for energy and carbon units for the major Annex I countries, as derived from the CLIMOX model. Positive bars show prices greater than the gas price, negative bars show that prices are below the gas price. The series on the right shows data for coal, the series on the left shows indices for refined oil. Differences are shown for major Annex I regions, and for each region the shaded bars show relative prices per unit of energy, and solid bars show prices per unit of carbon. The figure shows clearly that in all regions refined oil is substantially more expensive than gas, and in most regions coal is cheaper than gas, and this general result holds both for prices per energy unit and for prices per carbon unit.

The difference in price between refined oil and gas is smallest in the USA, where oil costs 52 per cent more per heating unit, and 24 per

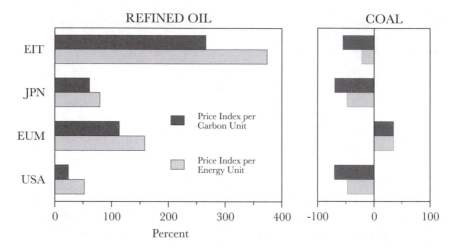

Figure 11.6:   Differences between Coal, Refined Oil, and Gas Prices in Per Cent of Gas Prices, per Energy Unit and per Unit of Carbon. 1995

cent more per ton of carbon, than gas. In Japan, an energy unit of oil costs 80 per cent more, and in the EU it costs 1.6 times as much as an energy unit of gas. The differences between gas and refined oil are less when prices are expressed per ton of carbon, because the carbon content of refined oil is higher than that of gas. Coal is cheaper than gas except in the EU, by 20 to 70 per cent. The price of coal is lower in terms of carbon units as compared with energy units, because of the higher carbon content of coal as compared with gas.

Figure 11.6 shows that adding a uniform carbon levy has very different relative effects on the three fossil fuels: the relative increase in the price of coal is much greater than the relative increase in the price of gas which in turn is much greater than the relative increase in the price of refined oil. Fuel switching will therefore take place away from coal, as intended, but also away from gas, which is not intended because gas has less carbon per energy unit than oil products. The existing taxes on fuels therefore distort the intended effects of carbon instruments and we should expect a stronger impact of climate change measures on gas and coal, than on oil.

In addition, oil serves the transport sector, which is often described as a captive market because substitution possibilities away from oil are severely limited. In contrast, electricity generation and energy intensive industries are the major markets for gas and coal, and at least in the latter oil products are competitive. Fuel switching can therefore be expected to be less important for oil, than for coal and gas. Also, several industrial sectors can more easily substitute away from energy, than transport or electricity generation. Again we would expect more impact on gas and coal.

Finally, it has been shown (in Chapter 9) that methane emissions from gas production and distribution are large. A large part of the adverse impact of climate change policies on gas is therefore due to the methane leaks, especially in the EIT region. To show this, we have performed additional simulations, where methane is not taken into account, both for a non-methane BaU scenario, and a non-methane Kyoto scenario. The new Kyoto scenario produces projections of gas use which are much nearer to the BaU projections, than in the basic Kyoto scenario. The difference is particularly evident in the EIT region: in the basic Kyoto scenario, gas use is lower than the BaU levels by 2.7 and 3.6 mb/d oil equivalent in 2010 and 2020. In the non-methane Kyoto scenario, gas use is reduced by 1.4 and 2.1 mb/d oe. Instead of a reduction from BaU levels of 6–7 per cent in the basic Kyoto scenario, this sensitivity analysis shows a reduction of 3–4 per cent. Nearly half the impact of climate change policies on gas is due to methane leaks in the EIT region.

Following this discussion, we can therefore expect to see large impacts on coal and in particular on gas because of the methane leaks, but only small effects on oil demand in the simulation results. As we shall see, the total demand for liquid fuels remains very nearly the same with an implementation of Kyoto. Nevertheless, demand for crude oil is reduced because of an increase in the competitiveness of hydrogen brought about by carbon policy instruments. In the BaU scenario, hydrogen production reaches 400 thousand and 4.8 million b/d in 2010 and 2020, respectively. In the basic Kyoto scenario, hydrogen increases to 3.2 and 9.5 million b/d in 2010 and 2020. This increase is sufficient to substitute for a decline in crude oil demand.

Again, we have performed sensitivity analysis to look at this aspect in more detail. To evaluate the importance of the existence of hydrogen in the model, we have performed simulations for a world without hydrogen. In this, the quantity of oil increases in the BaU case, to 104.4 mb/d in 2020, as opposed to 102 mb/d in the base version. The oil price rises by 40 per cent from the 1995 level, compared with an increase of 33 per cent in the base case. Total refined product availability is less than in the base case – 110 mb/d instead of 112 mb/d (as before, this figure includes refinery gains).

Implementing Kyoto then reduces the total production of oil to 101.1 mb/d in 2020, a reduction of 3.3 mb/d as compared to 5.3 mb/d in the simulations with hydrogen. The oil price increases by 35 per cent from the 1995 level, a 3.6 per cent drop from the BaU simulation, as opposed to 7 per cent in the base case. The impact of Kyoto on the oil market is therefore significantly less in a world without hydrogen as backstop fuel.

To conclude, contrary to *a priori* expectations based on partial equilibrium evaluation of carbon contents of fuels, climate change policies as envisaged in the Kyoto scenario have a strong impact on gas, almost as strong as on coal, the major culprit in the greenhouse debate. Existing taxation means that the impacts on oil are reduced, but technological development takes away some of the oil demand.

11.3.2 Conventional and Non-conventional Oil Supply

The Annex I countries are the major users of oil in the world and the implementation of the Kyoto Protocol obviously has an impact on the demand for oil and therefore also on prices and quantities produced. However, the impact on oil depends on elasticities of substitution in demand between different products, elasticities of substitution between fuels in the production of energy, and as pointed out in the last section the development of technology.

Figure 11.7 shows the global supply of oil (including Natural Gas Liquids), both from conventional and non-conventional sources. The dotted lines show the Business-as-Usual case. Total oil supply increases to 91.2 mb/d in 2010, continues rising to 100.2 mb/d in 2015, and

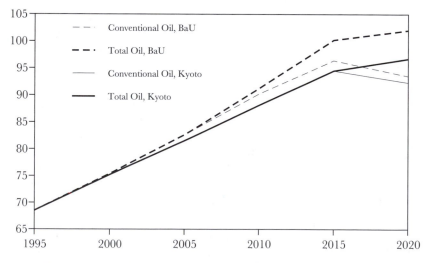

Figure 11.7:   Oil Production, BaU and Kyoto. Million Barrels per Day

102 mb/d in 2020. From 2010, an increasing share of total supply comes from non-conventional sources, with non-conventional oil production reaching 1 mb/d, 3.7 mb/d, and 8.5 mb/d in 2010, 2015, and 2020, respectively, which more than compensates for the decline in conventional oil production. The solid lines show the production of oil given the 'most likely' implementation of the Kyoto Protocol.

The policies set out in Chapter 10 lead to a decline in oil production of 3 mb/d in 2010, and 5.3 mb/d in 2020 as compared with the BaU projections. Most of this decline in volumes comes from non-conventional sources: under the Kyoto scenario, the production of non-conventional oil is delayed beyond 2015, and production increases over the next five years, to reach 4.3 mb/d in the final period. The Kyoto policies therefore reduce non-conventional oil production by the end of the projections period to half its BaU level. Conventional oil production is only about 2.1 mb/d and 1.2 mb/d in 2010 and 2020 below the projected BaU level.

The oil market is a truly global market, and reductions in the supply of conventional crude oil are therefore spread over the globe (presumably the supply reductions will be due to policy in the OPEC region and to a decline in investments in non-OPEC countries). The impact of the Kyoto scenario on the suppliers of conventional oil is accordingly smaller than the impact on total oil production. Because non-conventional oil is produced only in some regions, these regions are disproportionately hit by the impacts of Kyoto policies. The ROO

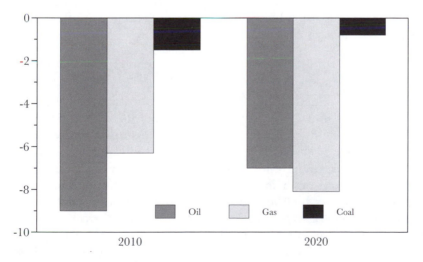

Figure 11.8: Fossil Fuel Prices, Changes from BaU. Per Cent of BaU. 2010 and 2020

region (mainly Canada) loses production of 1 million b/d, and the LAM region 800 thousand b/d in 2020. The call on Middle East oil increases from 24 mb/d in 1995 to 35.6 and 39.8 mb/d in 2010 and 2020 in the BaU case, and to 35.3 and 39.6 mb/d in the Kyoto case, with reductions of only 200–300 thousand b/d due to Kyoto.

11.3.3 Oil Prices

The flexible response of non-conventional crude supply to the reduced demand growth under Kyoto policies dampens the impact on prices. Figure 11.8 shows changes in fossil fuel prices in per cent of BaU prices for 2010 and 2020.

In a Business-as-Usual world, the oil price is projected to increase smoothly 11 per cent above the 1995 level in 2010, and 17 per cent in 2015 in real terms. Starting at a level of $18 in 1995, this means the oil price reaches $20 in 2010, and $21 in 2015. In the next five-year period, the oil price is projected to pick up sharply to reach $24 (in 1995 Dollars), or 33 per cent above the 1995 level in real terms by the end of the projections period.

As shown in Figure 11.8, the oil price falls from the baseline by 9 per cent in 2010 and 7 per cent in 2020. This means Kyoto 'costs' to the oil producers are a combination of the quantity reactions shown in the last paragraph, and a price response of 7–9 per cent of the price expected in the BaU case for both 2010 and 2020. As a result, traditional large producers of conventional oil will be more seriously affected than suggested by quantities alone. A discussion of impacts on oil revenues follows in Section 11.5.

11.3.4 Hydrogen

Most of the reduction in oil supply is substituted by hydrogen. Hydrogen is assumed to be a perfect substitute for refined oil, both in stationary uses and in transport. We further assume that hydrogen is produced without the use of fossil fuels, and is therefore a perfectly carbon-free fuel. Under these assumptions, hydrogen demand increases strongly with the price increases brought about by carbon policies. Figure 11.9 shows hydrogen production in the Kyoto scenario.

The user cost of hydrogen is assumed to be 15 per cent above the cost of refined oil initially. In addition, the market penetration of hydrogen is constrained by the necessity of a new distribution infrastructure, and the replacement of existing equipment using oil products, such as cars. This means that the market penetration of

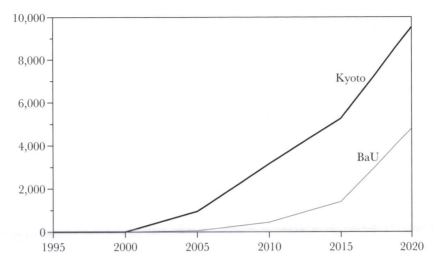

Figure 11.9:   Hydrogen Production, BaU and Kyoto. Thousand Barrels per Day
Oil Equivalent

hydrogen is constrained even when it becomes significantly cheaper than conventional oil products.

Compared with the BaU case, the Kyoto policies therefore increase the use of hydrogen from 440 thousand b/d to 3.2 million b/d oil equivalent in 2010, and from 4.8 to 9.5 million b/d in 2020. In the Kyoto scenario, non-carbon hydrogen captures almost 10 per cent of the market for liquid fuel in 2020. The total production of liquid fuels therefore is almost completely unaffected by Kyoto: in the BaU case as well as in the 'most likely' Kyoto case, global liquids supply is around 112 mb/d oil equivalent in 2020.[2]

Thus, in the case of oil the impact is greatly increased by the availability of a direct competitor, whereas coal and gas do not have such direct non-carbon alternatives. Solar electricity does not fulfil this role, because it is a competitor to conventional electricity. Although substantial, primary fuels make up only a certain percentage of electricity production costs, and prices therefore do not increase in parallel with increases in domestic prices of fossil fuels. The relative improvement of the competitiveness of solar power is therefore much

2. This is availability of refined oil. Note that oil production is 68.5 mb/d and refined oil production is 71.9 mb/d in 1995 due to refinery gains. Assuming the same ratio of crude to products this means oil production is 102 mb/d in 2020, hydrogen is 4.8 mb/d and total refined oil (including hydrogen) is 112 mb/d.

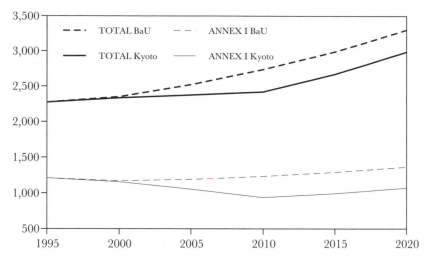

Figure 11.10: Coal Consumption, Total and Annex 1, BaU and Kyoto. Million
Tonnes per Year Oil Equivalent

smaller than in the case of hydrogen.

11.3.5 Impacts on Coal

This section shows the reductions in supply of and demand for coal.
Figure 11.10 shows coal use both globally and in the Annex I region.
In the BaU case, global coal use is projected to increase from the
current 2300 mtoe to 2700 mtoe in 2010 and 3300 mtoe in 2020. The
Annex I countries will have a declining share of the total, as coal use
is being reduced in Europe, and grows only very little in the other
OECD countries. The implementation of the Kyoto Protocol will
reduce coal use in the Annex I countries below current levels, to
around 900 mtoe and 1000 mtoe in 2010 and 2020 respectively. This
means a demand reduction compared with the BaU case in the Annex
I countries of 300 mtoe in 2010 and 2020.

   Unlike the cases of oil and gas, there is no increase in the demand
for coal in non-Annex I countries. This is due to a direct quantity
response to demand changes, and an indirect substitution effect.
Production of coal is more price responsive than oil production. Also,
transport costs of coal are higher which means that the coal market is
regionally disaggregated to a certain extent. Demand reductions mean
a fall in volume and a small fall in price. The price fall in some
markets, i.e. the Annex I region, is not sufficient to lead to a strong
rise in demand from the non-Annex I countries. In addition to this

direct effect, the relative fall in the international prices of oil and gas means that some coal is squeezed from the non-Annex I markets through substitution. In fact, the net result of direct and indirect effects is that coal use declines slightly from the BaU levels in the non-Annex I countries.

The average world producer price of coal decreases very little compared with the BaU case, as can be seen in Figure 11.8. The coal price increases by 4 and 9 per cent in the BaU case, and by 2 and 8 per cent in the Kyoto case in 2010 and 2020 respectively. Producer prices are high also because of the increase in the production costs for coal in the Annex I region, due to an increase in the costs of energy inputs into production, and to methane leaks in production. The energy used for coal production is almost exclusively coal, and the domestic price of coal increases substantially due to the price of carbon levied upon it.

11.3.6 Impacts on Gas

Together with oil and coal, climate change policies increase the prices paid by consumers for gas. The impact on gas is shown in Figure 11.11, both for the world and the Annex I region, for the Business-as-Usual and for the Kyoto scenarios.

World gas use falls by 230 bcm per year below BaU projections in 2010, and 280 bcm in 2020. Total gas demand is equivalent to 57.5

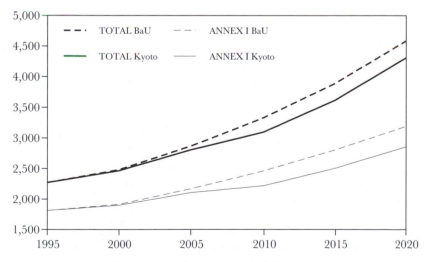

Figure 11.11: Gas Use. Total and Annex 1, BaU and Kyoto. Billion Cubic Metres per Year

and 79 million barrels per day in 2010 and 2020 respectively in the BaU case. Gas demand falls below the BaU levels by 4 mb/d of oil equivalent in 2010, and 4.8 mb/d in 2020 worldwide, 4.2 mb/d and 5.7 mb/d in 2010 and 2020 in the Annex I region. The adverse impact on gas is therefore larger than the impact on oil in 2010, both in absolute and in relative terms, as was explained in Section 11.3.1.

As in the case of oil, non-Annex I demand for gas increases due to price reductions relative to the BaU levels. Non-Annex I countries increase gas use by 11 and 56 bcm in 2010 and 2020 relative to the BaU levels, which is the equivalent of 190 and 962 thousand barrels of oil per day. This is only one-tenth and one-third of the 'leakage' observed in the oil market.

Figure 11.8 shows the price response underlying the quantitative developments. In the BaU case, the world average gas price declines in the first two periods, and increases 4 per cent and 18 per cent above the 1995 level in 2010 and 2020. In the Kyoto case, gas prices decline below the 1995 level until 2015, and rise by 8 per cent in 2020. Gas prices are therefore 6 and 8 per cent below BaU projections in 2010 and 2020. The price response of gas is larger than that for oil in 2020, and is also larger than for coal, because coal supply is more elastic to price changes.

11.4 Sectoral Demand for Fossil Fuels

11.4.1 Oil Products

Global demand for oil products is necessarily equal to oil supply, with only very minor year-by-year stock changes which average out over the five-year periods shown here. As mentioned above, the total availability and use of oil products including hydrogen is almost unaffected by Kyoto policies, with a reduction in demand by 350 thousand b/d and 600 thousand b/d in 2010 and 2020. This section discusses the development of oil products demand in the main economic sectors: electricity generation, energy intensive industries, other industries and services, and transport and household. It concludes with an overall comparison.

(a) Electricity generation.This sector accounts for only a small part of the total demand for oil, at least in the OECD countries. Fuel substitution is relatively easy in this sector, which is represented in the model with a high elasticity of substitution between fuels. The higher carbon

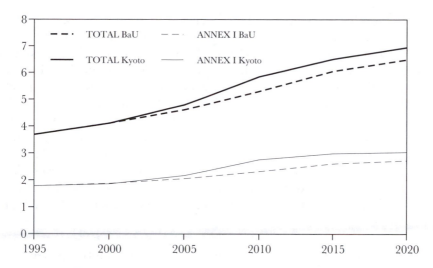

Figure 11.12: Demand for Refined Oil in Electricity Generation, BaU and Kyoto. Million Barrels per Day

content of coal means that the domestic price of coal increases by more than the gas and oil price, when climate change policies distinguish taxes or levies by carbon content. Figure 11.12 shows oil use in electricity generation in million b/d, both for the world as a whole and for the Annex I countries. In the BaU world, the use of oil products for generation of electricity increases from 3.7 mb/d in 1995 to 5.3 mb/d in 2010, and 6.5 mb/d in 2020. The 'most likely' implementation of Kyoto will increase the amount of oil used in the sector by 550 thousand b/d in 2010, and 460 thousand barrels in 2020. The sector therefore has a share in total oil demand of about 5 per cent, which does not change substantially with the Kyoto policies. It should be remembered here that hydrogen is a perfect competitor to refined oil in the simulation model, and therefore the demand for hydrogen is indistinguishable from the demand for oil products in the model results. At least some of the increase in the use of oil products in electricity generation should therefore be ascribed to the use of hydrogen in stationary fuel cells or hydrogen turbines.

*(b) Energy Intensive Industries.*These account for 16.2 mb/d of oil demand in 2010 in a Business-as-Usual world, increasing to 18.3 mb/d in 2020. The Annex I countries account for about half of the total. The income elasticities of demand for energy intensive products are relatively low, and structural change reduces their relative importance

in the developed countries. This is visible in the much lower growth rate in oil demand from the sector in the Annex I countries.

The implementation of the Kyoto Protocol leads to a small increase in the demand for oil from the sector by 150 thousand b/d in 2010 and 90 thousand barrels in 2020 above the respective BaU levels. Demand in Annex I countries declines by 320 thousand b/d and 520 thousand b/d from BaU levels in 2010 and 2020 respectively, but the lower oil price leads other countries to increase their demand. Partly this effect is due to the relocation of production into non-Annex I countries, which then export their goods to Annex I countries. This leads to a 'leakage' of CO_2 emissions, due to the fact that the Kyoto Protocol specifies emission targets only for one group of the world's countries.

(c) Other Industries and Services. This sector is even more diverse than energy intensive industries. It comprises manufacturing industries as well as private and public services. The energy costs are a smaller percentage of total input costs than in the sector discussed above. This sector uses 13.9 mb/d of oil in 2010 and 15.5 mb/d in 2020 in the BaU case, more than three-quarters of which is in the Annex I countries. Kyoto policies lead to a decrease in demand by about 290 and 390 thousand b/d in 2010 and 2020 in total, 530 and 720 thousand b/d in the Annex I countries. Again, some 'leakage' can be observed, which means that global demand reductions are smaller than those in the Annex I countries by about 250 thousand b/d in 2010 and 2020, because of demand increases in non-Annex I countries.

*(d) Transport and Households.*This is the most important sector for oil demand. As is visible in Figure 11.13, transport and household demand for liquid fuels increases from 34.5 mb/d in 1995 to 46.4 mb/d in 2010, and 54.9 mb/d in 2020. The substitution possibilities for transport fuel are much lower than in any of the other economic sectors, and the income elasticity of household demand for transport is high. In addition, hydrogen is an alternative fuel for a new generation of vehicles. As discussed above, hydrogen is a perfect competitor to refined oil in the simulation model, and indistinguishable from refined oil in the model results. Some of the increase in oil use in transportation is thus due to hydrogen. As a percentage of total sectoral demand, the impact of the Kyoto policies is therefore small. Demand is reduced by 450 and 390 thousand b/d in 2010 and 2020 as compared with the BaU case. Again a small 'leakage' effect can be observed.

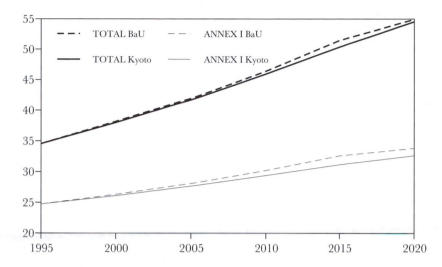

Figure 11.13: Demand for Refined Oil in Transport and Households, BaU and Kyoto. Million Barrels per Day

(e) Overall comparison. Table 11.3 shows sectoral demand data for the three fossil fuels. The Kyoto scenario shows a total decline in the demand for oil of only 350 and 600 thousand b/d in 2010 and 2020, due to the availability of hydrogen as a competitive backstop fuel. The global impact of this demand reduction is a result of reductions of 1.8 mb/d and 3 mb/d in the Annex I countries, mitigated by higher demand in the non-Annex I regions by 1.4 mb/d and 2.4 mb/d in 2010 and 2020. The highest 'leakage' rates are observed in energy intensive industries, where relocation of production could become an important effect.

11.4.2 Coal

The sectoral impacts on coal are much more pronounced than in the case of oil products, because direct substitutes for coal are not available. This section discusses briefly changes in coal use.

(a) *Electricity generation.* This is the most important sector for coal demand. In 1995, as shown in Figure 11.14, more than 1000 million tons oil equivalent of coal were used in this sector in the world, 670 mtoe in the Annex I region. This is projected to increase to 1450 mtoe and 770 in 2020 in the BaU case. Implementing Kyoto means a reduction from BaU by 180 mtoe and 170 mtoe in 2010 and 2020

Table 11.3: Changes in the Demand for Fossil Fuels by Sectors. Thousand Barrels per Day Oil Equivalent

Sector		Electricity	Energy Int.	Other Ind.	Transport + Household	Other	Total
Total							
Oil Products	2010	550	148	-288	-449	-314	-353
	2020	460	93	-387	-386	-381	-602
Coal	2010	-2,450	-826	-127	-98	-929	-4,430
	2020	-2,310	-754	-120	-156	-1,026	-4,366
Gas	2010	-856	-2,106	-366	-110	-595	-4,032
	2020	-1,178	-2,384	-192	-167	-831	-4,752
Annex I							
Oil Products	2010	437	-321	-531	-807	-572	-1,793
	2020	311	-520	-720	-1,200	-856	-2,984
Coal	2010	-2,331	-721	-86	-105	-907	-4,151
	2020	-2,174	-668	-83	-167	-1,012	-4,105
Gas	2010	-847	-2,208	-424	-111	-633	-4,222
	2020	-1,348	-2,836	-490	-171	-871	-5,715

Note: For coal, Transport and Household sector includes government, for gas, Electricity includes Gas Distribution sector.

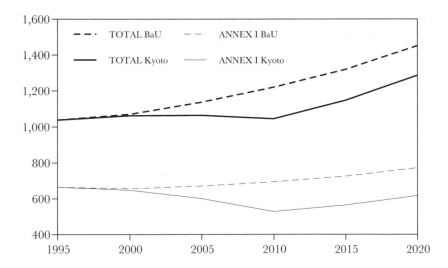

Figure 11.14: Demand for Coal in Electricity Generation, BaU and Kyoto, Million Tonnes per Year Oil Equivalent

globally, a little less in the Annex I region, which is equivalent to 2.3 and 2.2 million barrels of oil per day.

(b) *Energy Intensive Industries.* Coal demand from this diverse sector is only about half as large as from electricity generation, with a base level of 570 mtoe in 1995. Coal use is projected to increase to 800 mtoe in 2020 in the BaU case, 230 mtoe in the Annex I region. With an implementation of the Kyoto policies, coal use in energy intensive industries declines by 60 mtoe from the projected BaU levels in 2010 and 2020, which is equivalent to 700 thousand barrels of oil per day.

(c) *Overall Comparison.* Electricty and Energy Intensive Industries account for three-quarters of total coal demand. The reduction in the projected increase in coal demand in the two sectors adds up to 3.2 mb/d and 3 mb/d oil equivalent in 2010 and 2020, with total reductions of 4.4 mb/d for both periods. There is no 'leakage' from coal, as non-Annex I countries reduce coal use as opposed to oil use. The price response of coal is projected to be very small, and international mobility of coal is limited. This means non-Annex I countries substitute oil for coal as oil prices respond much more strongly. The total reduction of coal use is smaller than in the case of oil, because of the lack of a direct non-carbon competitor to coal, and the differential impact of increases in the consumer prices of coal and oil due to carbon permits or taxes. Table 11.3 summarises sectoral shifts in coal use.

11.4.3 Gas

The most important sectors for gas demand are electricity generation and energy intensive industries.[3] The discussion therefore concentrates on these two sectors.

(a) *Electricity.* It can be seen in Figure 11.15 that the sector accounts for 1000 billion cubic metres of gas use in 1995, 45 per cent of the total. Gas demand for electricity generation increases to 1400 bcm and 1900 bcm in 2010 and 2020. The Annex I region accounts for the major part of total gas demand initially, 900 bcm in 1995. This

---

3. In the GTAP database and therefore the CLIMOX model, a major part of total gas use is delivered to the gas distribution sector, and then to industries and households. It would have been difficult to trace gas use once it had entered the gas distribution sector, and electricity and gas distribution have therefore been grouped together in this discussion.

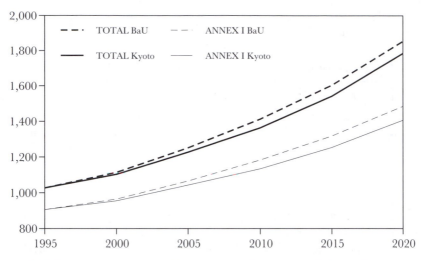

Figure 11.15: Demand for Gas in Electricity and Distribution, BaU and Kyoto.
Billion Cubic Metres per Year

increases to 1200 bcm and 1500 bcm in 2010 and 2020, which means
gas use grows less strongly in the Annex I region than in the rest of
the world. The non-Annex I share in gas use for electricity increases
from 12 to 20 per cent, a quadrupling of volumes. Implementing
Kyoto means a small reduction in gas use for electricity generation as
compared with the BaU levels. Total gas use for the sector lies 50 bcm
and 70 bcm below projected BaU levels in 2010 and 2020, which is
equivalent to 850 thousand b/d and 1.2 million b/d of oil.

(b) *Energy Intensive Industries*. Initially, this sector uses 500 bcm of gas in
the world, 90 per cent of which is in the Annex I region. This increases
to 800 and 1200 bcm in 2010 and 2020, and the share of the non-
Annex I region again increases strongly. Because the sector is diverse
and substitution possibilities exist, the implementation of Kyoto means
a stronger impact on gas demand in this sector than in electricity
generation. Gas demand from energy intensive industries reaches 700
bcm and 1100 bcm in the Kyoto scenario, a reduction from the BaU
projections of 120 bcm and 140 bcm in 2010 and 2020, which is
equivalent to 2.1 mb/d and 2.4 mb/d, or more than double the
impact in electricity generation in absolute terms. The reductions in
gas use in the sector are almost the same globally, as in the Annex I
region in 2010, but some 'leakage' can be observed in 2020, when the
reduction in gas demand is equivalent to 2.4 mb/d oil globally, and
2.8 mb/d oil in the Annex I region. This is another indicator for

relocation of production away from the Annex I region, in addition to changes in oil use in the sector discussed in Section 11.4.1.

(c) *Overall comparison.* As with coal, three-quarters of total gas is used in electricity and energy intensive industries. Reductions from BaU projections for these two sectors amount to 2.9 and 3.6 mb/d oil equivalent in 2010 and 2020 respectively, out of total reductions in gas demand of 4 and 4.8 mb/d oil equivalent. 'Leakage' in gas use is 200 and 900 thousand b/d oe for the two periods as world gas prices decline and non-Annex I countries substitute away from coal. Summary figures are shown in Table 11.3.

11.5 Oil Revenues

Changes in prices and volumes of oil sold translate into changes in oil revenues for oil producers. In Table 11.4 we show oil revenue indices for the regions in the model. In Table A2.11 we also present oil revenue indices by country. World oil revenues increase 48 and 98 per cent from the 1995 levels for 2010 and 2020, respectively, in the Business-as-Usual case. There are strong regional differences in this increase, as oil production in some regions declines and in others increases very strongly. The greatest increase for the regions is observed

Table 11.4: Oil Revenues. Change from 1995 in Per Cent of 1995, and Change from BaU in Per Cent of BaU

	BaU, Per Cent Change 1995–		Kyoto, Per Cent Change 1995–		Per Cent Change from BaU	
	2010	*2020*	*2010*	*2020*	*2010*	*2020*
USA	3	-4	-11	-14	-14	-10
EUM	-43	-66	-51	-69	-14	-9
ROE	16	-16	1	-23	-13	-9
ROO	35	158	19	94	-12	-25
EIT	75	195	40	116	-20	-27
CHN	46	57	30	44	-11	-8
IND	-14	-3	-24	-11	-11	-8
ANI	-22	-35	-31	-40	-12	-8
AOE	65	121	49	104	-10	-7
LAM	122	210	63	120	-27	-29
ROW	-2	41	-14	10	-12	-22
TOTAL CONV.	47	81	30	66	-11	-8
TOTAL OIL	48	98	30	74	-12	-12

in Latin America, where revenues more than double to 2010, and
more than triple to 2020 in the BaU case. Oil revenues in the Middle
East (AOE) also increase strongly, to more than twice their 1995 level.
The price and quantity reactions to the implementation of the Kyoto
Protocol mean that oil revenues worldwide increase less strongly than
in the BaU case. In the Kyoto case, average world oil revenues are 12
per cent lower than revenues expected under BaU in both 2010 and
2020, as shown in the last two columns of Table 11.4.

The regional differences are again strong, because non-conventional
oil suffers more from Kyoto policies. Producers of high amounts of
non-conventional oil in the BaU case see more of their revenue increase
dwindle, than producers of only conventional oil. Oil revenues in
Latin America fall by 27–29 per cent from the BaU levels, and also in
the EIT region, the postponement of non-conventional oil projects
means oil revenues fall by 20 per cent and 27 per cent from the BaU
levels in 2010 and 2020. The AOE region suffers relatively little, with
revenues 10 and 7 per cent lower in 2010 and 2020 than projected
under Business-as-Usual for these years. Oil revenues are still projected
to increase to more than double their 1995 levels by 2020.

11.6 Concluding Remarks

This chapter has shown the implications of the 'most likely'
implementation of the Kyoto Protocol, and of 'roll-over' of emission
targets in the years following the first commitment period. The EIT
region emerges as the only region selling emission permits. An assumed
'hot air' cartel limits the supply of permits in all periods, and increases
permit prices considerably. Limits on permit supply also mean that the
EIT region can carry over unused permits (banking) from 2010, and
has 'hot air' in the periods after the first commitment period. The EIT
region therefore does not have to undertake any abatement effort.
Kyoto assigned amounts plus banking give them room to increase
emissions according to the Business-as-Usual trajectory. The region
does however reduce emissions substantially, as it has relatively low
abatement costs and reductions allow it to sell emission permits
profitably.

Energy taxes in the EU lead to a high emissions abatement effort
inside the region. High emission permit prices due to the EIT monopoly behaviour further increase incentives to reduce emissions in the
region. This means the cap on trading proposed by the EU is not
binding during the projections horizon. The cap would limit the

international purchase of emission permits to 50 per cent of the required emission reductions in the EU. Actual trading falls below this amount.

Climate change policies as envisaged in the Kyoto scenario have a strong impact on gas, almost as strong as on coal, the major culprit in the greenhouse debate. Existing taxation means impacts on oil are reduced, but technological development takes away some of the oil demand. Oil demand increases during the whole projections period, and prices rise from the 1995 baseline. However, quantities and prices in the Kyoto scenario are lower than what could be expected under Business-as-Usual.

CHAPTER 12

THE IMPACT OF SPECIFIC POLICY INSTRUMENTS

12.1 Introduction

In this chapter we present and discuss the implications for fossil fuel markets arising from the adoption of single policy instruments instead of the policy package of the Kyoto scenario. Section 12.2 looks at impacts of national emission quotas or carbon taxes, Section 12.3 looks at energy taxes, and internationally traded emission permits are discussed in Section 12.4. Section 12.5 compares the three implementation options in terms of increases in domestic prices of energy. Conclusions follow in Section 12.6.

12.2 National Carbon Taxes or Emission Quotas

This section considers the impacts of implementing the emission restrictions set out in the Kyoto Protocol using purely domestic measures. Each country reaches the emission targets or assigned amounts domestically, i.e. international emission permit trading, joint implementation, and the Clean Development Mechanisms are ruled out. The policy instruments chosen here to achieve emission reductions are a domestic CO_2 trading system or carbon taxes. Under the domestic trading system, all energy users are allowed and able to trade emission permits, including individual households, and trading is assumed to be implemented efficiently and with very low transaction costs. The government auctions an amount of emission permits initially, which is equal to the national quota or assigned amount specified in the Kyoto Protocol. In this case, the shadow price of the quota, or the price of the traded permits, is equivalent to the carbon tax the government would otherwise choose to reduce emissions.

Institutionally, there are of course important distinctions between privately traded emission permits, and a carbon tax which increases government revenues. For the purposes of the macro-economic modelling undertaken here, we assume that carbon taxes are revenue and distribution neutral, i.e. the government returns the extra revenue received from carbon taxes, without re-distributive consequences for individuals. In the same way we assume that the government auctions emission permits and returns revenues, if permit trading is the chosen policy.

Emissions and Permit Prices. Emissions for the Annex I countries follow the Business-as-Usual trajectories until the year 2000. Interim targets have been chosen for 2005, because some emission restrictions will be implemented before the Kyoto commitment period to avoid a large economic shock in 2008. In the commitment period, emissions reach the targeted levels and stay at these levels in the subsequent periods, since we assume a roll-over of emission targets for the time after the commitment period. The emission reductions with respect to the BaU trajectories therefore increase after the first commitment period.

Emission reductions are achieved by increasing domestic costs of fuels through a national emission permit scheme. Figures 12.1 and 12.2 show the development of national permit prices in the Annex I regions. No emission restrictions apply in 2000, and permit prices are therefore zero. From 2005, permit prices increase, reaching an average of around \$24 per ton of CO_2 equivalent in 2010, and \$25–31 in 2020 for most of the Annex I regions with two exceptions: permit prices in the Rest of OECD Europe region (Norway, Switzerland, and Iceland)

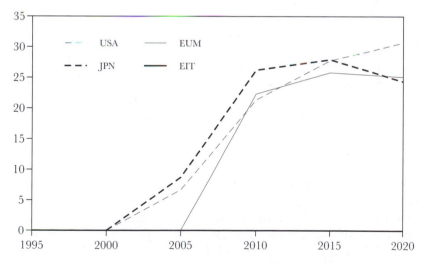

Figure 12.1:   Domestic Price of Emission Permits. Dollar per Tonne of CO_2 Equivalent

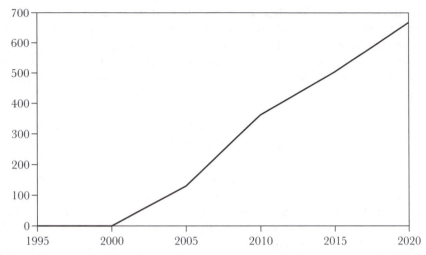

Figure 12.2:   ROE Domestic Price of Emission Permits. Dollar per Tonne of CO_2 Equivalent

rise much faster, reaching $360 in 2010 and $670 in 2020. This shows very high emission abatement costs in this region, which has little coal electricity generation, and low emissions from industry. Permit prices for the Economies in Transition stay at zero until 2020 as no emission restrictions apply because of 'hot air' and banking. In the last period in the projections, costs in the EIT region reach $4 per ton CO_2e.

The figures show the great differences in costs which the countries face when trying to achieve the Kyoto targets domestically. The Rest of Europe region obviously would benefit most from international flexibility in implementing Kyoto. In 2010, costs are lowest in the USA, followed by the European Union, and Japan. If trading was allowed, these regions would therefore buy more emission permits relative to their reduction requirements than the USA. In 2020, the USA is the region with the highest permit prices.

Impact on the Oil Market. The lack of international flexibility in implementing Kyoto means that emission abatement has to occur where it is relatively expensive, while cheaper options remain unused. This places a heavier burden on oil than would a more flexible implementation. Figure 12.3 shows the impacts on oil production of a national implementation of Kyoto. Conventional oil production lies 3.9 mb/d below the BaU case in 2010 and 2.2 mb/d below in 2020. This is a greater impact than in the 'most likely' implementation scenario where the reduction from BaU is 2.1 mb/d in 2010, and 1.2 mb/d in 2020.

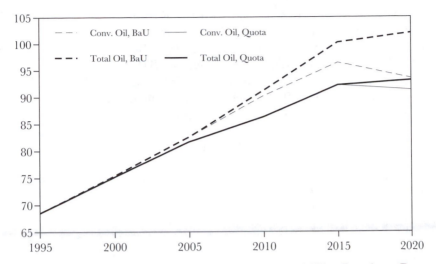

Figure 12.3:   Oil Production, BaU and National Quotas. Million Barrels per Day

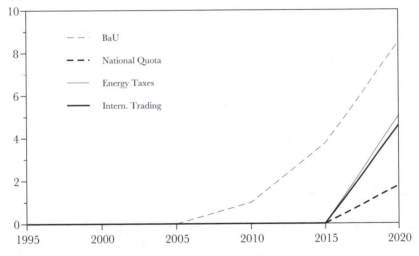

Figure 12.4:   Non-conventional Oil Production, Policy Instruments. Milllion
                   Barrels per Day

Figure 12.4 shows non-conventional oil production under the three
main climate change policy instruments discussed in this chapter, i.e.
national quotas, energy taxes, and internationally traded permits.
Under national implementation, non-conventional oil production is
delayed beyond 2015, and reaches around 1.8 mb/d in 2020, less than
half the level reached in the 'most likely' Kyoto scenario.

This strong reduction in non-conventional oil production is reflected in lower prices, when compared with the Kyoto scenario. Figure 12.5 shows that in the case of a national quota system, the demand reduction in 2010 is strong enough to reduce oil prices by 5 per cent below the 1995 level, and 17.3 per cent below the BaU level. Slow demand growth, met entirely by conventional crude until 2015, brings the price higher, and by 2020 it lies 13.6 per cent below BaU. The price response is stronger than in the Kyoto case, because emission reductions have to be made in the regions with a high oil share in energy use, in particular the Rest of OECD Europe region.

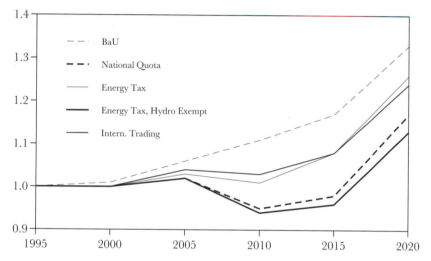

Figure 12.5:   Oil Price Index, 1995 = 1

12.3 Energy Taxes

Energy taxes are an excise levy on energy at the point of use. They are distinct from carbon taxes discussed earlier because they do not distinguish between the carbon content of the energy commodity used. The carbon content of coal is much higher than that of oil and gas. Therefore, energy taxes place a heavier burden on oil and gas, than a comparable carbon policy instrument. On the other hand, existing taxation increases the domestic price of oil products strongly above the prices for gas and coal. As shown in Chapter 11, the domestic price of coal is one-third the price of oil products per unit of energy in the USA, and one half of the price of oil in the EU. A levy on the unit of energy will therefore increase the domestic price of oil products relatively little.

This section presents simulation results based on the assumption that governments achieve the national Kyoto targets with energy taxes alone. In the model, energy taxes are determined by trial and error until a level is reached at which the countries reach emission targets. The strong differences in abatement costs manifest in the different carbon permit prices shown in the last section mean that levels of energy taxation have to differ strongly between regions in order to reach the Kyoto targets.

An increase in the domestic price of oil products due to carbon taxes makes hydrogen much more attractive, and therefore increases the impact of carbon instruments on oil. With energy instruments, it is not immediately clear whether hydrogen will be taxed or not. A strict policy of energy taxation would of course treat all sources of energy in an equal way, which means also that energy from non-carbon, renewable sources would be taxed. However, such a policy is not very likely to be implemented, at least insofar as the government uses climate change in arguing for the new tax. Even when new taxes are implemented on the basis of concerns for local pollution, it is not likely that hydrogen would be taxed equally as polluting oil products. We show therefore simulation results for two scenarios for energy taxes, one where hydrogen is taxed along with carbon energy, and one where hydrogen is exempted from taxes.

Impact on the Oil Market. Figure 12.6 shows oil supplies when the Kyoto emission targets are implemented using energy taxes only, and

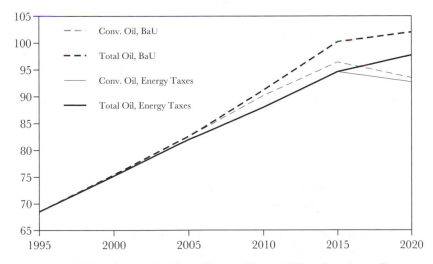

Figure 12.6:   Oil Production, BaU and Energy Taxes. Million Barrels per Day

hydrogen is taxed equally. Conventional oil supply in 2010 falls 2.3 mb/d below the BaU projections, a little less than in the Kyoto scenario. In 2020, the gap to the BaU trajectory still amounts to 0.8 mb/d. Non-conventional oil production is reduced strongly, and the total supply reduction in 2020 amounts to 4.3 mb/d from the BaU level.

As shown in Figure 12.5, all-out energy taxes have less impact on the price of oil than domestic carbon instruments, and the price increases by 1 per cent and 26 per cent from the 1995 level in 2010 and 2020 respectively. This scenario projects therefore an oil price fall from the BaU projections of 10 and 5 per cent in 2010 and 2020. However, energy taxes result in oil prices which are about the same as prices projected in the Kyoto scenario, although domestic energy taxes should place a much heavier burden on oil, with impacts at least as large as in the case of domestic carbon instruments discussed in the last section.

As mentioned in Chapter 11, in the Kyoto scenario the main impact on oil comes from the competitiveness of hydrogen, because the domestic price of hydrogen is not increased by carbon instruments. With energy taxes also on hydrogen, consumption reaches 300 thousand and 2.7 million b/d in 2010 and 2020, a drop from the BaU scenario by 1 and 2 mb/d, and less than one-third of the levels reached in the Kyoto scenario. The impact of energy taxes on oil is accordingly reduced compared to an implementation with carbon instruments, if in fact hydrogen is taxed alongside other energy sources.

Since it is not at all clear whether an energy tax regime would be applied across all sources of energy, we show in Figure 12.7 results of a simulation of energy taxes with an exemption for hydrogen. The high level of energy taxation necessary to achieve the Kyoto targets means a strong increase in the competitiveness of hydrogen, when this is exempt from taxes. This leads to a strong reduction in demand for oil. Conventional oil demand falls by 4.1 and 2.9 mb/d from BaU levels for 2010 and 2020, whereas non-conventional oil is almost not produced at all. Total oil production falls by 5.1 and 10.7 mb/d. Hydrogen production increases to 7.1 and 15.9 mb/d oil equivalent in 2010 and 2020, triple the BaU levels, and almost five times the levels reached under all-out energy taxes. Oil prices fall 15 per cent from the BaU levels, as compared with a fall of 10 and 5 per cent under all-out energy taxes for 2010 and 2020. As shown in Figure 12.5, of the policies compared in this chapter, energy taxes with an exemption for hydrogen have the strongest effect on oil.

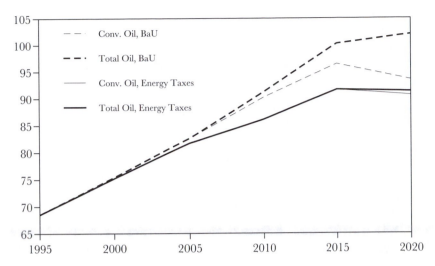

Figure 12.7:   Oil Production, BaU and Energy Taxes, Hydrogen Exempt. Million
Barrels per Day

12.4 International Emissions Trading

This section assumes that the Kyoto targets are achieved with full
flexibility between the Annex I countries. An emission restriction is set
for the region as a whole, and tradable permits are bought and sold
according to differences in emission abatement costs. It is assumed
that international permit prices are directly translated into domestic
prices. The effect is efficiency in reaching the Kyoto targets, meaning
that least-cost options for emission reductions are used.

Emissions and Permit Prices. As in the 'most likely' Kyoto scenario, we
assume a limit on the amount of 'hot air' tradable permits supplied by
the Economies in Transition. This 'hot air' reduces the reduction
efforts needed, and emission trajectories for the big Annex I countries
are similar to those shown in the 'most likely' Kyoto scenario. But the
level of trading is higher, and domestic abatement efforts especially in
Japan and the EU are lower, because these regions do not limit trading.
Figure 12.8 shows the development of the international permit price.

The permit price reaches $11 per ton of CO_2 equivalent in 2010.
By the end of the projection horizon, emission permits are traded at
$12 per ton. This is higher than the level of permit prices under the
'most likely' Kyoto scenario ($10 to $11), because domestic energy
taxes in the EU, and restrictions on trading in Japan lower the permit
price in the Kyoto scenario.

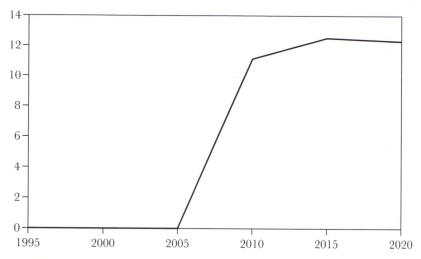

Figure 12.8:   Price for International Emission Permits. Dollars per Tonne of CO_2 Equivalent

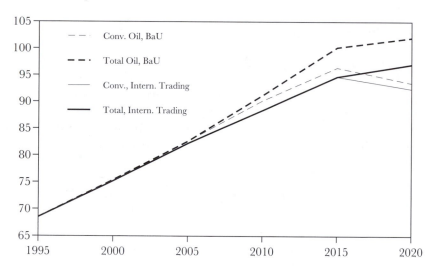

Figure 12.9:   Oil Production, BaU and International Trading. Million Barrels per Day

Impact on the Oil Market. Figure 12.9 shows total and conventional crude supplies (non-conventional crude supplies were shown in Figure 12.4) for the Business-as-Usual case and a Kyoto scenario with internationally traded emission permits. Conventional oil production is reduced by 1.8 and 1.1 mb/d below the BaU levels in 2010 and 2020 respectively. Non-conventional oil production is postponed until 2020 when it reaches 4 mb/d, about the same level reached in the 'most likely' Kyoto scenario. Hydrogen production doubles.

Figure 12.5 shows the price response to the flexible implementation of the Kyoto targets. Very little change to the BaU price trajectory is observed in 2005, because the 'hot air' supplied by the Economies in Transition (Russia and the Ukraine) means that no actual abatement effort is needed. In 2010, the oil price is 7.8 per cent below the BaU level, but still 3 per cent above the 1995 level. By 2020, the oil price falls 6.4 per cent below BaU. The use of flexibility mechanisms therefore means a lower impact of the implementation of the Kyoto Protocol emissions reduction on the oil market, but also in general. This shows the importance of flexible instruments to reduce the costs of implementing the Kyoto targets.

12.5 Energy Prices

An implementation of Kyoto with different policy instruments has different implications on energy prices in the Annex I countries. As the discussion above has shown, flexibility mechanisms lower the costs of implementation. Figure 12.10 shows increases in the price of the average bundle of energy sold in the USA, the EU, and the EIT region, for the three single policy instruments discussed in this chapter, and the 'most likely' Kyoto implementation in comparison.

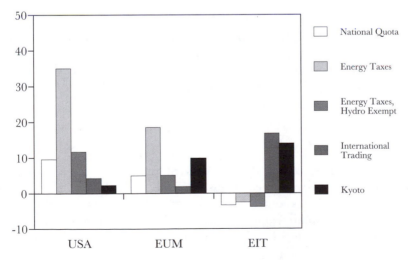

Figure 12.10: Energy Price Increase in 2020. Per Cent over BaU

The first bar in the charts shows energy price increases due to domestic carbon instruments. Energy prices in 2010 increase by 10 per cent in the USA, 5 per cent in the EU, whereas they decrease in the EIT region. In contrast, implementation of Kyoto using domestic energy taxes means energy prices increase by 35 per cent in the USA, and 19 per cent in the EU. In the EIT region, energy prices again show a net decrease, because of the reduction in fossil fuel prices due to policies in the other Annex I countries.

As in Section 12.3, we show increases of energy prices for an implementation of Kyoto with energy taxes, where hydrogen is exempt. In this case, energy prices in the USA increase 12 per cent, in the EU 5 per cent, and in the EIT region they show a decline of 4 per cent. This environmentally conscious energy tax scenario therefore has about the same costs in terms of energy price increase as the national quota system.

Using internationally traded carbon permits means energy prices increase much less in the major Annex I countries: by 4 per cent in the USA, one and a half per cent in the EU. In this case, energy prices increase by 16 per cent in the EIT region, because carbon becomes a valuable export commodity. By reducing domestic emissions substantially below the Kyoto target, the region obtains sizeable revenues in the emission trading market. The energy price increase shown in Figure 12.10 is therefore paid for by the other Annex I countries.

In the 'most likely' Kyoto scenario, energy prices increase by 3 per cent in the USA, 10 per cent in the EU, and 14 per cent in the EIT region. This shows the impact of restrictions on trading in Japan, and energy taxes in the EU. These diversions from full use of flexibility mechanisms reduce energy costs in the USA and the EIT region, and increase them in the EU and Japan. Restrictions on international flexibility therefore hurt the restricting countries, by increasing costs of climate change policies, and reducing international competitiveness.

12.6 Concluding Remarks

This chapter has shown the impacts of implementing Kyoto using different policy instruments. It has become clear that more flexibility in implementing emission restrictions generally benefits the oil markets, i.e. the more flexibility is given to economic agents to find cost-effective solutions to reduce fossil fuel use, the less impact will be felt in the oil market.

International flexibility greatly lowers the costs of reaching the Kyoto targets. Across the board energy taxes impose the least costs on oil producers, because they hit hydrogen as strongly as oil. It might not be very likely that governments would ever impose such a blind policy of energy taxation, which not only ignores the carbon content of fossil fuels, but even imposes taxes on non-carbon alternative energy. For a more environmentally conscious scenario, we have shown that an implementation of Kyoto on the basis of energy taxes with an exemption for hydrogen lowers the demand for oil and therefore oil prices rather drastically. International carbon trading should therefore be the preferred policy option for oil-producing countries.

CHAPTER 13

THE GLOBAL COMPROMISE SCENARIO

13.1 Introduction

Our Global Compromise scenario is intended to reflect a plausible state of affairs which is (i) in line with the FCCC's overall aim of stabilising Greenhouse Gas (GHG) concentrations at an acceptable level, and (ii) more ambitious in its abatement assumptions than our Kyoto scenario. The key difference between the present scenario and the Kyoto case is that we are now considering active abatement efforts by non-Annex I Parties. This will require additional assumptions concerning the FCCC process.[1] Specifically, we must make plausible suppositions concerning the modalities of developing country (DC) participation during the time-frame of the study, and, more generally, assumptions concerning post-Kyoto commitment targets both globally and for individual parties. The climate change regime of the scenario we have in mind develops in two stages.

13.2 The Global Compromise Regime

13.2.1 Stage One: up to 2010

While it is at least in principle possible that the Kyoto Protocol could be superseded by a completely new treaty with new and possibly stricter targets for a first commitment period (not necessarily the same as the Kyoto commitment period between 2008 and 2012), this seems to us highly unlikely, given the transaction costs that would be involved in such re-negotiations. Accordingly, we propose our Global Compromise set-up to begin with a sub-scenario (the 'Stage One'), covering

---

1. For the Kyoto scenario the issue of who is going to abate by how much was settled in the Kyoto Protocol, and the only 'FCCC-assumption' we had to make was our 'roll-over' assumption for the period after 2012.

the time up to the Kyoto commitment period and given by the Annex I assumptions of our Kyoto scenario together with certain additional assumptions concerning non-Annex I participation. In deference to the precedent established at Kyoto, we shall furthermore assume that any subsequent commitment period will be defined in terms of a five-year average and preceded by an adjustment period similar to the one adopted at Kyoto (i.e. around ten years). Accordingly, we shall consider a single post-Kyoto sub-scenario ('Stage Two'), with a second commitment period between 2018 and 2022, centred around 2020.

An active participation of developing countries in the FCCC abatement efforts in the period up to and including the Kyoto commitment period could be voluntary – as in the Clean Development Mechanism (CDM) or in the adoption of voluntary targets – or it could be by acceding to Annex I. The main problem with the 'participation-through-accession' option is the failure of the Kyoto Protocol to specify modalities about the way in which such an accession should be carried out. In particular, nothing is mentioned concerning the targets for such newcomers. The accession option thus allows for at least two further possibilities, namely

(i) Annex I accession under 'Kyoto-type' targets, i.e. grandfathering of a 1990 baseline minus x (with x in the region of 5 per cent).[2]
(ii) Annex I accession under 'tailor-made' targets, i.e. targets specific to the individual Parties wishing to accede.

Both these options would be more ambitious than the Kyoto scenario, at least insofar as the notion of 'targets' is assumed to involve some reduction of net emissions as measured against the BaU case. The most likely candidates for an accession under Kyoto-type targets are those developing countries which might derive a more or less immediate economic benefit from 'hot-air' trading in the Kyoto commitment period. For reasons to be discussed below, it is however highly unlikely that two of the key non-Annex I players – China and

---

2. The term 'grandfathering' generally refers to distributions proportionate to what has already been acquired in ('inherited from') the past, i.e. in proportion to a relevant historic base-line. In the case of distributing emission quotas this means, more precisely, a distribution in proportion to the emissions which the Parties have emitted in some base-line year or period. Although, strictly speaking, the Kyoto targets would only qualify as grandfathering targets under a uniform percentage cut, the deviations of the actual targets are sufficiently small to warrant the assumption that, fundamentally, the Parties at Kyoto implicitly agreed on grandfathering as the fairest starting point for negotiations on pure Annex I quotas.

India – would be willing to even contemplate such a grandfathering accession. They might, however, be tempted to accede if they were offered certain 'tailor-made' targets. The only problem with this is that there simply are not enough permits to satisfy both Annex I grandfathering and China and India's perception of acceptable 'tailor-made' Annex I accession targets.[3] This is why we dismiss the possibility of an accession of non-Annex I Parties to Annex I of the Kyoto Protocol.

By contrast, voluntary non-Annex I participation within the Kyoto framework – be it under the CDM, or, in the case of the more developed non-Annex I Parties (such as the ones in LAM and ANI), under the adoption of certain 'reasonable' voluntary targets – does seem plausible. We are, of course, aware that presently the dominant view amongst non-Annex I countries is to reject such voluntary measures; in particular, the idea of voluntary targets – be they 'reasonable' or not. For this reason we explain at some length in Annex 13.1 why we think that a change of mind in this respect may not be an implausible hypothesis. As concerns the 'reasonableness' of such voluntary requirements, we again propose to use precedent as our guide: in analogy to the obligations set for Annex I in the FCCC, we propose that voluntary targets should be defined as the stabilisation of emissions by the commitment period at 2000 levels. Such a voluntary participation would have the particular advantage of removing one of the main obstacles to the Kyoto treaty, namely the US precondition to implementing the Protocol requiring a meaningful participation of non-Annex I Parties.

In short, Stage One of our Global Compromise scenario is to be given by the assumptions that (i) the Kyoto Protocol is implemented as specified in our Kyoto scenario; and (ii) that non-Annex I regions may participate in CDM activities. LAM and ANI will adopt voluntary stabilisation for 2010 at 2000 levels.

13.2.2 Stage Two: 2010–2020

There are at least three options to be considered for our second commitment period:

3. According to our BaU projections, roughly 48 per cent of the global emissions total envisaged by the Kyoto Protocol in the first commitment period is allocated to Annex I. Under the per capita distribution, espoused by the key DCs, however, non-Annex I should be allocated around 78 per cent of permits (indeed, CHN, IND and ROW alone would jointly be allocated a percentage incompatible with the Kyoto allocation, namely 59 per cent).

(i) Stage One is carried over except for the introduction of a stricter total Annex I abatement target.

(ii) Stage One is carried over except for the admission of 'tailor-made' accession targets for non-Annex I Parties.

(iii) A new treaty (a 'Global Compromise Protocol'), with newly negotiated targets both for Annex I and non-Annex I Parties, is implemented.

The second of these options has to be the least plausible, for the very same reasons that we rejected 'tailor-made' accession targets for the first commitment period. The first option is also implausible, but for other reasons. In order to be an effective step towards satisfying the aim of the Framework Convention, Stage Two of our Global Compromise scenario will have to involve a global 2020 emissions level which is considerably lower than the one determined by the Kyoto scenario targets. Since all abatement under this first scenario option would be carried out by Annex I Parties, they would obviously face much more onerous abatement tasks than under the Kyoto scenario. And it is difficult for us to imagine that this would remain an acceptable option for them.

This leaves the last of our three options for Stage Two, where the Kyoto Protocol is superseded by a new protocol for the second commitment period. It goes without saying that the plausibility of such a Protocol being adopted, let alone implemented, stands and falls with the question whether an acceptable distribution of 2020 emissions quotas (for both Annex I and non-Annex I) can be found. Apart from purely economic considerations, this acceptability will crucially involve the question of distributive justice.

(a) Sizing the 'Cake'

Fairness is a matter of the proportions of the shares allocated to the relevant Parties. As such, it can be discussed in purely relative terms. Economic consequences, by contrast, can only be gauged from absolute figures (of assigned amounts). Given that our Global Compromise Protocol is meant to be a Protocol to the FCCC, these absolute amounts depend, in particular, on whether their sum total (the global emissions level) is consistent with the Convention's key aim of stabilising the emissions concentration at an acceptable level. Determining such an 'FCCC-consistent' global emission level for our second commitment period, however, is not unproblematic, for it is by no means self-evident what level of atmospheric GHG concentration would be a politically acceptable target. Our derivation of the 2020 global energy emissions target level of 14.4 per cent below BaU emissions – leaving us with a global energy emission level of 31.5 Gt CO_2e for the model – is based on an argument showing that the Kyoto Protocol implicitly reveals the acceptability of stabilising CO_2 concentration at 550 ppm ('parts per million'). For a detailed exposition of this argument and of the derivation of the global target level we refer to Annex 13.2.1.

(b) Distributing the 'Cake'

Given the 14.4 per cent global reduction target for 2020, the key problem for the envisaged Global Compromise Protocol is to find a distribution of these permissible global emissions which could plausibly be accepted by the main players of both Annex I and non-Annex I. Are there any indications as to conditions under which these major Parties would be willing to adopt legally binding emission caps?

By adopting the Kyoto Protocol, with its reduction targets defined in terms of 1990 baseline emissions, Annex I Parties have clearly revealed their willingness to join an abatement regime if the emission quotas ('assigned amounts') are allocated under a grandfathering scheme. The fact that, prior to Kyoto, 'African countries had started supporting a principle that emission entitlements should be allocated on a per capita basis [and that] China and, most stridently, India backed similar proposals',[4] in turn, suggests that the DC majority of non-Annex I might be willing to join an abatement regime under a per capita allocation of quotas.[5]

In other words, we do have an idea of the conditions under which the key players would be willing to join a Protocol subjecting them to legally binding emission caps. As in the case of 'tailor-made' targets discussed earlier, the problem is that these conditions are mutually incompatible. The only way forward towards an agreement of the type under consideration is to try to find an acceptable compromise between these two positions. Yet this is a more difficult task than might meet the eye, for the simple reason that the Parties in both camps consider their position to be equity based, i.e. they see their own position as the *only* fair way of distributing the quotas. This obviously does not create an atmosphere conducive to compromise. After all, why should one compromise if one clearly feels in the right?

The chances of compromise are indeed slim, unless the Parties

---

4. M. Grubb, *The Kyoto Protocol: A Guide and Assessment* (London: RIIA and Earthscan 1999), p.95.
5. Per capita distributions are distributions in proportion to the population figures in some base-line year.

bring themselves to admit that they are dealing with a morally complex situation, in which there is more than one morally justifiable position to be held.[6] However, when they come to this realisation, the way will be cleared for a compromise procedure, first introduced by Müller,[7] which we believe just might produce a distribution acceptable to both camps. The idea is simply to 'mix' the two incompatible distribution proposals – in a manner akin to the well-known 'Norwegian Formula' (see Box 13.1)[8] – by forming a 'socially weighted' arithmetic mean between them. Under the resulting compromise proposal – called 'Preference Score Distribution' – a Party is to be allocated an assigned amount (*PS*) determined by the formula:

$$PS = w_{GF} \cdot GF + w_{PC} \cdot PC$$

GF and *PC* are the assigned amounts the Party would have received under the grandfathering and the per capita proposal, respectively (see Table 13.1). The normalised[9] weights w_{GF} and w_{PC}, in turn, reflect the 'social desirability' of these proposals. They are determined by a simple

---

6. Both the grandfathering and the per capita position on emission quota distributions are equity based, i.e. they can both be justified in terms of moral principles, namely in terms of entitlement and egalitarian theories, respectively. For a detailed analysis of the equity issues involved in quota distributions, and indeed of the possibilities to reach a compromise solution, see Benito Müller, *Justice in Global Warming Negotiations: How to Achieve a Procedurally Fair Compromise* (OIES: Oxford, second edition 1999).

7. Ibid.

8. The compromise procedure which we have in mind, it has to be emphasised, is not limited to the sort of basic mixtures of two simple distributions considered in the present context. Indeed, its advantages only become self-evident in the context of mixtures of three or more base distributions, such as the one carried out in the Norwegian Proposal. The problem with this formula, however, is that it is not a compromise formula in our sense. Indeed, Asbjørn Thorvanger, one of its architects, confirmed in a personal communication that the formula was designed to introduce additional differentiation into a commonly accepted initial position (i.e. grandfathering amongst Annex I Parties), and *not*, as required in our present scenario, to create an acceptable compromise out of mutually incompatible positions. For more on the Norwegian formula, see Lasse Ringius, Asbjørn Torvanger and Bjart Holtsmark, 'Can Multi-Criteria Rules Fairly Distribute Climate Burdens? OECD Results from Three Burden Sharing Rules,' *Energy Policy* 26(10) (August 1998), pp. 777–93.

9. The term 'normalised' here simply refers to the fact that they are meant to add up to 1.

Box 13.1: The Norwegian Proposal

In a formula, the weighted sum of the above indicators for individual Parties could be related to the average for a group of countries (for example the Annex I Parties). If it is assumed that the group agrees on a target for the group as a whole, the indicators suggested could be used to determine the specific targets for individual Parties. Such targets should be determined as annual emissions relative to the projected level for a specified year. By attaching weights to the individual indicators, the three indicators could be combined and constructed as a multi-criteria indicator. By varying the values of the weights, varying importance could be attached to the different indicators.

An example of a formula in line with this proposal is given below. When an agreed protocol or another legal instrument is to be renegotiated at a later time, the weights in the formula can be adjusted in line with new knowledge.

$$Y_i = A[x(B_i/B) + y(C_i/C) + z(D_i/D)]$$

where Y_i is the percentage reduction of emissions for Party i. The relation of B_i to B is CO_2 equivalent emissions per unit of GDP for Party i relative to the average in the Annex I Parties. The relation C_i to C is the GDP per capita in Party i relative to the average in the Annex I Parties, while the relation of D_i to D is the CO_2 equivalent emissions per capita in Party i relative to the average of the Annex I Parties. A is a scale factor to ensure that the desired overall reduction in emissions is achieved. The coefficients x, y and z are weights, which add up to a total of 1.

FCCC/AGBM/1997/2, Art 98.2

---

preference score procedure carried out by the Parties in question: each of the Parties ranks the two base distributions according to its preferences and expresses this ranking by assigning what are called 'single preference scores', namely in the present two-option case, the score 1 to the one it prefers, and 0 to the other. While our two weights could be determined on the basis of these single preference scores, we prefer – for reasons explained in Annex 13.2.2 – to use 'global preference scores', given by multiplying the single scores by the population figures of the relevant Parties. Our two weights are then given by the normalised proportions of the total global preference scores assigned in this manner to the two base distributions. Thus if the per capita and the grandfathering option manage to attract, say, 4.9bn and 1.6bn global preference scores, respectively (Table A.13.5),

Table 13.1: Assigned Energy Emission Amounts (Including Banking). 2020

	Per Capita (Mt CO$_2$e)	Grandfathering (Mt CO$_2$e)	Preference Score (Mt CO$_2$e)
USA	1,442	6,852	2,768
JPN	665	1,465	861
EUM	1,986	4,027	2,486
ROE	63	94	70
ROO	270	1,075	467
EIT	3,297	6,339	4,043
CHN	6,407	4,253	5,879
IND	4,939	1,136	4,007
ANI	2,202	1,501	2,030
AOE	1,395	1,631	1,453
LAM	2,172	1,366	1,974
ROW	6,619	1,719	5,418
World	31,458	31,458	31,458

then the proportion $w_{PC} : w_{GF}$ is meant to be 4.9bn : 1.6bn, which – given that the weights are intended to add up to 1 – means that $w_{PC} = 0.75$ and $w_G = 0.25$. Figure 13.1 and Table A13.6 show the shares the different Parties would be allocated under the two base distributions and our compromise proposal, and Table 13.1 lists the absolute figures for the assigned amounts (including banked credits from the first commitment period) as used in the model.

We take this Preference Score distribution to be a plausible compromise between the grandfathering and the per capita camps *not* because everyone is supposed to accept it as the fairest solution. On the contrary, the idea is that (i) having accepted the moral complexity of the situation, the Parties would have realised that in this case accepting a compromise need not be a sign of lacking moral fibre, and (ii) they would accept the Preference Score proposal as sufficiently fair (due to the transparent and equitable nature of the procedure used in determining it) for it to be preferable to a break-down in negotiations.

Having said this, it must be emphasised that the acceptability of such a compromise quota distribution proposal is not only a matter of 'retrospective' distributional equity,[10] but also of the ensuing economic

---

10. The egalitarian and entitlement arguments put forward for the per capita and the grandfathering solution are arguments which are not based on potential effects of the possession of quotas. They see such quotas as 'rewards', which are not to be judged on the potential effects they might have on the recipient, but only on the merit accrued in the past or present.

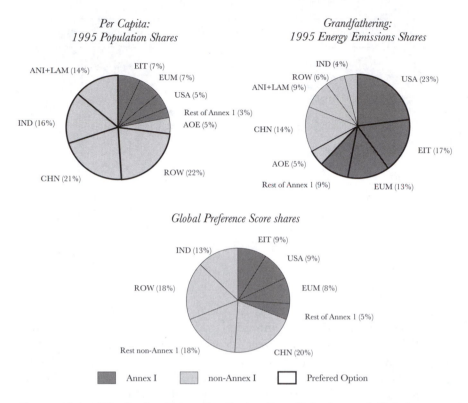

Figure 13.1:   Distribution Shares. Per Capita, Grandfathering, and Global
Preference Scores

implications, and, indeed, of the compatibility with the relevant legal
framework (the FCCC). For example, even though grandfathering may
be a morally perfectly justifiable position, in the context of our 2020
quota allocation it would entail a distribution which clearly would not
conform to the spirit of the FCCC, for it would allow Annex I Parties
to *increase* their emissions after 2010 by a staggering 40 per cent (Table
A.13.7). Both the Per Capita and the Preference Score distributions,
by contrast, require further Annex I abatement by 46 and 25 per cent,
respectively. (For a detailed discussion of these issues see Annex 13.2.2.)

13.3 Emission Reductions, Emission Trading, and the 'Hot Air Problem'

Having specified the environmental regime for our Global Compromise
scenario, in particular the assigned amounts for the two commitment

periods, we now turn to discuss some of its general economic implications, namely the ones arising from the use of international emission transfer mechanisms permitted under this regime. The aim of this discussion is to evaluate the acceptability of the envisaged Global Compromise distribution with respect to these specific consequences. We are, of course, aware that to give a proper consequentialist evaluation of the acceptability of the Global Compromise distribution, many other factors would have to be considered, in particular, the costs avoided through the mitigation efforts. However, as such an analysis would clearly go beyond the intended scope of this book – and, indeed, beyond the capacities of our model – we have to content ourselves with the following partial evaluation. Section 13.3.1 prepares the ground by describing the projected emission trajectories for the regions. In Secton 13.3.2 we turn to the actual analysis of emission trading under the Global Compromise assumptions, with particular reference to the issue of surplus permits. Section 13.3.3 puts these results into a somewhat more general context by describing some welfare implications estimated by our model.

13.3.1 Emissions by Region

The regional energy emission (combustion CO_2 and fugitive fuel CH_4) projections for the major emitters together with their emission targets ('assigned amounts'[11]) for the commitment periods are depicted in Figures 13.2 (Annex I) and 13.3 (non-Annex I).

As in the Kyoto scenario, the Economies in Transition (EIT) emerge as the suppliers of international emission permits in the year 2010. Business-as-Usual emissions for this year are far below their assigned amount. Again, the region limits the supply of 'hot air' emission permits to 2 per cent of total demand while at the same time reducing emissions by about 800 Mt to take advantage of monetary transfers through Joint Implementation. Limits on the sales of 'hot air' mean that the region has a large amount of unused permits in the first commitment period. Through banking, these can be carried over to the next commitment period, thus increasing the region's emission target for 2020 by 1,200Mt CO_2e.

---

11. To avoid misunderstandings, given the five-year average nature of our model parameters, we are strictly speaking dealing here with average annual parts of assigned amounts for the commitment periods. In other words, actual assigned amounts for the periods would be five times the figures quoted here.

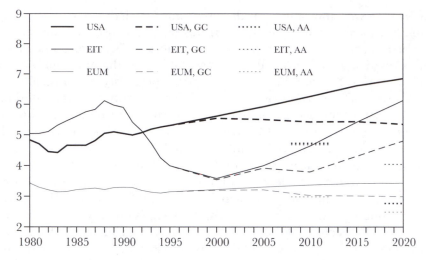

Figure 13.2:   Energy Emissions (Annex I). BaU, Global Compromise (GC), and Assigned Amounts (AA). Gt CO_2e

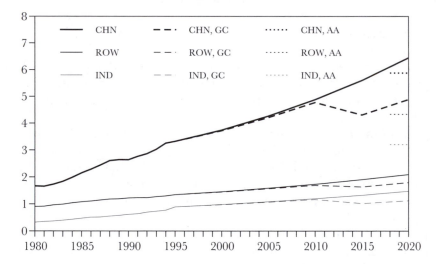

Figure 13.3:   Energy Emissions (non-Annex I). BaU, Global Compromise (GC), and Assigned Amounts (AA). Gt CO_2e

However, in contrast to the Kyoto scenario, these banked credits are insufficient for EIT to meet its emission target of 4,000Mt in the subsequent commitment period. The region therefore has to undertake significant domestic abatement or buy permits. Figure 13.2 shows that domestic emissions are reduced substantially, but remain above the assigned amount. The region meets about two-thirds of its 2020 abatement requirements by domestic action and one-third by the use of the flexibility mechanisms (Table 13.2). The USA, in contrast, buys two-thirds of its reduction requirement of 4,100Mt CO_2e, while the EU roughly balances its use of flexibility and domestic action at 500Mt and 400Mt, respectively.

For India and the Rest of the World (ROW) region, emission targets or assigned amounts for the year 2020 are well above BaU emissions, thus leaving the two regions with a substantial amount of surplus permits. China's BaU emissions lie by a small margin above assigned amounts, which means they have to undertake some domestic abatement in any case, whereas India and ROW have room to increase emissions even above their BaU paths.

The surplus permits of the latter two regions are of considerable economic importance. Emission levels shown in Figures 13.2 and 13.3 for the Global Compromise scenario are in total about 20 per cent below BaU emissions, given that India and ROW limit surplus permits to 80 per cent of their assigned amounts. If none of the surplus permits were available in the international permit market, global emissions would have to be reduced by an additional 10 per cent of BaU emissions below the levels shown in this chapter, i.e. global emission

Table 13.2: Surplus Permits, Permit Sales and Domestic Abatement Levels. 2020. Mt CO_2e

	Required Reduction[a] ('+'= Surplus)	Actual Reduction from BaU ('Domestic Action')	Permit Sales ('+' = sale, '−' = purchase)			Supplement-arity Level[c] (%)
			Total Permits	Surplus permits[b]	JI/CDM permits	
USA	-4,091	-1,506	-2,585			37
JPN	-418	-177	-241			42
EUM	-943	-439	-504			47
ROE	-25	-3	-22			12
ROO	-583	-153	-429			26
EIT	-2,092	-1,327	-764			63
CHN	-568	-1,561	992		992	
IND	2,887	-354	2,086	1,732	354	
ANI	-293	-279	-15			95
AOE	-1,670	-480	-1,190			29
LAM	-469	-602	133		133	
ROW	3,622	-296	2,538	2,242	296	

(a) Required reduction = assigned amounts (Table 13.1) − BaU.
(b) Under weak cartel quotas.
(c) Percentage of domestic action of the required reduction.

abatement would be almost 30 per cent of BaU emissions with accordingly much larger impacts on economies in general and fossil fuels in particular.

13.3.2 Emission Trading and the 'Hot Air Problem'

Figure 13.4 shows emission reductions and assigned amounts for the world. The amounts assigned to India and ROW under the Global Compromise Protocol are both over one and a half times greater than their projected 2020 BaU emissions. We assume that the two regions manage to create a surplus permit cartel, amounting to a self-imposed reduction of their assigned amounts by 20 per cent each. Still, India and ROW emerge as the biggest suppliers of internationally traded emission permits. India reduces emissions below her assigned amount by 350Mt CO_2e in 2020, and sells 2,100Mt worth of permits. The biggest supplier is the ROW region with 2,500Mt of permits sold. China reduces emissions by 1,600Mt from the BaU scenario, of which she is able to sell 1000Mt.

Global emissions are reduced by 19.5 per cent below BaU levels projected for the year 2020, as compared with 8 per cent in the Kyoto scenario. China, India, and Latin America reduce emissions the most in terms of per cent reductions from BaU levels, with reductions around

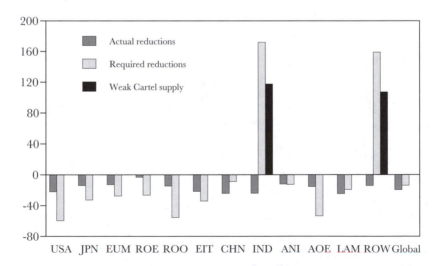

Figure 13.4:   Actual and Required 2020 Energy Emission Reductions.* Surplus Permit Supply. Per Cent of BaU Emissions

*Required Emission Reductions = Assigned Amounts minus BaU emissions

24 per cent of BaU emissions for 2020. Given low efficiency in the provision of energy in the two poorest regions in this overview, the potential for cheap emission abatement is large. However, all of the Indian effort and two-thirds of the Chinese one are paid for by the sale of emission permits, i.e. by the industrialised countries with high abatement costs. At around 22 per cent, the USA's and EIT's relative domestic abatement efforts are nearly as high as in China and India. ROE, ROO and AOE make the greatest use of international flexibility by buying emission permits and reducing domestic emissions less strongly (see Figure 13.5 and Table 13.2).

The more stringent global emissions constraint in the year 2020 as compared with the Kyoto scenario means that the global permit price for greenhouse gas emissions increases by 40 per cent from the Kyoto scenario. Already in 2010, emission permit prices in the Global Compromise scenario are higher, where permits are traded at $11 and $16 per ton of CO_2e, as opposed to $10 and $11 for the 'most likely' Kyoto case, in 2010 and 2020, respectively. This is due to voluntary restrictions of the ANI and LAM regions and arises even though the two regions do not take part in international permit trading in 2010. Their voluntary emission reductions however lead to lower prices for fossil fuels in the Global Compromise scenario as compared with the Kyoto scenario. The domestic price increases needed to reduce emissions in the Global Compromise scenario to the Kyoto targets in 2010 are then necessarily greater than in the Kyoto scenario. Emission permit prices therefore increase.

So-called 'hot air' – or, more precisely, 'hot air' trading – has had a rather bad press in environmental quarters. Michael Grubb, for

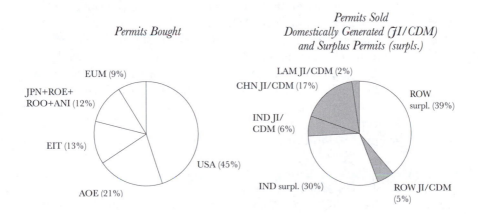

Figure 13.5:   Global Emission Permit Transfers

example, dedicates a substantial part of his discussion of the Kyoto mechanisms to the 'hot air problem', which he perceives to be a potential cause for breakdown of the climate change process:

> Potentially the most fatal aspect of hot air trading [under the Kyoto regime] is its implications for the expansion of the regime. If countries presently within Annex I are allowed both to obtain and then to trade assigned amounts that turn out to be far in excess of their needs, there would appear to be no politically plausible way of preventing other countries from joining on a similar basis in the future (at least as long as allocations remain based on ad-hoc national bargaining). Failure to tackle 'hot air' trading could thus lead to the whole Kyoto system ballooning.[12]

There is no doubt that the type of 'ballooning' described by Grubb would ultimately be incompatible with the aim of the FCCC, but this is not a problem of surplus permits per se, but of the ad hoc manner in which assigned amounts were allocated at Kyoto.[13] The surplus permits allocated in Stage Two of our Global Compromise scenario, by contrast, are environmentally completely benign, given our assumptions about the acceptable global 2020 emission level. Moreover, there is nothing morally shady in their allocation, for the recipients have a legitimate claim to the share they are allocated under the Preference Score distribution used in our Global Compromise scenario. Consequently, they are also entitled to maximise the income they can derive from this legitimately acquired resource. The surplus emission permits in the Global Compromise scenario should therefore really not be described as being 'hot' (with its stolen property connotations). If anything, they should be referred to as 'sweet air'.

As in the case of our Kyoto scenario, the size of resource transfers from emissions trading in the second commitment period – and, in particular, the income derived from the sale of surplus permits – depends again on the degree of supply cartelisation achieved. For example, sensitivity analysis has shown that if there is no cartel at all – i.e. if all the surplus permits in the system are traded – the permit price in 2020 reaches $9.70, about two-thirds of the level achieved through the supply restrictions adopted in the weak cartel of our Global Compromise scenario. In the 'no cartel' case, the OECD region pays on average, $35bn (0.1 per cent of BaU real income) each year

---

12. M. Grubb, *The Kyoto Protocol: A Guide and Assessment* (London: The Royal Institute of International Affairs, 1999), p.214.
13. The fact that the Kyoto allocations can be interpreted as an instance of the grandfathering principle does not alter the purely 'strategic' manner in which they were arrived at.

Table 13.3: Average Annual Resource Transfers from Emission Trading in the Second Commitment Period (2018–2022). Billion $ and Per Cent

	Kyoto ('roll over')		No Cartel		Weak Cartel		Strong Cartel	
	Billion $	%	Billion $	%	Billion $	%	Billion $	%
USA	-9.23	-0.08	-23.91	-0.20	-41.50	-0.35	-67.42	-0.56
JPN	-0.07	0.00	-2.23	-0.03	-3.87	-0.05	-4.23	-0.05
EUM	-0.50	0.00	-4.66	-0.03	-8.10	-0.06	-14.03	-0.10
ROE	-0.24	-0.03	-0.20	-0.03	-0.35	-0.05	-0.77	-0.11
ROO	-1.68	-0.10	-3.97	-0.25	-6.89	-0.43	-12.78	-0.79
OECD	-11.72	-0.03	-34.98	-0.10	-60.72	-0.17	-99.23	-0.28
EIT	11.73	0.63	-7.07	-0.38	-12.27	-0.66	29.89	1.61
CHN			9.18	0.32	15.93	0.56	46.85	1.65
IND			19.29	2.16	33.48	3.75	23.95	2.68
ANI			-0.14	0.00	-0.24	-0.01	4.29	0.11
AOE			-11.01	-0.58	-19.10	-1.01	-29.95	-1.59
LAM			1.23	0.03	2.13	0.06	14.14	0.37
ROW			23.48	1.15	40.75	1.99	22.12	1.08
GDG			51.95	0.90	90.17	1.56	92.92	1.61

of the commitment period and what we call the 'Green Developing Group' – GDG = CHN+IND+ROW, see Annex 13.1.3 – receives $52bn (0.9 per cent), as shown in Table 13.3.

Under a strong cartel, where the surplus permit suppliers manage to limit their supply to, say, 10 per cent of their BaU emissions, the situation will be quite different: permit prices increase to $33/t CO_2e, the OECD pays $99bn (0.3 per cent) and the GDG receives $93bn (1.6 per cent). Finally, under the Global Compromise scenario with its rather weak cartel, the permit price is $16/t, and the OECD pays $61bn (0.2 per cent) while the GDG receives $90bn (1.6 per cent).[14]

The total annual volume of the permit trade in our Global Compromise scenario is slightly higher at $92bn. As shown in Figure 13.6, almost two-thirds of this volume is bought by the USA (45 per cent) and the AOE (21 per cent) regions, highlighting a potential equity problem which will have to be addressed: Under all the global regimes discussed, the Middle East and North Africa region will face emission abatement costs which can justifiably be regarded as disproportionate to its level of development (see Table A.13.2). However, since these are costs incurred through mitigation efforts, it stands to reason that they would qualify for compensation under the

---

14. Given the rather large number of countries which would have to be involved in order to achieve such a high degree of cartelisation, we consider our weak cartel more plausible.

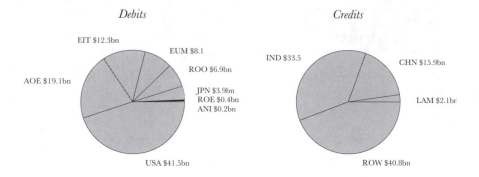

Figure 13.6: Global Compromise. Average Annual Resource Transfers from
Emission Trading (2018–2022)

FCCC, say through the Global Environment Facility (GEF).[15] We shall
return to this issue when we discuss the welfare implications of the
different regimes at the end of this section.

Compared with current annual aid flows from the members of the
OECD Development Assistance Committee of around 0.25 per cent
GDP, we believe that OECD countries would not be able to argue
convincingly that even the strong cartel is too costly. Given India's
base period (1995) export earnings of $30.5bn,[16] its permit earnings of
$33.5bn (under the Global Compromise assumptions) should also look
rather appealing. China, in turn, should at least find the economic
consequences of the strong cartel acceptable, under which it stands to
make an annual gain of $47bn. However, it is questionable whether it
would be able to impose such a cartel on India and ROW – who after
all own the surplus permits (Table 13.2) – since these two least
developed regions jointly stand to gain over 60 per cent more under
the weak cartel. The only 'hot air problem' in our Global Compromise
scenario is really a strictly economic question, namely whether the
surplus permit suppliers will be able to form a cartel or not, and if yes,
at which level.

The degree of surplus permit cartelisation, as mentioned before, has
an effect on the degree of global abatement which will have to be

---

15. Currently, the GEF (www.gefweb.org) provides funds to defray the added
    costs of making projects planned in developing countries and economies in
    transition 'environmentally friendly'. Yet this does not exclude the possibility
    that at a later stage, it could be used to defray more general added
    environmental costs.
16. IMF, *International Financial Statistics Yearbook 1996.*

attained. The less surplus permits available, the higher the degree of actual abatement which is required. Indeed, the global emission projections for 2020 range from our (presumed cost-effective) 14.4 per cent below BaU in the case of no cartel to 29 per cent below BaU for the strong cartel, with 19.5 per cent for the weak cartel. This means that, due to the cartelisation, the abatement undertaken in our Global Compromise scenario is globally less efficient than least-cost abatement under the no cartel option, but it would be rather 'blue-eyed' to think that the least developed countries would forsake the additional income they can derive from limiting the surplus permit supply just for the sake of 'global efficiency'.

13.3.3 Some Welfare Implications

In assessing the political acceptability of a treaty such as the one envisaged in our Global Compromise scenario, it would be unwise to focus exclusively on whether the environmental emission caps are distributed equitably when judged with the past actions or entitlements of the Parties involved. Another question which minimally must be addressed is the acceptability, and indeed fairness of the future (economic) welfare consequences which the treaty would entail.

In the context of our macro-economic modelling analysis, there are two welfare indicators which would generally be used for this purpose, namely Real Income (RI) and Gross Domestic Product (GDP). In this brief discussion we shall employ the former, for the latter, we believe, is not a good economic welfare indicator: GDP is an indicator of the level of domestic economic activity for it reflects only the value of goods produced domestically. It does not capture terms of trade effects of policy changes. RI is a much better indicator because it measures directly the amount of goods available to the domestic consumer.

Real Income calculated from the simulation results is based on both price and quantity changes for goods and services. We therefore have to compare situations where more of one and less of another good is available. Comparing simply values of goods and services does not give accurate information about welfare changes, and indices are needed instead.

There are two basic indices used in welfare comparisons: the Paasche and the Laspeyres index.[17] Consider two situations, a base or initial situation 1 and a simulated situation 2 after a parameter change

---

17. This section follows Dervis et. al., *General Equilibrium Models for Development Policy* (Washington D.C.: World Bank, 1982), 245ff.

characterised by consumption bundles C^1 and C^2 and price vectors P^1 and P^2.

The Paasche index, call it π, evaluates old and new consumption bundles both at new prices, so

$$\pi = \sum_s P_s^2 C_s^2 \bigg/ \sum_s P_s^2 C_s^1$$

where s stands for the commodities in the consumption basket.

If $\pi > 1$ then the new bundle of goods has a higher value than the old bundle if both are evaluated at new prices. The Laspeyres index, call it l, evaluates old and new consumption bundles at old prices. Evaluated at old prices, an index value greater than one shows that the new consumption bundle has a higher value than the old. If prices are determined in a competitive market and using the theory of revealed preference we can use both indices to compare consumer welfare between the two situations. A value greater than one for the Paasche index constitutes a sufficient condition for an increase in welfare, whereas the Laspeyres index can only give a necessary condition. We therefore use the Paasche index to compare impacts of international transfers from emission trading.

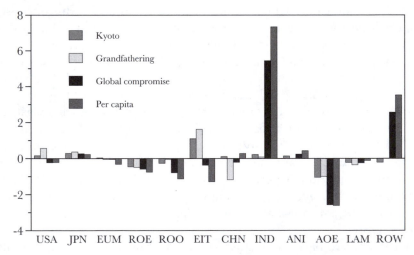

Figure 13.7:   Regional Changes in 2020 Real Income from BaU. Per Cent

Figure 13.7 shows the regional percentage changes in 2020 Real Income from the BaU situation as induced by the Kyoto scenario, the Global Compromise scenario, as well as certain modified versions of the latter. If changes of less than a percentage point can be said to be small (or even negligible), then there are only two discernible RI changes from BaU under the Kyoto scenario: EIT wins while AOE loses, both by just slightly more than 1 per cent. Whether a single percentage point change is indeed seen as significant or not depends, of course, on one's perspective, but it does pale in comparison with the sort of changes arising in the context of the Global Compromise scenario.

Under the assumptions of this Global Compromise scenario, we find EIT incurring a loss of 1.4 per cent, while AOE's loss increases more than two-fold its Kyoto level to 2.6 per cent, again almost exactly matching the gains of a winner, this time the second least developed of our regions (Table A.13.2), namely ROW. The most dramatic change, however, is reserved to our least developed model region, IND, which manages to improve its Real Income by an unquestionably impressive 5.4 per cent under the Global Compromise scenario.

Indeed, if it were not for the negative impact on EIT, and even more so on AOE, it could be argued that the welfare changes induced by the Global Compromise scenario are not only justifiable but desirable, by benefiting the least privileged (the regions with low Human Development Index) while leaving the others reasonably unaffected. Given the relatively large (annual) abatement costs incurred, say, by the AOE region of $26.7bn (1.4 per cent of BaU GDP),[18] however, it stands to reason that this negative impact could be significantly reduced by way of abatement assistance, as envisaged under the Framework Convention (and *mutatis mutandis* for EIT).

---

18. $19.1bn for permit acquisition and (a maximum of) $7.6bn for domestic action.

ANNEX TO CHAPTER 13

DETAILED ANALYSIS OF THE GLOBAL COMPROMISE REGIME

A13.1 The Issue of Voluntary Targets

Our Global Compromise scenario assumes two non-Annex I regions, LAM and ANI, as voluntarily participating in the abatement efforts under the Kyoto Protocol by stabilising their emissions at 2000 levels in the Kyoto commitment period, i.e. for the purposes of our model, in 2010. To assess the plausibility of this Stage One assumption, we have to say a few words about the GHG Policies of the non-Annex I Parties to the FCCC.

A.13.1.1 The Group of 77

The non-Annex I GHG policies are dominated by a coalition known as the 'Group of 77' (G77) – or 'Group of 77 and China'[1] – formed in 1964 to 'provide the means for the developing world to articulate and promote its collective economic interests and enhance its joint negotiating capacity on all major international economic issues in the United Nations System'.[2] This predominance will not be surprising, considering that more than 90 per cent of the non-Annex I membership is made up by G77 members –the most notable exceptions being Israel, Jordan, South Korea (OECD), and Mexico (OECD).[3]

Comprising roughly two-thirds of all the Parties to the FCCC, the G77 has the potential of being *the* dominant player in climate change

---

1. For the sake of simplicity we shall use 'G77', since China is actually a member of the Group of 77.
2. www.g77.org/geninfo/whatis77.htm
3. There are several G77 members – such as Afghanistan, Angola, Bosnia-H., Brunei, Iraq, Libya, and Somalia – which are actually not (as yet) Parties to the FCCC. Taiwan, not being recognised by the UN, is neither a member of G77 nor a signatory to the FCCC.

negotiations as a whole, simply on grounds of numerical superiority. However, this potential strength in numbers can only be realised if the numbers in question 'pull in the same direction'. The failure to actualise this potential is largely due to the multifarious positions and interest groups within the G77 membership. This heterogeneity, however, is not confined to climate change issues. Originally designed to represent the economic interests of developing countries, it now includes members of all levels of economic development. This becomes evident if we look at the distribution of its membership according to the UN Human Development Index (HDI): far from having members only from the lower end of the development spectrum, the G77 membership is divided almost evenly into Low- (35 per cent, incl. India), Medium- (35 per cent, China) and High- (29 per cent, Brazil) development countries (Figure A.13.1).

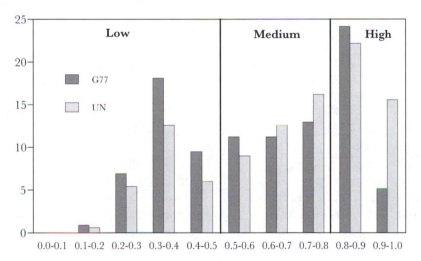

Figure A.13.1: Percentages of Membership at Different Levels of the Human Development Index (HDI). G77 & UN

On top of these economic differences, the G77 also faces strong internal tensions due to diverging interests concerning the climate change issue itself. The main concern of its OPEC members is that GHG abatement efforts, particularly amongst OECD countries, might have a detrimental effect on income derived from exporting crude oil and petroleum products. Consequently they have seen it in their interest to minimise if not prevent any such efforts. The Alliance of Small Island States (AOSIS) – a group of small, low lying island states – not surprisingly has a rather different attitude towards GHG abatement. They too fear a detrimental effect on their economies. But their fear is not about the loss of some GDP percentage points, they are rather worried that if abatement efforts are not stringent enough, they might end up with not having a GDP at all.

A.13.1.2 The G77 and Voluntary Targets

At COP1 (the first session of the Conference of the Parties to the FCCC in Berlin 1995), Germany proposed that progress should be made 'towards commitments to limit the rise of emissions in the case of certain advanced developing countries'. This proposal, perceived as an attempt by industrialised countries to draw India and China into making commitments to restrict GHG emissions, was vociferously rejected by India together with all other 'insidious moves to divide the developing countries into new categories'. Realising that the proposal was blocking the Protocol process, Germany, being the host, withdrew it. Another proposal, submitted by AOSIS demanded that developed countries should cut their CO_2 emissions by 20 per cent from their 1990 level by 2005. By contrast to the German proposal, there was no consensus amongst the G77 members as to whether the AOSIS demand should be supported or not, even though it originated from within the G77. The notion of abatement, let alone abatement on the scale envisaged by AOSIS, was anathema to OPEC, which feared that it might lead to unacceptable losses in oil revenues. Indeed, OPEC even refused to adopt the 'Berlin Mandate', the outcome of COP1, which was generally seen as a success for developing countries by affirming that the process which was to lead to the Kyoto Protocol would not introduce any new commitments for non-Annex I countries and instead reaffirm and advance the commitments of Annex I Parties to the FCCC. Interestingly, OPEC's steadfast refusal to accept a process aimed at the introduction of abatement targets for Annex I countries led to the formation of a new (albeit short-lived) 'Green Group' within the G77 which did not include OPEC, and this despite the preceding G77 rhetoric against introducing any kind of new categories amongst (DC) Parties.

The Ad Hoc Group on the Berlin Mandate (AGBM) met eight times between 1995 and 1997 in order to produce a draft Protocol to be deliberated at COP3 in December 1997 in Kyoto. At its final session before Kyoto, the United States declared that it would not assume binding obligations until there was 'meaningful participation from key developing nations,' and the draft Protocol submitted to the conference contained an article on voluntary commitments by non-

---

Box A13.1: India's Climate Change Policies

Almost 95 per cent of India's 1995 anthropogenic CO_2 emissions (881 Mt CO_2) are energy sector emissions, dominated by emissions from power generation (Power: 47%, Industry: 30%, Transport: 12%, Residential/ Commercial: 5.8%). Its methane emissions of 422 Mt CO_2e, by contrast, are primarily from the agriculture sector (Livestock: 63%, Rice Cultivation: 23%, Energy: 14%, Waste: 4%).

By the 1992 UNCED (UN Conference on Environment and Development) in Rio, it was clear that *global environmental* issues, such as climate change and sea-level rise, are low on the Indian policy agenda. Indeed, most of the problems listed as high priority issues by the Indian government were concerned with development, namely population growth, poverty, and agriculture. The only high priority environmental problem was local community waste. In order to promote this agenda, India had worked from the beginning with China to prepare a common position for the UNCED, not just for themselves, but with other major DCs in the G77. Being mainly an agenda for development, the G77 was seen as the most appropriate constituency. India and China soon emerged as the leaders of the G77 in all the preparatory negotiations for the Rio summit.

It is therefore not surprising that the G77 position in the preparatory negotiations concerned specifically with climate change (leading to the FCCC, signed at Rio) was dominated by developmental concerns. The Indian government, in particular, argued that the envisaged convention should not divert international development assistance into various forms of 'green aid'. Any funding for DCs under the convention should be additional to the existing commitment concerning development assistance (0.7 per cent of OECD GNP by 2000). Another main concern of the Indian government was to have the convention recognise certain key differences between ICs and DCs in the climate change context. India insisted on noting in the preamble to the convention that 'the largest share of historical and current global emissions of greenhouse gases has originated in developed countries, that per capita emissions in developing countries are still relatively low and that the share of global emissions originating in developing countries will grow to meet their social and development needs'.

Accordingly, India tabled a draft text for the convention advocating a per capita handling of national CO_2 emissions. Indeed, it proposed further that a convergence of per capita emissions over time should be required under the convention. Although neither of these points were included in the FCCC, they remain important for the simple reason that there have been no major changes in the Indian position in the period since. The main concerns of the Indian government remain:

Box 13.1: *continued*

- securing the commitments undertaken by the ICs, both with respect to the assigned amounts and the promises of technological and financial transfers to DCs.
- achieving equity in accordance with the principle of 'common but differentiated responsibilities' adopted in the FCCC.

Sources: Susanne Jacobson, *India's Position on Climate Change from Rio to Kyoto: A Policy Analysis* Centre for Development Research Working Paper 98.11, Copenhagen 1998; Joyeeta Gupta, *The Climate Change Convention and Developing Countries: From Conflict to Consensus*, Dordrecht: Kluwer, 1997

Annex I countries. According to this article, non-Annex I countries voluntarily taking on commitments would have been permitted to participate in joint implementation and emission trading. Interestingly, the two OECD non-Annex I countries, Mexico and South Korea, both issued declarations in support of such voluntary commitments. At Kyoto, however, this article was deleted after strong opposition by India and China who questioned the legality of creating a new category of Parties under the Convention. Another draft text, tabled by New Zealand, called for 'progressive engagement of developing countries according to relative levels of development' under which a process to set binding non-Annex I targets for future commitment periods was to be established by 2002. It was also rejected, not only by the G77 but also by the EU, mainly for not being helpful to the negotiations at hand. In accordance with the Berlin Mandate, the Kyoto Protocol was consequently adopted without any further reference to non-Annex I targets, voluntary or not.

The topic, however, was to reappear in its voluntary guise at COP4 in 1998 in Buenos Aires. While the issue was deleted from the provisional agenda put forward by the host, Argentina, at the instance of the G77, it resurfaced in the second week with the President of Argentina's announcement that it would undertake a voluntary abatement commitment at COP5. In what looked rather like an orchestrated move, the United States signed the Kyoto Protocol less than 24 hours after this declaration, stating that 'as the first developing country to make this pledge, Argentina demonstrates great leadership, real courage, and a deep appreciation that climate change is a truly global challenge that demands a truly global solution.' In contrast to the declarations by Mexico and South Korea at Kyoto, this statement of intent to adopt voluntary targets – and indeed the similar one issued by Kazakhstan – were of greater significance to the G77, for the simple reason that they came from within its own membership.

A.13.1.3 The 'Green Developing Group' (GDG)

Given the diversity of economic as well as environmental interests amongst the G77 membership, these contraventions of the agreed G77 position cannot really come as a surprise. Indeed, if anything is surprising and a credit to the negotiating skills of the leading G77 negotiators, then it is the fact that such a position was possible in the first place. The reason why the key players in the G77, India and China, have been trying to defend the unity of the G77 as a negotiating bloc has to be their perception that in doing so, they will retain a strength in numbers, meant to increase DCs' bargaining power. Although there have been some notable DC successes in the course of the FCCC negotiations, the overall effect of this insistence has been the opposite. By tying themselves to G77 consensus, India and China have actually debilitated their bargaining power, with the result that they have had no genuine option other than to pursue policies which were largely reactive to Annex I proposals. However, a group's bargaining power is not necessarily proportional to its size. The strength of the US position, for example, clearly depends on its economic strength. And yet, money is not the only source of bargaining power. Given that, according to our Kyoto scenario, China, India and the ROW region are projected to emit almost the same amount of Energy Emissions (combustion CO_2 + fugitive fuel CH_4) as the combined emissions of the OECD countries (Table A.13.1), it will be clear that these developing countries can wield a large 'environmental stick' in these negotiations, even though they, as yet, do not have the same sort of 'financial carrots' as the United States. In the medium to long run, nothing goes without China and India.[4]

If China and India were to form a coalition with countries genuinely sharing their economic and environmental concerns – a 'Green Developing Group' (GDG) as a version of the 'Green Group', restricted to non-oil-exporting Parties of, say, low or medium development (i.e. HDI < 0.8)[5] – they would not only gain further bargaining power in

---

4. India's potential GHG emissions in the near to medium run may be dwarfed by those of China, yet it has to be taken seriously, for it alone amongst the key players can claim to be representing the least developed countries. Moreover, under the Preference Score Distribution adopted by us, India will become the major single supplier of hot air in 2020 (Table 13.2).

Table A.13.1: Projection of Energy Emissions under the Kyoto Scenario. 2020

	(Mt CO₂e)	*% of Total*
USA	5,586	16.5
JPN	1,002	3.0
EUM	3,029	9.0
ROE	92	0.3
ROO	921	2.7
EIT	5,110	15.1
Annex I	15,741	46.6
CHN	6,409	19.0
IND	1,473	4.4
ANI	2,408	7.1
AOE	3,145	9.3
LAM	2,465	7.3
ROW	2,123	6.3
World	*33,764*	100.0

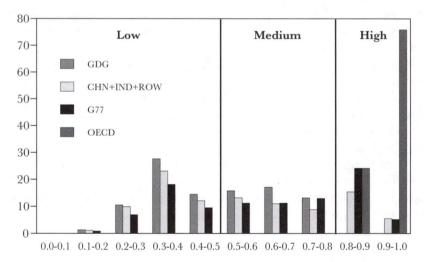

Figure A.13.2:   Percentages of Membership at Different HDI Levels: GDG, G77
& OECD

5.   The implementation of this GDG in our model poses some slight problems
     due to the make-up of our model regions. Considering population weighted
     aggregates of the HDIs (Table A.13.2), there is no doubt that CHN, IND
     and ROW would have to be in this grouping (although, due to its catch-all
     nature, ROW also contains some 20 per cent high-development countries).
     As for the other non-Annex I regions, it will be equally clear that LAM and
     AOE must be excluded from the GDG region for being high-development

terms of overall emissions, but they would still form a substantial bargaining bloc (more than 40 per cent of the Parties) within the FCCC. Moreover, it stands to reason that only such a streamlined alliance with a more unified range of positions could be a genuine counterweight to the high-development countries represented by the OECD.

Table A.13.2:   Development Indicators: HDI and GDP per capita. 1995

	UNDP Classification	HDI	HDI Range within region	GDP/cap. 1995 $ (PPP)	
	1995 Human Development Indices (pop. weighted aggregates)				
ROO		0.95	0.93 (Australia)- 0.96 (Canada)	26,573	USA
JPN		0.94		23,828	ROE
ROE	High:	0.94	0.93 (Switzerland) – 0.94 (Norway, Iceland)	21,930	JPN
USA	≥ 0.8	0.94		20,787	ROO
EUM		0.92	0.89 (Portugal) - 0.95 (France)	19,149	EUM
LAM		0.82	0.59 (Bolivia) – 0.89 (Chile)	6,387	LAM
EIT		0.75	0.58 (Tajikistan) – 0.89 (Slovenia)	5,860	ANI
ANI	Medium:	0.74	0.68 (Phillipines, Indonesia) – 0.9 (Thailand)	5,375	AOE
AOE	≥ 0.5	0.69	0.36 (Yemen) – 0.91 (Israel)	4,148	EIT
CHN		0.65	0.65 (China) – 0.91 (Hong Kong)	2,858	CHN
ROW	Low	0.46	0.19 (Sierra Leone) – 0.91 (Cyprus)	1,856	ROW
IND		0.45		1,422	IND

Source: UNDP 1998 Human Development Report

In view of the declared positions of China, India and OPEC, it would clearly be implausible to expect either our model-GDG (= CHN+IND+ROW) or AOE to adopt any voluntary abatement targets under the Kyoto regime. For the remaining non-Annex I regions (LAM and ANI), however, it does seem to us that, given their level of development, they could reasonably be expected to contribute actively to abatement efforts relating to the first commitment period (the

---

and/or oil-exporting regions. This leaves us with the region of the Asian newly industrialised countries. Given that its aggregate HDI is less than 0.8, ANI is a *prima facie* candidate for inclusion in our GDG region. However, of the seven ANI members, all but Indonesia and the Philippines have an HDI greater than 0.8. This, and the fact that the ANI's GDP per capita is much closer to our high-development Latin American region than to the other established GDG regions, are the reasons why we chose to exclude ANI from the GDG.

'principle of common but differentiated responsibility', after all, cuts both ways). Moreover, in view of the aforementioned declarations by Argentina, Mexico (LAM) and South Korea (ANI), we do believe such a participation to be a plausible option for the first stage of our Global Compromise scenario, in particular if the targets involved are justifiable ones.[6]

A.13.2 The Global Compromise Protocol

A.13.2.1 Acceptable Global 2020 Emissions

In order to make reasonable assumptions about emission targets (quotas) for post-Kyoto commitments one has to consider at least two inter-linked issues. An assignment of such targets will for one be a distributive problem. As such, the main concern will be the relative sizes of the allocated quotas, something inexorably linked with issues of distributive justice. However, a quota assignment also involves the choice of an acceptable absolute level of global emissions for the relevant commitment period. In other words, a decision will have to be made about an acceptable overall size of the 'cake' which is to be distributed under such an assignment of targets. Whether or not a proposed global emission level is acceptable must be judged on the basis of its social and economic consequences (which, in turn, cannot be gauged without taking into account its scientific implications). The decision itself, however, will ultimately remain a political one.

Unfortunately, there is very little in the manner in which the Kyoto targets were established which could guide us in choosing an acceptable global post-Kyoto emission level for our modelling purposes. None the less, Kyoto cannot be ignored. The decision taken at Kyoto provides us with a 'fixpoint' for acceptable global emissions trajectories. In other words, by virtue of the political decision taken at Kyoto, we can reasonably assume that there are at least some emission trajectories

---

6. One of the reasons why the notion of voluntary targets is often rejected is the fear that a Party proposing to adopt such a target might choose this target in a manner which is not in line with the aim of the FCCC. However, the notion 'voluntary', in this context, does not necessarily mean that the Parties in question can actually choose which target they want to adopt voluntarily. On the contrary, reasonable targets should, in our view, be offered on a 'take-it-or-leave-it' basis by the international community, and their reasonableness determined by reference to plausible precedents, such as the stabilisation targets under the FCCC.

through the Kyoto level which would be deemed acceptable. But which are they?

Up to this point talk has been about 'acceptable emission levels' and, more generally, about 'acceptable emission trajectories'. What we have not mentioned, so far, is the fact that, in both cases, the notion of 'acceptability' derives its meaning from the aim of stabilising atmospheric GHG *concentrations* at an acceptable level: emission levels are acceptable only as part of an acceptable emission trajectory, and emission trajectories can only be acceptable if they lead to such a stabilisation.

The literature on these issues generally focuses on CO_2 concentrations. The CO_2 concentration levels which have been most frequently considered in this context range from 450ppm (less than twice the pre-industrial concentration of 280 ppm) to 650 ppm. While there are still many different global CO_2 emission trajectories under which stabilisation could be achieved at any of these concentration levels, it will be clear that some of them would be more costly than others. Indeed, in a recent letter to *Nature*, Ha-Duong, Grubb and Hourcade[7] have analysed least-cost stabilisation trajectories for CO_2 concentration levels in this range. Having adapted their findings to our

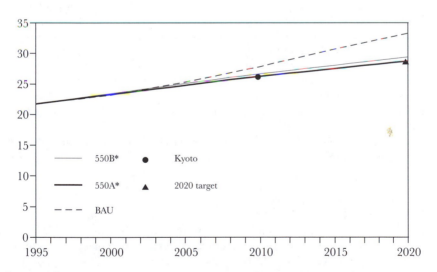

Figure A.13.3: Global CO_2 Combustion Emissions. Gt CO_2

7. M. Ha-Duong, M.J. Grubb, and J.-C. Hourcade, 'Influence of socio-economic inertia and uncertainty on optimal CO_2-emission abatement', *Nature*, vol. 390 (20 Nov.) 1997.

Box A.13.2:
The 550A Abatement Strategy and the 550A* Trajectory

Ha-Duong, Grubb and Hourcade are interested in the effect of socio-economic inertia and uncertainty on cost effective CO_2 emission abatement. The uncertainty involved concerns the acceptable concentration level, while 'socio-economic inertia' refers to the fact that certain socio-economic structures relevant to GHG emissions cannot be changed over night. The analysis is carried out by applying a dynamic integrated CGE-model to two families of scenarios, one with the said uncertainties and one in which the acceptable level is assumed to be known from the outset. The 550A scenario, as it happens, belongs to the latter family, i.e. it is assumed that the socio-economic consequences of stabilising the global CO_2 concentration level at 550ppm are politically acceptable.

There are two exogenous parameters common to all the scenarios with the 550ppm stabilisation assumption considered by the authors: they are all based on reference emissions provided by an IPCC 'business-as-usual' scenario (IS92a), and they all involve the assumption of a technical progress rate of 1 per cent per annum. The difference between the four 550 scenarios discussed is given in the assumptions concerning the social (risk-free) discount rate (3 or 5 per cent) and the characteristic time of energy systems (20 vs. 50 years). If interpreted purely in terms of capital depreciation, the two values for the inertia parameter correspond to depreciation rates of 3.5 and 1.4 per cent per annum, respectively. The former, the authors argue, is a reasonable average rate of renewal of appliances, cars, power stations and refineries. The reason for considering the lower rate is the existence of other GHG-relevant factors with higher inertia, exemplified by the fact that 'without specific policies, new energy sources have taken about 50 years to penetrate from 1% to 50% of their ultimate potential.'

Abatement costs C, in the model used by Ha-Duong *et al.* vary with the reference emissions (normalised by the initial emission level), i.e.

$$C(t) = E^{ref}(t) / E^{ref}(t_0) \leftrightarrow \Phi(t, K)$$

The problem with the authors' conclusions for our purposes is that the values of this normalised emissions parameter for IS92a emissions figures are not the same as the ones for our BaU emissions. For one, our initial BaU emission level is about 9 Gt CO_2 lower than the one used by Ha-Duong *et al.*, which obviously made it impossible to use their trajectories without some adjustment. On the assumption that the 'shape' of the minimal cost trajectories will not substantially, if at all, be altered if the reference emissions are changed by a constant amount, we decided to adapt their minimum cost trajectories by subtracting this difference in

---

Box A.13.2: *continued*

initial emissions (the resulting adjusted trajectories are marked by an asterisk). However, even this does not guarantee that the resulting adjusted trajectories are really minimum cost, for we also find that our BaU figures steadily outgrow the IS92a* ones, ending up 9 per cent higher in 2020. Our adaptations of the IS92a based minimal cost trajectories must therefore be taken *cum grano salis*.

The 550A scenario assumes a discount rate of 3 per cent and a characteristic time of 50 years. Not surprisingly, it is the most demanding of all the 550 scenarios discussed by the authors, namely (in increasing order of 2020 emissions): 550A (3%, 50yrs), 550D (3%, 20yrs), 550C (5%, 50yrs), 550B (5%, 20yrs). By using the *550A** emissions trajectory to determine the 2020 emissions target we might to some extent be paying over the odds to what is minimally required for a 550ppm stabilisation (the 'actual' inertia of the systems involved might be less than 50 years). But as Kyoto will already have put us on the 550A track, we might as well take this risk in order to ensure a 550ppm stabilisation in light of this 'inertia uncertainty'.

BaU CO_2-emission projections, we find that one of their 550 ppm stabilisation scenarios (referred to as '550A', see Box A.13.2) leads to a minimum-cost trajectory (*550A**) which passes through our Kyoto CO_2-target level, or, to be more precise, its 'full hot-air' version of 26.3 Gt CO_2.[8]

Under the *550A** emission trajectory, stabilisation at 550 ppm is achieved in 2100. The global CO_2 emission levels continue to rise until they reach their apex in 2050 at 33.5Gt CO_2. In 2020, the *550A** trajectory reaches a level of 28.6Gt CO_2, which, taken as abatement target, requires a global emission reduction of about 14.4 per cent of the BaU level. Compared with the level of reduction required of the Annex I Parties by the Kyoto Protocol – ranging between 9.7 and 16.1 per cent, depending on the amount of hot air put on sale (see Table A.13.3) – this first global abatement target could *prima facie* be regarded as less ambitious than the Kyoto target. This, however, would be misleading, for the proper reference point for such a comparison has

---

8. According to our projections, there will be 0.9Gt CO_2 of hot-air in the Annex I trading system in 2010. The global CO_2 emission level under compliance with the Kyoto requirements will vary with the amount of hot-air actually used in complying, namely between 26.3 (with all hot air) and 25.4Gt CO_2 (without any hot air).

to be the range of *global* reductions implied by the Kyoto regime, namely between 5.4 and 9.0 per cent below BaU. Moreover, the ambitiousness of an abatement scheme can really only be judged with respect to the targets assigned to the individual Parties/regions, which we will turn to shortly.

Table A.13.3:   Modelling Targets for CO_2 Combustion Emissions

---

Kyoto Scenario

	BaU 2010 Emissions Gt CO_2	2010 Target Gt CO_2	Required Reduction with hot air Gt CO_2	Required Reduction with hot air % of BaU	Required Reduction without hot air Gt CO_2	Required Reduction without hot air % of BaU
Annex I	15.5	14.0	1.5	9.7	2.5	16.1
non-Annex I	12.3	n.a.	n.a.	n.a.	n.a.	n.a.
World	27.8	26.3	1.5	5.4	2.5	9.0

Global Compromise Scenarios

	BaU 2020 Emissions Gt CO_2	2020 Target Gt CO_2	Required Reduction Gt CO_2	Required Reduction % of BaU
Annex I	17.5			
non-Annex I	15.9			
World	33.4	28.6	4.8	14.4

In order to include non-CO_2 GHGs (specifically methane), we propose to generalise our CO_2 results by adopting the assumption that the overall size of acceptable GHG emissions in the second commitment period is to be given analogously as 14.4 per cent below the relevant 2020 BaU emissions of 36.7Gt CO_2e.[9] In other words, we propose to adopt a global 2020 emission limit for our model of 31.5Gt CO_2e.

A.13.2.2 Distributing Assigned Amounts

Having established the size of the 'cake' – i.e. the level of global 2020 emissions which we deem to be plausible as an acceptable global

---

9. We are, of course, aware of the fact that this analogy may not preserve the least cost character of the 550A CO_2 emission trajectory established by Ha-Duong *et al.*, but given the predominance of CO_2 in the Kyoto basket of GHGs, we believe our assumption to be justifiable in the present context.

emissions cap within the constraints given by the FCCC – our task must now be to justify what we consider to be a plausible distribution of these quotas ('assigned amounts') between the Parties to the FCCC. As mentioned previously, there are essentially two opposing camps facing one another. On the one hand the industrialised countries firmly persuaded that the proper way of distributing the quotas is to 'grandfather' them, i.e. distribute them in proportion to a baseline *emission* profile. DCs, on the other hand, are convinced that the quotas ought to be distributed on a per capita basis, proportional to a baseline *population* profile.

In order to assess the compatibility of these positions, both with one another and with 'exogenous' constraints such as the ones given by the FCCC, we must make a decision where the relevant baseline is to be drawn. As witnessed by the choice of 1990 as the Kyoto baseline, with its ensuing complications concerning the issue of EIT 'hot air', such a choice of baseline can be a very delicate matter. However, it does seem to be reasonable to assume that the baseline year ought to be earlier than the negotiations, if only to avoid certain undesired incentives.[10] As far as our model is concerned, the simplest and least problematic baseline option is, of course, our base period of 1995, given the exogenous character of all its parameter values.

Considering therefore the world in 1995 (Table A.13.4) as our baseline, it becomes immediately apparent that the positions of our two camps are mutually incompatible: indeed the OECD's emissions grandfathering claim of 45 per cent and the GDG per capita claim of 59 per cent alone add up to more than can possibly be distributed. Clearly, if there is to be a treaty such as the envisaged 2020 Protocol (i.e. one assigning quotas to all FCCC Parties), then there has to be some compromise between the two camps.

For there to be such a compromise, at least one of the two camps must be willing to give way and abandon their initial position. Arguably the simplest way in which this might be achieved is if the two camps were to 'meet each other half way' by agreeing to accept the simple arithmetic mean of what they would have obtained under the two competing distribution proposals. This solution would indeed be quite

---

10. To choose a grandfathering baseline later than the negotiations would obviously produce the incentive to emit as much as possible in the baseline year, while – as Michael Grubb has pointed out on several occasions – a similar per capita baseline might provide disincentives concerning population growth control measures (although the latter seems to us much less probable than the former).

Table A.13.4: The World in 1995. Population, GDP and Energy Emissions

	Population		GDP (PPP)		GDP/cap	Energy Emissions		EE/cap.
	Million	%	Billion $	%	$	(Mt CO$_2$e)	%	(t CO$_2$e)
USA	271	4.8.8	7,206	21.5	26,573	5,348	22.7	19.7
JPN	125	2.2	2,743	8.2	21,930	1,143	4.8	9.1
EUM	374	6.6	7,152	21.3	19,149	3,143	13.3	8.4
ROE	12	0.2	281	0.8	23,828	74	0.3	6.2
ROO	51	0.9	1,057	3.1	20,787	839	3.6	16.5
OECD	832	15	18,439	54.9	22,152	10,546	45	12.7
EIT	391	6.9	1,621	4.8	4,148	3,995	16.9	10.2
CHN	1,205	21.2	3,444	10.3	2,858	3,319	14.1	2.8
IND	929	16.3	1,321	3.9	1,422	887	3.8	1.0
ANI	414	7.3	2,426	7.2	5,860	1,172	5.0	2.8
AOE	262	4.6	1,411	4.2	5,375	1,273	5.4	4.9
LAM	408	7.2	2,609	7.8	6,387	1,066	4.5	2.6
ROW	1,245	21.9	2,311	6.9	1,856	1,342	5.7	1.1
GDG	3,379	59.4	7,076	21.1	2,094	5,548	23.5	1.6
World	5,687	100.0	33,582	100.0	5,905	23,600	100.0	4.1

Sources: various

plausible, were it not for the fact that we are dealing with equity-based initial positions. The problem with this 'halfway house' solution, in other words, is that the initial positions in question are not just strategic gambits, but positions which are perceived by their proponents as morally justified positions. Being equity-based in this sense makes them much more resilient to compromise, even if such a compromise would entail some sort of economic benefit.

(a) Single National Preference Scores. However, we believe that even under these circumstances, compromise may be possible provided the compromise proposal itself is determined in a manner generally regarded as fair. This, in turn, may plausibly be achieved by using a method in which preference scores are used to determine the weights under which the base proposals – in our case the grandfathering and the per capita distribution – are aggregated by way of forming a ('socially'[11]) weighted arithmetic mean: Each of the Parties involved

11. The weights established in this manner reflect, if we wish, the social desirability of the base-distribution in question. A more detailed discussion of the ideas behind this 'preference score method' can be found in Benito Müller, *Justice in Global Warming Negotiations: How to Achieve a Procedurally Fair Compromise* (OIES: Oxford, second edition,1999).

ranks the initial proposals admitted for consideration according to (moral) preference and expresses this ranking by assigning numbers from a given pool of preference scores, in our case 1 for the preferred distribution and 0 for the other. The weight under which a particular proposal enters into the weighted average compromise formula is then given by its preference score total, or rather its proportion of the sum of all the preference scores.

For example, if we assume that all the Parties to the FCCC were to rank our two base proposals purely on the basis of self-interest, the method described would generate a total score – or, to be more precise a 'single national preference score' – of 63 for grandfathering and 116 for the per capita proposal (see Table A.13.5), which would leave us with preference score weights of 0.35 and 0.65, respectively.[12] In other words, under the preference score compromise formula, a Party with a grandfathering share of *GF* and a per capita share of *PC* would receive the preference score share

$$0.35 \ GF + 0.65 \ PC$$

There is, however, a slight problem with the method as described so far, for it is not strictly 'collusion proof' in the sense that Parties could not gain an advantage by forming new Parties.[13] Of course, Parties cannot gain by unification – such as if the EU member states were to forfeit their status in favour of a single EU Party – but they can gain if they were to segregate.[14] In practice the question as to who is to count as a Party is settled by reference to the UN system at large, and it seems unlikely that one would be able to play such 'collusion games'. Nevertheless, the question as to the fairness of the procedure in question – which is, of course, crucial to its intended purpose of bringing about an acceptable compromise – remains pertinent and needs to be addressed.

---

12. $63/179 = 0.35$, $116/179 = 0.65$.
13. The sensitivity of the PS-weights to this sort of 'collusion' becomes clear if we consider the case where the Parties involved are the twelve regions of our model. In this case we would have a PS-weight of $7/12 = 0.58$ for grandfathering and $5/12 = 0.42$ for the per capita distribution.
14. If, say, the USA, following the EU example, were to be counted as 50 different Parties representing the individual States, plus, for good measure, one representing the Federal Administration, then we would be dealing with a sum total of 229 Parties, and the PS-weights for grandfathering distribution preferred by the USA would rise from 0.35 to $113/229 = 0.49$, thus leaving us essentially with the above mentioned halfway house solution.

Table A.13.5:   Preference Scores

	Global Scores (millions)[a]		Single National Scores[b]	
	Per Capita	Grandfathering	Per Capita	Grandfathering
USA	0	292	0	1
JPN	0	127	0	1
EUM	0	378	0	18 [c]
ROE	0	12	0	4
ROO	0	56	0	3
EIT	0	391	0	21
CHN	1,304	0	1	0
IND	1,082	0	1	0
ANI	473	0	6	0
AOE	0	335	0	15
LAM	471	0	13	0
ROW	1,569	0	95	0
Total	4,900	1,591	116	63

	Global		Single National	
PS-weights	0.75	0.25	0.65	0.35

(a)   Based on projected 2005 population figures.
(b)   As at 6 June 1999, the FCCC Secretariat had received instruments of ratification or accession from 179 Parties.
(c)   Apart from the 15 EU member states, EUM contains three further FCCC Parties: Monaco, San Marino and the EU itself.

(b) Global Preference Scores. The solution is quite simple. All we need to do is to allow all the Parties in question to (hypothetically) segregate as much as they possibly could, i.e. to the level of individual inhabitants. Assuming the negotiations did take place in, say, 2005, we would – according to our adopted UN medium projection – be left with a total of 6.5 billion Parties. At this level of disaggregation, there clearly can no longer be an objection to the 'single Party, single score' principle used so far. The original Parties would then be simply allocated the sum total of the allocation to their inhabitants. This 'individual preference score method', as fair as it may be, is naturally completely impracticable.[15] However, under certain reasonable simplifying assumptions, it yields precisely the same result as is obtained under

15. While it would not be difficult to establish the per capita share of an individual person, establishing actual emission levels for each individual is clearly not practically feasible.

'global preference scores',[16] where the scores by each Party are multiplied by the number of its inhabitants. This, and the fact that the resulting 'global preference score method' is strictly collusion proof, is the reason why we have chosen to base our analysis on global (rather than single national preference scores), given by the formula:

$$0.25 \ GF + 0.75 \ PC$$

The distribution of assigned energy emissions amounts which would result from this formula (in the absence of a 'banking' mechanism) are listed, together with the assignments that would have been made under the two base distribution, in Table A.13.6.

Table A.13.6:   Assigned Energy Emission Amounts (Without Banking). 2020.

	Per Capita ($Mt\ CO_2e$)	%	Grandfathering ($Mt\ CO_2e$)	%	Preference Score[a] ($Mt\ CO_2e$)	%
USA	1,500	4.8	7,128	22.7	2,880	9.2
JPN	692	2.2	1,524	4.8	896	2.8
EUM	2,066	6.6	4,189	13.3	2,587	8.2
ROE	65	0.2	98	0.3	73	0.2
ROO	281	0.9	1,118	3.6	486	1.5
EIT	2,161	6.9	5,325	16.9	2,937	9.3
CHN	6,665	21.2	4,425	14.1	6,116	19.4
IND	5,139	16.3	1,182	3.8	4,169	13.3
ANI	2,290	7.3	1,562	5.0	2,112	6.7
AOE	1,452	4.6	1,697	5.4	1,512	4.8
LAM	2,259	7.2	1,421	4.5	2,054	6.5
ROW	6,886	21.9	1,788	5.7	5,637	17.9
World	31,458	100	31,458	100	31,458	100

(a)   Based on Global (2005) Preference Scores.

(c) Eco-friendly Banking. The assigned amounts listed in Table A.13.6, however, are not very realistic, as it is unlikely that a 2020 Protocol would be adopted without some provision for 'banking' unused assigned amounts from the Kyoto commitment period. Given our assumptions

16. The idea here is simply to switch, if we wish, from actual inhabitants to a hypothetical 'average inhabitant' and to assume that the position of the Party is the same as that of its 'average inhabitant'. In other words, all allocations to a Party are divided evenly amongst its inhabitants and it is assumed that the Party and its average inhabitant has the same (moral) preference structure as concerns the ranking of the distribution proposals in question.

about the hot-air cartel during the Kyoto commitment period, EIT (see Table 10.2) would have the substantial sum of 1,2Gt CO_2e of bankable assigned amounts from that commitment period, which it clearly would not wish to go to waste.

There are at least two ways in which this 'credit' could be incorporated into the 2020 Protocol: for one, we could simply follow the Kyoto Protocol provision[17] and add it to EIT's assigned amount under the distribution of our acceptable global 2020 target level of 31.5Gt CO_2e as listed in Table A.13.6. The other option would be to subtract it from this global target before applying our distributive formula, and then credit it to EIT. Given the 'climate first' approach which we have used to determine the global emissions level, however, the latter seems to be more justified, for unlike the other, it keeps our abatement efforts on track with stabilising the climate at the chosen acceptable level.

The total amount of acceptable emissions unspoken for at 2020 is therefore 30.3Gt CO_2e (= 31.5Gt CO_2e −1.2Gt CO_2e), which are distributed under our preference score formula. Adding the 'credits' banked in the Kyoto commitment period brings the global emissions level back to our acceptable 31.5Gt CO_2e and leads to the assigned amounts for the 2020 commitment period listed in Table 13.1.

(d) The Ambitiousness of the 2020 Targets. In our discussion of the global target level for the '2020 Protocol', we mentioned the fact that, as concerns targets, the ambitiousness of such a protocol must be judged by reference to individual country targets. Judging the assigned amounts given by our three distribution proposals relative to the situation in our Kyoto commitment period (2010), it becomes first of all patently obvious that pure grandfathering is not compatible with the FCCC: after all, it could hardly be seen in the spirit of this convention if those Parties (i.e. Annex I) which were required to stabilise their emissions at 1990 levels by 2000, and even to reduce on average to 5.2 per cent below it by 2010, were then permitted to increase their emissions in 2020 by 40 per cent over the level they reached in 2010 (see Table A.13.7), while the developing world, as represented in our GDG, would actually be required to reduce emissions by 7 per cent.

---

17. 'If the emissions of a Party included in Annex I in a commitment period are less than its assigned amount under this article, the difference shall, on request of that Party, be added to the assigned amount for that Party for subsequent commitment periods'[Art. 3.13 Kyoto Protocol]

Table A.13.7:   Assigned Amounts for 2020 (from Table 13.1) in Percentage Changes from the Projected 2010 Global Compromise Levels

	2010 Level ($MtCO_2e$)	Per Capita %	Grandfathering %	Preference Score[a] %
USA	5,428	-73.4	26.2	-49.0
JPN	1,058	-37.1	38.4	-18.6
EUM	3,027	-34.4	33.0	-17.9
ROE	88	-28.7	7.1	-19.9
ROO	827	-67.3	29.9	-43.5
OECD	10,428	-57.6	29.6	-36.2
EIT	3,794	-13.1	67.1	6.6
Annex I	14,222	-45.7	39.6	-24.8
CHN	4,773	34.2	-10.9	23.2
IND	1,165	324.0	-2.5	244.0
ANI	1,365	61.3	10.0	48.7
AOE	2,255	-38.1	-27.7	-35.6
LAM	1,279	69.8	6.8	54.4
ROW	1,691	291.4	1.7	220.4
GDG	7,629	135.5	-6.8	100.6
World	26,750	17.6	17.6	17.6

(a)   Based on Global (2005) Preference Scores.

The same cannot be said for the other two distribution proposals. Indeed, the per capita proposal and, to a lesser degree, the preference score distribution are both very onerous on Annex I countries and undeniably favourable, not only to the GDG, but to all non-Annex I regions except AOE. Given, in particular, that under the PS-proposal Annex I is given a total assigned amount of 25 per cent below the 2010 level, it will be clear that target-wise our Global Compromise Protocol is indeed more ambitious than the Kyoto Protocol.

CHAPTER 14

THE IMPLICATIONS OF A NEW CLIMATE CHANGE AGREEMENT (THE GLOBAL COMPROMISE SCENARIO)

14.1 Introduction

The Global Compromise scenario describes a world which is serious about reducing climate change. It is based on the Kyoto scenario for the years up to 2010, and policies in the Annex I countries being the same as in the Kyoto scenario for that year. For the non-Annex I countries, the Asian Newly Industrialised countries and Latin America take on voluntary commitments to stabilise emissions at the level reached in the year 2000 for the Kyoto commitment period 2008–12. From 2018, all regions of the world enter a new climate change agreement with new emission targets, and take part in unimpeded global emissions trading. All regions make use of 'no regrets' improvements in energy efficiency and EUM imposes a 10 per cent tax on energy as in the Kyoto scenario.

The difference between the impacts of the Kyoto and the Global Compromise scenarios for 2010, therefore, result only from the voluntary commitments of the two developing country regions. Global emissions fall by 3500 Mt CO_2 equivalent from the baseline for 2010, as compared with a reduction by 2400 Mt CO_2e in the Kyoto scenario. Much more stringent emission reduction targets apply for 2020, when all world regions are included in the new agreement, with emissions falling 7100 Mt CO_2e below the baseline. This reduction is 4100 Mt CO_2e greater than in the Kyoto scenario. Regional emission profiles, emission trading, and monetary transfers resulting from trading were discussed in Chapter 13. We will in this chapter present energy price increases by region, the impacts on the fossil fuel markets, and finally oil revenues.

14.2 Energy Prices

The development of domestic prices for the average unit of energy is shown in Figures 14.1 and 14.2. As in the Kyoto scenario, of all the Annex I regions, energy prices increase most strongly in the EU due to the energy taxes imposed disregarding carbon contents of fuels. EU energy prices increase on average by 13 per cent by the first commitment period, and 23 per cent towards the end of the projections

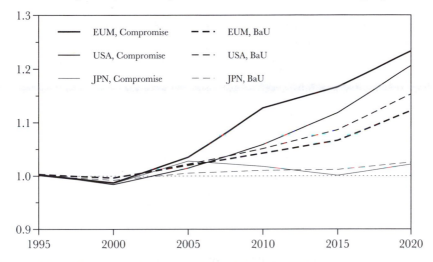

Figure 14.1: Price Index for Average Unit of Energy. 1995 = 1

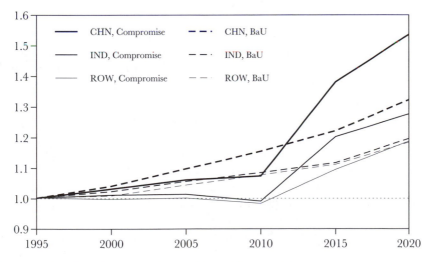

Figure 14.2: Price Index for Average Unit of Energy. 1995 = 1

horizon, 9 and 11 percentage points above BaU levels. US energy prices increase more than EU prices in the BaU case because of the high oil component in the fuel mix. Climate change policies increase US energy prices by 5 percentage points. Japanese energy prices end the projection horizon at the BaU levels.

The Asian Newly Industrialised countries and Latin America voluntarily commit to a stabilisation of their emissions at year 2000 level by the first commitment period, yet they do not take part in international emissions trading until 2020. The strong domestic abatement effort required by the two regions decreases producer prices of fossil fuels in the first commitment period. Domestic energy prices for the three non-Annex I regions shown in Figure 14.2 therefore decrease relative to BaU projections until 2010, where these regions do not undertake abatement, and increase later.

In the non-Annex I countries, domestic prices for the average unit of energy fall between 2005 and 2010, reaching almost their 1995 levels, a fall of about 10 per cent below the BaU levels. By the end of the projections horizon, energy prices in China have increased 20 percentage points, in India 10 percentage points above BaU levels. This increases Chinese energy prices by 54 per cent over the next twenty years.

14.3 Impacts on the Fossil Fuel Markets

14.3.1 Conventional and Non-conventional Oil Supply

The accession of two regions without participation in international trading in the first commitment period, and the much stronger abatement effort in later years mean a significant impact on the demand for oil. This comes despite the assumption of a wide use of flexibility mechanisms for the implementation of the Global Compromise successor agreement to the Kyoto Protocol. Figure 14.3 shows supplies of conventional and total oil, both for the BaU case and for the Global Compromise scenario. Conventional oil production has to adjust before 2015, because of the low level of non-conventional oil production in earlier periods in the BaU case. In 2010, conventional oil production reaches 86.5 mb/d, a decline from BaU projections by 3.7 mb/d.

The response of conventional oil is reduced in later periods, where flexibility mechanisms allow a more efficient implementation of climate change policies. Also, the postponement of non-conventional oil production brings relief to the oil market.

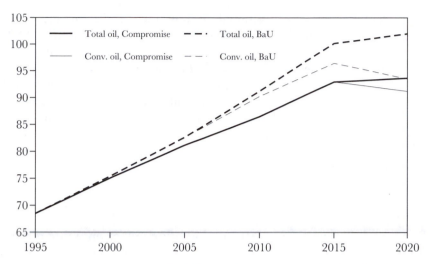

Figure 14.3: Oil Production, BaU and Global Compromise. Million Barrels per Day

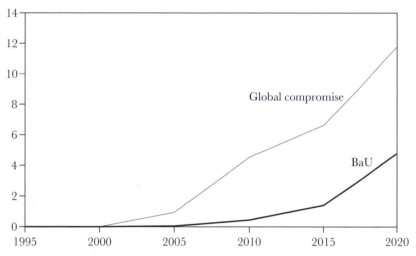

Figure 14.4: Hydrogen Production, BaU and Global Compromise. Million Barrels per Day Oil Equivalent

The capital intensive, long-term non-conventional oil projects are undertaken only if demand projections are strong, and are postponed or cancelled when climate change policies lead to sluggish growth or demand reductions. Non-conventional oil production however, is small in the BaU case in 2010, at a level of about 1 mb/d and conventional oil has to suffer the difference.

Production of non-conventional oil only starts during the last period of the projections horizon, and reaches a level of 2.5 mb/d in 2020, as opposed to 8.5 mb/d in the BaU case. In contrast, hydrogen production increases by 7 mb/d from the projected BaU level, to reach 11.8 mb/d, as shown in Figure 14.4. Hydrogen is drawn into the market already in 2005 at 1 mb/d oil equivalent, and reaches 4.5 mb/d in 2010, where almost no hydrogen (as liquid fuel substitute) was used in the BaU case. Market penetration and infrastructure constraints still keep the level of hydrogen market share at around 10 per cent in 2020, up from about 4 per cent in the BaU world.

14.3.2 Oil Prices

Demand reductions in the 2010 period are much stronger than in the Kyoto scenario, because of the voluntary commitments of the two non-Annex I regions with strong emission restrictions. Figure 14.5 shows the oil price projections resulting from the Global Compromise scenario. The international price of oil actually falls by about 5 per cent in real terms from 1995 levels, instead of rising by 11 per cent as in the BaU case. After the first commitment period, the inclusion of all non-Annex I countries into an international emissions trading system reduces the impact on oil.

This inclusion helps oil because of the large share of coal in the energy mix of the large developing countries China and India. A contribution by these countries to the international emission reduction

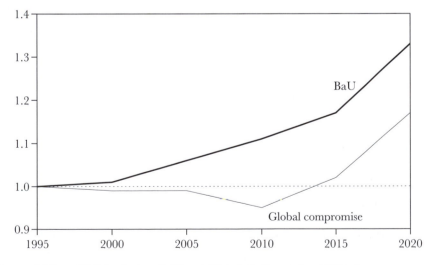

Figure 14.5: Oil Price Index, BaU and Global Compromise. 1995 =1

efforts therefore puts a higher burden on coal, instead of oil. The oil price recovers from the slump to increase 2 per cent above the 1995 level in 2015, and 17 per cent in 2020. Still, the oil price is about 11 per cent below the BaU level in 2020. The Global emission restrictions take away about half of the oil price increase expected under BaU, but the price still increases.

14.3.3 Impact on Coal

As discussed in Chapter 11 on the Kyoto scenario, the heaviest burden of an efficient implementation of climate change policies is placed on coal because of its higher carbon content per energy unit, and relatively low initial consumer prices. Coal production and use therefore decline in the Global Compromise scenario between 1995 and 2015. Figure 14.6 shows coal use in the Annex I region and globally.

World coal production and use increase very little towards the end of the projections horizon. In 2020, world coal production is 2400 mtoe, as compared with 2300 mtoe in 1995, and 3300 mtoe in 2020 in the BaU case. This is a reduction from BaU of 900 mtoe, equivalent to 12.5 mb/d of oil. Annex I countries reduce coal use by 330 mtoe below BaU level, non-Annex I countries 570 mtoe in 2020.

This strong drop in demand is accompanied by a small increase in the producer price. World coal prices are 2 percentage points below BaU projections in 2010, but 11 percentage points above BaU

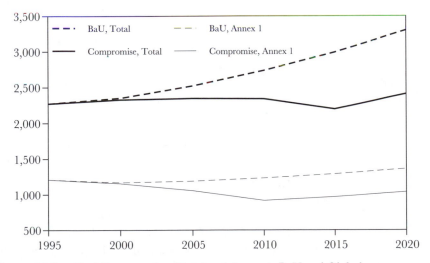

Figure 14.6:   Coal Consumption, Total and Annex 1, BaU and Global Compromise. Million Tonnes Oil Equivalent

projections in 2020. This is due to an increase in production costs brought about by carbon taxes on the energy used in production and on the methane leaking during production.

14.3.4 Impact on Gas

The voluntary reduction commitments by the two non-Annex I regions increase also the impact on gas in the Global Compromise scenario. In the Compromise scenario, gas demand in the Annex I region is 330 bcm below BaU level, in the non-Annex I region gas use falls by 160 bcm below projections for 2010. In 2020, Annex I uses 430 bcm less, and non-Annex I 320 bcm less than projected under BaU. Gas use projections for BaU and the Global Compromise scenario are shown in Figure 14.7.

In oil equivalent units, gas use reaches 49 mb/d and 66 mb/d in 2010 and 2020, as compared with 57.5 mb/d and 79 mb/d in the BaU case, a reduction by 8.5 mb/d and 13 mb/d in 2010 and 2020. Again, the impact of the climate policies on gas is as strong as on coal, as discussed in Chapter 11.

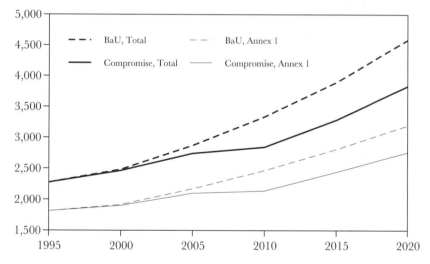

Figure 14.7:   Gas Use, Total and Annex 1, BaU and Global Compromise. Billion Cubic Metres

World gas prices on average fall below their 1995 levels until 2010, from which point on they rise by 2 per cent in 2015, and 7 per cent in 2020 above the 1995 levels. The Global Compromise scenario therefore produces a price drop as compared with the BaU scenario of 6 per cent and 11 per cent in 2010 and 2020. This gap is only 1 percentage point larger than in the Kyoto scenario.

14.4 Sectoral Demand for Fossil Fuels

14.4.1 Oil Products

Demand for oil products amounts to 96.2 mb/d and 112 mb/d in 2010 and 2020 in the BaU case, and 95.5 and 110.6 mb/d in the two periods in the Global Compromise scenario. As in the Kyoto scenario, total availability of liquids is changed little by the climate change policies, due to the strong increase in hydrogen production. This section shows changes in oil demand in the main economic sectors.

Electricity Generation. Climate change policies place a heavy tax burden on coal, which is more carbon intensive than oil or gas. Part of the coal used in electricity generation is therefore substituted by liquid fuels, especially in developing countries with a low level of gas infrastructure development. Also, as discussed in Chapter 11, the user price increase for oil products is reduced by the competitiveness gain of hydrogen, which is not affected by carbon policy instruments. As shown in Figure 14.8, the demand for oil from electricity generation therefore increases by about 1 mb/d in 2010, and 1.3 mb/d in 2020 above the BaU case. More than half of the increase in the first commitment period is due to increased oil use in the Annex I region. This level of extra oil demand for electricity generation in Annex I countries continues until 2015, and amounts to 500 thousand barrels oil equivalent per day in 2020. The other half of the extra demand in 2010 is due to the stringent emission restrictions implemented in the Asian Newly Industrialised and Latin America regions. By 2020, non-Annex I countries use 800 thousand b/d oe more in electricity generation than in the BaU projections. The overall share of the electricity sector in total oil demand remains low. As in the Kyoto scenario, this increase in oil demand reflects the increase in the availability of hydrogen as perfect competitor for oil products.

Energy Intensive Industries. Oil demand in energy intensive industries changes very little between the BaU and the Global Compromise scenarios. Annex I countries reduce demand by small amounts, and non-Annex I countries compensate for this reduction, as production is relocated into these countries. Oil demand in the sector is down by

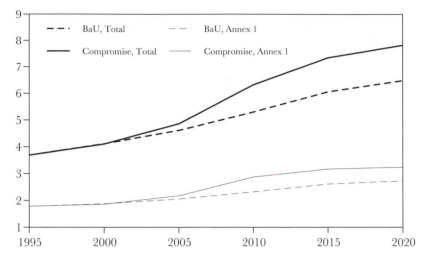

Figure 14.8: Demand for Refined Oil in Electricity Generation, BaU and Global Compromise. Million Barrels per Day

300 thousand b/d in Annex I, and up by 550 thousand b/d in non-Annex I countries, with a small positive total effect.

Other Industries and Services. The demand reductions dominate in the most diversified sector in the projections. Oil demand is reduced as compared with the BaU projections by 620 thousand b/d in the Annex I region, with only a very small increase in the non-Annex I region, and a total effect of a reduction of 420 thousand b/d in 2020.

Transport and Households. The substitution possibilities in this sector are very low, and the response to the climate change policies is therefore small in percentage terms. Because it is the largest source of demand for liquid fuels however, the response is large in absolute terms. Demand for transport fuels declines by 1.2 mb/d in 2020 in the Annex I countries, and remains almost unchanged in the non-Annex I region, therefore we obtain a reduction from BaU projections by 1.2 mb/d for the world as a whole. Table 14.1 summarises sectoral effects in the oil market.

14.4.2 Coal Demand

World coal use is reduced from 3300 to 2400 million tonnes oil equivalent in 2020 under the Global Compromise scenario. This section shows changes in coal demand in the most important economic sectors.

Table 14.1: Changes in the Demand for Oil Products by Sectors. Thousand Barrels per Day

Sector	Electr.	Energy Int.	Other Ind.	Transp. + HHD	Other	Total
1995	0	0	0	0	0	0
2000	-10	-23	-36	-262	-32	-364
2005	245	-11	-165	-469	-195	-595
2010	1,019	98	-318	-701	-778	-680
2015	1,287	170	-520	-1,643	-1,396	-2,101
2020	1,338	268	-416	-1,193	-1,395	-1,398

Electricity Generation. The sector accounts for almost half of total coal use in the world, 1000 mtoe out of 2300 mtoe in 1995, which increases to 1500 mtoe in 2020. The Annex I region accounts for two-thirds of the total in 1995, but the non-Annex I demand for steam coal increases much faster, such that non-Annex I market share is about 50 per cent in 2020. Coal demand from the sector declines by 380 mtoe from the level projected under the BaU scenario for the world as a whole, from 1500 to 1100 mtoe in 2020. In the Annex I region, reduction from the BaU scenario is about 200 mtoe. The reductions are equivalent to 5.3 and 2.4 million barrels of oil per day for total demand and demand in the Annex I region in 2020 compared with the BaU levels.

Energy Intensive Industries. While this sector initially has a global share in the coal market about half the size of the electricity sector, it grows faster than generation. Also, much more of the demand for coal from the sector comes from non-Annex I countries, with Annex I demand almost stagnant at 230 mtoe between 1995 and 2020. The Global Compromise climate change policies reduce coal demand from the sector by 200 mtoe in 2020 on a global level, 50 mtoe in the Annex I region below levels projected under BaU. The reductions are equivalent to 3 million b/d oil for the world, 700 thousand b/d for the

Table 14.2: Changes in the Demand for Coal by Sectors. Thousand Barrels per Day Oil Equivalent

Sector	Electr.	Energy Int.	Other Ind.	HHD + Govt.	Other	Total
1995	0	0	0	0	0	0
2000	-158	-80	-17	-17	-55	-326
2005	-1,165	-672	-92	-47	-456	-2,432
2010	-2,896	-1,105	-195	-155	-1,182	-5,532
2015	-4,796	-2,710	-559	-393	-2,660	-11,118
2020	-5,343	-2,980	-642	-492	-3,039	-12,496

Annex I region. Table 14.2 summarises sectoral effects of the Global Compromise scenario on the coal market.

14.4.3 Gas Demand

The most important economic sectors in the gas market are the same as in the coal market, namely electricity and energy intensive industries. We now discuss these sectors.

Electricity and Distribution. Of the 2300 bcm of gas used in the world in 1995, more than 1000 bcm were used in electricity generation and the distribution system.[1] The Annex I region accounts for 90 per cent of the total. As with coal, demand in the non-Annex I region grows much faster than in the Annex I region, from 100 bcm in 1995 to almost 400 bcm in 2020. Implementing the Global Compromise policies reduces gas demand from the sector by 140 bcm below the level projected under BaU, which is equivalent to 2.5 mb/d of oil.

Energy Intensive Industries. Gas demand in this diverse sector is projected to increase to 1200 bcm per year under Business as Usual, with growth about equal in the different regions in the model. Implementing the Global Compromise policies reduces projections to 980 bcm for the world, and 780 for the Annex I region in 2020, which means a reduction by 260 and 210 bcm below BaU projections. The reductions are equivalent to 4.5 mb/d of oil globally, 3.5 mb/d of oil in the Annex I region. Table 14.3 summarises sectoral effects in the gas market.

14.4.4 Overall Comparison

The electricity sector is the only main economic sector in which we observe a strong switch of fuels in the simulations. The use of oil products increases strongly, while coal and gas demand declines. Overall demand for fossil fuels declines by 6.4 mb/d oil equivalent, with a decline in coal and gas use by 7.8 mb/d oe, and an increase in the use of liquid fuel by 1.3 mb/d. As discussed in Chapter 11, much of the increase in liquid fuel use should be ascribed to the increase in availability of hydrogen in stationary fuel cells. Given that

---

1. The CLIMOX model cannot trace gas through the distribution system into other industries or households. We have therefore grouped all gas going into the distribution system together with the electricity sector.

Table 14.3: Changes in the Demand for Gas by Sectors. Thousand Barrels per Day Oil Equivalent

Sector	Electr. + Gas Distr.	Energy Int.	Other Ind.	HHD + Govt.	Other	Total
1995	0	0	0	0	0	0
2000	-207	-15	-5	-24	-70	-322
2005	-675	-568	-226	-79	-675	-2,223
2010	-1,898	-3,227	-1,019	-179	-2,138	-8,461
2015	-2,157	-3,735	-1,383	-215	-3,039	-10,529
2020	-2,478	-4,535	-1,845	-273	-3,847	-12,978

hydrogen production increases by much more than 1.3 mb/d in the Compromise scenario as compared with the BaU projections, we can safely assume that actual oil use in electricity generation is decreasing.

As in the Kyoto scenario, the impact of climate change policies on gas is greater than the impact on coal. As shown in Chapter 11, this is to a large extent due to the methane leaks in gas production, and the increase in production costs of gas once climate policies are implemented. The model cannot identify options for reducing gas leaks, and gas could expand its market share substantially if repairs of pipelines turn out cheaper than reductions in gas use.

14.5 Oil Revenues

Under the BaU scenario, world oil revenues increase by 98 per cent above their 1995 levels until 2020. As shown in Table 14.4, quantity and price changes produced by an implementation of the Global Compromise climate change agreement mean that revenues rise less strongly, and reach 61 per cent above their 1995 levels, a drop from the projected baseline by 19 per cent. As in the Kyoto scenario, the countries with significant non-conventional oil production in the BaU case are most strongly affected. Latin American oil revenues are projected to reach 3.1 times their 1995 levels in 2020 in the BaU case. Under the Global Compromise scenario, oil revenues reach only 2.5 times the initial level, a shortfall below BaU projections of more than 19 per cent.

A higher impact is observed in the ROO region, where the shortfall between projections under BaU and projections for the Global Compromise scenario reaches 38 per cent. In the AOE region, oil revenues are projected to increase to 2.2 times their 1995 levels in the

BaU case, and 1.9 times their 1995 levels under the Global
Compromise scenario. The Compromise scenario therefore means a
fall in revenues by 15 per cent. This impact is lower than for the world
as a whole. As in the Kyoto scenario, it becomes clear that suppliers
of conventional oil are less strongly affected by climate change policies
than countries which are projected to supply significant amounts of
non-conventional oil under the BaU scenario. Table 14.4 and Figure
14.9 summarise the changes.

Table 14.4: Oil Revenue Index, BaU and Kyoto. 1995 = 1

| | | BaU | | | Global Compromise | |
	2010	2015	2020	2010	2015	2020
USA	1.03	0.94	0.96	0.80	0.74	0.80
EUM	0.57	0.42	0.34	0.45	0.34	0.29
ROE	1.16	1.01	0.84	0.92	0.82	0.72
ROO	1.35	1.74	2.58	1.09	1.28	1.61
EIT	1.75	2.50	2.95	1.28	1.69	1.93
CHN	1.46	1.48	1.57	1.20	1.24	1.36
IND	0.86	0.92	0.97	0.70	0.76	0.82
ANI	0.78	0.65	0.65	0.63	0.54	0.56
AOE	1.65	1.94	2.21	1.40	1.64	1.92
LAM	2.22	2.69	3.10	1.84	2.21	2.52
ROW	0.98	1.13	1.41	0.80	0.88	0.93
TOTAL CONV.	1.47	1.65	1.81	1.21	1.38	1.56
TOTAL OIL	1.48	1.72	1.98	1.21	1.38	1.61

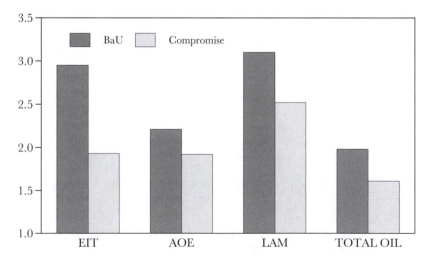

Figure 14.9: Oil Revenue Index, BaU and Global Compromise. 1995 = 1

14.6 Concluding Remarks

This chapter has shown the impacts of the new Global Compromise climate change agreement which could take the place of the Kyoto Protocol after 2012, as described in Chapter 13. The results shown here point out the importance of flexibility mechanisms in implementing the climate change policies: voluntary emission reductions by the Asian Newly Industrialised Countries (ANI) and Latin America (LAM) lead to a strong impact on the world oil price in 2010, because these countries have to achieve lower emissions by means of domestic measures alone. In later years, the impact on oil is mitigated by the inclusion of all regions into the new climate change agreement, despite more stringent emission reductions. The big non-Annex I countries, India and China, have a very high share of coal in their energy mixes. Inclusion of these countries into international permit trading reduces the global impact on oil, because it is relatively cheaper to reduce the use of coal, than it is to reduce the use of oil. International flexibility then means that coal use especially in China and India can be reduced more than oil use.

World oil revenues under the Global Compromise scenario therefore still increase 61 per cent above their 1995 levels, as compared with a 98 per cent increase in the BaU case, and a 74 per cent increase in the Kyoto scenario. Oil revenues will be 19 per cent below BaU under the Global Compromise scenario, as compared with 12 per cent below BaU under the Kyoto scenario.

CHAPTER 15

SENSITIVITY ANALYSIS

15.1 Introduction

This chapter tests the sensitivity of results to some of the most important exogenous parameters in the model. The assumptions tested here concern the functioning of the oil market, the availability of oil, economic growth, demand and supply elasticities, and 'hot air' cartels. As argued in Chapter 3, we have modelled the oil market in two tiers, one for conventional, the other for non-conventional oil. In the main scenarios, conventional oil supply is inflexible to demand changes, whereas non-conventional oil comes into the market to fill excess demand, and therefore reacts more flexibly to demand changes. In Section 15.2 we assume instead an inflexible response also of non-conventional oil supply, and look at the impacts of Kyoto on oil under this new specification.

In Section 15.3 the assumptions for oil supply capacity are changed. In the previous chapters, we projected oil supply to increase to about 100 million b/d by 2020. This is now increased by about 10 per cent. Price and quantity responses to the implementation of Kyoto are shown. Section 15.4 analyses the impacts of Kyoto in a world which is growing faster than the 2.5 per cent per year assumed in previous chapters. Economic growth is increased to 3.1 per cent on average. Again, the impact on oil prices and quantities are shown for both a BaU and a Kyoto scenario using this new assumption.

Section 15.5 looks at the sensitivity of results with respect to changes in major exogenous elasticity parameters specified in CLIMOX. In choosing elasticity parameters, modellers mainly rely on scant econometric evidence, and estimated guesses. In this section, we show effects of Kyoto on oil, first with a change in the elasticities of substitution between fuels in the main economic sectors, and second with a change in the elasticities of substitution between capital and resources in the fossil fuel production functions.

In Section 15.6 we make different assumptions about the supply of surplus trading permits to international emission trading. As explained in Chapter 10, we assumed for the Kyoto scenario that the EIT region limits quite strongly the amount of 'hot air' supplied to international trading. Likewise, we discussed in Chapter 13 limits to the supply of surplus permits by India and the Rest of the World region. Here we show impacts of different assumptions concerning 'hot air' and surplus permits; we show impacts of Kyoto without the EIT 'hot air' cartel, and impacts on results of the Global Compromise scenario for both less stringent surplus permit limits ('no cartel') and more stringent limits ('strong cartel'). Conclusions follow in Section 15.7.

15.2 Inflexible Oil Supplies

The supply of conventional oil has limited flexibility to respond to current market developments. Installed capacity determines to a large extent the supply of oil, and capacity is installed on the basis of long-term, and sometimes strategic decisions, which are not always well adjusted to short- and medium-term market developments. In the main scenarios, we assumed that the supply decisions for non-conventional oil are made on the basis of demand expectations, in contrast to decisions on conventional oil. As a result, the total supply of crude to the world is able to respond to some extent to demand changes resulting from climate change policies. In this section, we treat conventional and non-conventional oil in the same way, i.e. we assume that non-conventional oil projects are built as in the BaU case even when Kyoto is implemented. This means that oil production capacity grows as in the BaU case despite the demand shortfall resulting from Kyoto, because of the small price elasticity of both conventional and non-conventional oil supplies. In the model, this means the distinction between conventional and non-conventional oil disappears.

Figure 15.1 compares total oil supplies in the BaU case, and in the case of an implementation of Kyoto with the new oil market assumption. The climate change policies lead to a decrease in the supply of oil of 1.6 mb/d in 2010, but almost no change in 2020, as compared with the BaU projections. Obviously, the price response must be larger than in the Kyoto scenario to produce demand high enough for this level of supplies.

In a Kyoto scenario with inflexible supplies, the oil price stays flat at the 1995 level until 2010 and then increases by 12 per cent in 2020. The difference between the projections here and those in the Kyoto scenario in Chapter 11 are small for the period up to 2010, because

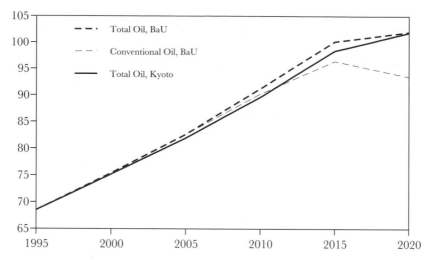

Figure 15.1:   Oil Production, Inflexible Supply. BaU and Kyoto. Million Barrels
per Day

of the already low level of non-conventional oil production in this
period in the BaU case. The difference between the impact of flexible
and inflexible supplies of these small amounts is naturally small. For
later periods, the difference in results is more significant. Under the
inflexibility assumption, the oil price falls by 11 per cent and 16 per
cent below the BaU levels in 2010 and 2020 respectively, as opposed
to 9 and 7 per cent in the Kyoto scenario. The important conclusion
is that some flexibility in oil supplies does reduce the adverse impact
of Kyoto on oil prices.

A stronger price response to climate change policies means lower
revenues than in the Kyoto scenario (see Table 15.1). Total oil revenues
of world producers increase to almost double their 1995 level in 2020
in the BaU case. With inflexible supplies, the implementation of the
Kyoto Protocol reduces the projected increase in world oil revenues by
12 and 16 per cent from the BaU levels in 2010 and 2020, respectively,
as compared with 12 per cent for both periods in the original Kyoto
scenario. The regional divergences from the world average in the
Kyoto scenario are caused by the difference between quantity responses
of conventional and non-conventional oil. In the Kyoto scenario, the
traditional suppliers of conventional oil suffer less than producers of
large amounts of non-conventional oil in the BaU case. Here the
regional divergences are small, because the reactions of producers of
both conventional and non-conventional oil are inflexible.

Table 15.1: Changes in Oil Revenues Between BaU, Kyoto, and Sensitivity Scenarios, 2010–20. Per Cent

	Kyoto Scenario		Inflexible Supply, Kyoto		High Oil Supply		High Economic Growth	
	2010	2020	2010	2020	2010	2020	2010	2020
USA	-14	-10	-17	-19	-13	-15	-10	-14
EUM	-14	-9	-12	-11	-13	-14	-10	-14
ROE	-13	-9	-13	-11	-12	-13	-9	-13
ROO	-12	-25	-14	-18	-12	-21	-24	1
EIT	-20	-27	-14	-16	-13	-23	-32	-12
CHN	-11	-8	-11	-13	-10	-11	-8	-13
IND	-11	-8	-12	-15	-11	-12	-9	-13
ANI	-12	-8	-7	-8	-11	-12	-9	-13
AOE	-10	-7	-11	-16	-9	-10	-8	-12
LAM	-27	-29	-12	-16	-10	-13	-12	-10
ROW	-12	-22	-13	-8	-11	-15	-9	-29
TOTAL CONV.	-11	-8	-11	-8	-11	-12	-8	-13
TOTAL OIL	-12	-12	-12	-16	-11	-14	-13	-12

15.3 High Level of Oil Availability

The level of oil production in the next twenty years is highly uncertain. In the main scenarios, total hydrocarbon liquid production reaches around 100 million barrels per day in 2020. We show here the impacts of Kyoto given higher capacity projections for oil. As discussed in Chapter 3 and in the model description in Chapter 5, capacity is given exogenously and production is allowed some flexibility around the given capacity level. Table 15.2 shows regional capacity projections. The capacity assumption here is set at 103 mb/d in 2020 but production, given substitution of capital for the resource in the CLIMOX model, reaches 111.7 mb/d in 2020. In contrast to the oil supply projections in the main scenarios, conventional oil supply increases between 2015 and 2020, and the volume of non-conventional oil supply is much lower as it only reaches 2.8 mb/d in 2020.

Figure 15.2 shows the resulting production profiles, for total oil supplies and conventional oil supplies in the 'high oil' BaU case, and for a new Kyoto simulation. The high level of conventional oil availability means that the requirement for non-conventional oil is fairly low. With an implementation of Kyoto in this 'high oil' scenario, conventional oil supplies are 90 mb/d and 106.3 mb/d in 2010 and 2020 respectively, whereas non-conventional oil is not competitive. Oil

Table 15.2: Oil Capacity Projections, High Oil Supply, 1995–2020. Thousand Barrels per Day.

	1995	2000	2005	2010	2015	2020
USA	8,626	8,434	8,248	8,000	8,000	8,000
EUM	3,485	2,887	2,288	2,000	2,000	2,000
ROE	2,905	3,300	3,150	3,000	3,000	2,800
ROO	3,071	3,170	3,354	3,600	4,000	4,200
EIT	7,339	8,355	9,270	12,000	14,000	16,000
CHN	2,990	3,287	3,611	3,800	3,800	3,800
IND	750	733	676	600	600	550
ANI	2,375	2,064	1,795	1,500	1,150	1,000
AOE	23,951	27,165	30,544	35,050	40,000	44,000
LAM	8,799	8,803	11,211	13,180	15,730	16,000
ROW	4,364	6,024	5,782	5,460	5,700	5,010
TOTAL	68,655	74,222	79,929	88,190	97,980	103,360

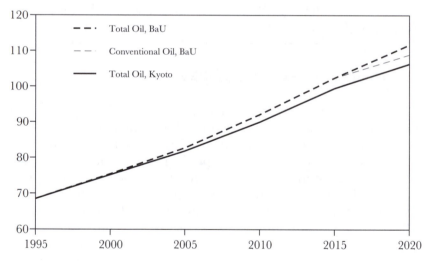

Figure 15.2: Oil Production, High Oil Supply. BaU and Kyoto. Million Barrels per Day

production falls by 2.1 mb/d in 2010 and 5.4 mb/d in 2020 from the new BaU levels.

Relatively low prices are needed to place the larger oil supplies in world markets. In the new BaU case, oil prices increase by 11 and 19 per cent in 2010 and 2020 from the 1995 levels, instead of 11 and 33 per cent in the main BaU scenario in Chapter 4. The implementation of the Kyoto Protocol results in lower price increases than shown for the new BaU case, but oil prices in 2020 are still higher than in the base year. They reach the end of the projections period at about 8 per cent above the 1995 level. The implementation of Kyoto in this simulation therefore brings the oil price 8 and 10 per cent below the BaU levels in 2010 and 2020 respectively, as compared with 9 and 7 per cent in the main Kyoto scenario.

As in the last section, we shall consider the effects of an implementation of Kyoto on oil revenues, when oil production is high. Table 15.1 shows changes in per cent in oil revenues between a BaU case and a Kyoto scenario, both with high oil supplies.

In this case, world oil revenues increase to 1.94 times their level in 1995 in a Business-as-Usual world. The implementation of Kyoto then leads to oil revenues lower than in BaU in 2020, but they still reach 1.67 times their 1995 levels, which means that Kyoto brings world oil revenues below the new BaU levels by 11 and 14 per cent in 2010 and 2020 respectively.

Oil revenues with high oil supplies are lower in 2020 in the BaU case, than projected in the main BaU scenario, where they reach 1.98 times the 1995 level, showing the importance of production restraint to protect revenues. The relative impact of an implementation of Kyoto however is about the same as in the Kyoto scenario in Chapter 11.

15.4 High Economic Growth Scenario

World economic growth in the main scenarios was assumed to be 2.5 per cent per year. To show the sensitivity of results to different growth assumptions, we have now changed the economic growth assumptions for every region, such that world growth averages 3.1 per cent per year. Higher economic growth has been implemented through increases in the total factor productivity, savings, and government expenditure growth rates by 0.6 per cent per year for OECD countries, and 1 per

Table 15.3: Average Growth of GDP. Per Cent Per Year

	1995–2020		1995–2020
USA	2.5	IND	5.1
JPN	2.4	ANI	5.4
EUM	2.6	AOE	4.9
ROE	2.6	LAM	4.5
ROO	2.7	ROW	3.4
EIT	4.4		
CHN	5.8	WORLD	3.1

cent for developing countries. The resulting growth rates are shown in Table 15.3.

The oil demand increase resulting from these high economic growth rates pushes prices higher and thereby leads to some increases in supply, in particular supply of non-conventional oil. Figures 15.3 and 15.4 show oil supplies and oil price indices for the high growth scenario.

In the new Business-as-Usual case shown in the two figures, oil production increases to 105.6 mb/d in 2015, and falls thereafter to

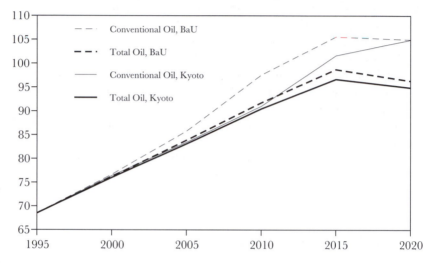

Figure 15.3:   Oil Production, High Economic Growth. BaU and Kyoto. Million Barrels per Day

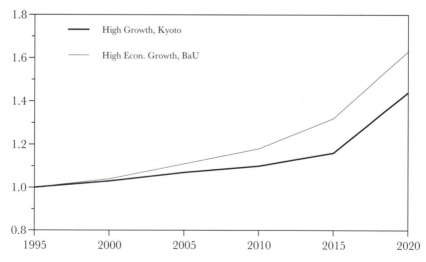

Figure 15.4:   Oil Price Index, High Economic Growth. BaU and Kyoto. 1995 = 1

105 mb/d. Higher rates of economic growth and the oil price increase shown in Figure 15.4 lead to increases in the production of conventional oil of 1.6 mb/d and 2.8 mb/d in 2010 and 2020, and increases in non-conventional oil of 4.9 mb/d, compared with the main scenarios based on a lower economic growth assumption. As before, the implementation of Kyoto decreases conventional oil production very little, whereas non-conventional oil production is 10 per cent below its BaU level in 2010. Remarkably however, non-conventional oil production picks up strongly in the last period, and total oil production in 2020 is virtually unchanged from the new BaU level. Hydrogen production reaches 2.4 mb/d in 2010 and 12.3 mb/d in 2020 in the new BaU case, and increases to 7.1 and 15.4 mb/d in the respective years in the new Kyoto case.

The strong oil demand expansion in the high economic growth scenario means that the oil price increases much more strongly than under the growth assumptions in the main chapters. Prices increase by 18 per cent in 2010, and 63 per cent in 2020 compared with their 1995 levels. This leads to a real price of oil in the year 2020 of about $30 in the new BaU case. The price response to the implementation of Kyoto policies in a high growth world is in the beginning very similar to the response obtained in the main Kyoto scenario. In 2010, the oil price falls 7 per cent below the new BaU level. In 2020, the oil price ends up 12 per cent below the BaU level as compared with a fall by 7.5 per cent in the Kyoto scenario. Under high economic growth, the oil price is projected to reach 44 per cent above the 1995 level in 2020 with the implementation of Kyoto.

Strong demand from a faster growing world means higher oil revenues. Table 15.1 shows changes in oil revenues between the new BaU and Kyoto scenarios. In the new BaU case, world oil revenues increase 2.5 fold between 1995 and 2020, as compared with a 98 per cent increase in the base case. An implementation of Kyoto in this fast growing world still has about the same effect on oil in relative terms as in the main Kyoto scenario. Oil revenues fall 13 and 12 per cent below the new BaU projections in 2010 and 2020 respectively. Strongest revenue reductions are observed in the countries which produce a high volume of non-conventional oil in the BaU case.

15.5 Changes in Elasticity Parameters

Elasticity parameters are the weakest point of any analysis based on computable general equilibrium models. As explained in Chapter 5,

CLIMOX is based on the GTAP database, which consists of regional social accounting matrices, with input-output tables and national accounts data, and an international trade matrix. Supplies of and demands for factors and goods in the model are based on multi-level nested constant elasticity of substitution (CES) functions. There are two types of parameters for the functions: the first, levels of supplies and demands, and factor shares, are determined from the database. The second are elasticity values, i.e. elasticities of supply of resource factors, elasticities of substitution between input factors, and substitution between goods in consumption. These elasticity values have to be determined exogenously by the modeller, and their empirical basis is weak. Elasticity estimates in the literature depend on the specification of the estimation model, time-frame of estimation, and regional and sectoral aggregation. Time series data usually do not exist for large parts of the world. Thus, estimated elasticity values are not obtainable, or not applicable for most of the functions in CGE models.

Modellers therefore have to enter elasticity values into their CGEs which are based on a judgement. The only way then to obtain credible CGE models is by using calibration and sensitivity testing. Models are calibrated by changing parameters until solutions reproduce actual parameter values, and where these are not obtainable, for example because models cover the future as in the case of CLIMOX, solutions are fitted to expectations and 'guesstimates' by the modellers. Sensitivity testing is then performed in order to show changes in modelling results due to changes in assumptions. This is indeed the task undertaken in this chapter. In this section, we show results of changes in elasticity values.

15.5.1 Demand Elasticities

Elasticities of demand for fossil fuels are not directly specified in CLIMOX. Demand for energy is derived from demand for inputs in production, and from linear expenditure systems with given income elasticities for households and governments. Elasticities of substitution between the different fuels, and between energy and non-energy goods are specified.

Three different elasticity values apply to the different sectors. For agriculture (including rice and livestock), the elasticity of substitution between different non-electric energy inputs is unity; for the energy commodities (oil, coal, gas, refining), the transport sector, and private and government demand, the elasticity is 0.2; for electricity generation, energy intensive and other manufactured goods, the elasticity of substitution is 5, implying highly flexible technology.

In this section, we show results of reducing the elasticities of substitution in the electricity and non-energy sectors. Instead of values of 1 (for agriculture) and 5 (for electricity and manufacturing), we have run CLIMOX with a uniform elasticity parameter of 0.2 across all sectors and consumers, i.e. we have changed our assumption for industrial sectors from highly flexible to highly inflexible. With the new elasticity values, we have simulated a new Business-as-Usual world, and an implementation of Kyoto.

With inflexible technology, the demand for oil is higher in the new BaU case, than in the previous chapters. Inflexibility means the price rise has to be stronger for firms and households to substitute away from oil when capacity growth is below demand growth in later periods. The new BaU price profile therefore projects an increase in the oil price of 40 per cent between 1995 and 2020, as compared with 33 per cent in the main chapters. Oil supply in 2020 increases to 103.8 mb/d as compared with 102 mb/d in the earlier chapters.

Implementing Kyoto with inflexible technology results now in a drop in the oil price of 12 per cent and 9 per cent in 2010 and 2020, respectively, from the levels projected under the new BaU for the two years, as compared with 9 and 7 per cent in the Kyoto scenario in Chapter 11. The production of oil is reduced to 99.8 mb/d in 2020, a drop of 4 mb/d from the new BaU projection, as compared with 5.3 mb/d in the main chapters.

Oil revenues of world producers increase tremendously in the new BaU case, by 52 and 112 per cent above 1995 levels for 2010 and 2020, respectively. Implementing Kyoto lowers oil revenues, by 16.6 per cent and 12.6 per cent below the new BaU projections for 2010 and 2020. The stronger price effect of Kyoto compared with results presented in Chapter 11 means a stronger effect on revenues than in the Kyoto scenario. Note that the dramatic change in substitution elasticities leads only to a relatively small change in the negative impact of Kyoto on oil revenues.

The inflexibility of production technology means that the consumer price increases needed to reduce fossil fuel use and emissions both for industrial and private consumers are larger than in the main chapters. Therefore, with the new set of elasticities, the prices of internationally traded emission permits reach \$20.40 and \$21.20 per ton CO_2e in 2010 and 2020, respectively, roughly double the prices obtained in the Kyoto scenario.

15.5.2 Supply Elasticities

Fossil fuel production is determined to a large extent by increases in physical production and transportation infrastructure, which do not react swiftly to current demand. With a given infrastructure, a limited amount of supply flexibility exists, for example through an increase in pipeline pressure, or some additional equipment with low installation costs. In CLIMOX, fossil fuel production is controlled by exogenously specified growth of the resource factor in the CES production function nesting, and limited substitution between resource factor and capital.

As shown in Chapter 5, Table 5.2, the elasticity of substitution between resource factor and capital, $K{:}F$, is 0.5 in the case of coal, 0.2 for gas, and 0.15 for oil. In this section, we show results of running CLIMOX with $K{:}F$ equal 2 for the three fossil fuels, i.e. for a hypothetical world in which fossil fuel production can react strongly to current demand signals by using more or less capital equipment.

In this flexible world, oil production increases in the new BaU scenario to 108.3 mb/d in 2020, as compared with 102 mb/d in the main chapters. Implementing Kyoto reduces world oil production to 103.8 mb/d, a reduction of 4.5 mb/d, as compared with 5.3 mb/d in the Kyoto scenario in Chapter 11. Oil prices fall by 2.7 and 3 per cent below the new BaU projections for 2010 and 2020, respectively, less than half the price fall observed in Chapter 11. Oil revenues in the new BaU projection are smaller than in the main chapters, highlighting the need for production restraint to maintain oil revenues.

The impact of Kyoto is a fall in revenues by 2.3 and 7 per cent from BaU levels projected for 2010 and 2020. Again, the impact of Kyoto is smaller than in Chapter 11. This confirms our earlier conclusion that some flexibility in the oil market reduces the impacts of Kyoto on oil revenues. Prices for internationally traded emission permits reach $8 and $11.20 per ton of CO_2e in 2010 and 2020 in the new Kyoto simulations.

15.6 Unrestricted 'Hot Air' and Surplus Permit Supply

In previous chapters – the Kyoto scenario and the Global Compromise scenario – it was assumed that countries with a high level of surplus and 'hot air' quota allocations form cartels and limit the supply of permits to international emissions trading. In the Kyoto scenario, emission targets for the EIT region are substantially above emissions projected in the BaU case. The region therefore has a fair amount of 'hot air' potentially available for trading. Following policy statements, we have assumed in the Kyoto scenario that the region limits 'hot air' supply to 2 per cent of required emission reductions in the other Annex I countries. In Section 15.6.1, we drop the supply limit and assume instead that the region supplies the full amount of 'hot air' permits to the international emissions trading market, i.e. there is no 'hot air' cartel. In the next two sub-sections, we show results of changing the surplus permit supply in the Global Compromise scenario.

15.6.1 Kyoto Without 'Hot Air' Cartel

The initial limit on 'hot air' supply in 2010 allowed the EIT region to carry over emission permits to the next period through 'banking'. The region therefore still had a substantial amount of 'hot air' permits in 2020.

Without a 'hot air' cartel, there will be no banking. All available 'hot air' permits are sold in 2010, and BaU emissions increase fast enough to surpass emission targets in 2020. This means that the EIT region has no 'hot air' in the last period. Total Annex I permit supply in the first commitment period therefore is here substantially greater, but in the last period supply will be lower than in the original Kyoto scenario.

The increase in permit supply lowers the price of international emission permits from $10 in the Kyoto scenario to $1.60 per ton of CO_2e in 2010. This reduces both the cost of implementing Kyoto for the Annex I countries and the incentive for domestic emission cuts for all the regions, because buying permits becomes cheaper. Lower reduction efforts reduce the impact of the implementation on the oil market in the first commitment period.

Emission restrictions then become more severe in the later periods, increasing the permit price from $11 in the Kyoto scenario to $13 per ton CO_2e in 2020. The impact of the Kyoto 'roll over' is therefore stronger in the last period, than shown in Chapter 11. Oil supplies show very little response to the 'no cartel' implementation of Kyoto in 2010, but the impact is more significant in 2020. Total conventional oil is reduced by only 1.3 mb/d in 2010 and 2020, and non-conventional oil is reduced by 1 mb/d in 2010 and 4.4 mb/d in 2020. Total oil supply is reduced by 5.7 mb/d in 2020.

Figure 15.5 shows oil supplies and the oil price index for BaU and Kyoto under unrestricted 'hot air' supply. The oil price index shows the same development as oil supply changes: the impact of Kyoto policies is mitigated in the first period, and later increased by the 'no

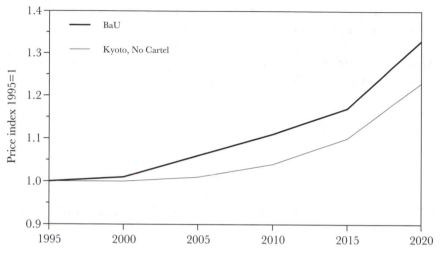

Figure 15.5:   Oil Price Index, BaU and Kyoto, No Cartel. 1995 = 1

cartel' policy in the EIT region as compared with the impacts in the original Kyoto scenario in Chapter 11.

15.6.2 The Global Compromise Scenario Targets without Surplus Permit Cartel

As explained in Chapter 13, India and RoW are assigned emission amounts far in excess of BaU emissions under the Global Compromise formula. However, these should not be called 'hot air' because the surplus amounts are different in nature from those which arose in the EIT region. In the Global Compromise, the surplus reflects a right acquired by the relevant parties, not the accidental result of historical developments. We have assumed in the Global Compromise scenario that India and the RoW region would form a surplus permit cartel. The assumption was that the two regions reduce their amounts of tradable permits by 20 per cent below their assignments under the Global Compromise formula. This section reports the results of simulating an implementation of the Global Compromise targets without surplus permit cartel.

The surplus permit allocations for India and the RoW region are very large. A free supply of all surplus permits to the international trading system means that global emissions are reduced by 14.4 per cent below BaU level in 2020, as opposed to 20 per cent in the Global Compromise scenario in Chapter 13. The permit price is therefore lower. Starting at $9.70 in 2010, the permit price drops to $9.30 per

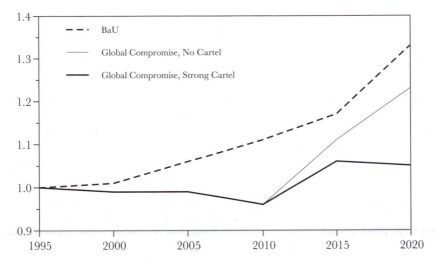

Figure 15.6: Oil Price Index, BaU and Global Compromise, No Cartel and Strong Cartel. 1995 = 1

ton CO_2e in 2020, compared with \$16 in the Global Compromise scenario. The 'no cartel' supply of surplus permits reduces the price of international emission permits by 40 per cent as compared with the Global Compromise scenario.

Lower emission reduction requirements mean a more benign impact on the oil market. In 2010, the quantity reduction from the BaU case is the same here as in the Global Compromise scenario because the same targets apply. By 2020, less emission reductions will be required because of the unrestricted surplus permit supply. Oil supplies are reduced by 6.2 mb/d in 2020 as compared with 8.3 mb/d in the Global Compromise scenario.

The price development is shown in Figure 15.6 for both the 'no cartel' scenario and a 'strong cartel' scenario discussed in the next subsection. Again, the development shown here is the same as that shown in Chapter 14 for the period until 2010. From then on the price reductions from BaU projected levels become smaller with full supply of surplus permits in the 'no cartel' case. By 2020, the price of oil is 8 per cent below the BaU level, as compared with 12 per cent in the Global Compromise scenario.

15.6.3 The Global Compromise Scenario Targets with a Strong Surplus Permit Cartel

Instead of supplying all surplus permits to the international emission

permit trading, we assume here that India and the RoW region form
a strong cartel and do not supply any surplus permits to the market,
i.e. they sell emission permits only according to emission reductions in
the two regions. The international availability of emission permits is
reduced substantially, and permit prices increase. Permit prices reach
$34.60 per ton of CO_2e in 2020, more than double the level obtained
in the Global Compromise scenario in Chapter 13. This permit price
increase is not in the best interest of the cartel countries. Despite the
strong price increase, their revenues from permit trading decline (see
Table 13.3). In this sense, the case is therefore not so much
representative of a 'strong cartel', but more of an irrational cartel.

The higher permit prices require a higher emission reduction effort
in the non-cartel regions, and therefore a stronger impact on the oil
market. Figure 15.7 shows oil supplies in the strong cartel case. Total
oil supply in 2020 is 13.9 mb/d below the BaU projections, as opposed
to 8.3 mb/d in the Global Compromise scenario. Non-conventional
oil production is completely squeezed out of the market.

The price response shown in Figure 15.6 is also much larger than
in the Global Compromise scenario. Oil prices in the strong cartel
case increase 5 per cent above the 1995 level, as opposed to 33 per
cent in the BaU case, and 17 per cent in the Global Compromise
scenario.

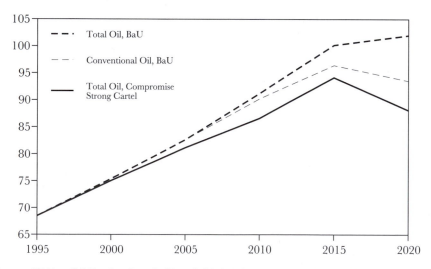

Figure 15.7:   Oil Production, BaU and Global Compromise, Strong Cartel.
Million Barrels per Day

15.7 Concluding Remarks

From the sensitivity analyses shown in this chapter we conclude that the main results of the previous chapters are fairly robust. Changes in assumptions about economic growth and the oil market only lead to small variations in the relative impact on the oil market of implementing Kyoto. In simulation analyses based on models like CLIMOX, it is the relative impact of policy changes rather than absolute levels that is of most interest. Actual levels of oil supply over the next twenty years, as other economic variables, are highly uncertain, yet modelling provides us with a good idea of the differences that alternative policies can make.

It has been shown that flexibility in the supply of non-conventional oil is important for mitigating the quantity and price adjustments in conventional oil production. There is a conflict of interest here between those countries projected to produce large volumes of non-conventional oil in the BaU case, and those which supply only conventional oil. If non-conventional oil production reacts flexibly to slower demand growth in a Kyoto scenario, those countries producing it will see their oil revenues increase much less than in the BaU case. They then lose out doubly, by not producing non-conventional oil, and because of lower prices on the conventional oil they produce. If they do not curb non-conventional production, they will lose more on their conventional oil production; but because overall production is higher, total oil revenues suffer less. It is therefore not in their best interest to postpone non-conventional production. Countries producing only conventional oil on the other hand will be less affected by Kyoto when non-conventional oil is flexible, than when it is inflexible.

Naturally, high levels of oil production mean lower oil revenues than when production restraints are applied. We have also seen that high economic growth ensures high oil prices and revenues, but again the impact of the Kyoto Protocol is about the same in relative terms. The main results of the analysis – the changes to be expected in the oil markets in relative terms – are therefore remarkably robust to changes in underlying assumptions about the oil market and economic growth.

The two sensitivity runs in Section 15.5 have shown that results depend to some extent on elasticity values. However, the changes in elasticities implemented here are very large. We have gone from a highly flexible specification of input demand in production and consumption to a highly inflexible specification, resulting in changes in oil revenues of about 30 per cent in 2010, and very little change in

2020. A larger change in results concerning oil revenues was observed in Section 15.5, where we have gone from a highly inflexible specification of fossil fuel supply to a highly flexible substitution of resources and capital. Modelling of the supply side of fossil fuel markets therefore seems to be much more crucial for the results than the modelling of the demand side, as shown not only by the results here, but also in Section 15.4, where we changed assumptions about economic growth.

Section 15.6 has shown that the impacts of the implementation of climate change agreements are very sensitive to assumptions made concerning surplus permits. It should be kept in mind that the 'surplus permit countries' can be expected to place some limits on supplies, if only to 'save up' permits to be used in later periods. On the other hand, any permit restriction policy will have to take into consideration the effect it has on international permit prices and revenues. We have tried to make a realistic assessment of supply limits, but a more detailed analysis would be needed to determine optimal supply behaviour for the different countries.

CHAPTER 16

COMPARISON WITH OTHER STUDIES

16.1 Introduction

The climate change issue in general, and the negotiations leading up to and following the Kyoto conference have attracted a fair amount of attention. It is therefore no wonder that the literature contains a large number of papers on the subject. Several of these are based on modelling exercises, and we will review a selection of these.

Comparisons of results are difficult, because modellers use different starting periods, methodologies, and scenarios, and in general only some of the assumptions are explicitly stated. It is clear that assumptions and methodologies, and in particular the type of models used have an influence upon the results of the analyses. Space and time constraints usually mean that limited information is made available concerning the sensitivity of results to the assumptions and the structure of the models.

A review like the one undertaken in this chapter is therefore a dangerous matter. Because of the limitations under which the reviewer has to work, it can be little more than a listing of differences in results. Such differences should not be interpreted as an 'expression of hapless ignorance of the analysts, but as a manifestation of the uncertainties inherent in projecting how the future will unfold'.[1]

Analysts have different beliefs about the future, and about the mechanisms at play. These beliefs are translated into choices of methodology and assumptions underlying the models. Differences in modelling results are therefore to a large extent due to differences in opinion about the functioning of the world economy, the availability of natural resources, the substitutability of inputs in production, and the availability of new technologies. All are highly uncertain, and no amount of analysis and literature search will provide definite guidelines.

---

1. John P. Weyant and Jennifer Hill (eds), 'The Costs of the Kyoto Protocol: A Multi-Model Evaluation', *The Energy Journal*, Special Issue, 1999, p. VIII.

The comparison in this chapter should ideally provide a concise analysis of the impacts of modellers' choices on results of climate change policy analysis. This would better enable the reader to judge from his or her own view of the world which modelling exercises are more credible and useful than others. Alas, such a review is a major research project on its own, and we can only go a small way towards that goal.

Keeping this in mind, we will proceed first with an overview of modelling approaches, second a comparison of marginal abatement costs of emission reductions, and third a comparison of oil market projections as obtained from the models.

16.2 Modelling Approaches

We have reviewed a number of models listed in Table 16.1, without claim to completeness. The table shows the model names, a brief description of the models reviewed, and their institutional origin. Most models used for climate change analyses can be distinguished in five basic categories, although of course many models display features of more than one category: (1) Aggregate cost function models, (2) Detailed energy sector models, (3) Computable general equilibrium models, (4) Macro-econometric models, (5) Integrated climate/economy models.

Aggregate Cost Function Models. The first category of models has the most aggregate treatment of the economic process. Each country or region is represented by an aggregate production function, in which GDP is produced using carbon as an input. Abatement cost functions can be derived from the production function using simple algebra. Reducing the amount of carbon available for production – an emission abatement regime – translates directly into economic costs. The models RICE and FUND included in Table 16.1 would fit into this category.

Detailed Energy Sector Models. The models sometimes have elaborate specifications of the energy sector, and only an aggregate production function to determine GDP. The detailed energy sector modelling is based on engineering studies of different energy technologies. Technology options are emphasised from a bottom-up perspective, and the models determine which technologies would be employed for a given set of relative prices using non-linear optimisation techniques. CETA, MERGE, and POLES are examples.

Computable General Equilibrium Models. Our CLIMOX is a typical example of this category. The models consist of sets of simultaneous equations, representing both supply and demand of factors, goods, and services. Energy and non-energy sectors are usually distinguished in some detail, and international trade in inputs and outputs is accounted for. General equilibrium models are firmly based on neo-classical economic theory and focus on interactions of firms and consumers in various sectors and industries. General equilibrium theory is static, which means the models are solved for a particular point in time. Because the theory assumes smooth adjustment of all economic sectors to a new set of prices, without unemployment of resources and without looking at transitional costs, this point in time is usually interpreted as an average over a medium-term period, say three to five years.

For analyses over a longer time horizon, CGEs make different assumptions about inter-temporal expectations. CLIMOX is a recursive model, i.e. economic agents are myopic and base their decisions only on price signals in the current period. The model is solved for a given period, after which stock variables, e.g. labour and capital supply, are updated to form the basis of a new solution representing a period further along the time path. Besides CLIMOX, examples are AIM, EPPA, GREEN, SGM, and WorldScan.

In contrast, a few models incorporate some form of foresight, where agents maximise discounted utility over the modelling period. Economic agents are assumed to take the future course of the economy into account in decisions for the current period, and the models are therefore solved simultaneously for the entire modelling horizon. Examples are ABARE-GTEM, G-Cubed, GemWTrap, and the MS-MRT model. Most CGEs look only at the real side of the economy, and the financial sector and money demand and supply are not represented. Inflation and nominal exchange rate changes therefore cannot be modelled. G-Cubed is the only counter-example in our sample, with an adequate modelling of the financial sector.

Macro-econometric Models. These consist of sets of simultaneous equations which are estimated statistically from time-series data of economies. Functional forms and equation structure are determined primarily by ability to explain the data-sets, and are not based on a priori theoretical assumptions. Originally, econometric models were designed as short-term forecasting tools, and are therefore sparse in economic feed-backs between demand and supply side. 'Their results become unrealistic (or chaotic!) when used over the long time periods which [other] models simulate'.[2]

Their advantage lies in their ability to analyse adjustment processes, with unemployment and capital shortages. Advances in econometrics, for example cointegration theory, and more detailed modelling of the supply side of economies has allowed the development of modern macro-econometric models which can be used for the long-term analyses required for climate policy advice. In Table 16.1 we have included the Oxford Economic Forecasting and EGEM models, which are general macro-econometric models, and the IEA and OWEM models, which are econometric energy models with a more aggregated treatment of the economy.

Integrated Climate/economy Models. The fifth category of models used for climate policy advice combines economic models with models of the physical aspects of climate change. This allows feed-backs between economies and the climate, and therefore an integrated assessment of benefits and costs of policy action, which is especially important for very long-term analyses, say over a period of one hundred years. Examples shown in Table 16.1 are CETA, FUND, and GRAPE.

16.3 Emission Abatement Costs

Because of differences in focus and methodology, comparison between results from different modelling exercises is difficult. Models do not have the same base year, and they look at a different set of parameters. There are for example very few studies which look in detail at the impact of climate policy on fossil fuels, and an indicator for this impact cannot therefore be used to compare model results. Nevertheless, for all the models shown in Table 16.1 we were able to collect at least some values for comparable endogenous economic parameters: prices of nationally or internationally traded carbon emission permits for an implementation of the emission constraints given in the Kyoto Protocol. These are shown in Table 16.2.

Most of the papers written on the basis of the modelling exercises reviewed here list results for different scenarios referring to an implementation of Kyoto. We have listed prices for domestic carbon trading for an implementation of Kyoto without international flexibility, and prices of emission permits traded within the Annex I region. Model names are shown in alphabetical order in the first row, and

2. N. Mabey, *Arguments in the Greenhouse: The International Economics of Controlling Global Warming*, (London: Routledge, 1997) p. 53.

Table 16.1: Models Analysing Kyoto Implementation Scenarios

Model Acronym (Full Model Name)	Model Description	Home Institution
ABARE-GTEM (Global Trade and Environment Model)	Multi-region dynamic CGE, 18 regions, 16 goods, based on GTAP V3	Australian Bureau of Agriculture and Resource Economics (ABARE, Australia)
AIM (Asian-Pacific Integrated Model)	Multi-region recursive CGE, 21 regions, 11 goods	National Institute for Environmental Studies (NIES, Japan) Kyoto University
CETA (Carbon Emissions Trajectory Assessment)	Intertemporal equilibrium model, detailed energy sector, aggregated. Rest of the economy, integrated climate model	Electric Power Research Institute Teisberg Associates
EGEM	Macro-econometric, 8 OECD regions, aggregated economy, detailed energy demand	London Business School
FUND (Climate Framework for Uncertainty, Negotiation, and Distribution)	Aggregate cost functions, integrated climate model, 9 regions	Vrije Universiteit Amsterdam (Netherlands)
G-CUBED (Global General Equilibrium Growth Model)	Multi-region dynamic CGE, 8 regions, 12 industries	Australian National University, University of Texas, U.S. Environmental Protection Agency
GEMWTRAP	Multi-region, dynamic CGE, technological sub-model of electricity generation, 7 regions, 12 sectors	Ministry of Equipment/Atomic Energy Agency (France)
GRAPE (Global Relationship Assessment to Protect the Environment)	Dynamic, intertemporal optimisation, integrated climate model, 10 regions	Institute of Applied Energy (Japan), Research Institute of Innovative Technology for Earth (Japan), University of Tokyo
GREEN	Multi-sector recursive CGE, 10 regions, 10 sectors, based on GTAP V4	OECD
IEA	Econometric energy demand, 10 regions	International Energy Agency
MERGE 3.0 (Model for Evaluating Regional and Global Effects of GHG Reductions Policies)	Intertemporal equilibrium model, detailed energy sector, aggregated. Rest of the economy, 9 regions	Stanford University, Electric Power Research Institute

Table 16.1: *continued*

Model Acronym (Full Model Name)	Model Description	Home Institution
MIT-EPPA (Emissions Projection and Policy Analysis Model)	Multi-region, recursive CGE, 12 regions, 12 sectors	Massachusetts Institute of Technology (MIT)
MS-MRT (Multi-Sector Multi-Region Trade Model)	Multi-region, dynamic CGE, 10 regions, 6 sectors, based on GTAP V4,	Charles River Associates, University of Colorado
OWEM (OPEC World Energy Markets)	Econometric energy demand, 11 regions	OPEC Secretariat
Oxford Model (Oxford Economic Forecasting)	Macro-econometric, 22 regions, aggregate production functions	Oxford Economic Forecasting
POLES	Bottom-up Energy Sector Model, 26 regions	IEPE/CNRS (France)
RICE (Regional Integrated Climate and Economy Model)	Optimal growth model, 13 regions, aggregate production functions	Yale University
SGM (Second Generation Model)	Multi-region recursive CGE, 12 regions, 9 sectors	Batelle Pacific Nothwest National Laboratory
WorldScan	Multi-region recursive CGE, 12 regions,	Central Planning Bureau/ Rijksinstituut voor Volksgezondheid en Milieuhygiene (RIVM) Netherlands
CLIMOX	Multi-sector recursive CGE, 12 regions, 12 sectors, based on GTAP V4	OIES

Sources: Models are described in papers in John P. Weyant and Jennifer Hill (eds) 'The Costs of the Kyoto Protocol: A Multi-Model Evaluation', op.cit. In addition, for the IEA model: International Energy Agency, *World Energy Outlook*, 1998 edition, Paris: IEA; for EGEM: N. Mabey et al., *Arguments in the Greenhouse: The International Economics of Controlling Global Warming*, op.cit.; for GemWTrap: A.L. Bernard and Marc Vielle, 'Efficient Allocation of Global Environment Cost Between Countries: Tradable Permits VERSUS Taxes or Tradable Permits AND Taxes? An Appraisal with a World General Equilibrium Model', 1999, Ministry of Equipment, Transports and Housing; for OWEM: Shokri Ghanem, Rezki Lounnas and Gary Brennand, 'The Impact of Emissions Trading on OPEC', *OPEC Review*, 1999, vol.XXIII, no.3.

prices are shown for the reference year listed in the second row. The next four rows show prices in base-year $ per tonne of carbon for domestically traded emission permits for the USA, Japan, Other OECD Countries, and the European Union, as far as they are given in the papers reviewed. The last row shows prices for emission permit trading between Annex I countries.

The range of permit prices in Table 16.2 is large. Domestic implementation of the Kyoto target for the USA can be achieved for anything between $50 (Worldscan) and $410 (Oxford Economic Forecasting) per tonne of carbon. The overall highest permit price for domestic implementation in the comparison table is from the Oxford Economic Forecasting model with $1100 per tonne carbon for Japan. Despite this wide range of results, a general pattern can be observed. In most models, permit prices in the USA are significantly lower than prices in Europe, and these are lower than in Japan, although several models show abatement costs in Europe surpass those in Japan.

The last column contains simple arithmetic averages for the permit prices shown, which have not been adjusted for the different base years of the models. According to these, reaching Kyoto will be achieved at $200 per tonne of carbon in the USA, $410 per tonne in Japan, $270 in other OECD countries, and $330 in Western Europe. CLIMOX figures shown in the column to the left of the averages are significantly below average, except for Other OECD countries.

The last row of the table shows modelling results for permit trading between Annex I countries, similar to our Kyoto scenario. Permit prices range between $20 (Worldscan) and $275 (EGEM) per tonne of carbon. Again, we show a simple arithmetic average in the last column, which is $100 per tonne of carbon. The permit price from CLIMOX in the Kyoto scenario shown in Chapter 11 translates to $40 per tonne of carbon. Our modelling results therefore seem at the lower end of the range.

Although we have confidence in our results, it is helpful to look at two specific assumptions which reduce permit prices in our simulations. We have therefore also shown a permit price for CLIMOX for an additional simulation: we implement Kyoto without non-carbon liquid fuels and without 'no regrets' measures included in the model, which reduce the permit prices in the policy scenarios. Taking away these favourable options for implementation of the Kyoto Protocol therefore increases adjustment costs. In Table 16.2, we show that the permit price for the new simulation (CLIMOX-NN) is $70 per tonne of carbon, much closer to the average shown in the last column.

This highlights the importance of non-carbon alternatives and 'no

Table 16.2: Comparison of Simulated Prices for Internationally Traded Emission Permits from Different Models. 2010

Models	Abare-GTEM	AIM	EGEM	EPPA	G-Cubed
Units	1992$	1992$/tC	1990$/tC	1990$/tC	1995$/tC
Permit Prices					
USA	350	150		240	90
Japan	690	240		590	110
Other OECD				280	260
EU	710	200	275*	310	
Annex I trading	110	65		90	60

Models	GEMWTRAP	GRAPE	GREEN	IEA	MERGE
Units	1990$/tC	1990$/tC	1995$/tC	1998$/tC	1990$/tC
Permit Prices					
USA	120		230		
Japan	160		180		
Other OECD					240
EU	250		190	250**	
Annex I trading	35	70	90		

Models	MS-MRT	OWEM	Oxford Economic Forecasting	POLES	RICE
Units	1995$/tC	1998$/tC	1997$/tC	1990$/tC	1994$/tC
Permit Prices					
USA	270	250			
Japan	470		410		
Other OECD	250	330	1100		
EU	210	480	950		
Annex I trading	90	150	220	80	65

Models	SGM	Worldscan	CLIMOX	Average Unadjusted $/tC
Units	1992$/tC	1992$/tC	1995$/tC	
Permit Prices				
USA	170	50	80	200
Japan	460		100	410
Other OECD			250	270
EU	140	85	80	330
Annex I trading	70	20	40 (70)	100

* refers to OECD-wide tax required to stabilise emissions at 1990 levels. ** preliminary results, described as 'carbon value' ... using the price response coefficients estimated for the OECD regions', see International Energy Agency, *World Energy Outlook*, 1998 edition, p. 55.

regrets' measures in our analysis. It is widely believed that some attractive alternatives to liquid fuels exist, and that energy efficiency increases can be achieved at little or no cost once incentives exist. Both options to reduce emissions lead to lower permit prices in the simulation. Most of the other models reviewed do not include these features of reality, and some of the differences between the other studies and the CLIMOX results can be explained by this omission.

In Figure 16.1 we have ordered models according to international permit prices. Four models clearly have very high permit price results, EGEM, IEA, Oxford Economic Forecasting, and OWEM. The majority of the studies shows permit prices between $60 and $80. CLIMOX results are at the low end of the spectrum, but higher than GemWTrap and Worldscan results. The permit price for the CLIMOX-NN simulation for Annex I trading now lies well within the range of the majority of the studies.

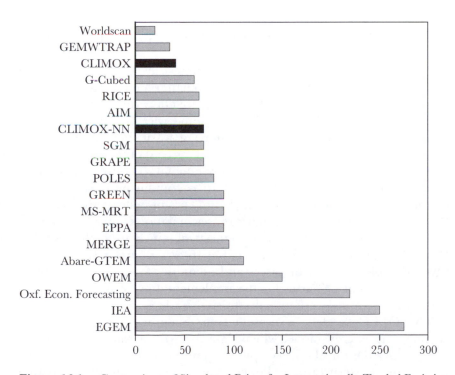

Figure 16.1: Comparison of Simulated Prices for Internationally Traded Emission Permits from Different Models, 2010. $ per Tonne of Carbon

Source: Based on Table 16.2.

From the figure, it seems that econometric studies show relatively high abatement costs, in comparison to other analyses. This could be due to the short-term focus of traditional macro-econometric models. In the short term, relocation of factors of production is very costly, and abatement costs are therefore high. On the other hand, these models are based on estimated elasticities of substitution and they could therefore give answers much closer to the truth than the other models.

As mentioned in the introduction to this chapter, it would make an interesting research project to compare modelling approaches in detail, and try to determine whether indeed the results from the macro-econometric studies shown here come closer to the truth than the results of the other studies. If so, it would mean that meeting the Kyoto emission targets is much more expensive in general economic terms than shown in this book, although the impact on the fossil markets need not be much different.

16.4 Modelling Effects of Climate Policies on Oil Markets

To our knowledge, there are very few studies in the literature which explicitly look at the impacts of climate change policies on fossil fuel markets. Of course, all the studies which are concerned with economic analyses of climate change policies, in some way or another have to make assumptions about the availability of fossil fuels, because they are the source of the large majority of greenhouse gas emissions. However, some studies look at aggregate CO_2 emissions, without specifying the sources, while other studies contain oil, coal, and gas, but neither production profiles nor the impacts of policies are discussed. We therefore confine this comparison to simulation results by Ghanem et al. (1999) from the OPEC Secretariat obtained from their OPEC World Energy Model (OWEM).[3] Table 16.3 compares CLIMOX and OWEM projections for oil prices and quantities for 2010, under BaU, and two different scenarios for the implementation of Kyoto, national carbon taxes, and international emission trading.

The OPEC model, as presented in Section 16.2, is a macro-econometric energy model which describes the world in six regions, namely OECD, OPEC, Developing Countries excluding OPEC, FSU, China, and Eastern Europe. Projections are carried out for the period

---

3. Shokri Ghanem, Rezki Lounnas, and Garry Brennand, 'The Impact of Emissions Trading on OPEC', *OPEC Review*, 1999, vol. XXIII, no. 3.

1997 to 2020. The model does not calculate oil prices endogenously, rather, an exogenously determined price is fed into the model, which then solves for regional oil demand. Supply is then computed to fill that demand. The analysis therefore starts with exogenous assumptions about the oil price (OPEC Reference Basket of crude) under business-as-usual. From a level of $12.30 in 1998, this is assumed to reach $14.50 in 1999, and $17 in 2000. From then on, prices rise by 1.5 per cent per year in real terms, reaching (in 1998 prices) $19.40 per barrel, whereas world oil production reaches 87.9 million barrels per day in 2010, and 99 mb/d in 2020. In comparison, in CLIMOX oil production reaches 91.2 mb/d and 102 mb/d in 2010 and 2020, respectively, and the oil price is $20 per barrel in 1995 Dollars for dated Brent crude in 2010.[4]

The OPEC Secretariat has analysed several different scenarios for an implementation of the Kyoto Protocol, and Table 16.3 shows results for four implementation scenarios in which emission trading is not allowed (national carbon taxes), and one scenario for international emission trading within the Annex I region. Since the OWEM does not compute prices endogenously, the scenarios have to involve assumptions about prices. The argumentation for the scenarios shown in Table 16.3 nevertheless is in terms of the production response of oil producers to the introduction of climate change policies necessary to maintain prices at a given level.

CLIMOX projections for an implementation of Kyoto on the basis of national carbon taxes show total oil production of 86.3 mb/d at a price of $17.1 in 2010. This results in a fall in oil revenues for the world oil producers of 19.1 per cent from BaU levels. For an implementation with intra-Annex I trading, CLIMOX shows a fall in producer revenues by 10.3 per cent.

The OPEC analysis shows two main scenarios for an implementation of Kyoto, namely (a1) with only national carbon taxes, and (b1) with inter-Annex I trading, and with producers in both cases maintaining prices at BaU levels. In the case of national taxes, as shown in Table 16.3, the OWEM model shows a fall in production by 7.3 million barrels per day from BaU levels in 2010, which leads to overall revenue losses of 8.3 per cent from BaU. In the case of intra-Annex I trading (b1), production falls by 3.8 mb/d, with revenue losses of 4.3 per cent. In the two scenarios for an implementation of Kyoto, the revenue

---

4. The USA consumer price deflator translates this into $21.4 in 1998 prices. The difference between Brent crude and the OPEC reference basket in 1998 moved in the range of $0.1 to $1.0.

losses from Kyoto projected by OWEM are therefore less than half the losses projected by CLIMOX. However, it is not clear which of the implementation scenarios for OWEM we should compare with CLIMOX.

The Ghanem et al. paper shows three additional scenarios which differ by the producer response to an implementation of Kyoto with national carbon taxes. In the first (a2), it is assumed that OPEC producers restrain oil production strongly, in order to maintain the same level of OPEC oil revenues as projected under BaU. Total oil supply falls to 79 mb/d, and prices reach $22.70 as compared with $19.40 under BaU in 2010. Second (a3), OPEC maintains production at the BaU level, with limited production response from non-OPEC, and prices fall sharply to $11.20. In the third sensitivity scenario (a4), OPEC and major non-OPEC producers curb production sufficiently to leave overall oil revenues almost unchanged from BaU. Production reaches 79.4 mb/d, at a price of $21.20 per barrel.

Changes in revenues for world oil producers calculated from the quantity and price figures for OWEM are also shown in Table 16.3: the revenue changes from Kyoto in the national carbon tax cases (a1-a4) range from plus 5.2 to minus 44.7 per cent of BaU revenues for 2010. The results highlight the importance of the producer response to demand changes. The Ghanem et al. paper concludes that careful production restraint can minimise the impact of Kyoto on oil revenues, although co-operation between OPEC and non-OPEC producers may be needed to avoid free-riding and a strong loss of market share for OPEC. This supports our conclusion that flexibility in production in general, and careful planning of non-conventional oil capacity, are important to reduce the impact of Kyoto on oil producers (see Chapter 11).

In order to compare OWEM and CLIMOX simulation results more directly, Table 16.3 shows two additional OWEM scenarios, which we have calculated by simple extrapolation of prices and quantities presented in the OPEC paper. The first (a5) starts with the CLIMOX price response to Kyoto, which is a fall by 14.5 per cent from BaU. In the OWEM projections, this corresponds to a price level of $16.60 per barrel, which according to our extrapolation would be obtained with an oil production of 81.7mb/d. This means oil revenues fall by 20.5 per cent below the level obtained in the BaU scenario for 2010, as compared with 19.1 per cent in the CLIMOX simulation. The second extrapolation scenario (a6) starts with the quantity response simulated by CLIMOX, a drop by 5.4 per cent from BaU. This translates into a production volume of 83.2 mb/d in OWEM, which

Table 16.3: Comparison of Oil Market Results, CLIMOX and OWEM, BaU and Different Kyoto Implementation Scenarios, 2010.

BaU

	CLIMOX	OWEM
Oil Production	91.2	87.9
Oil Price*	20.0	19.4

Kyoto, national carbon taxes

Scenario	CLIMOX	(a1) OWEM maintain price	(a2) OWEM, maintain OPEC revenues	(a3) OWEM, maintain OPEC production
Oil Production	86.3	80.6	79.0	84.2
Oil Price*	17.1	19.4	22.7	11.2
Change in Revenue (% of BaU)	-19.1	-8.3	5.2	-44.7

Scenario	(a4) OWEM joint production restraint	(a5) OWEM with CLIMOX price response	(a6) OWEM, with CLIMOX quantity response
Oil Production	79.4	81.7	83.2
Oil Price*	21.2	16.6	13.1
Change in Revenue (% of BaU)	-1.3	-20.5	-36.2

Kyoto, international emission trading

Scenario	CLIMOX	(b1) OWEM maintain price
Oil Production	88.4	84.1
Oil Price*	18.5	19.4
Change in Revenue (% of BaU)	-10.3	-4.3

* OWEM oil prices refer to OPEC reference basket of crude, CLIMOX oil prices are dated Brent

implies a price of $13.10 per barrel, and revenue losses of 36.2 per cent of BaU revenues for 2010, according to our extrapolation.

It is obvious that demand in OWEM is much more inelastic than in CLIMOX. Price elasticity of demand is estimated to be around −0.13 for OWEM, and −0.55 CLIMOX over the range of scenarios shown in Table 16.3, i.e. a price drop of 10 per cent would lead to an increase in oil demand by 1.3 per cent in OWEM, and 5.5 per cent in CLIMOX. According to OWEM, a policy of maintaining a similarly high level of oil production in the face of an implementation of Kyoto as the one shown in CLIMOX would lead to a sharp reduction in the price of oil, and large revenue losses. On the other hand, a policy of cutting production sufficiently to lower prices in OWEM by a similar margin as in CLIMOX would lead to revenue losses very similar to those shown in CLIMOX. Obviously, the inelastic demand in OWEM gives much more scope to producers' influence on revenues, and the impact of Kyoto on revenues, than the more elastic demand in CLIMOX.

Estimates of the price elasticity of demand for oil in the literature vary strongly with the time-frame of the analysis. It is clear that the elasticity is very low in the short term, and increases over time. The OWEM results for 2010 show an average for a period of ten years (2006–15), whereas CLIMOX results are for five years. Adelman discusses the changing price elasticity of demand, and estimates the long-term elasticity as –0.75.[5] The OWEM structure therefore seems better suited to predict short-term behaviour.

---

5. See Morris Adelman, *The Economics of Petroleum Supply* (MIT Press: Cambridge, 1993). See also Robert S. Pindyck, On Monopoly Power in Extractive Resource Markets, Energy Laboratory Working Paper No. MIT-EL 84-008WP, 1984, Center for Energy Policy Research, Massachusetts Institute of Technology, p. 13, who estimates long-term elasticity 'probably less than -1.5'; also, more recently Hashem M. Pesaran, Ron P. Smith, Takamasa Akiyama, *Energy Demand in Asian Developing Economies* (Oxford University Press: Oxford, 1993) p. 28, estimate own price elasticities for ten Asian countries in a range between -0.3 and -1.6.

CHAPTER 17

SUMMARY AND CONCLUSIONS

Last but not least, it is time to step back and reflect on the major results presented in this book, with a critical eye on the limitations we faced, as much as any other researchers, in the study of such a diverse and complex issue as our subject here, and with a healthy detachment from the particular methodology and assumptions necessary for the analysis. The main purpose of the study presented in this book is to assess the effects of climate change policies on fossil fuel markets with special attention to the oil market – that is demand, supply, prices and producers' revenues. The time horizon of this study is the period between the base year 1995 and the year 2020.

17.1 Methodology

Fossil fuels are quite literally the engine of the global economy, and their use pervades all economic sectors as intermediate inputs, and reaches every private household. The study looks at effects of the implementation of policy measures designed to reduce emissions of greenhouse gases from the fossil fuel sectors. The extensive national and international linkages between fossil fuels and the rest of the world economy make this an impossible task without the use of a complex but consistent framework. We have developed such a framework in the form of a global computable general equilibrium model, which we have called CLIMOX.

The model represents the world economy in twelve regions, with simultaneous production, demand, and foreign trade equations for twelve economic sectors, and solves for prices and quantities of factors and goods for each of the regions. CLIMOX is a recursive model, which means each solution represents averages for a period of five years, and after each solution we update stock variables, i.e. labour, capital, resources, and technology to account for growth. The model projects emissions of CO_2 from fossil fuel burning at the point of consumption, and methane emissions (converted into CO_2 equivalent units on the basis of a 100-year global warming potential) from fugitive fuels during production and transportation of fossil fuels.

We also project the production of two alternative sources of energy, carbon-based non-conventional oil and hydrogen, which are direct competitors to oil products.[1] They are more expensive to produce than conventional liquids, and therefore enter the market only after substantial price increases – due to a scarcity premium – of conventional oil. Non-conventional oil supplies make up less than 8 per cent of liquid fuel supply in 2020. Hydrogen supplies 4 to 14 per cent of the market for liquids in 2020 in the different simulations. Nuclear power is included implicitly in the model. We do not project major increases in nuclear power generation over the time horizon of the study above what is already planned mainly in developing countries as a response to climate change policies. Nuclear energy is not seen as the answer to the climate change problem, because of safety concerns.

The CLIMOX model is a useful framework in which to analyse impacts of policies, but at the same time, the methodology imposes certain restrictions on what can be analysed, and what the outcomes will be. A number of assumptions are needed which to a large part have to be based on judgement, or 'estimated guesses', and inevitably will be disputed by people with different judgements. Our defence is two-fold: first of all, the use of a computer model, and the description of the model in the book, mean that the analysis has to be internally consistent, because it is trapped in the brutal logic of binary numbers, and that all major assumptions are clearly stated and openly accessible to the critics. Secondly, we have performed a large number of additional simulations, which test the robustness of the results of the analysis with regard to changes in major assumptions.

17.2 Scenarios for Policy Analysis

The economic impact assessment of climate change policies is based on a comparison of different scenarios for the development of the world economy between 1995 and 2020. To assess the impacts of policies, we first project values of economic variables for a reference or business-as-usual scenario, which shows how the world develops without the climate change policies. We then compare this scenario

---

1. Hydrogen is used as a generic term for very low carbon alternatives to liquid hydrocarbon fuels.

with simulation runs in which all the exogenous parameters in the model stay the same, except for the implementation of a set of climate change policies. Because CLIMOX is a recursive model with discrete time periods, the analysis uses comparative statics, i.e. economic variables are compared for distinct points in time, which are taken to represent five-year averages.

We show impacts of two main scenarios for an implementation of climate change policies: the first is the Kyoto scenario, which assumes that the Kyoto Protocol is implemented, and that emission targets assigned in the Protocol for the First Commitment Period 2008–12 are rolled-over to 2020. The policy instruments for emission reductions chosen in the scenario are based on public statements from the governments concerned, and reflect what we consider as the most likely policies, if Kyoto is implemented at all. The scenario relies predominantly on trading of CO_2 equivalent emission permits between Annex I countries, significant additional energy efficiency improvements, and modest energy taxes in the EU.

The second policy scenario is the Global Compromise scenario, which assumes that a new, global agreement is reached sometime after 2012, in which all countries in the world commit themselves to a policy regime which leads to much more substantial emission reductions than the Kyoto Protocol, and puts the world on a path for an eventual stabilisation of greenhouse gas concentrations in the atmosphere.

In the Business-as-Usual world, economic growth of 2.5 per cent per year on average produces robust growth in the demand for energy, despite technological progress and energy efficiency improvements. Oil prices are projected to rise by about one-third over the study horizon, and gas prices also rise significantly, whereas coal prices stay more or less flat. The strong rise in consumption of fossil fuels means global greenhouse gas emissions from these sources rise by more than 50 per cent.

These projections should not be taken as predictions of actual quantities and prices in 2020. CLIMOX is a simulation model, and not a crystal ball. We produce a possible state of the world, in order to compare it with states of the world which differ only by the introduction of climate policies from the first. The actual development of the world will inevitably be very different from the one shown in this book. First and foremost, this is due to the stochastic nature of the real world, as opposed to the deterministic nature of the CLIMOX. The reality will always consist of small, and sometimes, large swings, which is why we interpret parameter values obtained from each model solution as five-year averages. In particular in the case of oil prices, the development over much of the 1980s and 1990s was characterised by sometimes sudden movements within a range which extended between a low of $7 and a high of $42 per barrel, and there is no reason why this should be much different in the future. This means net oil revenues can move up and down by a factor of more than five in a relatively short time. The effects of Kyoto on oil markets presented in this book – a reduction in oil revenues by 10–20 per cent – are easily swamped by this volatility. However, the implementation of Kyoto means that oil revenues will be lower on average than without implementation, and swings will be around this lower average.

17.3 Emission Reductions

Table 17.1 and 17.2 at the end of this chapter show the main results of the research presented in this book. They summarise simulation outcomes for emissions, conventional and non-conventional oil production, oil prices and oil revenues. Initial values are shown for the base year of the study, 1995, and projections for 2020, for a business-as-usual world, and for the two main policy scenarios, Kyoto and Global Compromise.

It is obvious that the impact of the Kyoto Protocol is relatively small, in terms of global emission reductions, economic costs, and effects on oil. The Kyoto Protocol is only a partial agreement, in which a subset of countries, albeit the richest and most energy-intensive ones, commit themselves to reduce emissions collectively by 5.2 per cent below the 1990 level. For one region of countries, the Economies in Transition, the choice of the base year 1990 for the Protocol means that emissions are projected to remain below target in a BaU world until around 2020, because of the economic collapse in the region since the early 1990s. The Protocol therefore allocates a large amount of surplus emission credits to the region.

While the industrialised countries are responsible for the largest share of global greenhouse gas emissions in the base year 1995, other countries which are not committed to emission reductions grow faster, and will be responsible for a fast rising share of emissions in the future. With an implementation of Kyoto extended to 2020, global emissions are therefore reduced by only 8–10 per cent from where they would have been in a business-as-usual world in 2020. In comparison, the reduction from business-as-usual levels required by that year in order to stabilise atmospheric greenhouse gases by the end of the twenty-first century at twice the pre-industrial level is generally estimated at between 20 and 30 per cent, two to three times what is required under the roll-over Kyoto Protocol. Such a stabilisation would still be associated with substantial global warming and sea-level rise.

It is clear that the impacts of the Kyoto Protocol on fossil fuel markets will also be small compared with the much stronger reductions necessary for stabilisation, as simulated in the Global Compromise scenario. This should not be interpreted as diminishing the significance of an implementation of the Kyoto Protocol. The Protocol was designed with limited aims, under many political constraints, and nobody could claim that its implementation would be sufficient to address the climate change problem. But this implementation is probably a necessary condition for a stabilisation regime, in the sense that developing countries are unlikely to be persuaded to join such a regime at a later stage without developed countries taking the lead by implementing the Kyoto Protocol. It also has to be expected that the modalities of implementation of the Kyoto Protocol – the extent to which international emission trading is allowed; the inclusion of gases other than CO_2, non-fuel emissions and different sinks; and the provision of funds to worst affected parties – will have strong inertia in any subsequent emission reduction regime. In other words, the rules of the game will be defined before the Kyoto commitment period, and it would be unwise to dismiss Kyoto. Interested parties should engage themselves constructively in the process, to shape the things to come.

17.4 Fossil Fuel Markets

The three fossil fuels, oil, coal, and gas, are affected differently by an implementation of climate change policies. Oil production in the Kyoto scenario is 3 per cent below BaU in 2010 and 5 per cent in 2020. Almost all of the fall in demand for oil is matched by an increase in the demand for hydrogen and other non-carbon fuels. The biggest oil demand comes from the transport sector, and substitution away from liquid fuels is much more difficult than reducing gas and coal consumption. The demand reduction for oil is therefore to a large extent due to our assumption that non-carbon alternatives are available at prices which become much more competitive when climate change is addressed. In fact, sensitivity analysis has shown that the impact on oil of Kyoto is reduced by half, if non-carbon alternatives are not available.

The non-carbon alternatives to oil currently available are much more expensive than oil products, and substantial technical progress has to occur to make even the modest market share in our projections possible. However, efforts are under way, and the major manufacturers of automobiles and generation equipment seem to believe strongly in sources of energy. In our projections, non-carbon liquids react strongly to climate change policies, which increase their competitiveness by increasing the price of conventional fuels. It is debatable to what extent technological progress is induced by policies and prices, as opposed to being autonomous and depending only on a stochastic process of inventions. It should be kept in mind, however, that sudden technological breakthroughs, whether induced by direct policies, changes in relative prices, or autonomous bouts of ingenuity, can have a strong impact on the market for oil, probably much stronger than any direct impacts from increases in consumer prices through carbon taxes.

Coal production suffers much more from climate policies than oil production, because of the high carbon content per energy unit of coal, with a reduction of 12 per cent from BaU in 2010, and 9 per cent in 2020, while gas is reduced by 7 and 6 per cent in 2010 and 2020, respectively. The quantitative impact of Kyoto on natural gas is therefore stronger than on oil; in fact, in absolute terms the reduction in gas demand is as strong as the reduction in coal demand. This is a somewhat surprising result, given that natural gas is usually seen as the cleanest fossil fuel, and the energy source of the future.

Oil has very specific uses, especially in the transport sector, and substitution away from oil is more difficult, than from coal and gas, which are used in diversified industries. Another important factor which works against gas is fugitive fuel methane emissions. Natural gas production, transportation and distribution is associated with methane leaks, which constitute important greenhouse gas emissions. While the carbon content of gas per energy unit is lower than for the other fuels, these methane emissions mean that gas is not the big winner from climate change policies. If methane emissions are taxed as CO_2 equivalent emissions, consumer prices for gas will increase substantially. About half the impact of Kyoto on gas is due to fugitive methane, as was shown in Chapter 11 where gas demand falls by 3–4 per cent only from BaU in a sensitivity simulation where we have taken methane out of the CLIMOX.

A caveat has to be made which qualifies this result. In the simulations, fugitive fuel emissions are determined using fixed coefficients associated with the production and transportation of fossil fuels. The only way to reduce emissions of methane in the model is therefore to reduce fuel production. However, it could well be that plugging gas leaks is much cheaper than reducing gas use. Relatively modest investment in new infrastructure would mean that consumer prices for gas increase much less than in the simulations, and gas would be a more competitive fuel. The extent of fugitive fuel emissions in particular in Russia is highly uncertain, and costs of reducing emissions are even more uncertain. It seems that most gas leaks occur in old, low-pressure distribution systems, not high-pressure, long-distance pipelines. Repairing distribution systems in cities might be very costly, whereas exchanging valves or even whole sections in long-distance pipelines is not. In the case of Russia, this would mean high gas prices for consumers in cities with old distribution systems, whereas gas prices in the European export markets may not be affected very much.

The overall effect of Kyoto on gas markets as shown in this book is therefore highly uncertain, especially in Europe. This should focus attention on the problem of fugitive fuel, and on the fact that gas is not so clearly the 'clean' fossil fuel.

The issue of initial consumer prices of fuels deserves some more attention than given to it in this book. Current energy taxation is heavily skewed against oil products, for revenue purposes and to reduce local pollution and road congestion. On the other hand, coal is subsidised in some industrialised countries, notably in Germany, for structural reasons. A 'green' tax reform to implement Kyoto, instead of additional penalties on fossil fuels from climate change policies, would probably reduce taxation on oil products, and increase consumer prices in particular for coal substantially. Emission reductions would then in principle be achieved with very small impacts on the oil market. It is not clear, however, how this could be reconciled with concerns for local pollution and road congestion.

17.5 Oil Revenues and Instrument Choice

In the Kyoto scenario, global oil revenues fall by 12 per cent below the levels projected under business-as-usual for 2020. We have discussed four additional scenarios for an implementation of the Kyoto Protocol, to test the impact of specific policy instruments as opposed to a mix of instruments implemented in the Kyoto scenario. The four scenarios show an implementation of Kyoto using national carbon taxes, national energy taxes on all fuels, national energy taxes with non-carbon fuels exempt, and international carbon permit trading. The choice of policy instrument for the implementation of emission cuts can lead to strongly different results: for the year 2020, reductions in oil revenues from business-as-usual range between 9 and 24 per cent. It becomes clear that energy taxes are an inefficient instrument for the implementation of climate change control, because they do not recognise the different carbon contents of fuels. However, it is quite possible that energy taxes will be used in some countries, and in fact it seems that in the EU at least they will indeed be implemented, but it is highly unlikely that energy taxes on renewable energy will be politically acceptable. The high level of energy taxes necessary to meet the Kyoto commitments boosts the competitiveness of alternative fuels, which strongly increases the reduction in oil demand.

The change in oil revenues from climate change policies matters more than changes in coal or gas revenues, because there is a set of countries which are heavily dependent on oil revenues, largely in the Middle East and North Africa. In most of the developing countries in this region, oil exports constitute by far the biggest source of foreign exchange and government revenue. No country is similarly dependent on gas or coal exports, and impacts of climate change policies on fossil fuel markets will therefore be most strongly felt in the Middle East and North Africa.

With the strong differences in impacts shown here, oil producers should have an incentive to lobby internationally against an implementation of Kyoto on the basis of energy taxation, and in favour of the international flexibility mechanisms included in the Kyoto Protocol. International carbon permit trading should be the policy of choice both on the grounds of economic efficiency for all countries concerned, and for the oil producers because it has significantly less impact on the oil markets than the other policy instruments.

Sensitivity analysis has shown that simulated impacts of Kyoto on oil revenues are remarkably robust to changes in major assumptions. Oil revenues fall by 12–16 per cent from BaU for different assumptions about economic growth, and availability of oil. Even the specification of substitution in demand between different fuels does not have a major impact on results. Some differences in results can be observed however, in simulations with changes in supply side specifications.

Flexibility in the supply of oil therefore seems to be important to reduce impacts on oil producers, by reducing the change in oil prices necessary to equate supply and demand. In particular, investment in highly capital intensive, non-conventional oil production capacity should be made only after careful consideration of the supply and demand balance in the oil market over the project lifetime, and of the impact of carbon penalties on the competitiveness of the project, given that some non-conventional oil resources have a much higher carbon content than conventional oil.

17.6 Emission Trading and Excess Permits

We have performed additional simulations with different assumptions about the climate change control regime. The Kyoto Protocol assigns emission targets to the countries in Eastern Europe and the Former Soviet Union, which are far above emission levels in the 1995 base year of our analysis. Because of the economic collapse since the beginning of the 1990s, the Economies in Transition as a whole are projected to reach these targets in the BaU scenario only towards the year 2020, whereas during the Kyoto commitment period 2008–12 their BaU emissions are significantly below the targets. This is the so-called 'hot air' problem: they have no incentive to actively reduce emissions. In addition, if international emission trading is allowed, the region can sell substantial amounts of emission permits without undertaking any abatement efforts, which would allow other Annex I countries to reduce emissions by a lesser amount than otherwise.

Two countries in the region are widely believed to be the only major suppliers of 'hot air' permits, Russia and the Ukraine. In our Kyoto scenario, these countries form a duopoly in the emission market, and reduce permit supply. The resulting increase in permit prices not only increases revenues from trading, but also induces other countries to undertake joint implementation projects in Russia and the Ukraine, with associated benefits from technology transfers.

The self-imposed limits on 'hot air' supply by Russia and the Ukraine increase the impact of Kyoto on global emissions strongly in 2010, with emission reductions of 8 per cent instead of 4 per cent. High permit prices also mean that all Annex I countries undertake substantial abatement efforts at home, and caps on emission trading proposed by the EU in 1999 become meaningless.

17.7 A New Global Climate Change Agreement

In the Global Compromise scenario, emission reductions are much larger than in the Kyoto scenario, increasing in 2010 from 8 to 12 per cent of BaU emissions because of voluntary commitments by some regions, and in 2020 from 8 to 20 per cent because of the participation of all regions in a global agreement. Global oil demand falls by 8 per cent below BaU levels in 2020, coal demand by 27 per cent, and gas demand by 16 per cent. Despite a more than double impact on emissions, the impact on oil in this scenario is only about 50 per cent higher than in the Kyoto scenario, because of the high share of coal in the big developing countries, India and China, who participate in the global reduction effort. Oil revenues fall by a substantial 19 per cent from BaU levels in 2020, and by 32 per cent from BaU if trading in excess permits is not allowed. This clearly has very substantial impacts on the economies of oil-exporting countries. Negative impacts in the major industrialised countries however are modest, while developing countries make substantial gains from emission trading.

If climate change is taken seriously by the world, a stabilisation of greenhouse gases in the atmosphere has to be attempted sooner rather than later, and we believe that our Global Compromise scenario shows a possible way to go. It is possible both in terms of inducing developing countries to join the global efforts, because it is based on principles of fairness and justice, and in terms of aggregate economic consequences, because impacts on world growth will be limited. However, a long-term solution to the climate change problem has to take into account regional differences both in effects of global warming, which probably cannot be avoided anymore, and effects of emission abatement, which will be felt most strongly in oil-exporting countries.

17.8 Non-energy Emission Abatement and Sinks

All the scenario projections in this study, and most other studies in the literature, are based on energy emissions – i.e. CO_2 emissions from fossil fuel combustion and methane emissions from fugitive fossil fuels – which in 1995 amounted to 87 per cent of all Annex I GHG emissions. In other words, we did not take into account the full basket of GHGs allowed for under the Kyoto Protocol, mainly because of modelling limitations: energy emissions are directly related to the use of fossil fuels, and abatement usually means a reduction in fuel use. Impacts of climate policies on fossil fuel emissions can be modelled easily in a general equilibrium framework, which has maximising agents taking price increases into consideration. Non-energy emissions, and to some extent also fugitive fuel emissions from gas leaks as was already discussed, can be reduced through investment in distinct projects, and these would have to be modelled separately in a bottom-up fashion, which goes far beyond the scope of this study. In view of the relative size of energy emissions, the omission of non-energy GHGs was felt to be justifiable. Likewise, we have made no attempt to include the possibilities of carbon sequestration in the soil, the seas, or bio-mass, so called sinks, as an alternative to emission abatement. The reasoning here has less to do with modelling limitations, than with data limitations. The scientific basis for calculation of sink potentials is slim, with a partial exception in the case of bio-mass, i.e. we have some knowledge over how much carbon is taken up by plants, but very little when it comes to soil and seas.

However, in drawing our policy conclusions, it would be unwise to completely ignore the abatement options which non-energy emissions and sinks might afford. In the case of methane emissions, the second most important greenhouse gas, the relevant total methane abatement potential is already estimated to be several times larger than the total required emission reductions from the Kyoto Protocol. Most of the abatement potential for methane is in non-Annex I countries. This means that if projects in non-Annex I countries are allowed for in meeting Kyoto commitments through the Clean Development Mechanism, the possibility exists in principle to implement the Kyoto Protocol purely on the basis of non-energy emissions and sinks. Since all researchers face the same uncertainties and modelling difficulties with regard to non-energy options, most analyses are confined to energy sources, and other options are ignored. While a non-fossil-fuel implementation of Kyoto is highly unlikely, the omission of these other options overstates the costs of Kyoto, both in general and in terms of impacts on fossil fuel markets.

It is in the oil producers' interest to argue that non-energy sources of emissions should be looked at, and that they should be included in the modalities for the implementation of Kyoto which are under negotiation mainly before and during the Conference of the Parties (COP6) session in 2000.

17.9 Policy Implications

The major lessons to be drawn from the research presented in this book can be summarised in three points, which involve direct policy recommendations. Firstly, the choice of policy instruments to address the climate change problem matters. Economic costs in general, and impacts on fossil fuels in particular, differ greatly with different instruments. Emission trading between Annex I countries, and participation of non-Annex I countries through the Clean Development Mechanism should be the preferred policy option. This internationally flexible implementation should be based on the six gases and the sink potentials specified in the Kyoto Protocol. Oil-exporting countries have a role to play in this regard in the international negotiations leading up to and during the sixth session of the Conference of the Parties in the autumn of 2000, where major decisions about the modalities of the implementation of Kyoto will be taken.

Secondly, market information, and the formation of correct demand expectations is important to ensure an orderly functioning of the oil market. Non-conventional oil plays a crucial role beyond 2010 in filling the gap between conventional oil supplies and oil demand. It is important that investments in non-conventional oil are made in a timely manner. Because of the time lags involved between investment decision and project completion, expectations concerning demand have to be formed. The danger is always that expectations are too low, and capacity is not ready when conventional oil production capacity falls short of demand, or that expectations are too high, and demand growth does not materialise, which puts downward pressure on the oil price. In our analysis, we have shown that an adaptation to the implementation of Kyoto of investments into non-conventional oil production capacity is crucial.

Thirdly, the development of technology matters. The moot question is whether climate change policies will bring about technological breakthroughs that will ultimately lead to the demise of oil, especially in the car industry. And if so, when will this happen, and how long will it take for the composition of the car stocks in the world to change significantly? It is quite possible that a breakthrough will come without much direct inducement from prices or policies. In the scale of things, the development of transport technology may prove to be a more potent cause of worries to oil-exporting countries than Kyoto as framed today. To say that these are worries about the long term, that is for times beyond 2020, the end of our period of study, is no great consolation. The development challenge that faces the oil-exporting developing countries also involves a very long-term horizon. The diversification of their economies which began in the 1970s will not provide a base for self-sustained economic growth, in many cases, until well into the twenty-first century. This is the challenge that calls for all the attention of their governments and their citizens and for the support of the international community.

Table 17.1: Summary of Results: Emissions and Oil Production, all Scenarios. 1995 and 2020

		Global Emissions Mt CO_2e	Emissions Reduction Per Cent of 2020 BaU	Total Oil Production Million Barrels per Day	Reduction from BaU Million Barrels per Day
Base Level	1995	23,679	-	68.5	-
Business-as-Usual	2020	36,750	-	102.0	-
Kyoto	2020	33,764	-8.1	96.7	-5.3
Single Policy Instrument					
National CO_2 Quotas	2020	33,391	-9.1	93.1	-8.9
Energy Taxes	2020	33,466	-8.9	97.7	-4.3
Energy Taxes, Hydrogen Exempt	2020	33,094	-9.9	91.3	-10.7
International CO_2 Trade	2020	33,739	-8.2	97.0	-5.0
Sensitivity					
High Economic Growth, BaU	2020	39,986	-	105.0	-
High Economic Growth, Kyoto	2020	36,862	-7.8	104.9	0.0
High Oil Supply, BaU	2020	37,424	-	111.7	-
High Oil Supply, Kyoto	2020	33,857	-9.5	106.3	-5.4
Demand Elasticities, BaU	2020	36,983	-	103.8	-
Demand Elasticities, Kyoto	2020	33,751	-8.7	99.9	-4.0
Supply Elasticities, BaU	2020	37,504	-	108.3	-
Supply Elasticities, Kyoto	2020	33,790	-9.9	103.8	-4.5
Inflexible Oil Supply, Kyoto	2020	33,818	-8.0	101.8	-0.1
Kyoto, No Cartel	2020	33,461	-8.9	96.3	-5.7
Global Compromise	2020	29,573	-19.5	93.7	-8.3
No Cartel	2020	31,456	-14.4	96.2	-5.8
Strong Cartel	2020	25,953	-29.4	88.1	-13.9

Table 17.2: Summary of Results: Non-conventional Oil Production, Oil Prices and Oil Revenues, all Scenarios. 1995 and 2020

	Non-conventional Oil Production Million Barrels per Day	Oil Price Per Cent Change from BaU	Oil Revenue Per Cent Change from BaU
Base Level	-	-	-
Business-as-Usual	8.5	-	-
Kyoto	4.3	-7.0	-11.8
Single Policy Instrument			
National CO_2 Quotas	1.8	-11.9	-19.6
Energy Taxes	5.0	-5.0	-9.0
Energy Taxes, Hydrogen Exempt	0.6	-14.9	-23.8
International CO_2 Trade	4.6	-6.4	-11.0
Sensitivity			
High Economic Growth, BaU	8.6	-	-
High Economic Growth, Kyoto	10.0	-11.5	-11.6
High Oil Supply, BaU	2.8	-	-
High Oil Supply, Kyoto	0.0	-9.6	-14.0
Demand Elasticities, BaU	9.5	-	-
Demand Elasticities, Kyoto	7.1	-9.1	-12.6
Supply Elasticities, BaU	2.9	-	-
Supply Elasticities, Kyoto	9.5	-3.0	-7.0
Inflexible Oil Supply, Kyoto	n.a.	-15.9	-16.0
Kyoto, No Cartel	4.1	-7.5	-12.7
Global Compromise	2.5	-11.5	-18.7
No Cartel	4.1	-7.6	-12.9
Strong Cartel	0.0	-21.2	-31.9

APPENDICES

APPENDIX 1

The aim of this appendix is to draw together the greenhouse gas (GHG) emissions data used to calibrate the initial period of the CLIMOX model, and to provide a list of methane abatement potentials, based on IPCC figures and CLIMOX estimates.

1995 Greenhouse Gas Emissions

All the Annex I figures have been taken from the National Communications mandated under the UN Framework Convention on Climate Change, as summarised by the FCCC secretariat in two documents, namely CP/1998/11/Add.2 and CP/1998/INF.9. The data for non-Annex I countries were obtained from the World Resources Institute (WR). 'EIT1' refers to the Annex I countries of our EIT region.

Table A.1.1 gives an Annex I summary of all anthropogenic GHG emissions in 1995, and, for comparative purposes, in 1990 (the Kyoto baseline). Tables A.1.2 to A.1.4 contain further (global) CO_2 data, while Tables A.1.5 and A.1.6 are devoted to Annex I methane (CH_4) and nitrous oxide (N_2O), respectively. Table A.1.7, in turn, summarises anthropogenic CO_2 emissions from and removals by land-use change and forestry, impact on total CO_2 emissions, and CO_2 emissions from international bunker fuels.

Methane Abatement Potentials

Table A.1.8, finally, lists our 2010 and 2020 estimates (based on IPCC percentage figures) of methane abatement potentials for the agricultural, waste-disposal and energy sectors.

Table A1.1: Annex I Anthropogenic GHG Emissions. 1995 and 1990. Thousand Tonnes CO_2e and Per Cent of Total by Party/Region

1995	CO_2 (Gg)	%	CH_4 (Gg)	%	NO_2 (Gg)	%	Other GHGs (Gg)	%	Total (Gg)
USA	5,214,710	84.8	650,475	10.6	144,801	2.4	136,669	2.2	6,146,655
JPN	1,218,377	88.1	32,487	2.3	34,131	2.5	98,542	7.1	1,383,537
EUM[a]	3,195,971	79.9	455,700	11.4	294,221	7.4	51,829	1.3	3,997,721
ROE	84,332	76.3	15,078	13.6	7,812	7.1	3,344	3.0	110,566
ROO	823,617	73.0	220,080	19.5	73,873	6.6	10,223	0.9	1,127,793
OECD Total	10,537,008	82.5	1,373,820	10.8	554,838	4.3	300,607	2.4	12,766,273
EIT1[b]	2,969,407	82.3	523,131	14.5	78,182	2.2	38,980	1.1	3,609,700
Annex I Total	13,506,414	82.5	1,896,951	11.6	633,020	3.9	339,587	2.1	16,375,972

1990	(Gg)	%	(Gg)	%	(Gg)	%	(Gg)	%	(Gg)
USA	4,960,432	85.5	621,138	10.7	131,750	2.3	88080	1.5	5,801,400
JPN	1,124,532	89.8	33,075	2.6	32,643	2.6	61474	4.9	1,251,724
EUM	3,316,507	75.8	484,596	11.1	527,775	12.1	43,630	1.0	4,372,508
ROE	82,761	74.8	14,490	13.1	8,339	7.5	5,062	4.6	110,652
ROO	761,800	72.3	210,966	20.0	65,875	6.3	14,410	1.4	1,053,051
OECD Total	10,246,033	81.4	1,364,265	10.8	766,382	6.1	212,656	1.7	12,589,336
EIT1	4,288,709	79.7	909,573	16.9	137,702	2.6	42,124	0.8	5,378,108
Annex I Total	14,534,742	80.9	2,273,838	12.7	904,084	5.0	254,780	1.4	17,967,444

(a) Other GHG data not available from Greece, Ireland, Luxemburg, Monaco, Portugal, Spain.
(b) Other GHG data available only from Czech Republic, Russia, Slovakia.

Table A1.2: Anthropogenic CO_2 Emissions by FCCC Sector. 1995. Thousand Tonnes CO_2 and Per Cent of Total

	Fuel combustion (Gg)	%	Energy Fugitive fuel (Gg)	%	Total Energy (Gg)	Industrial processes (Gg)	%	Waste (Gg)	%	Other (Gg)	%	Total (Gg)
USA	5,144,626	98.7	6,200	0.1	5,150,826	63,884	1.2		-		-	5,214,710
JPN	1,138,478	93.4		-	1,138,478	61,236	5.0	18,663	1.5		-	1,218,377
EUM	3,049,300	95.4	19,044	0.6	3,068,344	113,499	3.6	7,784	0.2	6,345	0.2	3,195,971
ROE	70,758	83.9	1,873	2.2	72,631	10,014	11.9	1,365	1.6	322	0.4	84,332
ROO	770,354	93.5	15,441	1.9	785,795	34,588	4.2	754	0.1	2,481	0.3	823,617
OECD Total	10,173,516	96.6	42,558	0.4	10,216,074	283,221	2.7	28,566	0.3	9,148	0.1	10,537,008
EIT1[a]	2,890,884	97.4	22,805	0.8	2,913,689	54,564	1.8	1,154	0.0		-	2,969,407
Annex I Total	13,064,400	96.7	65,363	0.5	13,129,762	337,785	2.5	29,720	0.2	9,148	0.1	13,506,414
EIT[b]	3,296,612	97.4	26,006	0.8	3,322,618	60,459	1.8	1,716	0.1		-	3,383,521
CHN[c]	2,906,257	89.4	10,379	0.3	2,916,635	333,074	10.6		-		-	3,249,709
IND[c]	825,841	94.0	2,814	0.3	828,655	52,322	5.6		-		-	880,976
ANI[c]	1,138,524	91.5	6,623	0.5	1,145,147	92,309	8.0		-		-	1,237,456
AOE[c]	1,077,973	88.1	68,313	5.6	1,146,285	71,157	6.3		-		-	1,217,442
LAM[c]	961,025	91.8	23,603	2.3	984,628	61,079	5.9		-		-	1,045,706
ROW[c]	1,192,129	89.7	80,490	6.1	1,272,620	38,382	4.2		-		-	1,311,002
World	21,571,877	94.4	260,785	1.1	21,832,662	992,001	4.3	30,282	0.1	9,148	0.0	22,862,820

(a) Annex I EITs: FCCC data not available for Croatia, Lithuania, Romania, Slovenia and Ukraine. They were supplied by EIA and WR (Industrial processes = 1.5 Cement, as suggested by the FCCC data for EIT countries).

(b) Total emissions were calculated on the basis that total energy emissions are 98.2 per cent (as in EIT1), Industrial process and waste emissions were then calculated in accordance with the EIT1 distribution.

(c) Energy figures from EIA statistics (Fugitive fuel: WR); Industrial processes = WR cement figure x 1.5 (according to EIT proportion).

Table A1.3: Annex I CO_2 Fuel Combustion Emissions by FCCC Sector. 1995. Thousand Tonnes and Per Cent of Total

	Energy industries (Gg)	%	Industry (Gg)	%	Small combustion (Gg)	%	Transport (Gg)	%	Other (Gg)	%	Total (Gg)
USA	1,811,186	35.2	1,099,118	21.4	597,105	11.6	1,598,375	31.1	38,842	0.8	5,144,626
JPN	359,385	31.6	346,492	30.4	177,084	15.6	242,123	21.3	13,393	1.2	1,138,478
EUM	1,096,133	35.9	541,833	17.8	642,611	21.1	747,094	24.5	21,629	0.7	3,049,300
ROE	10,213	14.4	8,602	12.2	20,989	29.7	29,907	42.3	1,048	1.5	70,758
ROO	322,238	41.8	128,576	16.7	90,846	11.8	226,621	29.4	2,073	0.3	770,354
OECD Total	3,599,155	35.4	2,124,621	20.9	1,528,635	15.0	2,844,120	28.0	76,985	0.8	10,173,516
EIT1	1,611,928	55.8	519,202	18.0	488,111	16.9	257,799	8.9	13,856	0.5	2,890,884
Annex 1 Total	5,211,083	39.9	2,643,823	20.2	2,016,746	15.4	3,101,919	23.7	90,841	0.7	13,064,400

Table A1.4: Global CO_2 Energy Emissions by Fuel Type. 1995. Thousand Tonnes and Per Cent of Total[a]

	Solids	%	Liquids	%	Gases + Flaring	%	Total
USA	1,814,792	35.2	2,203,267	42.8	1,132,767	22.0	5,150,826
JPN	281,576	24.7	720,521	63.3	136,380	12.0	1,138,478
EUM	807,752	26.3	1,647,183	53.7	613,409	20.0	3,068,344
ROE	4,268	5.9	57,877	79.7	10,486	14.4	72,631
ROO	252,799	32.2	336,994	42.9	196,002	24.9	785,795
OECD Total	3,161,187	30.9	4,965,842	48.6	2,089,044	20.4	10,216,074
EIT1	1,109,166	38.1	702,440	24.1	1,102,083	37.8	2,913,689
Annex I Total	4,270,353	32.5	5,668,283	43.2	3,191,127	24.3	13,129,762
EIT	1,210,414	36.4	852,859	25.7	1,259,344	37.9	3,322,618
CHN	2,372,990	81.4	507,068	17.4	36,577	1.3	2,916,635
IND	573,524	69.2	211,656	25.5	43,475	5.2	828,655
ANI	248,395	21.7	748,563	65.4	148,189	12.9	1,145,147
AOE	27,546	2.4	704,915	61.5	413,824	36.1	1,146,285
LAM	71,837	7.3	697,319	70.8	215,473	21.9	984,628
ROW	599,682	47.1	504,548	39.6	168,390	13.2	1,272,620
World	8,265,574	37.9	9,192,771	42.1	4,374,317	20.0	21,832,662

(a) Totals from Table A1.2. Percentages supplied by EIA

Table A1.5: Annex I Anthropogenic Methane (CH_4) Emissions. 1995. Thousand Tonnes CO_2e and Per Cent of Total by Party

| | Energy | | | | Agriculture | | | | Waste | | Other | | Total |
| | Fuel combustion | | Fugitive fuel | | Livestock | | Other | | | | | | |
	(Gg)	%	(Gg)	%	(Gg)	%	(Gg)	%	(Gg)	%	(Gg)	%	(Gg)
USA	16,821	2.6	196,287	30.2	190,659	29.3	10,269	1.6	236,439	36.3	-	-	650,475
JPN	2,205	6.8	3,549	10.9	9,555	29.4	8,274	25.5	7,833	24.1	1,071	3.3	32,487
EUM	15,582	3.4	75,978	16.7	178,773	39.2	8,736	1.9	167,160	36.7	9,471	2.1	455,700
ROE	588	3.9	903	6.0	5,355	35.5	-	-	8,211	54.5	21	0.1	15,078
ROO	3,444	1.6	59,535	27.1	111,468	50.6	6,174	2.8	37,779	17.2	1,680	0.8	220,080
OECD Total	38,640	2.8	336,252	24.5	495,810	36.1	33,453	2.4	457,422	33.3	12,243	0.9	1,373,820
EIT1[a]	5,712	1.1	321,510	61.5	103,404	19.8	2,919	0.6	80,388	15.4	9,198	1.8	523,131
Annex I Total	44,352	2.3	657,762	34.7	599,214	31.6	36,372	1.9	537,810	28.4	21,441	1.1	1,896,951

(a) No data available for Croatia, Lithuania, Romania, Slovenia and Ukraine.

Table A1.6: Annex I Anthropogenic Nitrous Oxide (N_2O)Emissions. 1995. Thousand Tonnes CO_2e and Per Cent of Total

	Energy				Industrial processes		Agriculture		Waste		Other		Total
	Transport		Other										
	(Gg)	%	(Gg)	%	(Gg)	%	(Gg)	%	(Gg)	%	(Gg)	%	(Gg)
USA	33,790	23.3	11,160	7.7	32,550	22.5	67,301	46.5	-	-	-	-	144,801
JPN	4,278	12.5	17,143	50.2	7,409	21.7	2,821	8.3	2,046	6.0	434	1.3	34,131
EUM	19,902	6.8	40,982	13.9	91,853	31.2	123,287	41.9	2,635	0.9	15,562	5.3	294,221
ROE	868	11.1	403	5.2	1,674	21.4	4,650	59.5	93	1.2	124	1.6	7,812
ROO	18,073	24.5	3,813	5.2	11,935	16.2	39,091	52.9	62	0.1	899	1.2	73,873
OECD Total	76,911	13.9	73,501	13.2	145,421	26.2	237,150	42.7	4,836	0.9	17,019	3.1	554,838
EIT1[a]	837	1.1	14,074	18.0	9,517	12.2	51,863	66.3	310	0.4	1,581	2.0	78,182
Annex I Total	77,748	12.3	87,575	13.8	154,938	24.5	289,013	45.7	5,146	0.8	18,600	2.9	633,020

(a) No data available for Croatia, Lithuania, Romania, Slovenia and Ukraine

Table A1.7: Annex I Anthropogenic CO_2 LUCF Emissions (negative = sink) and Bunker Fuel Emissions. 1995. Thousand Tonnes

	Total Emissions (Gg)	Sinks (Gg)	Sinks % of Total Emissions	Net Emissions (Gg)	Bunker Fuels (Gg)
USA[a][f]	5,214,710	-428,000	-8.2	4,786,710	
JPN	1,218,377	-94,619	-7.8	1,123,758	37,328
EUM[c]	3,195,971	-186,311	-5.8	3,009,660	185,240
ROE[d]	84,332	-18,737	-22.2	65,595	5,107
ROO[e]	823,617	-42,593	-5.2	781,024	16,083
OECD Total	10,537,008	-770,260	-7.3	9,766,748	243,758
EIT1[b][g]	2,945,015	-719,707	-24.4	2,225,308	11,406
Annex I Total	13,482,023	-1,489,967	-11.1	11,992,056	255,164

(a) US figures only.
(b) The only sink figures available for Lithuania, Slovenia, and Ukraine are for 1990, which were taken over for 1995. No figures available for Romania and Croatia.
(c) No sink figures for Greece.
(d) No sink figures for Iceland.
(e) No sink figures for Canada.
(f) No data provided by USA.
(g) Bunker fuel data provided only by Bulgaria, Hungary and Russia

Table A.1.8: Methane Abatement Potentials. 2010 and 2020. Million Tonnes CO_2e

Source	Average percentages 1995–2020	Abatement Potentials		Required Reductions	
		2010	2020	Kyoto[a] (2010)	Global Compromise[b] (2020)
Non-energy Emissions					
Rice	97% non-Annex I	781	1,189	1,417	7,170
Livestock	73% non-Annex I	1,134	1,603		
Solid Waste	61% Annex I	282	502		
Total		4,207	5,314		
Annex I		502	775		
Fugitive Fuel Emissions					
Coal	66% non Annex I, 17% EIT	539	665		
Gas	57% Annex I, 45% EIT	666	943		
Total		1,205	1,608		
Annex I		563	764		
EIT		391	537		
Sum Total		5,412	6,922		

(a) The Kyoto reduction level assumed here is predicated on full 'hot air' trading.
(b) The Global Compromise Scenario Reduction is calculated at 14.4% below the relevant BaU emissions (see Ch 13).

APPENDIX 2

Table A2.1: Energy CO_2 and Fugitive-Fuel CH_4 Emissions, BaU and Changes from BaU, Different Scenarios. 1995–2020. Million Tonnes CO_2 Equivalent.

BaU

	1995	2000	2005	2010	2015	2020
USA	5,307	5,613	5,921	6,257	6,617	6,859
JPN	1,149	1,209	1,256	1,297	1,314	1,279
EUM	3,146	3,219	3,301	3,368	3,420	3,429
ROE	74	80	86	90	93	95
ROO	830	874	920	968	1,012	1,050
EIT	3,994	3,579	3,993	4,632	5,412	6,135
CHN	3,322	3,741	4,266	4,882	5,599	6,447
IND	891	980	1,083	1,197	1,324	1,473
ANI	1,181	1,365	1,580	1,809	2,065	2,323
AOE	1,353	1,651	1,958	2,311	2,703	3,123
LAM	1,088	1,280	1,500	1,762	2,077	2,443
ROW	1,343	1,454	1,586	1,731	1,905	2,092
TOTAL	23,679	25,044	27,450	30,305	33,541	36,750

Difference, Kyoto – BaU

	1995	2000	2005	2010	2015	2020
USA	0	-73	-417	-849	-1,085	-1,273
JPN	0	-6	-254	-295	-312	-277
EUM	0	-25	-126	-354	-391	-400
ROE	0	0	-2	-2	-3	-3
ROO	0	-8	-54	-134	-139	-129
EIT	0	-40	-74	-754	-924	-1,025
Annex I	0	-152	-928	-2,389	-2,854	-3,106
CHN	0	-5	-23	-39	-43	-38
IND	0	-1	-1	-4	-3	0
ANI	0	2	19	57	95	84
AOE	0	0	2	6	12	22
LAM	0	1	4	8	12	22
ROW	0	0	3	4	12	31
Non-Annex I	0	-5	5	33	85	121
TOTAL	0	-157	-923	-2,357	-2,769	-2,986

Table A2.1: *continued*

Difference Global Compromise – BaU

	1995	2000	2005	2010	2015	2020
USA	0	-72	-417	-829	-1,182	-1,506
JPN	0	-5	-199	-240	-172	-177
EUM	0	-24	-89	-341	-406	-439
ROE	0	0	-2	-2	-3	-3
ROO	0	-7	-54	-141	-152	-153
EIT	0	-41	-77	-837	-1,109	-1,327
Annex I	0	-149	-838	-2,390	-3,024	-3,606
CHN	0	-20	-56	-108	-1,290	-1,561
IND	0	-9	-16	-32	-306	-354
ANI	0	-4	-110	-444	-244	-279
AOE	0	-14	-31	-57	-364	-480
LAM	0	-4	-170	-482	-439	-602
ROW	0	-12	-21	-40	-271	-296
Non-Annex I	0	-62	-402	-1,164	-2,913	-3,571
TOTAL	0	-211	-1,240	-3,554	-5,936	-7,177

Table A2.2: Oil Production, BaU 1995–2020, and Changes from BaU, Different Scenarios, 2020. Million Barrels per Day Oil Equivalent

	Business-as-Usual Levels			Kyoto Targets, Change from BaU in 2020					
	1995	2010	2020	Kyoto Scenario	National Quota	Energy Tax	Energy tax (non-carbon exempt)	International Carbon Trading	Inflexible Supply
USA	8.6	8.0	6.2	-0.2	-0.5	-0.2	-0.8	-0.2	-0.3
EUM	3.3	1.7	0.9	0.0	0.0	0.0	0.0	0.0	0.1
ROE	2.9	3.0	1.8	0.0	-0.2	-0.1	-0.2	0.0	0.1
ROO	3.1	3.7	4.3	-0.1	-0.2	-0.1	-0.2	-0.1	1.5
ROO NON-CONV	0.0	0.0	1.7	-1.1	-1.7	-0.9	-1.7	-1.1	-1.7
EIT	7.3	10.6	12.6	-0.3	-0.4	-0.2	-0.4	-0.3	3.7
EIT NON-CONV	0.0	1.0	3.7	-1.0	-2.0	-0.8	-3.1	-0.8	-3.7
CHN	3.0	3.9	3.5	0.0	-0.1	0.0	-0.1	0.0	0.1
IND	0.8	0.6	0.5	0.0	0.0	0.0	0.0	0.0	0.0
ANI	2.4	1.7	1.2	0.0	0.0	0.0	0.0	0.0	0.1
AOE	24.0	35.6	39.8	-0.2	-0.4	-0.1	-0.5	-0.2	0.0
LAM	8.8	17.6	19.0	-0.2	-0.3	-0.1	-0.5	-0.2	1.5
LAM, NON-CONV.	0.0	0.0	1.5	-0.9	-1.5	-0.7	-1.5	-0.8	-1.5
ROW	4.4	3.8	3.6	0.0	-0.1	0.5	-0.1	0.3	1.5
ROW NON-CONV.	0.0	0.0	1.5	-1.2	-1.5	-1.1	-1.5	-1.2	-1.5
TOTAL CONV.	68.5	90.2	93.5	-1.2	-2.2	-0.8	-2.9	-1.1	8.3
TOTAL NON-CONV.	0.0	1.0	8.5	-4.2	-6.7	-3.5	-7.9	-3.9	-8.5
TOTAL OIL	68.5	91.2	102.0	-5.3	-8.9	-4.3	-10.7	-5.0	-0.1

Table A2.2: *continued*

	Kyoto Targets, Change from BaU in 2020					Global Compromise Targets, Change from BaU in 2020		
	High Oil Supply, Kyoto	High Econ. Growth, Kyoto	Kyoto, No Cartel	Demand Elastic	Supply Elastic	Global Compromise	No Cartel	Strong Cartel
USA	-0.5	-0.2	-0.2	-0.2	0.1	-0.4	-0.2	-0.9
EUM	-0.1	0.0	0.0	0.0	-2.2	0.0	0.0	-0.1
ROE	-0.1	0.0	0.0	0.0	-1.4	-0.1	0.0	-0.1
ROO	-0.1	-0.1	-0.1	-0.1	-0.4	-0.1	-0.1	-0.3
ROO NON-CONV	-0.5	1.0	-1.2	-1.3	1.8	-1.7	-1.1	-1.7
EIT	-0.8	-0.4	-0.4	-0.5	-3.1	-0.5	-0.3	-1.2
EIT NON-CONV	-1.8	0.3	-1.1	0.8	2.3	-1.5	-1.0	-3.7
CHN	-0.1	0.0	0.0	0.0	-1.6	-0.1	0.0	-0.2
IND	0.0	0.0	0.0	0.0	-0.1	0.0	0.0	0.0
ANI	0.0	0.0	0.0	0.0	-3.7	0.0	0.0	-0.1
AOE	-0.4	-0.2	-0.2	-0.3	1.8	-0.6	-0.4	-1.2
LAM	-0.3	-0.2	-0.2	-0.2	-0.5	-0.4	-0.2	-1.0
LAM, NON-CONV.	-0.5	0.6	-0.9	-0.9	1.1	-1.3	-0.9	-1.5
ROW	-0.2	-0.6	0.2	-1.1	1.4	-0.1	0.1	-0.3
ROW NON-CONV.	0.0	-0.5	-1.3	0.0	0.0	-1.5	-1.4	-1.5
TOTAL CONV.	-2.6	-1.4	-1.3	-1.5	-11.1	-2.3	-1.4	-5.4
TOTAL NON-CONV.	-2.8	1.4	-4.4	-2.4	6.6	-6.0	-4.4	-8.5
TOTAL OIL	-5.4	0.0	-5.7	-4.0	-4.5	-8.3	-5.8	-13.9

Table A2.3: Oil Demand, BaU 1995–2020, and Changes from BaU, Different Scenarios, 2020. Million Barrels Oil Equivalent

| | Business-as-Usual Levels | | | Kyoto Scenario | Kyoto Targets, Change from BaU in 2020 | | | | |
	1995	2010	2020		National Quota	Energy Tax	Energy tax (non-carbon exempt)	International Carbon Trading	Inflexible Supply
USA	15.11	18.79	19.47	-3.58	-8.69	-3.23	-10.93	-4.40	-1.89
JPN	4.56	5.20	4.76	-1.06	-1.06	-0.69	-0.84	-0.57	-1.01
EUM	12.57	14.21	13.91	-2.62	-1.73	-1.17	-2.09	-0.96	-2.11
ROE	0.55	0.66	0.65	0.10	-0.27	-0.26	-0.26	0.01	0.14
ROO	2.45	2.90	3.03	-0.29	-0.80	-0.76	-0.68	-0.33	-0.23
EIT	4.56	5.00	6.58	-0.89	-0.30	-0.29	-0.35	-1.19	-0.92
CHN	3.11	4.79	5.87	0.28	0.42	0.18	0.47	0.27	0.61
IND	1.22	1.86	2.27	0.12	0.15	0.08	0.16	0.10	0.21
ANI	5.01	7.56	8.68	0.87	1.30	0.60	1.51	0.75	1.75
AOE	8.85	15.13	19.16	0.88	0.90	0.54	0.95	0.62	1.45
LAM	6.34	9.68	11.43	0.56	0.84	0.51	0.94	0.49	1.12
ROW	4.16	5.42	6.17	0.31	0.36	0.20	0.40	0.22	0.75
TOTAL OIL	68.49	91.20	101.98	-5.32	-8.87	-4.30	-10.72	-4.99	-0.13

Table A2.3: *continued*

| | Kyoto Targets, Change from BaU in 2020 | | | | | Global Compromise Targets, Change from BaU in 2020 | | |
	High Oil Supply, Kyoto	High Econ. Growth, Kyoto	Kyoto, No Cartel	Demand Elastic	Supply Elastic	Global Compromise	No Cartel	Strong Cartel
USA	-2.55	-1.57	-3.99	-3.17	-1.83	-4.28	-2.55	-7.28
JPN	-1.21	-0.86	-1.05	-1.30	-0.18	-0.53	-0.32	-1.02
EUM	-3.44	-2.55	-2.66	-2.50	-0.87	-2.52	-2.42	-2.90
ROE	0.12	0.15	0.10	0.13	-0.04	0.12	0.10	0.18
ROO	-0.52	-0.12	-0.32	-0.38	-0.13	-0.33	-0.24	-0.54
EIT	-1.23	-1.11	-0.99	-1.09	0.45	-1.26	-0.71	-2.06
CHN	0.32	0.62	0.31	0.35	-0.47	0.81	0.59	1.20
IND	0.13	0.25	0.13	0.15	-0.14	0.01	0.01	-0.05
ANI	1.10	1.51	0.91	1.24	-0.83	-0.53	-0.23	-1.24
AOE	0.92	1.72	0.94	1.33	-0.32	-0.16	-0.25	-0.43
LAM	0.64	1.30	0.62	0.81	-0.09	0.15	0.12	-0.03
ROW	0.34	0.61	0.33	0.49	-0.04	0.19	0.09	0.26
TOTAL OIL	-5.39	-0.04	-5.68	-3.95	-4.49	-8.32	-5.80	-13.90

Table A2.4: Coal Production, BaU 1995–2020, and Changes from BaU, Different Scenarios, 2020. Million Tonnes Oil Equivalent per Year

	Business-as-Usual Levels			Changes from BaU Kyoto Scenario	Global Compromise
	1995	2010	2020	2020	2020
USA	554	611	679	-176	-197
JPN	4	3	4	-1	0
EUM	127	68	43	-4	-4
ROE	0	0	0	0	0
ROO	174	208	244	-18	-8
EIT	340	350	409	-84	-94
CHN	662	965	1,272	-21	-449
IND	152	180	209	-3	-85
ANI	41	65	89	-2	-7
AOE	1	1	1	0	0
LAM	25	47	72	-1	-5
ROW	192	237	277	-2	-44
TOTAL	2,272	2,736	3,300	-312	-893

Table A2.5: Coal Demand, BaU 1995–2020, and Changes from BaU, Different Scenarios, 2020

Million tonnes oil equivalent per year

| | Business-as-Usual Levels | | | Changes from BaU | |
| | | | | Kyoto Scenario | Global Compromise |
	1995	2010	2020	2020	2020
USA	509	563	617	-174	-193
JPN	75	75	75	-15	-13
EUM	227	200	198	-15	-17
ROE	1	1	1	0	0
ROO	74	79	83	-19	-21
EIT	325	314	388	-71	-81
Annex 1	1,210	1,233	1,363	-293	-325
CHN	647	965	1,283	-12	-406
IND	159	209	254	-2	-84
ANI	68	100	134	-4	-21
AOE	8	12	16	0	-3
LAM	20	24	29	0	-5
ROW	161	192	220	-1	-49
Non-Annex 1	1,062	1,503	1,937	-19	-568
TOTAL OIL	2,272	2,736	3,300	-312	-893

Million barrels oil equivalent per day

| | Business-as-Usual Levels | | | Changes from BaU | |
| | | | | Kyoto Scenario | Global Compromise |
	1995	2010	2020	2020	2020
USA	7.13	7.89	8.64	-2.44	-2.70
JPN	1.04	1.05	1.06	-0.21	-0.18
EUM	3.17	2.80	2.77	-0.20	-0.24
ROE	0.02	0.02	0.02	0.00	0.00
ROO	1.03	1.11	1.17	-0.26	-0.29
EIT	4.54	4.40	5.44	-0.99	-1.14
Annex 1	16.94	17.26	19.09	-4.10	-4.55
CHN	9.05	13.51	17.96	-0.16	-5.68
IND	2.22	2.92	3.56	-0.03	-1.17
ANI	0.96	1.39	1.88	-0.05	-0.29
AOE	0.11	0.17	0.22	0.00	-0.04
LAM	0.28	0.34	0.41	0.00	-0.07
ROW	2.25	2.69	3.08	-0.01	-0.69
Non-Annex 1	14.86	21.04	27.11	-0.26	-7.95
TOTAL	31.80	38.30	46.20	-4.37	-12.50

Table A2.6: Gas Production, BaU 1995–2020, and Changes from BaU, Different Scenarios, 2020. Billion Cubic Metres per Year

	Business-as-Usual Levels			Changes from BaU Kyoto Scenario	Global Compromise
	1995	2010	2020	2020	2020
USA	541	614	678	-30	-36
JPN	2	3	3	0	0
EUM	207	234	267	-13	-16
ROE	34	81	89	-5	-6
ROO	199	276	347	-11	-12
EIT	744	1091	1,513	-171	-250
CHN	20	50	103	-2	-4
IND	20	31	43	-4	-16
ANI	111	211	324	-7	-16
AOE	237	364	503	-8	-77
LAM	102	253	487	-16	-291
ROW	56	127	228	-10	-30
TOTAL	2,273	3,335	4,585	-276	-753

Table A2.7: Gas Demand, BaU 1995–2020, and Changes from BaU, Different
Scenarios, 2020

Billion cubic metres per year

| | Business-as-Usual Levels | | | Changes from BaU | |
| | | | | Kyoto Scenario | Global Compromise |
	1995	2010	2020	2020	2020
USA	628	822	1,014	-40	-57
JPN	69	109	141	-27	-14
EUM	341	449	531	-39	-49
ROE	6	8	8	0	0
ROO	109	147	180	-16	-24
EIT	661	933	1,318	-210	-290
Annex I	1,814	2,467	3,192	-332	-433
CHN	20	55	121	7	36
IND	21	36	55	2	-7
ANI	74	142	235	14	-31
AOE	186	334	491	10	-133
LAM	104	205	347	11	-158
ROW	55	96	145	12	-28
Non-Annex I	459	867	1,393	56	-320
TOTAL	2,273	3,335	4,585	-276	-753

Million barrels oil equivalent per day

| | Business-as-Usual Levels | | | Changes from BaU | |
| | | | | Kyoto Scenario | Global Compromise |
	1995	2010	2020	2020	2020
USA	10.83	14.16	17.47	-0.70	-0.99
JPN	1.19	1.87	2.43	-0.46	-0.24
EUM	5.87	7.74	9.15	-0.67	-0.84
ROE	0.10	0.13	0.14	0.00	0.00
ROO	1.88	2.53	3.11	-0.27	-0.41
EIT	11.40	16.07	22.71	-3.63	-4.99
Annex I	31.26	42.52	55.00	-5.71	-7.46
CHN	0.34	0.94	2.08	0.11	0.62
IND	0.35	0.62	0.95	0.04	-0.12
ANI	1.28	2.44	4.04	0.25	-0.53
AOE	3.20	5.75	8.46	0.17	-2.29
LAM	1.79	3.54	5.98	0.18	-2.72
ROW	0.95	1.65	2.49	0.20	-0.48
Non-annex I	7.91	14.95	24.01	0.96	-5.52
TOTAL	39.17	57.47	79.01	-4.75	-12.98

Table A2.8: Oil Demand by Main Economic Sectors, BaU, 1995–2020.
Thousand Barrels per Day

Total Sectoral Demand, BaU

Sector	Electricity	Energy Int.	Other Ind.	Transp. + HHD	Other	Total
1995	3,687	12,324	10,856	34,542	10,486	71,894
2000	4,110	13,582	11,830	38,173	11,450	79,144
2005	4,611	14,732	12,740	41,921	12,776	86,781
2010	5,297	16,203	13,919	46,378	14,405	96,202
2015	6,055	17,748	15,173	51,441	16,206	106,625
2020	6,486	18,253	15,541	54,927	16,868	112,075

Annex I Sectoral Demand, BaU

Sector	Electricity	Energy Int.	Other Ind.	Transp. + HHD	Other	Total
1995	1,783	7,093	7,441	24,745	5,196	46,257
2000	1,875	7,493	7,863	26,323	5,108	48,661
2005	2,054	7,768	8,211	28,073	5,464	51,569
2010	2,320	8,212	8,726	30,195	5,965	55,418
2015	2,610	8,648	9,255	32,580	6,538	59,631
2020	2,726	8,527	9,188	33,810	6,720	60,971

Table A2.9: Coal Demand by Main Economic Sectors, BaU, 1995–2020. Million
Tonnes Oil Equivalent per Year

Total Sectoral Demand, BaU

Sector	Electricity	Energy Int.	Other Ind.	Transp. + HHD	Other	Total
1995	1,038	566	108	143	417	2,272
2000	1,070	587	111	151	430	2,350
2005	1,137	626	119	176	463	2,521
2010	1,220	676	129	207	503	2,736
2015	1,319	735	141	245	550	2,990
2020	1,451	807	157	284	601	3,300

Annex I Sectoral Demand, BaU

Sector	Electricity	Energy Int.	Other Ind.	Transp. + HHD	Other	Total
1995	665	228	29	62	225	1,210
2000	656	220	27	54	213	1,170
2005	671	218	27	59	216	1,190
2010	694	220	27	68	223	1,233
2015	725	226	28	79	232	1,290
2020	772	234	29	87	240	1,363

Table A2.10: Gas Demand by Main Economic Sectors, BaU, 1995–2020. Billion Cubic Metres per Year

Total Sectoral Demand, BaU

Sector	Electricity and Gas Distribution	Energy Int.	Other Ind.	HHD and Govt.	Other	Total
1995	1,027	489	96	138	523	2,273
2000	1,114	554	114	133	568	2,482
2005	1,251	684	151	142	642	2,870
2010	1,412	836	190	155	742	3,335
2015	1,603	1,019	237	171	863	3,894
2020	1,854	1,244	307	186	994	4,585

Annex I Sectoral Demand, BaU

Sector	Electricity and Gas Distribution	Energy Int.	Other Ind.	HHD and Govt.	Other	Total
1995	906	438	56	123	292	1,814
2000	965	486	63	115	287	1,915
2005	1,066	591	82	121	312	2,171
2010	1,183	708	99	131	347	2,467
2015	1,317	843	116	144	389	2,809
2020	1,485	990	138	155	424	3,192

Table A2.11: Oil Revenues, Indices 1995 = 1 for BaU 2010–2020, and Different Scenarios, 2020

	Business-as-Usual			Kyoto Scenario	Global Compromise Scenario
	2010	2015	2020	2020	2020
USA	1.03	0.92	0.91	0.85	0.80
Canada	1.39	1.62	1.94	1.80	1.71
Mexico	1.45	1.84	2.08	1.93	1.84
Total North America	1.19	1.24	1.35	1.25	1.19
Argentina	1.48	1.72	1.59	1.48	1.41
Brazil	1.89	2.25	2.35	2.19	2.08
Colombia	1.60	1.69	1.57	1.46	1.39
Ecuador	0.84	0.74	0.67	0.63	0.59
Peru	0.80	0.66	0.64	0.59	0.56
Trinidad & Tobago	0.72	0.59	0.57	0.53	0.50
Venezuela	2.10	2.46	2.69	2.50	2.38
Other S. & Cent. America	0.59	0.49	0.42	0.39	0.37
Total S. & Cent. America	1.77	2.03	2.12	1.97	1.88
Denmark	0.59	0.43	0.35	0.32	0.31
Italy	1.00	0.82	0.66	0.62	0.59
Norway	1.13	0.95	0.76	0.71	0.67
Romania	0.72	0.50	0.47	0.44	0.42
United Kingdom	0.61	0.43	0.34	0.31	0.30
Other Europe	0.76	0.67	0.60	0.56	0.53
Total Europe	0.86	0.69	0.55	0.52	0.49
Caspian	2.83	4.94	5.41	5.03	4.79
Russian Federation	1.41	1.68	1.79	1.67	1.59
Other Former Soviet Union	0.51	0.53	0.60	0.56	0.53
Total Former Soviet Union	1.54	2.00	2.15	2.00	1.90
Iran	1.45	1.59	1.62	1.50	1.43
Iraq	9.67	11.24	13.85	12.88	12.26
Kuwait	1.48	1.56	1.77	1.64	1.56
Oman	0.77	0.68	0.61	0.57	0.54
Qatar	1.69	1.66	1.73	1.61	1.53
Saudi Arabia	1.63	2.11	2.54	2.36	2.25
Syria	0.56	0.29	0.22	0.21	0.20
United Arab Emirates	1.55	1.64	1.85	1.73	1.64
Yemen	0.64	0.50	0.38	0.35	0.34
Other Middle East	1.11	1.17	1.33	1.23	1.17
Total Middle East	1.71	2.01	2.31	2.15	2.05

Table A2.11: *continued*

	Business-as-Usual			Kyoto Scenario	Global Compromise Scenario
	2010	*2015*	*2020*	*2020*	*2020*
Algeria	1.52	1.87	1.81	1.68	1.60
Egypt	0.60	0.51	0.43	0.40	0.38
Libya	1.39	1.71	1.66	1.54	1.47
Nigeria	1.56	1.76	1.79	1.67	1.59
Other West Africa	1.40	1.65	1.77	1.65	1.57
Other Africa	2.97	2.35	2.21	2.06	1.96
Total Africa	1.37	1.59	1.59	1.48	1.41
Australia	1.14	1.20	1.29	1.20	1.14
Brunei	0.64	0.54	0.46	0.42	0.40
China	1.49	1.41	1.46	1.36	1.30
India	0.84	0.89	0.92	0.86	0.82
Indonesia	0.63	0.52	0.50	0.47	0.45
Malaysia	0.92	0.73	0.73	0.68	0.65
Papua New Guinea	0.56	0.59	0.66	0.62	0.59
Vietnam	1.11	1.17	0.88	0.82	0.78
Other Asia Pacific	1.52	1.33	1.21	1.12	1.07
Total Asia Pacific	1.11	1.04	1.06	0.98	0.94
Total OPEC	1.71	2.00	2.26	2.11	2.00
Total NOPEC (excl. FSU)	1.15	1.16	1.18	1.09	1.04
Total World	1.41	1.58	1.70	1.58	1.51

Note: Oil revenue indices by country are based on the capacity projections described in Chapter 3. They do not take into account quantity changes due to price increases in the BaU case, and lower price increases in the Kyoto case. The indices shown here are therefore lower than actual, because prices increase both in BaU and in the policy scenarios. Also, the figures here do not include revenues from non-conventional oil. Country indices based on regional production as projected in CLIMOX.

INDEX